AGAINST
THE EVIDENCE

The Becker-Rosenthal Affair

AGGAINST THE EVIDENCE

The Becker-Rosenthal Affair

ANDY LOGAN

The McCall Publishing Company

NEW YORK

For the lost boys,
Andrew and Alexander Lyon

AGAINST
THE EVIDENCE

The Becker-Rosenthal Affair

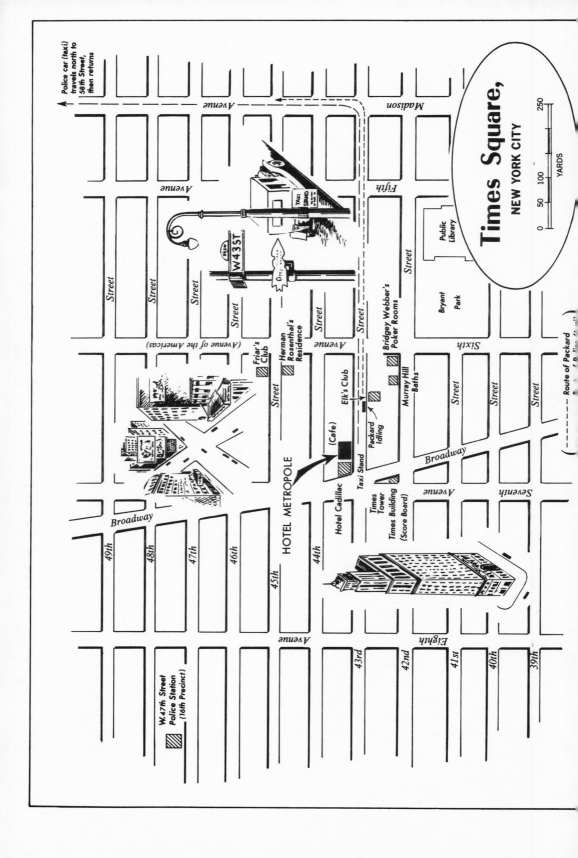

Times Square,
NEW YORK CITY

YARDS

0   50   100   250

I

No one who was born after the Second World War knows what a summer night was once like in a large American city. In 1912, for example, the population of New York was not much more than the four million that O. Henry's collection of urban vignettes had recently claimed for it. Yet in the late evening of July 15—it was St. Swithin's Day as the New York *Herald* with its usual attention to ceremony had pointed out that morning—the city's arc-lit cafe and theater district looked many times as crowded as it would on a July night in the last half of the century when it would be the gaudy center of fun for nearly twice as many New Yorkers. By the 1970s every lighted canopy would lead to a cool oasis whose windows, shuttered and sealed against the heat, also sealed off the customers from the sights and noises of the street. In 1912, however, when the now seedy area radiating out from Times Square was known as the Tenderloin—a word that symbolized all that was glittering and splendid and corrupt in the city—every window was thrown open that July night in the hope of trapping a stray breeze. On Forty-third Street between Broadway and Sixth Avenue, for instance, men and women leaned on the sills panting, sweating, and trading hot weather bromides with strangers on the sidewalk below. There were half a dozen hotels in the block, but prosperous citizens who had to stay in town were little more comfortable on a hot evening than slum dwellers. On every fire escape, at every window, there was the rhythmic motion of hand fans. Later that night when police lifted from the sidewalk the body of a man who had just been murdered in the block they would find beneath him a cardboard fan that apparently had been hoarded from year to year like any other recurrent necessity of life. It advertised "Henderson's Waterproof Celluloid Collars, Cuffs and Shirt Bosoms—Economical, Durable, Indispensable," although celluloid collars, cuffs, and shirt bosoms had been dispensable for a decade.

The heat wave had gripped the city for more than a week. There being little else to write about (the Democratic National Convention in Chicago had finally closed down after nominating Woodrow Wilson, and the Newport season was "dull, dull, *dull*," as the *Herald* complained), most of the local newspapers each day gave over their lead columns to the horrors of the weather— so many dead, so many prostrated, so many driven insane as a result of the heat (this last being a routine high temperature statistic of the time). The problem of crosstown traffic was worse than ever because of the bodies of sunstruck horses clogging the streets. One local sufferer had climbed twenty stories up on the network of red steel bars and crossbeams of the Woolworth Building, then under construction, and had sat there swinging his legs, hoping to catch a breeze off the North River. And only the day before an editor at the *Evening Post,* mopping his brow, had written that he wasn't at all surprised to learn from a recent Police Department report that New Yorkers committed more murders in July than in any other month. Fortunately, fresh revelations about a perennial concern of local editors—the liaison between gamblers and grafting policemen—had cropped up in the last few days to give the newspapers something beside the heat to carry on about.

By one o'clock of the night that would add another murder to the July statistics—the last-minute details of the crime were at that moment being worked out in a second-floor poker room around the corner at Forty-second Street and Sixth Avenue— women, except for prostitutes and a few actresses, had generally retired from the Forty-third Street scene, and lights had finally gone out in most of the upstairs rooms. Groups of perspiring men still backed and filled on the sidewalks, however, most of them painfully overdressed for the tropical weather in dark suits, long-sleeved shirts with high, starched collars, and, of course, hats—

another commodity that would later turn out to be not wholly indispensable. The throng was especially dense in front of the Hotel Metropole, a narrow, six-story building on the north side of Forty-third Street fifty yards from the corner of Broadway, but no one could blame this on the weather. Whatever the temperature, the people who hung around the Metropole were the kind that slept through most of the daylight hours and got their bearings after dark—actors, prizefighters, gamblers, minor politicians working their special angles, and various sporting types, all of whom used the hotel as a listening post and gossip mart for their often interlocking trades. Fortunately the Cafe Metropole, which opened off the hotel lobby, had an all-night license to accommodate them. It had had no trouble getting this valuable piece of paper a few years back since the hotel was owned by the Considine brothers, Jim and George, in partnership with Big Tim Sullivan. No matter who was head of the local Democratic machine at Tammany Hall—it was a man named Charley Murphy at the moment—Big Tim, currently state senator and, anytime it suited him better, United States congressman from the Lower East Side, had for two decades been the man to see if you wanted to do business in the Tenderloin. If a fellow was short of the specified payoff money, he could still qualify if he was one of the boys from Big Tim's old East Side clubhouse for whom the politician felt a sentimental attachment—someone, for example, like Herman Rosenthal, the man who was about to be murdered.

Passersby in the daytime had noticed recently that the Metropole was beginning to look a little run-down, and in fact it would file a suit in bankruptcy later that week. From the street on this July evening of the murder, however, the place looked inviting enough, with its two brightly lighted entrances, one leading into the hotel itself and one directly into the cafe. Their revolving doors had been folded flat against the jambs because of the heat, and the festive goings-on within the cafe were visible from the street. In the mechanical breeze set off by two giant electric fans just inside the doors lace curtains fluttered at the windows and the potted palms that lined the steps leading up to the cafe swayed a little. Candles flickered behind red shades at each table. It was a Monday night, usually such a slow time that members of the five-piece Hungarian orchestra took it as their day off. In their absence the Considines had provided a ragtime piano player whose cheerful versions of the "Bunny Hug" and "Oceana Roll" could be heard out on the sidewalk through the open windows. Now and then a husky female voice accompanied him. One of the women sitting at a table near the piano had just closed in a Broadway revue and after a few late evening drinks was feeling generous enough to entertain the other diners for nothing. Sitting at the table with her was Billy File, an off-duty police detective. File, a tall, well-muscled young fellow, was a former sparring partner of Gentleman Jim Corbett, the former heavyweight champion, whom he liked to think he resembled. He was a regular at the Metropole, where he enjoyed hanging out with the theatrical crowd. The late hours kept by the Metropole kitchen made it a convenient place for actors to gather for a bite after a show. A number of them were on hand that night, sitting in their usual insular clumps, hashing over backstage gossip. As the night wore on, apparently neither they nor any of the other diners sitting near the windows happened to notice that there were fewer people standing in front of the Metropole than there had been a short while before and that most of those left were—as they would be described in the newspapers the next day—"East Side types."

In 1912 New Yorkers using the phrase "East Side" didn't mean just anywhere on the east side of Manhattan. Except in Yorkville, the German neighborhood in the Eighties, the population of the Upper East Side, still disfigured by the New York Central cut up the middle of Park Avenue, was at this time comparatively sparse and nondescript. An East Sider was someone from the vast festering slum east of Broadway and below Fourteenth Street. Twenty-five years earlier when a New Yorker had said "East Siders" he had meant the Irish. By 1912 he meant the new immigrant hordes who had taken over the Rivington and Stanton street tenements, the Jews. On the night of the murder, however, the few witnesses who were willing to be quoted at all and who spoke of "East Side types" were talking about the young Jewish criminal class that had begun to flourish south of Fourteenth Street in the past decade. Specifically, they meant the owners of low-class gambling houses and the gangsters who worked for them, a fraternity that reporters, anxious to show off their inside expertise, would refer to the next day as "the old Hesper crowd," in honor of one of the gamblers' former recreation centers, the Hesper Club on lower Second Avenue.

Beside actors, the customers inside the Metropole that night included some of the crowd that had come up from the fights at Madison Square Garden (still at Madison Square), a quartet helping a New Rochelle insurance man celebrate his fortieth birthday, several representatives of the timeless breed known as "promoters," and quite a few of those men who, like their counterparts out on the sidewalk in front of the Metropole, were usually found at this hour engaged in what the New York *Sun* in a recent fancy moment had called "aleatory pursuits." (Aleatory: depending on an uncertain event or contingency . . . pertaining to luck.) Although they were no longer entirely unknown around the velvet-draped roulette and faro tables of the west Forties, the natural habitat of these particular gamblers was a shabbier storefront kind of establishment south of Fourteenth Street, featuring a game called stuss, which was also known as Jewish faro. One of the gambling-house proprietors who came to the Metropole that night was Herman Rosenthal, who, with Big Tim Sullivan's help, had moved up from the world of stuss houses and set up shop in the Tenderloin only the fall before.

In the weeks that followed a number of the customers in the Metropole that evening were called to testify before various official bodies. When Rosenthal had bustled up the steps to the cafe a little before one o'clock, their stories agreed, a sudden silence fell at a table in the corner near the door where several downtown gamblers were clustered, and the piano player stopped playing in mid-bar. Rosenthal stood for a moment in the doorway while the gamblers stared at him. At first none of them spoke to him. Rosenthal was acquainted with them all, however, and he was entirely at home at the Metropole. As one of Big Tim's boys, he had treated it for years as his uptown fraternity house, pub, and occasional small-loan office. Swabbing his round face with a large yellow silk handkerchief, Rosenthal slumped down at the nearest empty table. A few minutes later he was joined there by three hangers-on of the East Side gambling crowd named Fat Moe Brown, Butch Kitte, and Boob Walker. At the other table the gamblers, after cautiously returning his greeting, went back to talking among themselves, not looking in his direction. The piano player began to pound out a new tune. When the waiter came,

Rosenthal ordered a horse's neck—ginger ale and a twist of lemon peel—and an expensive Havana cigar. He told the waiter that he wouldn't have anything to eat, that he might be called away at any time. From then on he kept his eye on the door. He didn't seem nervous, witnesses insisted. "Excited" was more the word, they said. "He was the picture of a man whose mind was working too actively for the repose of his body," as the *Sun* described it the next day. Although later Fat Moe, Butch, and Boob swore they couldn't remember a thing he had said or even the topic of conversation, he was seen waving his pudgy hands about and talking to them in an animated way for the next half hour. Above all things Herman Rosenthal was a talker.

He was a short, dapper man with dark wavy hair, a low forehead, small black eyes behind round glasses, and full red lips. He dressed expensively and usually sparkled and gleamed as he moved around, weighed down by numerous pieces of jewelry. Lately, however, these embellishments had been reduced to the gold cuff links, gold tie clasp, and gold belt buckle he was wearing tonight. On each of these the initials "H.R." were visible halfway across the room, a piece of vanity that presumably had reduced their value at the pawn shop. After his death there was a tendency to portray Rosenthal as a pathetic, inconsiderable figure, a born loser. In fact he had had a string of fat years that had begun to go sour about two and a half years before, at about the time he had launched a one-man vendetta against the New York Police Department. If he had made matters uncomfortable for a number of individual policemen during this period, he had hardly bettered his own circumstances. His lone surviving gambling house, two blocks north of the Metropole at 104 West Forty-fifth Street, a place he also used as a residence, had been raided three months before. The police had kept it under around-the-clock police guard ever since to make sure it stayed closed.

In the past few days Rosenthal had made several desperate moves. On the Thursday before, he had locked the day shift police guard inside the house. When the night shift man discovered the situation, reinforcements were sent for. They arrived bearing axes and one of the new hydraulic jacks the police used to break down particularly resistant doors. Watching from the sidewalk nearby, Rosenthal had hastily changed his mind and produced the keys. With the temperature in the mid-nineties, he had then announced that he planned to start up the coal furnace full blast and roast the interlopers out. (Once out of the house they could not break back in again, as the law read, without getting another warrant on fresh evidence.) But, again changing his mind, Rosenthal had instead, on that Friday, July 12, sworn out a warrant at the West Side Magistrate's Court for the arrest of Inspector Cornelius Hayes of the Third Inspection District that covered most of the midtown West Side and Captain William Day of the Forty-seventh Street police station, charging that the stationing of the guard in his house constituted "oppression."

To buttress the complaint, Rosenthal's lawyer quoted copiously from an opinion by a former State Supreme Court judge who had written of a police captain who kept his officers in a dining room above a saloon that was under suspicion as a gambling house: "He is . . . evidently under the dangerous illusion that he is an official of unlimited powers and free to exercise force and violence over any person or place in his precinct. . . . He is either grossly ignorant or else a willful and dangerous criminal." The judge who had so attacked the misuse of police powers a few years earlier was William Jay Gaynor, who was now mayor of New York and thus, ironically, the man ultimately responsible for the uniformed squatters in Rosenthal's gambling house. The magistrate before whom Rosenthal appeared had told him his evidence was insufficient for a warrant and advised him to prepare an affidavit demonstrating malice on the part of the police officers. Rosenthal did this, describing in the affidavit various meetings he had had with Inspector Hayes and Captain Day in which they had boasted they would keep the police guard at his place for as long as they pleased. He had delivered this document to the West Side court that very afternoon of July 15, a few hours before he turned up at the Metropole. (The case against the officers would eventually be dismissed on a very simple ground: no living complainant.)

All these Rosenthal antics had been found highly diverting by the local press. Reporters had dwelt at length on the comical figure cut by Herman's full-breasted wife, Lillian, as she leaned out of an upstairs window in her lace wrapper, shaking a fist at the uniformed figures every time there was a changing of the guard. They had described the morose expression on the face of the police guard as, coatless and gasping in the noonday heat, he stared across the way at the Friar's Club, from the windows of which leading theatrical figures, sipping tall, cool drinks, goggled back at him. Newspapers had also reported during the past weeks Rosenthal's unsuccessful attempts to see the mayor, District Attorney Charles Whitman, the police commissioner, and the president of the Board of Magistrates to register more of his chronic complaints about police oppression and, it was said, make charges of grafting against certain policemen. Two weeks earlier he had unsuccessfully tried to sell to a newspaper the story of a thousand-dollar payoff demanded of him by Inspector Hayes. About the same time, by waylaying the district attorney as he left his Madison Avenue apartment, Rosenthal had finally won a few minutes with Whitman. Whitman had told him that his story didn't amount to a rap without supporting evidence by other witnesses. Rosenthal's last desperate move had been made in collaboration with a young reporter on the *World* named Herbert Bayard Swope.

Swope spent almost as much time in gambling houses, where Rosenthal had got to know him, as he did in the *World's* city room. For many weeks Rosenthal had been trying to persuade the reporter to print his tale of police persecution. Late in the previous week, Swope had decided to risk it. On Friday he and Rosenthal had put together a long, sensational affidavit that had covered much of the first two pages of the *World* on Sunday, July 14—the day before Rosenthal's appearance at the Metropole— and had been reprinted in substance in later editions of every paper in the city. In this document Rosenthal did not mention the charges he had been making around town against Inspector Hayes, Captain Day, and others in the Police Department. He devoted all of his attention to the wrongs done him by a man who hadn't even been mentioned in his complaint to the Magistrate's Court—Lieutenant Charles Becker. Becker was the head of one of the department's three special task forces, popularly called "strong arm squads," whose chores included stamping out gambling in the city. Rosenthal had announced in the *World* that Becker had been his secret business partner in the Forty-fifth Street gambling house. The alleged partnership had followed a meeting "by appointment" with the police officer the previous New Year's Eve at an Elks' Club ball.

"We had a fine evening together and had a lot of champagne to drink," Rosenthal's affidavit had said. "Becker and I had been talking together through the night and he seemed very anxious to win my friendship. When we were all feeling so good he got up at the table, put his arms around me and kissed me. I was surprised at his action, but he waved his hands to the crowd and said: 'Anything in the world for you, Herman. I'll get up at three o'clock in the morning to do you a favor. You can have anything I've got.' " Then Becker had called over three members of his squad and introduced them, saying, "This is my best pal and do anything he wants you to do." After this episode, Rosenthal's affidavit had gone on, "I met Becker pretty often and we soon became very good friends . . . the best friends in the world . . . Sometimes we would meet at the Lafayette Turkish Baths and other times we would meet at the Elks' Club." Becker had kept telling him he "was getting hold of a lot of money" in his strong arm squad job. Rosenthal was anxious to open his Forty-fifth Street house and Becker had asked to be let in on it. According to Rosenthal, the lieutenant had put up fifteen hundred dollars in return for 20 per cent of the profits and a chattel mortgage on the furniture and gambling equipment.

The day after this account of the cozy relationship between a member of the police force and a well-known gambler appeared in the *World*, Rosenthal had been formally received by District Attorney Whitman for the first time. An appointment had been made for another meeting. It was set for 8 A.M. Tuesday, a little over six and a half hours from this moment when Rosenthal sat holding forth at his table in the Cafe Metropole.

"What do you boys think of the papers lately?" he called out suddenly to the group of gamblers at the next table. "You aren't sore at me, are you?"

"You're a damned fool, Herman," one of them told him—or so the other gambler would claim the next day.

At about one-thirty Bridgey Webber, a small, dapper figure who was well known to all those in the gamblers' corner, arrived at the Metropole. Bridgey, who had a sharp, dark face, black eyes, and a long, thin nose, was getting to be a big man in the gambling world, running houses both uptown and downtown. Some of them, it was said, also carried opium to go. Webber, as a boy, had stolen pet dogs and held them for ransom. Later he had run an opium den on Pell Street in Chinatown. His proper first name was Louis, his nickname tracing back to an ancient alliance with a prostitute named Bridget. He now came through the wide entrance to the cafe, made a swift circuit of the room, and went out again.

"Hello, Herman," he said when he saw Rosenthal.

"Hello, Bridgey," said Rosenthal. He did not show any surprise at Webber's affable tone although he and Webber had been not only rivals in the gambling business but bitter personal enemies since boyhood.

"When you found Rosenthal, did you speak to him?" the defense attorney asked Webber in court three months later.

"I said, 'Hello, Herman.' "

"In a friendly way?"

"Yes, sir," said Webber.

"When you went to the Metropole, for what purpose did you look for him? Was it for the purpose of having him murdered?"

"Yes, sir," said Webber, politely.

As Bridgey left the cafe that night Rosenthal said—according to an anonymous witness quoted in several newspapers the next day—"You see, Bridgey's all right. I'll get my money." Webber, for his part, showed no surprise at seeing Rosenthal sharing a table with a party that included Boob Walker, although for many years Boob had been Bridgey's bouncer, lookout, and hired thug, who from time to time had been assigned to put Rosenthal's hired thugs or even Rosenthal himself out of action. Boob reportedly had trailed the gambler to the Metropole and in fact, at Webber's orders, had been trailing him all day. But why it was that the grudge-bearing Rosenthal was suddenly willing to sit around with Boob in such chummy fashion, no one involved cared to clear up afterward. The lawyers for the defense in the murder trial would contend that Rosenthal was under the impression that the town's gamblers, including Bridgey, were about to give him a large sum of money to get out of town and that he sat chinning with Boob simply because he was feeling expansive and looking for anybody to talk to.

Soon after Webber left the hotel, all the taxicabs that usually lined up in front of the Metropole to haul away the night-blooming free spenders began to disappear, along with most of the casual pedestrians. From twenty minutes to two on, any taxi that paused there was dispatched on some mysterious errand. After a look at the unofficial dispatcher the hackie usually took off rapidly without asking questions. Most of those on foot made swift tracks when one of the East Siders suggested they move on. It was as if the area were a stage set, being cleared for some extraordinary special performance.

There are always a few nosy types, however, born eyewitnesses who nip out of the way as advised and nip back later to find out what's going on. After being waved off, Thomas Ryan, a young taxi driver, went around the block, parked his cab in the shadows, and walked back to a point just east of the Metropole. Louis Krause, a Hungarian currently grossing eight dollars a week as a waiter at Reisenweber's in Coney Island, was on his way to see about a better job at the Geneva Club, a West Forty-fourth Street social center run by the waiter's union. Stopping to mop his face, he was told to move along by a man later identified as Max Kahn, an East Side pickpocket. Krause, with the insurrectionary spirit of a man who had learned the Declaration of Independence by heart before he emigrated, asked whether Kahn owned the sidewalk. The look he got in return for this sally sent him scuttering all the way across Forty-third Street—but no farther. There he remained on the sidewalk, watching, waiting, sensing that something unusual was about to happen.

Thomas Coupe, the Limey desk clerk at the Elks' Club, which stood on the other side of the street from the Metropole and further east on Forty-third, was busy by the front window writing a letter to his family. He did not know what was about to happen. Nor did Charles Gallagher, an unemployed cabaret tenor now approaching the Metropole to see about a singing job, or Giovanni Stanich, a recent arrival from Austria, who was standing in front of the Hotel Cadillac, just west of the Metropole, negotiating with a prostitute. Bridgey Webber knew, of course. After his visit to the cafe he had gone back to his poker rooms above the United Cigar store at the northwest corner of Forty-second Street and Sixth and delivered a message.

"Herman's at the Metropole," he told the group assembled at a long table in the back room, a group that included four professional gunmen. Most of those at the table drank the last of their drinks, grabbed their hats, and headed, by foot or car, for the Metropole. Soon afterward Bridgey had returned to the hotel, taking up an inconspicuous post west of the entrance.

By ten minutes to two Bridgey's junior partner, Harry Vallon, was crouched on the other side of the entrance. Just inside the hotel door was Dave Mendelsohn, Bridgey's steerer and outside man. A gambler named Bald Jack Rose by this time stood talking to someone in one of the dark doorways across the street, and another East Side gambler named Sigmund (Beansey) Rosenfeld was posted near the Hotel Cadillac. Several anonymous witnesses afterward insisted that Big Jack Zelig, the East Side gangster, was also somewhere nearby in the shadows. In all, by one-fifty-seven, which was the moment of the murder, there were—padding about the sidewalks and in the street, standing flat in the door-ways near the Metropole, talking in low voices, pulling on cigars, and sweating—perhaps thirty men who had had a long associa-tion with Herman Rosenthal in the gambling trade south of Fourteenth Street. Meanwhile in other parts of the city—or so the story would be told the next day—in poker rooms and crap parlors in Harlem, in the dim arcade outside Madison Square Garden, in stuss houses on the East Side, in opium dens in Chinatown, and in many of the grander roulette houses uptown men who also knew what was about to happen waited near telephones for the word to come that the deed was done, that Herman had got his.

A few minutes before the murder a slate-colored seven-passenger touring car, a 1909 Packard, had turned into Forty-third Street from Sixth Avenue, made a U-turn, and paused, its motor running and its headlights on, on the south side of the street about a hundred feet east of the Metropole. A number of short, swarthy men—some said five, some said three, but the prevailing estimate was four—piled out of the car and moved up close to the sidewalk in front of the hotel. They were all wearing soft felt hats and dark suits. One short, swarthy man stayed for a brief time beside the driver—also short and swarthy—and then got out. Some witnesses—before they hastily withdrew them-selves from the roster of possible deponents and left town, in some cases permanently—said that the fifth passenger then went into the hotel and came out, followed by Herman Rosenthal. Others said he merely stood by the rear car door, holding it open, keeping the getaway car at the ready. Eventually the prosecution in the trials that followed would take the position that there had been no fifth passenger in the car at all.

A little earlier, at one-thirty, about the moment that Bridgey

Webber arrived for the first time that night at the Metropole, another touring car, a five-passenger Simplex carrying Lieutenant Charles Becker, Rosenthal's alleged gambling partner, came speeding up Sixth Avenue. At Forty-second Street the Simplex paused for a moment just below Bridgey Webber's poker rooms, to let off a passenger, a man named Jacob Reich who called himself Jack Sullivan. (An observer who relied only on names could be seriously misled about the numbers of Irishmen still living on the East Side.) Reich, who was planning to stop off at Bridgey Webber's, swore to the end of his days that he did not know what was about to happen although, curiously, the next years of his life would have been far simpler if he had agreed that he had been in on every detail of the murder plan to the point of having held the murderer's coats. As for Lieutenant Becker, who was then driven to his home on West 165 Street in northern Manhattan, two juries would find he not only knew the crime was about to take place but also had ordered the murder done.

About twenty minutes before two, Rosenthal stood up at his table in the cafe and said in a loud voice: "I guess the morning papers must be up." He found a newsboy near the main entrance and bought a copy of the *World*, the lead story of which was a follow-up on his charges against Lieutenant Becker. The first edition of Hearst's *American*, with matching headlines, was also on the streets. Rosenthal bought one of these and then, after looking them both over, bought seven more copies of the *World*, which put more credence in his story, and climbed back up the steps to the cafe.

"What about that for a headline?" he asked the gamblers at the next table, waving a paper at them. But all of them, as well as Boob Walker and his two companions, were on their feet, about to leave. Either they were anxious to move out of the line of fire, cynics said later, or they wanted to get out front and see the fun. Rosenthal shoved copies of the *World* into the hands of several of them as they went outside.

Rosenthal stayed behind, sitting at a table alone. He was bent over the front pages, smiling to himself when a man ("well-dressed" and "undersized" were the only adjectives witnesses later agreed on) came through the door and walked up to him. Five minutes earlier Bridgey Webber's sidekick Harry Vallon had approached a gambler named Chick Beebe at the main hotel entrance and asked him to step inside and tell Herman Rosenthal to come out. "Do it yourself, I'm not your lobbygow," Beebe said he told Vallon, using the East Side slang term for a hanger-on or high-class lackey—a term often applied to Vallon in his relations with Bridgey Webber.

Apparently Vallon got himself another messenger. Whoever the man was—some claimed it was Bridgey's outside man Dave Mendelsohn, some that it was a gambler named Sam Schepps, some that it was Harry Vallon himself—no one ever identified him publicly. Later on when it became expedient for the prosecution to downgrade the part played in the affair by certain men who had turned state's witnesses, the district attorney declared that there never had been a messenger, that Rosenthal had just decided on his own to leave the cafe. On the day after the murder, however, others who had been on hand insisted they had heard the new arrival say to Rosenthal:

"Can you come outside a minute, Herman? I got somebody out here wants to see you."

Immediately, eagerly, as if this were the summons he had been waiting for, Rosenthal got to his feet, slapped a dollar on the table to cover an eighty-cent tab, gathered up his scarf and the bundle of newspapers, put on his hat, and walked toward the door, still holding his burning cigar in his hand. Those watching in the street saw another man—also never formally identified—come out the door ahead of him, lift his hand to his hat brim in a signal, and then run down the steps to the sidewalk. Rosenthal had started down the steps, looking around him, clutching his cigar, blinking in the brilliant arc lights, when the four men who had arrived in the touring car—joined, some said, by a fifth man—moved in close. Five shots rang out. One shot went wild, lodging in the door frame, one hit him in the neck, one in the nose, and two on the side of his head. The shots were at such close range there were powder burns on one side of his face.

"I gotcha!" the cabdriver, Ryan, heard one of the gunmen say exultantly. Blue smoke from the guns filled the street and drifted back into the cafe. As, blood streaming, Rosenthal fell to the sidewalk on his back, the bundle of newspapers slid from his arms and spread out across him so that he seemed to lie in a grotesque shroud of early editions of the New York *World*, whose next edition would appear an hour and a half later with its headlines sensationally revised.

In that month of July in New York City there were thirty other murders, half a dozen of them described by the police as—like that of Herman Rosenthal—involving East Side gangsters. The morning after the Rosenthal shooting, for example, two men went into a barber shop at 261 East Tenth Street, spotted a customer known as Rocco, pumped eight slugs into his chest, and walked out. A few hours later a crap game proprietor walking along Second Avenue was shot ten times by unknown gunmen. None of these other gang murders was ever solved, nor was much public notice taken of the oversight. Because of the death of Herman Rosenthal, however, five men died in the electric chair at Sing Sing. Another man was executed more informally behind the bar of his saloon on East Ninth Street. The shooting down of a prominent gangster in October 1912 was also widely believed to be a related event. And there were sensible citizens who always believed that the death on the Yonkers train tracks of Big Tim Sullivan in August 1913 was a similar execution to prevent him from telling what he knew of the Rosenthal murder.

The murder made District Attorney Whitman governor of New York and an active candidate for the presidency of the United States. It helped bring to an end the political career—and, many thought, caused the death in office—of Mayor Gaynor. The furor that followed it had much to do with launching the judicial career of Justice Benjamin Cardozo. The murder promoted an obscure judge named Samuel Seabury to the highest court in the state. It established Herbert Bayard Swope as the best-known newspaperman of his generation. And it led the political bosses and outlaw elements of the city to conclude that the financial arrangements between their two groups would have to be put on a more businesslike basis, a resolution that caused them to install a ruthless and wily gambler named Arnold Rothstein as the czar of the New York underworld.

Herman Rosenthal was a small-time criminal whose loss to the living seems to have been singularly slight. Yet when District Attorney Charles Whitman declared a few weeks later at a mass meeting at Cooper Union that the crime must be avenged as "a challenge to our very civilization," the old building resounded to its wrought-iron beams with the cheers of aroused citizens. To the death of Herman Rosenthal attention would be paid.

II

IMMEDIATELY after the murder the men who had done the shooting raced across Forty-third Street and vaulted into the waiting car, which then "hurtled toward Sixth Avenue at fully thirty-five miles an hour," as the *Evening Post* described it later that day. Most witnesses quoted by the district attorney's office in the next few days said there were either six or seven men in the car as it sped away. The first official police report thought it was eight. All these men, it was agreed, were rather short, slightly built, dark-complected, clean-shaven, and, of course, dressed as before in dark suits and soft dark hats pulled down over their foreheads. These accounts seemed to promise some problem with identification. Fortunately for the prosecution, witnesses would be found who had no doubt about whom they had seen when it came time to testify in court.

At the sound of the shots the off-duty cop, Billy File, jumped up from his seat in the cafe, pulling his gun as he ran, and bowled over a waiter on his way to the door, moving so fast that, as his lady companion would point out in his defense at his later departmental trial for neglect of duty, he had actually forgotten to take his hat. By the time he got to the door it was blocked. There had been a stampede of cafe customers to get out and see what was going on at the same moment that dozens of people in the street were charging inside to get out of the way of further shooting. The touring car had already started its race toward Sixth Avenue.

Stowing his gun and shoving his way through the crowd, File ran to the taxi stand in front of the Cadillac Hotel, on which two fellow officers were already converging from their fixed posts on Broadway. The three men flung themselves into a taxi and ordered the driver to take off after the gray car. First, however, the driver had to crank up the cab (fortunately he had just filled its radiator from a gallon can in the Cadillac areaway) and then make a U-turn, and by the time they were headed toward Sixth the Packard had been out of sight for several minutes. As the taxi neared Sixth a man—it turned out to be Coupe, the Elks' Club clerk—ran into the street and shouted the license number after them: "New York 41313!" At Forty-third and Madison the pursuers screeched to a halt and asked advice of the driver of a milk wagon, who told them the car had veered north on Madison. The taxi did the same, but when it reached Fifty-eighth Street and there was still no sign of the getaway car, File and his fellow officers gave up the chase and returned to the Metropole. District Attorney Whitman would say the next day that they had made "little more than a pretense of pursuing the killers."

In front of the Metropole the crowds had moved in fast in the moments after the murder. Patrolman William Brady, whom his fellow policemen had left behind to cope, immediately had someone telephone for reinforcements. Forty of them arrived in short order by taxicab, but they had their hands full. Next day the crowd counters put the total at between three and five thousand people. Within two minutes of the murder, reported the *Sun*, "the Tenderloin was astir and wild with excitement. Men in evening clothes and in ordinary garb came pouring into Forty-third from clubs, hotels and restaurants." Jack's, the famous Tenderloin cafe, had "emptied itself at the first shot. The Elks' Club gave up its resident membership. The streets became almost impassable from Broadway to Sixth Avenue. And, singularly enough, half the people who came rushing to the scene seemed to know without being told that the dead man was Rosenthal, the troublemaker." In a suspiciously pat account the *Times* insisted that "immediately a cry went up from the crowd, 'Why, it is Herman Rosenthal, the gambler, who accused Lieutenant Becker of the police Strong Arm Squad!'" (In a spectacular piece of miscasting, the *Times* reporter who came to the scene, puffing, panting, and asking questions in a high-pitched voice, was a fat young man in eyeglasses named Alexander Woollcott, who would soon be switched by mutual consent to the theater desk.) As Rosenthal lay there under the glaring lights of what was still called a porte-cochere, "street walkers, gamblers, soft-treading gentry of ill-chosen professions," as the *American* described them, "and chorus girls and their rattle-brained escorts joked heartlessly."

"Hello, Herman," said one gambler, looking down at the body. "Good-*bye*, Herman!" There was laughter from his friends in the crowd.

"Is he dead? Then we collect," said another of the fraternity, showing the true aleatory spirit. A few minutes later, however, the East Side contingent—the soft-treading gentry—faded away from the scene as if on signal. Among them, observed loping toward Broadway, was Bridgey Webber, who had located Rosenthal for his executioners.

At the moment of the murder, according to his later testimony, Jacob Reich, also known as Jack Sullivan, the man who had ridden uptown with Lieutenant Becker and had been let off half an hour before at Forty-second and Sixth Avenue, was sitting in a shop next to the George M. Cohan Theatre on Forty-second Street near Broadway, having a soda. At the sound of the shots all the other customers rushed out, but he stopped to put his diamond stickpin under his lapel "because I've had experience with those kind of people." He then hurried around the corner to the Metropole. Seeing the enormous crowd, he took advantage of his trade, which was running a newspaper distribution service. Shouting "Press! Press! Press!" he was allowed to push his way through. Reich and Herman Rosenthal had been friends most of their lives since the days when they had sold newspapers side by side at the Manhattan end of the Brooklyn Bridge. During Reich's brief career as a welterweight Rosenthal had helped promote some of his fights. When Reich had gotten married eighteen months earlier, Rosenthal had been best man. He had even helped pay for the big spread at the Cafe Boulevard after the ceremony. Now Reich leaned over the body. "I asked him, 'Who did it, Herman?'" he testified later. "But he was dead already."

No doubt Reich would have preferred to stay around for the formalities for his old friend. But first things first. Although his claim to being a newspaperman had been a bluff, he found it useful to pal around with working reporters and often boasted of his pull with them. Here was a golden chance to pile up credit. Reich sprinted to Broadway, hailed a horse-drawn brougham, and drove to a favorite uptown hangout, the Garden Restaurant at Eighth Avenue and Fiftieth Street, where he knew he'd find a telephone. There he called the New York *American,* Hearst's morning paper. Reich did not ask to speak to the *American* reporter he knew best, Henry—better known as "Deacon"—Terry, who had been the Hearst man at the Criminal Courts Building for a decade. He and Reich and Lieutenant Becker had been together from eleven o'clock on that evening, when they had run into each other after the fights at Madison Square Garden. At about twelve-thirty Becker and Reich, riding in a car that Becker had borrowed for the evening, had let Terry off at the Thirty-third Street and Sixth Avenue entrance to the Hudson tube line that tunnels under the river to New Jersey. Before the reporter got out Becker had urged Terry to let him drive him to his home in Jersey City. Terry had said no, thanks, that it was easy enough to go by the tubes.

On this hairline decision Charles Becker's life may well have hung in the balance. Becker would write Terry to this effect much later in one of his last letters. "See how fate played against me," he wrote. "Had you said yes to my proposition, Sullivan [Reich] and I would have been in Jersey with you instead of I passing near the scene of the foul murder a short time before its commission. . . . Poor Sullivan would not have been charged with being near the murder scene . . . What a vast lot of circumstances that were made to appear damning would have been avoided!"

Since he knew that reporter Terry would, by then, be home in bed in Jersey City, Reich gave the news of the murder to the first person he spoke with at the *American* city desk. He then headed for Bridgey's place to find out, he said later, what in hell was going on. By this time Jim Considine, the Metropole proprietor, had ordered a waiter to bring a white tablecloth and drape it over Rosenthal's body. At two-twenty a doctor appeared from Flower Hospital and went through the formality of pronouncing him dead. The police ambulance, its bell slowly clanging, removed the body ten minutes later. It was delivered to the back room of the Forty-seventh Street station house between Eighth and Ninth Avenues. At the desk there a lieutenant began writing up the official report.

Sudden death 2:40 A.M. Herman Rosenthal, aged 38,
white, U.S., 104 West 45th Street, Gambler. . . . At
about two this A.M. while standing in front of the Hotel
Metropole. . . . Rosenthal was shot and killed by four
unknown men about 24 years, white, 5 feet 5 or 6,
smoothfaced, dark complection and hair, dark clothes,
soft dark hats, who after shooting Rosenthal jumped into
a waiting automobile No. 13131 N.Y. or 14131 N.Y.
(slate-colored touring car) which contained four other
young men, smooth faces, dark-complected. . . .

Some thirty hours later District Attorney Charles Whitman
would wave a piece of paper at newspapermen in his office. "I
have in my hand," he would say, "the police blotter report of the
murder, showing seven license numbers of the murder car, everyone of them wrong." Some of them, he told reporters, bore no
resemblance to the correct number. Whitman was overstating his
case. Both of the two numbers listed bore some resemblance to
New York 41313, the proper number. But they *were* wrong.
Whether this was the result of faulty reporting by other witnesses
or of police skullduggery was never established, but the public
would agree with Whitman that the police performance had been
odd indeed.

It wasn't until half an hour after the shooting that someone
remembered there was a Mrs. Rosenthal. Two reporters raced two
blocks north from the Metropole and hammered at the door of
Rosenthal's gambling house. The police guard wouldn't open up,
thinking it was some ruse to get him out of there, but Mrs. Rosenthal finally came downstairs. A massive woman with dyed red
hair, she said, weeping, that she had begged her husband not to
go out that night but that he had said he had an appointment to
meet someone at the Metropole.

"Were you surprised to hear that he was lying dead in front of
that place?" asked a reporter from the *Globe*.

"No, I wasn't too surprised," she told him. She threw an automobile duster over her nightgown and hurried to the scene of the
crime, but by the time she got there Rosenthal's body had been
removed.

Up in Police Commissioner Rhinelander Waldo's suite at the
Ritz-Carlton the telephone rang about two-thirty. One of his assis-

tants broke the news. The commissioner's response was "Ye Gods!" (On occasion he also used such expressions as "Balderdash!") Waldo asked dutifully about police deployment and was assured that all was under control. Apparently it never occurred to him to pile out of bed and go down and take charge of things at the precinct station. Waldo had stern notions about protocol and the division of authority, and taking charge of bodies was clearly a lineman's job. Police commissioners (and their deputies) were then civilians, not men who had come up through the ranks. Still, one of his nonuniformed predecessors, Teddy Roosevelt, almost certainly would not have been able to resist the cue to plunge into the midst of the murder melodrama.

Waldo—whose name was in the Social Register, his mother being one of *the* Rhinelanders—was a baby-faced, well-meaning young man with beautiful manners who had been the darling of anxious mothers in the cotillion set until his marriage two years earlier to the widow of John Heckscher of the coal family. He fancied himself as the leading American expert on police science, having made several trips abroad to study British and continental systems, and the tables and shelves of his Ritz quarters were cluttered with fat, leather-bound volumes on the subject. His hope, he had told reporters when he had arrived at 100 Centre Street as the new police commissioner in the spring of 1911, was to be remembered in history as the man who transformed the New York force into another Scotland Yard. As it turned out, he would be remembered only for the fact that, like Mayor Gaynor, he had proved totally unable to counter—or even, apparently, to understand—the extent and significance of the storm that broke over Centre Street as the result of the Rosenthal murder.

After graduating from West Point, Waldo had been sent by the army in 1901 to the Philippines, where he stayed on for several years as part of the occupation force in Mindanao. At loose ends after returning to New York and to civilian life, he had had the luck to find that the new police commissioner, a retired army general named Theodore Bingham, was an acquaintance of his and had been appointed Bingham's deputy early in 1906. Now, after some years away from Police Headquarters, he had taken over as police commissioner. This murder in the course of an urban tribal feud—as he judged Rosenthal's death to be on this early morning of July 16—must have reminded Waldo that the city was in many ways more of an alien jungle to him than the southern Philippines. At this moment he did nothing more than to sit disconsolately on his bed at the Ritz beside the telephone, leafing through a book on the new Bertillion fingerprinting system and pondering whether he would get a worse tongue-lashing if he woke up Mayor Gaynor now or if he waited and let the old Irishman hear the news hours after the fact.

Between these two men of different backgrounds and generations—Waldo was thirty-five and Gaynor sixty-four—a remarkably amiable relationship had developed in the fourteen months since Gaynor had named Waldo police commissioner. "Waldo, with one exception I consider you the Creator's noblest work," would be the caption a week later under a *Tribune* cartoon showing the mayor with a fond, protective arm around Waldo. The rapport between the two was not easily explained. Gaynor did *not* have beautiful manners, for example. One of his biographers, Mortimer Smith, has described him as "by a wide margin the most cantankerous man ever to sit in City Hall." The last time word of a shooting had really shaken the city Gaynor himself had been the victim. In August 1910 he had been strolling on the deck of the *Kaiser Wilhelm der Grosse*, about to sail for Europe, when a deranged city employee had come up behind him, pressed a gun to his neck, and fired. The other photographers had done their work and left, but as a reward for being late the man from the *Evening World* was on hand to snap one of the most frequently reprinted of all news pictures, showing Gaynor just before he crumpled to the deck. (Charles Chapin, the city editor of the *Evening World*—a man who, according to his staff of reporters, had a legendary imperviousness to human suffering, especially theirs—had been overjoyed. "Blood all over him!" he had cried, clutching the print, "and exclusive, too!")

On this early morning after the Rosenthal murder, Waldo finally decided to wait to call Gaynor—who had, of course, survived the attempted assassination—until the old man was likely to be awake anyhow. Fortunately the mayor was an early riser. "Got him, did they?" said Gaynor when he heard the news. He didn't sound surprised.

By the time Waldo talked to Gaynor he was able to tell him that the getaway car had been found. In years to come the shooting was often incorrectly referred to as the first murder in which a car was involved. The *Times* would describe it as such in its 1947 obituary of Charles Whitman. With an insistence on quotation marks a bit excessive even for the *Times*, it reported that Rosenthal's murderers "were the first 'gangsters,'" as that term later became familiarly used, to use an automobile to "rub out" a "squealer." On the day after the murder several newspapers mentioned an earlier gang killing in which a car had played a role.

This had been the shooting down in April 1910 of Spanish Louis, a free-lance gang leader, whose services Herman Rosenthal had frequently chartered. One of his assignments for Rosenthal had been to waylay and beat to death Bridgey Webber on lower Second Avenue one night in late 1909 while Rosenthal watched from across the street. Bridgey had managed to survive, however, and after a crowd gathered, Rosenthal, all Good Samaritan, had come along and taken him to a hospital. A few months later Spanish Louis had been mowed down on lower Second Avenue by a rifle barrage from a 1908 Pierce Arrow. "Boob Walker was reported to have been in the neighborhood that night," noted the *American* a few days after Rosenthal's murder, adding that Boob, who had shared Herman Rosenthal's last table, was, of course, an employee of Bridgey Webber's. Also in the car on the night of the Spanish Louis murder, said the Hearst paper, were three gunmen named Gyp the Blood, Whitey Lewis, and Lefty Louie. No arrests had ever been made in the case. There had been considerable astonishment in the congregation when Boob, Whitey, Gyp, and Louie had turned up as pallbearers and chief mourners at Spanish Louis' elaborate East Side funeral. Later it was reported that Bridgey, to throw everybody off further, had even paid the funeral bill.

But the guerilla warfare among the riffraff of lower Second Avenue was at this time so constant that it rarely made the papers, and to the average citizen the appearance of the gray Packard on the Rosenthal murder scene represented something new and bizarre in the annals of homicide. It gave the whole thing an extra excitement. "It proves that New York must be as modern as possible," noted the *Sun* in a tone verging on civic pride. (The shift in idiom from the horse-drawn era had not entirely caught on, however. One paper reported that the getaway car had traveled "at a rapid gait." A policeman described an automobile that had tried to follow it and developed a flat tire as having "lost a shoe.") Having called attention to the new gasoline-powered brand of thuggery, the *Sun* editors went on at length about how it all made them pine for the days of Bret Harte's stagecoach-riding gamblers and their picturesque ways. Then, remembering themselves, they concluded sternly: "But the root of the matter is that a pack of cutthroats has executed a man in a public street."

To District Attorney Whitman the root of the matter was something else. The headline in the *World* on Wednesday, July 17, which the newsboys were hawking twenty-four hours after the shooting, read: "WHITMAN SAYS 'I ACCUSE POLICE, THROUGH CERTAIN MEN, OF ROSENTHAL'S MURDER.'" The "system" through which criminals paid off the Police Department, he said, was "a great and powerful secret organization which can defy the law as it pleases. The time and place of the murder were meant to inspire terror in the hearts of those the system had most to fear." It was "intended to be an example of what anyone might expect who dares to assail it." The crime, Whitman went on, had been "the greatest shock to the administration of justice that this city has ever known. My duty will be to show the people that justice cannot be blocked by terrorists in or out of the Police Department." The statement was given to all reporters, but the man who stood at the district attorney's side as he handed a copy of it around was Herbert Bayard Swope of the *World*.

By this time the Rosenthal murder was not only the biggest story in all of New York's fourteen daily papers but had also made the front pages of most papers all over America as they welcomed with open arms this sensational example of sin in the big eastern city. It had aroused enormous interest in the press abroad for similar reasons. The London correspondent of the New York *Sun* noted that all over Europe newspapers had found that the death of a gambler on a New York street had "furnished an occasion for their anti-American outlook." "Many futile attempts have been made to purify American politics, but they have been hopeless," declared the Berlin *Morgenpost* later that week. "The evil is in the very blood of the nation. It manifests itself in the same way as breathing, eating and sleeping do in the normal life." If America had not been a country rich in natural resources, the German editorial went on, it would have been "long ago destroyed by moral blood poisoning. . . . The worst criminals of all are the New York police who love to call themselves the 'finest.' "

Within a day after the crime District Attorney Whitman would be making it clear to all chroniclers of the city's wickedness that he had a particular member of New York's finest in mind when he spoke of police terrorism. Long afterward he told Becker's lawyer that his suspicions of Becker had first been aroused because of the lieutenant's appearance at the Forty-seventh Street police station hardly more than an hour after Herman Rosenthal's body had been turned out on a slab in its back room.

III

"I concede freely that no public official has ever performed a service more valuable to the community which had honored him than you did in appearing at the station house immediately after the Rosenthal murder . . ." began one paragraph in an impassioned statement that Charles Becker sent thirty-six months later to Whitman, by this time governor of New York, a statement the policeman hoped would bring about a reconsideration of his death sentence for first-degree murder. He agreed that his own presence at the station had been a serious error and to a degree the cause of his current desperate plight.

Both Whitman and Becker had gone to the station house as the result of peremptory telephone calls from newspapermen. It was only about fifteen minutes after the shooting that Swope called Whitman at his home in an apartment hotel at Twenty-sixth Street and Madison Avenue, explained what had happened, and told him to get over to the Forty-seventh Street station fast. Whitman didn't see why he couldn't wait until morning.

"No, you've got to come right now," said Swope.

"But I'm in *bed*. I've got my *pajamas* on," said Whitman (or so Swope would tell it in years to come). Finally the reporter hailed a cab and went down to Whitman's apartment on Madison Square. Whitman was still in his pajamas, but Swope finally talked him into getting dressed and going to the station house. They arrived shortly after 3 A.M.

Becker got there a little before four. The car he had borrowed had let him off about two o'clock at the Belleclaire Court Apartments on Edgecombe Avenue at West 165 Street. He had gone upstairs to his four-room flat on the fourth floor, where he took off his hat, coat, and collar. His wife Helen was awake and got up to make him a roast beef sandwich. They were a very close, loving couple—a fact that would come in for constant attention in the ensuing months—and presumably he talked over with her the events of his crowded day. There were two telephones in the apartment, one with an unlisted number. Just before a quarter to three the unlisted phone rang. On the other end was Fred Hawley, a young police reporter for the *Sun* with whom Becker was on especially friendly terms. According to Hawley's later testimony as a defense witness, the conversation went like this:

HAWLEY: Hello, Charley.
BECKER: Who's this?
HAWLEY: It's Hawley. Have you heard the news?
BECKER: No, what?
HAWLEY: Rosenthal's been killed.
BECKER: You're kidding me.
HAWLEY: No, Charley, I'm serious. He was shot down outside the Metropole.
BECKER: I think you've got a hangover.
HAWLEY: No, Charley, it's true. I'm on the story, and I'd like a statement from you.
BECKER: Well, I don't know what I can say. I don't know anything about the shooting. But I'm sorry he's been shot, because I wanted to show up the son-of-a-bitch.
HAWLEY: I think you ought to come down. . . . I think you ought to get on the job.

Becker hung up and talked the conversation over with his wife. "When Hawley called and asked me if I wasn't coming downtown, I didn't know what to do," he told a *Times* reporter later that week. "I told Hawley if I come downtown people may think that I have come down to gloat over the death of the man who has attacked me. If I don't come down the newspapers will say that when told about Rosenthal's death I evinced no interest or emotion. Hawley convinced me I should come downtown and I did." He did not rush, however. At three minutes to three he was still at home when another call came asking if he had heard the news of the murder. It was Bald Jack Rose, the East Side gambler. Becker claimed later that he could not recognize the voice of the caller, that he had only said, "Yes, some reporter told me," and hung up.

Becker came up out of the Times Square station at the Forty-third Street exit, his suit clinging to him and his thick hair damp on his forehead. Even at 3:30 A.M. the mercury was still in the eighties. Looking east on Forty-third he could see that the street was quiet. He decided, he said later, that the whole thing must have been a cruel practical joke. Cussing Hawley out, he turned back toward the subway entrance. At this moment Hawley came around a corner and, like a stage extra on cue, a newsboy ran up hawking an early edition of the *World*. "All about the big murder! Extra! Rosenthal shot down in the street!" ("GAMBLER MURDERED IN POLICE FEUD" was the headline over Rosenthal's picture in the *World* that Becker made a grab for. The headline in the *Tribune*, a paper less dedicated to the crooked-cop issue, was "ROSENTHAL KILLED IN GAMBLERS' WAR.")

"My God, you're right," Becker told Hawley. He and the reporter stopped by the darkened Metropole, then took a trolley to Forty-seventh Street and Seventh Avenue and walked half a block west to the station house.

The West Forty-seventh Street station, headquarters of the Sixteenth Precinct, was a gloomy brick building on the south side of the street. Its walls were spotted and peeling, its ceilings scorched by smoke from the coal stove that heated it in winter, and its rough board floors and rickety tables and chairs charred with cigar burns. Ten years earlier it had been one of the stations condemned by a committee of police surgeons as a menace to public health. The stone steps of its low, wide stoop on the early morning after the Rosenthal murder were dark with the lounging bodies of newspapermen. Becker stood talking with them for a few minutes. About four o'clock a taxi pulled up. Two of his fellow policemen jumped out and went inside, dragging between them a prisoner dressed in a pair of coveralls. A short while afterward Becker followed them through the open double doors.

Becker was not on duty or in uniform—he wore a brown suit, a pin-striped shirt, and a straw hat—and this was not his precinct. The strong arm squads worked out of the central office at Police Headquarters down on Centre Street. But he had been detailed to the Sixteenth earlier in his career and had dropped by there frequently since Waldo had assigned him the previous fall to the drive against gambling. He had been on the force nearly nineteen of his forty-two years, and any precinct station was a part of the world he knew best. His step was strong and confident as he strode through the door of the Sixteenth, which was swarming with other policemen in uniform and plainclothes.

Although Becker's heritage was Bavarian, he was not the traditional blond Aryan type of German. "His eyes are brown and look straight at you," Swope would write in the *World* a few days later. "He is dark in hair and skin. His nose is big and straight . . . jutting out uncompromisingly over a long upper lip, a mouth like the cut of a knife, and a chin that sticks out squarely at the end of a jaw that looks like a granite block." In Becker's left cheek, however, was a deep dimple. The other cops teased him about the dimple and called him "Handsome Charley." Well over six feet tall, Becker was broad-shouldered and strongly built. His hands were unusually large. "He could kill a man with a punch," an admirer of his once wrote, offering it as a compliment. The admirer did not claim to have seen it done. Without stopping to check in with the desk lieutenant across the room, Becker walked toward the separate office at the right of the entrance that was called the "captain's room." Here Captain William Day usually sat at the main desk. Day had not yet arrived. He had called in from his home about 3 A.M. and asked if it would be necessary for him to make the long trip from Brooklyn. He was told coldly by the man who answered the phone that indeed it would be. The man on the phone had been District Attorney Whitman.

Whitman now sat bolt upright in the captain's swivel chair. His face was pale and tense with excitement. Still, he had a certain air of being at home there. In fact, as close students of his career could remember, he had been in this very room on another climactic early morning of his life. Like Becker, he had thick, waving brown hair and a jutting chin. His eyes were hazel, however, and he was more delicately put together. His lips were unusually thin; if he was aware of this, possibly he wondered from time to time at the injustice of the fact that in fiction the adjective "thin-lipped" guarantees that the character described will not turn out to be a warm, outgoing fellow. Physically, he had the look of a schoolmaster in a boys' academy, a job he had in fact held for some years after graduating from Amherst. He was forty-four, two years older than Becker, and considerably shorter, well under medium height. He had no dimple to be teased about. In any case he was not a man acquaintances were inclined to tease.

In the captain's room with Whitman as Becker approached the door were Second Deputy Police Commissioner Dougherty, Inspector Edward Hughes, and the prisoner, a small, dark, terrified-looking man whose name was Louis Libby. Dougherty had moved into his police job a little over a year before after a long career as head of the New York office of the Pinkerton Detective Agency. Inspector Hughes was a career policeman to whom Waldo had taken a special liking. He had been promoted twice since the young blueblood had come in as commissioner, and was now the inspector in charge of all the members of the force who worked out of the central office, a category that included Becker.

As for the prisoner, Libby was an East Sider, a member of the old Hesper Club, a small-time entrepreneur on the fringe of the gambling-gangster world below Fourteenth Street. A year before he had paid two hundred dollars down on a four-cylinder Packard once owned by former heavyweight champion John L. Sullivan and taken in a partner named William Shapiro to spell him at the wheel. Since the Packard's stand was in front of the Cafe Boulevard on the corner of Second Avenue and Tenth Street, they called themselves the Boulevard Taxi Service. For fifty dollars a night the car was at the disposal of East Side customers for excursions about the city, only a moderate percentage of which had ended in bloodshed. Not many automobiles were then for hire in the city, and only a few were regularly available to the East Side crowd. One they had access to was an Imperial often hired in his flush days by Herman Rosenthal. The Imperial was kept in the same garage at 75 Washington Square South that Libby patronized, and so was a Pierce-Arrow used in a recently head-lined jewelry heist. It was Libby's Packard that had now been identified as the murder car in the shooting of Rosenthal.

Standing beside Whitman at the captain's desk, talking rapidly into a telephone at this moment, was the tall, red-haired figure of reporter Swope. There were also a number of patrolmen and sergeants in the room, taking notes, fumbling with records, standing close by Libby to prevent his escape and jumping to gratify

Whitman's slightest request. Although this was police territory, there was no question about who was in charge. All eyes were turned on the captain's chair in which the district attorney sat barking questions at prisoner Libby.

If any one of the cops on the premises had been asked why Whitman was being allowed to treat the Forty-seventh Street station as a conquered province, his unprintable answer undoubtedly would have included the name of Gallagher. As soon as the murder car had swept by him on West Forty-third Street and, on a reflex, he had noted the license number, Gallagher, the cafe singer who had been on his way to apply for a job at the Metropole, had followed the surging crowd to the bloody scene in front of the hotel. "Why, I don't know," he said later. "I had already realized from the smoke that it had been a shooting, and I wasn't keen on getting mixed up in it." There he heard various members of the crowd giving policeman Brady the number of the getaway car.

"All those numbers are wrong," he stepped up and told Brady. "The right number was New York 41313."

Gallagher was not given a pat on the back for his public-spirited gesture. Instead, Brady told him to stand aside. Nevertheless, when reinforcements arrived from the Sixteenth Precinct Gallagher repeated his story to one of them. This time the policeman grabbed him and hauled him to the station house where the desk lieutenant booked him as a material witness. He was then thrown, kicking and shouting, into a cell. "They didn't even give me a chance to explain that I only wanted to help them," Gallagher said later in an aggrieved voice.

This was certainly very curious behavior by the police. For years to come it would be cited as proof that even the minor cops on the scene were in league with Charles Becker to obstruct the investigation of the crime. Perhaps they were. It is also likely that, whatever their relationship with Becker, they had less than the proper enthusiasm for bringing to justice the murderer of a gambler notorious for making trouble for countless members of the force. In addition they must have believed that their obstructive tactics would please their immediate superior, Captain Day, as well as Day's boss, Inspector Hayes, Day and Hayes being, of course, the two policemen Rosenthal had most recently tried to have arrested.

Unfortunately for them, the Gallagher incident did not go unobserved. A number of reporters were in and out of the station during the first hour after the crime. As soon as Whitman arrived, they told him what had happened. He instantly demanded that the singer be released. Gallagher, badly shaken, was brought upstairs from the cell area by a suddenly solicitous escort. Within a few minutes the police had traced the car to Libby, who had then been arrested in his Stuyvesant Street rooming house and brought to the station. Whitman apologized over and over again to Gallagher for the shameful treatment he had received at the hands of the police. So, for that matter, did Inspector Hughes, who arrived fifteen minutes later. The whole episode had been the result of a terrible misunderstanding, he assured Gallagher. A few minutes afterward, however, he took the precaution of directing that all newspapermen get the hell off the premises. This did not include Swope, who remained as Whitman's right hand.

Thus from the beginning of the investigation the district attorney was at least two up on the Police Department. Thanks to Swope, he had arrived on the scene before any important police figure was there to take charge. And he had the large moral advantage of having caught members of the force in a suspicious and reprehensible act. From that moment on the public had the impression that if the district attorney had not been on hand that morning, the murderer would never have been found. "On the night of the murder, had Charles Whitman not gone to the Forty-seventh Street police station, no one can doubt that Becker would today be a free man," Richard Harding Davis wrote a few months later in *Collier's*. "For the moment the District Attorney took on the crowd at that police station and released from a cell, into which the police had thrown him, the only man who knew or who would tell the number of the 'murder car' the case of the people was in safe hands." Becker himself described the district attorney's ferreting out of the number as a great public service three years later in his final appeal to Whitman. But when Thomas Coupe, the Elks' Club desk clerk, was brought into the station about a quarter to five on the morning of the murder he reminded Whitman that he too had caught the right license number and not only had shouted it after the pursuing taxi carrying Detective File but had given it to newspapermen on the scene. With the number in the hands of the press, New York 41313 would have been traced in the uproar that followed the murder. Presumably the garage favored by gangland chauffeurs would have been checked by police or by reporters who were soon engaged in a fierce rivalry to show them up, and the gray Packard would have been found. At the time, however, the Coupe development only gave Whitman the opportunity to point out, with justice, that neither Coupe nor Gallagher was a trained observer as policemen were supposed to be. "It seems mighty strange to me," he told the press, "that these cops missed what rank amateurs had no trouble seeing."

Because of his size and assertive manner—arrogance would come to be the well-worn word for it; *hubris* would probably have been put to use had it been one of the fad words of the day— heads usually turned when Becker entered a place, and, under the circumstances, his arrival at the station that early morning was bound to cause some stir. In the months to come, those who believed him guilty often would refer to the presumption of his turning up at the station unasked. Becker dealt with this in his last formal plea to Whitman. After mentioning Whitman's remark about his appearance there having first led the district attorney to suspect him, Becker wrote: "And yet, sir, I went there for precisely the same reason that led you to go there. When I heard of the murder, I said to my wife, 'I never now can meet and disprove the charges Rosenthal made against me. This will hang like a cloud over me in the department.' There was only one way to off-set the injury his death threatened to cause me and that was by discovering some clue to his murder that would greatly enhance my reputation on the force."

More probably Becker went to the station because the shooting was an extraordinary development in the case, and he couldn't bear not to know what was going on. Later those who thought him guilty considered his arrival there (to plant false evidence? to obstruct the pursuit of the killers?) certain proof of his guilt. The few outside the force who believed him to be innocent considered it a compelling argument for the opposite theory: Only an innocent man would have failed to calculate the danger of showing his face at the station at such a moment. On one point all agreed: Guilty or innocent, he would have done himself a big favor if he had finished out the night in bed with his wife in the Belleclaire Court Apartments.

As it was, he had barely reached the doorway of the captain's room and taken one step in, assuming his welcome, when Inspector Hughes quickly raised his hand and waved him out. All those in the small room turned to look at the intruder, and Whitman's and Becker's eyes met. In the months to come the police lieutenant's stolid composure under harrowing circumstances would astonish, even infuriate, those who watched him in the courtroom. At this moment, however, his black eyes were startled and angry. Whitman's expression was cool, speculative. The dramatic confrontation—almost certainly the last time they met outside of a courtroom—lasted only a few seconds. Then Becker turned and walked out the door.

For a time he leaned in sullen silence against the iron railing in front of the station. Soon, however, he sat down on the steps and began to talk about the murder with the other exiles from the center of excitement, the newspaper reporters. At one point, they later remembered, he said, "I'll lay you five to one it was some of Spanish Louis' gang." The reporters took turns ducking across the street to a saloon that was illegally open—not unheard of in 1912, even a hundred feet from a police station. The saloon had one telephone from which they called in to their city desks the arrivals and departures at the precinct and the latest developments in the case as they learned them from friendly cops inside the big doors. Hawley, the *Sun* reporter, later swore in court that, except for two such five-minute absences to telephone and one trip to the men's room, and except for Becker's time inside the station, which had no rear exit, the police lieutenant was not out of his sight from 3:30 to 8 A.M.

In time Whitman would publicly favor the theory that Becker's appearance at the station that morning had been for the purpose of planting a gun on Rosenthal's body, a plot the D.A. believed he had foiled by getting there first. (It was never clear what good it would have done the policeman to prove that Rosenthal had been armed). Three years afterward, Whitman recalled that Becker had come up to him at the station and said he was about to inspect Rosenthal's body. Whitman said he told him: "Never you mind going near it. I've been all over that body." However, Whitman didn't remember this conversation in time to repeat it in his appearance on the stand. Inspector Hughes would testify that he had come outside about four-thirty, tapped Becker on the shoulder, and asked him if he had seen the body.

"I said 'no,'" Becker recalled later. "Hughes said, 'We'll get a look at it.' We went to the rear yard and viewed the corpse." Both men were used to examining bodies whose heads had been partially shot away and were not put off by the grisly sight on the slab in the back room of the station.

"Whoever done him, done him good," Hughes said to Becker. Then, Hughes recalled, Becker said he was sorry since he had an affidavit "that would put it all over him." He had patted the pocket of his jacket, bulging with a copy of that day's *Morning Telegraph,* which contained the text of a "document of vile and hideous import," as the *Tribune* later described it. This was an affidavit from Herman Rosenthal's first wife, Dora Gilbert, in which she declared that in the years after their marriage some fifteen years earlier Rosenthal had acted as a procurer for her one-woman call house and had lived high on the proceeds. Becker had arranged to have her swear to this as part of the campaign he had just launched to discredit Rosenthal as a reliable witness against a respected police officer. He did not make the mistake of thinking that it was any good to him now. "Only tonight I completed one of the last bits of necessary work to be done on this case, in my opinion," he had told reporters when he first arrived at the station. The Gilbert statement "added to the facts and figures I have been seeking in regard to this man, his character, his career, and his standing in his own world and the world at large." With Rosenthal dead he wouldn't discuss what the affidavit said. "I merely refer to it as an indication of my desire to combat this man in the only fair way by meeting all his charges before the proper authorities."

When Becker and Hughes came back into the main part of the station, they found a line-up in progress. Libby in his greasy coveralls and chauffeur's cap—the police had ordered him to put these on when they arrested him, he said later—was in the middle of a row of plainclothesmen, all wearing business suits. Coupe, the Elks' Club clerk, was asked to identify the man he had seen in the driver's seat of the getaway car. Without hesitation he was able to pick out Libby who, it would turn out, had indisputably been upstairs in his rooming house quarters all evening. Coupe declared also that there had been only one killer and that

Libby was the man who had fired all five shots. Whitman went to
the front steps of the station and announced Coupe's identification of the murderer to the reporters. "He will make a splendid
witness," he told them.

A few moments later the murder car was driven up in front of
the precinct. The 1909 Packard—very high off the ground with a
wide running board, steeply arched fenders, enormous headlights,
and a cut-glass flower vase—had its top down as it had on its
murder run. Whitman, the senior police officers, and the reporters
hurried down the front steps to inspect it. Becker was with them,
he insisted later, standing within four feet of Whitman. Apparently the district attorney did not notice him, for he would testify
on the stand that he had not seen Becker at the station after
four o'clock.

At about five Whitman and Swope came out of the station,
hailed a cab, and went off to pay a visit to Mrs. Rosenthal. According to Hawley he and Becker soon afterward walked west to
Eighth Avenue to an all-night cafeteria for some ham and eggs.
Like other reporters who had been near the scene Hawley had
sent for reinforcements soon after the murder, and half a dozen
other *Sun* men were now fanning out through the city, taking
statements, usually not for attribution, and burrowing into underworld lore. If Becker had really had any notion of investigating
the murder on his own and turning up evidence that would
redound to his credit in the department, he clearly abandoned the
idea early in the game. He and Hawley had a leisurely breakfast
in which they were joined by three of the precinct policemen. As
they returned to the station about seven, Whitman and Swope
were just getting out of a cab in front of the door. Soon afterward
William Shapiro, Libby's partner, was brought in in handcuffs. It
was Shapiro, it turned out, who had driven the murder car. Libby
now admitted that when Shapiro had come home about two-thirty
that morning—the two of them lived in the same rooming house
—Shapiro had waked him up and told him that his night's fares
had "done a little shooting uptown," but Libby had thought
nothing of it, he said.

Becker hung around the station for an hour more. Before he
left at about eight he gave the press a formal statement.

"Coming as this does at this psychological moment, it is most
unfortunate," said Becker. "It ought to be needless for me to say—

and I think I ought not to be asked to say—what you newspapermen know to be the fact, that I know absolutely nothing about the
crime—who perpetrated it, what the motive was, or what was to
be gained by it. I want to say now that I have said this much—
and perhaps I am violating a rule of the department by so
saying—that it was to my best and only advantage that Rosenthal
should have been permitted to live for many years. I bear this
man no malice. He set himself up as my enemy. I have explained
every move I made with this man to the satisfaction of my
superiors." Thus within a few hours of a murder he would be
accused of having arranged, Becker seemed to be worrying only
about satisfying his superiors at headquarters, about breaching
department protocol.

The business of the mortgage could be easily explained, he
insisted. His meeting with Rosenthal on New Year's Eve hadn't
been by any appointment. "And of course I didn't get stewed and
kiss him or anything like that," he added. "I don't even drink. In
three more days the whole thing would have been over . . . the
last suspicion lifted by documentary, legal evidence." He watched
the press write all this down and then started off toward the
subway, walking briskly, swinging his hat.

IV

At first District Attorney Whitman didn't have everything his own way. His statement in the *World* the day after Rosenthal was shot, accusing the New York police force of having committed the murder "through certain men," moved the *Sun* to call him "unfortunately excitable." Whitman backed away a bit. He had made the charge "as an individual and not as District Attorney," he said. "No right-minded person would have suspected either that any policeman had a direct hand in the murder or that it was instigated on behalf of any member or set of members on the force," the *Times* scolded him. The crime was probably the result of an old grudge among East Side gamblers and their gangster friends, the paper said.

As a politician Whitman didn't welcome this theory. Intramural crimes among Second Avenue low life weren't the kind of antic that would stir up continuing headlines or further prosecutors' careers. Of a murder so clumsily handled that those in charge of the car bearing the murderers from the scene had not concealed the license number, he now commented, "Oh, it was a clever job. . . . No dull gangster ever laid out the work of that night!" He taunted the five policemen stationed within two blocks of the crime for not having got to the Metropole fast enough after the shooting. "Even the policeman posted farthest away—at Seventh Avenue and Forty-fourth Street—could have got to the hotel in fifteen seconds if he'd been on the job," the D.A. insisted. He speculated publicly on why the driver of the getaway car hadn't been arrested for making an illegal U-turn. Naturally he also referred often to the Gallagher incident. "POLICE QUEERLY IN-COMPETENT IN TRACING THE MURDER" read an accommodating headline in the *World*.

Whitman lost no time in zeroing in on Becker. "The case against Lieutenant Becker will be pushed through with all possible vigor though it is apparent that no conviction can result," he had said in his first interview with Swope after the murder.

"You mean the graft case, don't you?" other reporters asked him the next day. Whitman smiled and raised his eyebrows. One of his visitors inquired about his own theory of who was responsible for the murder.

"Why any newspaperman with a newspaperman's intelligence who has been reading the newspaper for the last week must be able to advance a suspicion of his own," the district attorney answered. "The trail is leading where I thought it would," he added, smiling at the reporters meaningfully.

If it hadn't been for his friend Swope at the *World*, Charles Whitman wouldn't have had such an obvious defendant. For that matter, if it hadn't been for the *World*, there might have been no murder. There was no doubt in anyone's mind that Rosenthal's statements about the corrupt relationship between gamblers and the police had been the immediate cause of his being shot down in front of the Metropole. His revelations had appeared in two separate articles in the *World*. On Saturday, July 13, a news story had been published in which Rosenthal charged that a certain anonymous police lieutenant assigned to enforcing the gambling laws had been his business partner. The next day his far more sensational affidavit had named Becker as the culprit and elaborated on their unseemly palship. Swope was the only person the gambler had found in the city who would pay attention to his lugubrious tale, and it was clear the high-powered reporter must have had some control over the story told for publication by the near-illiterate and overanxious gambler.

"I never met Becker nor knew anything of him until last fall when he made a raid on 155 Second Avenue," Rosenthal's affidavit of July 14 had begun. The gamblers running the Second Avenue place, he said, were Beansey Rosenfeld and Bald Jack Rose. After the raid Rose, an occasional employee of Rosenthal's, had cozied up to Lieutenant Becker, and the two had worked out "a sort of partnership" in which Rose had collected graft payments for the policeman from the major gamblers in town. Rosenthal then described his alcoholic evening with Becker at the Elks' Club and Becker's later investment in the Forty-fifth Street gambling house. The policeman hadn't handed over the fifteen hundred dollars directly, he said, but a lawyer known to Becker had given him the money after he had signed a chattel mortgage made out to a dummy. Becker had also specified, according to Rosenthal's affidavit, that his new sidekick, Bald Jack Rose, be installed at the gambling club as a co-manager to keep an eye on the policeman's investment.

Things had gone along all right at the Forty-fifth Street place, said Rosenthal, until one day Becker told him that Police Commissioner Waldo insisted the place be raided. After some stalling the raid had come off. During it, said the affidavit, one of Becker's men had told Rosenthal, "It's all right. It's Charley making the raid and it's all right." Becker himself, said Rosenthal, had told the gambler's wife not to worry, that he was sorry about the raid and that Rosenthal could consider the mortgage satisfied. One of the men taken in the raid, however, had been Lillian Rosenthal's young nephew. Rosenthal said Becker explained that the boy would get off in court, he would see to that. Instead, the young man had been indicted by the grand jury on the testimony of Becker's men. Moreover, the gambling equipment had been badly damaged. When Rosenthal complained, the affidavit claimed, Becker had taken vengeance by stationing the police guard in the Forty-fifth Street house.

When Rosenthal's first charges against him had been published that Saturday before the murder, identifying him in all but name to anyone in the police or gambling world, Lieutenant Becker had hired a lawyer named John Hart, who had been in the district attorney's office for many years and had recently left because he couldn't get along with Whitman. Early Monday morning after a conference with Commissioner Waldo, Becker got ready to start libel proceedings. Some aspects of Rosenthal's story in the *World* were true, he admitted. Bald Jack Rose *had* gone to work for him after the Second Avenue raid. Becker insisted that Rose had worked as his stool pigeon rather than his graft collector, as Rosenthal claimed. (Probably he was both.) It was true that

Becker's squad had raided Rosenthal's house on Waldo's order, but he had never discussed this with the gambler ahead of time or exchanged a word with Mrs. Rosenthal during the raid, Becker said. As for the New Year's ball, he and his wife *had* sat next to the Rosenthals. He suspected at the time, he would say later, that Bald Jack Rose had staged the encounter. On the other hand, Rosenthal was known to have pulled this trick in the past, contriving to be seen with people whose acquaintance would be useful to him. The Rosenthals, Becker would insist, had come and sat down next to him and his wife without being asked. Knowing the fellow's reputation for getting cops into trouble, he had said as little to the gambler as possible and had left right after dinner. Later, on the stand during Becker's two trials for murder, Bald Jack Rose supported Rosenthal's version. But a week before the policeman's execution, when the books on the case were closed, Bald Jack would indicate that Becker's story of the evening was substantially true, even agreeing that the policeman had changed places with his wife so he wouldn't be sitting next to the importunate gambler.

The Elks' Club ball had been a crowded public affair. At the table where Rosenthal and Becker sat were some two dozen other revelers, and all the tables were jammed close together in the big ball room. The drunken kissing scene Rosenthal described would have had hundreds of possible witnesses. (People weren't as aware of homosexuality early in the century or as nervous about it as they would be later. According to Lincoln Steffens, Jacob Riis, the Lower East Side reporter who had led anything but a sheltered life, angrily refused to believe that such practices existed. A charge such as Rosenthal's would have different overtones today, but there was never any indication at the time that Becker's alleged misconduct amounted to more than fraternization with a criminal.) Rosenthal's affidavit described Becker, a conspicuous man, as "waving to the crowd" while he stood embracing his new friend. This would have been particularly reckless since the guests at the Elks' Club that night had included George Dougherty, deputy police commissioner and head of the department's detective bureau, who undoubtedly would have caused immediate trouble for any member of the force making a spectacle of himself with a cop-baiting gambler. Yet no casual Elks' Club customer apparently saw the painful scene. Nor would any witness testify in court that he had encountered the police lieutenant with Rosenthal on their many sociable nights out together during the time when they were "the best friends in the world," as Rosenthal had put it in his affidavit.

As for Rosenthal's most damaging charge that Becker had been a partner in his gambling house, the lieutenant later concluded that Rosenthal had probably honestly believed this to be true, that Bald Jack Rose might well have told him it was Becker who had put up the fifteen hundred dollars with the proviso that Bald Jack be taken on as his assistant. Previous business arrangements between Rosenthal and Bald Jack had often ended in bitterness with Rose convinced he had got the short end of the stick. No doubt he thought this outcome would be less likely, Becker suggested, if Rosenthal believed Bald Jack was now a stand-in for a raiding cop. Rose also knew that in view of their past history of mutual treachery Rosenthal wasn't likely to give him a mortgage on the gambling house equipment. Sometime in February 1912, Becker would say, Rose had come to him, said he wanted to put money in Rosenthal's new house, and asked for the name of a lawyer, which Becker had given him. His usual Second Avenue lawyers were no good, Rose had told him, because he didn't want word to get around to his many creditors that he now had some cash in hand. (He was getting between 15 and 25 per cent of the collections he made for Becker, Rose would say in court.) This was the same reason Rose gave to the lawyer named for wanting a dummy's name on the mortgage papers. It was Rose who had brought the money to him, the lawyer would testify, and also Rose who, three weeks after the raid on Rosenthal's place, had told him he'd gotten his money out and to mark the mortgage as satisfied. Although he later repudiated it, some forty hours after the murder Rose himself would sign an affidavit agreeing that this was the way things had happened, that Lieutenant Becker had never been Rosenthal's partner no matter what the dead gambler had told the *World*.

Long afterward Becker would write in his last appeal to Charles Whitman: "That anybody could believe I would hold such a conversation (as the one reported at the Elks' Club) . . . with Rosenthal at our first meeting or . . . that among all the gamblers in New York I would select for a partner such a man

. . . is conceivable only where preconviction of my guilt has become an immovable mental obsession."

Becker had spent much of the seventy-two hours before the murder gathering evidence for his libel suit. Charles Plitt, an informal press agent whom Becker, a vain and ambitious man, had encouraged to ply the newspapers with tales of his strong arm squad exploits, had told him that the previous fall Rosenthal had approached him and offered him twenty-five hundred dollars (fifty dollars on account) if Plitt would help the gambler get close to Becker. To show that Rosenthal had been engaged in a long campaign to trap him into a compromising position, the lieutenant got a sworn statement about this from Plitt who was a man who'd swear to anything, as it turned out. He also asked Bald Jack Rose, who had told him about Rosenthal's unhusbandly behavior with his first wife, to see if Dora Gilbert would swear to this before a notary. And about one o'clock on Sunday morning when the first edition of the *World* containing Rosenthal's dramatic affidavit came off the presses Becker and Hart were at the World Building in the office of the paper's legal counsel, Isaac White. Before they left, White had lent them the *World's* morgue file on Rosenthal.

Much later that morning, after Rosenthal's charges reached most of the city's readers, Becker's phone at the Belleclaire Apartments began to ring so continuously that, he would say later, he told the downstairs switchboard not to put through any more calls. Early in the afternoon he and his wife, Helen, packed a picnic lunch, put on comfortable clothes, and took the subway downtown. While Helen Becker waited, her husband returned the Rosenthal clippings to Isaac White, picked up a certified copy of the Rosenthal affidavit for purposes of his libel action, and talked to the *World* lawyer, who was apparently anxious about the paper's liability. Becker and his wife then had taken the subway to Brighton Beach, beyond Coney Island. It was so hot they stayed there long after dark and did not get back home until nearly midnight. During the whole day, Helen Becker would insist later, they never mentioned the name Rosenthal.

On Monday afternoon, twelve hours before the murder, Becker had met with a dozen reporters in lawyer Hart's office. Hart handed out a statement demanding a full investigation of the Rosenthal charges on behalf of his client, pointing out the gambler's extensive history of illegal activity (conveniently culled from the *World* clippings) and quoting Rosenthal's frequent boast that any man who had ever raided him had got into bad trouble. Earlier in the day Becker had learned that Dora Gilbert was willing to make a statement and had arranged to have Bald Jack Rose, Plitt, and a notary go to her house on East Twenty-seventh Street that evening. Not averse to fighting headlines with headlines, Becker also got in touch with the raffish racing sheet, the *Morning Telegraph*, where his friend Bat Masterson, formerly the sheriff of Dodge City, was the sports editor. The *Telegraph* agreed to publish Dora's affidavit if it were delivered in time for the next day's edition. When he returned to Police Head-quarters after the press conference, Becker—according to an affidavit sworn to many years later by Jacob Reich—had a visit from Deacon Terry of the *American*. Reich said he heard Terry say he had a message for the lieutenant from District Attorney Whitman. (Before Swope came along, Terry had been the re-porter with the most direct line to the D.A.'s office.) The reputed message was that Becker wasn't to worry about the Rosenthal business, that Whitman was aware of his good work on the force, that the charges would be dealt with fairly. Did Becker have any evidence that would help show up Rosenthal for what he was? The policeman, according to Reich, mentioned the Gilbert state-ment and promised to send a copy to the district attorney.

Becker, a fight fan, had tickets for a bout at Madison Square Garden on the night of the murder. A colonel in the National Guard who owned a gray Simplex often let favored members of the police force use it, for reasons that were never specified. Becker borrowed the car for the evening. At the garage where he picked it up he invited the chauffeur and the garage bookkeeper to join him at the Garden. By eleven o'clock Buck Crouse had beat Joe Worthing in ten rounds in the main bout. On the way out Becker had run into Reich and Deacon Terry. They had a mid-night snack at the St. George Hotel on East Twenty-second Street and then set off for Park Row where most of New York's news-papers were then published. It was on this trip downtown that they had detoured to let Terry off at the tube station. At Park Row Reich had cased the *American* offices to see how they were handling the story while Becker went, one last time, into the *World* building to talk with Isaac White. When the first edition of the *World* came upstairs he took one and joined Reich, who had already reached the car with copies of the next day's *American* and the important *Morning Telegraph*. From the beginning of the case, like other principals involved, Becker never underestimated the power of the press. All the papers carried Hart's statement. They also carried some remarks of District Attorney Whitman that were clearly designed to damp down the furor over Rosenthal's charges.

"Lieutenant Becker smiled when he read what Whitman had said," Reich testified later. "He said he was very relieved." The Simplex started uptown. It was then a little more than half an hour before the murder.

District Attorney Charles Whitman had also put in a busy time of it in the few days before the shooting. However, his slight tan that reporters would notice the morning after the crime was the result of sunny afternoons at Bailey's—rather than Brighton—Beach. On Thursday, July 11, Whitman had left the raucous gamblers' side show behind him and departed by train for another kind of circus—the social scene at Newport. He and his wife had been invited to spend a few days there with that sprightly and unconventional grande dame, Mrs. Oliver Hazard Perry Belmont. Mrs. Belmont was the lady who in 1895 had locked her young daughter Consuelo in her room until she agreed to augment the family splendor by becoming Duchess of Marlborough. Shortly thereafter, in a day when a divorcee was treated as virtually a member of the demimonde, the indomitable mother had divorced a Vanderbilt (William K.) to marry a Belmont, which she regarded as a step upward since the Belmonts had been Society for two generations whereas the Vanderbilts, with her help, had only just bulled their way in. The Newport invitation to the Whitmans represented a significant step upward in their social progress. In addition, Mrs. Belmont was excellent company. Not to mention the fact that the city was at this point a grubby furnace. When a telephone call came early Saturday morning from young Swope telling him that all hell was breaking loose in the Rosenthal matter and that he should return to town at once, Whitman gave a flat no. Would he issue a statement to the *World* promising that the D.A.'s office would take action on Rosenthal's charges? "I *would* not," said Whitman, hanging up. In desperation Swope took the next train for Newport.

His great Rosenthal scoop would fall apart and probably be quashed as dangerous libel if the district attorney refused to take the gambler's charges against Becker seriously. Swope had demonstrated many times before, however, that Whitman found him a persuasive customer. For about a year and a half the two of them had been working closely together to their mutual profit, with Whitman giving Swope the inside rail on stories out of the D.A.'s office and the reporter, in the articles that followed, playing up Whitman as a political hero. Matters had reached the point where the district attorney of New York County—that is, Manhattan—sometimes would have to wait a quarter of an hour on the telephone line until the imperious reporter at the *World* was ready to receive his call. The extraordinary sway that Swope had over the district attorney had become a matter for satiric comment in other papers, according to E. J. Kahn, Jr., in *The World of Swope*. At the time of the tragic Triangle Building fire in March 1911, a rival journal reported that Swope had burst into a conference Whitman was having with other newspapermen in his office.

"That will be enough, boys!" Swope shouted. "The Triangle Building's on fire and I think the D.A. ought to be there." Swope had then convoyed the whole gathering to the scene of the fire and, sometime later, back to the Criminal Courts Building. "I think this is what the D.A. should say about the fire for the morning papers," he had announced, and, according to the *Sun*, Whitman had meekly approved the story that Swope then dictated.

When Swope approached Whitman in Newport that Saturday evening before the murder, however, he was not so co-operative. In a snit about having his fashionable holiday interrupted—or so Swope would describe it in later years—he finally agreed to take a look at a copy of Rosenthal's affidavit and the news story about it. If it didn't persuade the district attorney of his obvious duty, presumably he was won over by Swope's proposed lead on the article. The names of Rosenthal and Becker did not appear until well down in the piece, which began, after a Newport dateline: "District Attorney Whitman, who is here with his wife as a guest of Mrs. O. H. P. Belmont, showed keen interest in the story in the *World* today. . . ." Within the hour Whitman and Swope had got up a statement, telegraphed immediately to the *World* city desk, in which Whitman finally promised that Rosenthal would have a chance to tell his story to the grand jury.

"I have no sympathy with Rosenthal, the gambler," said the statement, "but I have real use for Rosenthal who, abused by the police, proposes to aid decency by revealing startling conditions. . . . The trail leads to high places. . . . The situation is best described as 'rotten.' " Whitman did insist on adding cautiously, "Rosenthal's story lacks legal corroboration and so far my men have not uncovered any legal evidence." The *World* was satisfied, however. "WHAT YOU SENT SAVED THE STORY," Swope's city editor wired him.

Whitman then had hurried off to dress for a ball at Crossways, Mrs. Stuyvesant Fish's forty-room cottage on Bellevue Avenue. Swope adjourned to the tables at Newport's famous Nautilus Club. Not only did he win, but later he also collected a tidy sum in space rates for a story on the Newport gambling scene, published in the *World* on the day of the murder. On Sunday morning after the Crossways affair, however, Whitman again gave Swope a bad time, seeing no reason why he should cut short his visit among the stately pleasure domes of Newport on account of a gambling-house hassle. When he reluctantly agreed to go back to town, Swope made sure the D.A. didn't defect at the last moment. He gave up another lucrative night at the Nautilus and took the train back with him. But the heat of the city was like a blow in the face. That night Whitman, in a very cross mood, apparently had some more second thoughts.

Herman Rosenthal appeared by appointment at his office in the Criminal Courts Building at nine o'clock Monday morning. When the gambler came out after half an hour, he looked discouraged. "No matter what anybody says," he told reporters waiting for him on the steep steps, "I'm going to see this thing through." The gambling fraternity had also sent out scouts who fell in with him on the way to the subway. "The lid will come off," an *American* reporter heard Rosenthal boast defiantly to a runner from an East Side stuss house. Rosenthal stopped by the World Building and then went to Magistrate's Court to present his amended affidavit charging Inspector Hayes and Captain Day with oppression for maintaining the guard in his house—the document that peculiarly, considering his recent statements to the *World*, did not mention Charles Becker. Several newspapers that came out that afternoon, twelve hours before his death, reported widespread rumors that Rosenthal's life was in danger.

What Whitman had pointed out to Rosenthal after he heard the gambler's story again that Monday morning, was that from a legal point of view nothing had changed since Rosenthal had talked to him weeks before: There was still no corroboration all the way down the line. Rosenthal had then given him the names of certain possible witnesses and agreed to come to Whitman's apartment the next morning, bringing promises from them to support his testimony before the grand jury. But the names he had given Whitman were those of the same men who had refused to support his story when he had tried them before: Bridgey Webber, Bald Jack Rose, gamblers Dollar John Langer and Sam Paul, and a man known as Abe the Rebbeler. The previous Thursday he had made the rounds of the East Side, nagging them to join him in his complaints about the police graft situation. "The gamblers in this town are a bunch of quitters," he had told a *Tribune* reporter the next day. "They snubbed me last night, but they'll look on me as some hill of beans if I win out."

By the time Rosenthal left, Whitman was very cold indeed on the situation. He called up Rhinelander Waldo and made a date with the commissioner to have lunch at the Union League Club. Waldo had just returned to the city from Toronto, having come back posthaste on orders of Mayor Gaynor after the mayor had seen the Rosenthal affidavit. The commissioner wasn't happy about having to cut *his* visit short either. He was to have been the star speaker at a police chief's convention on the subject, "How to Wipe Out Police Graft."

Although Mayor Gaynor detested Whitman, the district attorney and the amiable Waldo were on good terms. Waldo was a birthright member of the society that Whitman was just beginning to move into and had reportedly put the latter's name up for several clubs. Now Waldo assured him that Becker was one of his best men, that he was being victimized by a gambler sore about a raid, that Becker was suing the *World* for libel. No doubt he also reminded Whitman that—as he would write the district attorney later that week—in spite of all the overblown stories in the press Becker was only "a subordinate police officer, who has never been intrusted with any special power," or, as Mayor Gaynor would later put it, "just a little lieutenant."

With the D.A.'s office about to turn tail on the issue, Swope's position at the *World* was not enviable. Clearly he did not dictate the typewritten statement Whitman handed out to waiting reporters late that afternoon. Herman Rosenthal probably would not be called before the grand jury at all, the district attorney indicated. "This office is ready to present to the grand jury any evidence, properly corroborated, which involves the corruption of the Police Department or any other city department, but the time of the grand jury is limited and its work is heavy. I have no right to waste the grand jury's time by presenting to it witnesses whose statements consist of little more than rumors or hearsay and upon which no action would be justified," Whitman concluded.

These were the remarks that Lieutenant Becker would read and smile over when they appeared in the early edition of the morning papers just before the murder. Whitman would never again refer to his final public statement about Rosenthal before the killing. Certainly the last thing he would be anxious to admit was that less than an hour before the gambler was shot Charles Becker, thanks to a statement given to the press by the district attorney, had had reason to believe that this crisis in his life was over, that he could stop worrying about Herman Rosenthal.

But then had come the murder, which had changed everything.

V

"ROSENTHAL had in his hands the proof—or a close equivalent—
of the alliance between the police and crime. Just as he was
preparing to come to my home with additional information, just
as the situation shaped up most dangerously for the police involved, he was killed, and with him dies his evidence." So Whitman declared in an interview given to his favorite reporter on the
World the afternoon after the murder, twenty-four hours after he
had dismissed the gambler's evidence as not worth the time of the
grand jury. The contrast between his view of Rosenthal before he
was murdered and after suggested that witness Rosenthal dead
and unavailable for cross-examination was far more valuable to
the district attorney's office than witness Rosenthal alive. Whitman seemed unembarrassed by this implication and by the fact
that he had offered his valuable witness no protection. He agreed
that the gambler had expressed fears for his life and that he had
laughed at him. "Oh, you may laugh, but the gangs are already
around my house," an assistant district attorney remembered
Rosenthal's saying. He hadn't offered the gambler a bodyguard
because Rosenthal hadn't asked for one, said Whitman. Besides,
this was New York, wasn't it?—not the Wild West. But not all of
those who were following developments in the case had been as
surprised as the district attorney at the blood on the sidewalk in
front of the Metropole.

"Rosenthal was all right, but he had a big mouth . . . He

talked of things that would have meant the death of any man in his position," a henchman of Big Tim Sullivan's told the *Sun* on the day after the murder. And many of the bearded patriarchs sipping *kvas* in the coffee houses along Stanton Street must have believed that his violent end was a judgment on him for having turned his back on the old ways like so many of the younger Jewish immigrants, for spending his time with criminals and goys.

Born in one of the Baltic provinces of Russia, Rosenthal had arrived on the East Side at the age of five. He pulled out of home and school at fourteen, sold newspapers and hired on as a runner for a pool room, and discovered early in the game that the way to get ahead in the New World was to hang around Big Tim Sullivan's district headquarters. He and Sullivan, who always had a soft spot for former newsboys like himself, hit it off at once. In what Big Tim's other followers would later consider one of his first signs of mental instability, Sullivan made a special pet of young Rosenthal. For the rest of his life the gambler's fortunes would flourish and decline in tandem with those of the big Tammany Irishman.

"There is only one man in the world can call me off, that is the big fellow, Big Tim Sullivan, and he is as honest as the day is long and I know he is in sympathy with me," Rosenthal had told reporter Swope three days before the murder. "He don't want to see anybody else hurt. . . . My fight is with the police. It is purely personal with me . . . if I can't go through this without bringing anybody else in I'll quit. . . . The police know that I think more of Big Tim Sullivan than anybody else alive. They know that the only way they can hurt me is by trying to involve him with me— by trying to show that he is, or was, my partner in the gambling business. They know this is not true—that it is a dirty lie. He is not and never was interested with me to the extent of a penny. I hope that his name will not be brought out in this connection." It was true, said Rosenthal, that when he had needed cash to open his gambling places Sullivan had lent it to him, but "it was a legitimate transaction. I knew him as a boy," he went on. "I would lay down my life for him, and on more than one occasion he proved his friendship for me. If I need money I can go to him for it and he will give it to me or get it for me. I believe I could get anything he's got. It is purely a matter of friendship, and he never

expected to make a nickel profit out of it . . . I would do anything that Big Tim wanted me to do and would lose my life rather
than do this friend a wrong. He is the only man that could call me
off."

This proclamation that Big Tim's word was his command was
a part of Rosenthal's full statement on gambling in New York,
now appearing in print for the first time on the front page of the
World on Wednesday, July 17, the day after the murder. The
gambler's statement had been taken down at the *World* offices the
previous weekend, Swope reported, and it was from this account
that the affidavit dealing with Lieutenant Becker had been prepared. In his original statement Rosenthal had branded a number
of other policemen, including Inspector Hayes and Captain Day,
as grafters and preyers on the city's gamblers. Why they had been
left out of the affidavit was never made clear. The references to
Big Tim were presumably deleted by Rosenthal himself in the
hope that his name "will not be brought out in this connection."
Within hours after the shooting word was streaking around the
city that between the time Rosenthal had talked to Swope and the
time of the murder the "only man that could call me off," in
Rosenthal's words, had in fact made a strenuous effort to call
him off.

Rumors of this soon appeared in most local newspapers with
the exception of the *World*, which from the beginning ignored
most evidence suggesting that the person or persons responsible
for Rosenthal's death had any reason to think the problem of
shutting Herman up might have been solved short of murder. On
the afternoon before he died, reported the *Tribune*, Rosenthal had
told newspapermen that various politicians and agents of politicians had been visiting and calling him during the past forty-eight
hours, urging him to get out of town. Three or four hours before
he was killed "he received a summons to appear before one of the
highest politicians of Tammany Hall who had been his friend for
years. 'Herman, you have gone too far,' said the friend. 'It's time
you pulled in your horns. You're spoiling things.' " The *American*
had this same "very well-known East Side politician" telling
Rosenthal that if he did not shut up "I wash my hands of you."
The district attorney's office also reported that after the murder
Mrs. Rosenthal had told Whitman that Big Tim was among those
who had been in touch with her husband twice the afternoon

before his death, telling him he should "go away for a while." Big Tim himself had left the city for the Catskills sometime on the evening before the murder. He would not return to town for several weeks. Despite the published reports of his part in the prologue to Rosenthal's death—and in spite of more specific evidence of his involvement that would come out much later and that Charles Whitman would declare he had known all along—Sullivan's name would never be mentioned in the courtroom where Becker was twice tried for Rosenthal's murder.

Fame is freakish. Sullivan, a powerful figure in New York life for over two decades—at once feared, hated, deplored, and loved —is entirely forgotten today. When he died in 1913 the *Times* observed that "his face was better known to more thousands of New Yorkers than that of any other person within the limits of the Greater City." Certainly this was true on the East Side, politically the old Fourth Ward, where a large tinted lithograph of him hung in a place of honor in nearly every coffee house and saloon and over the mantel in most tenement flats, much like that of a reigning sovereign in a minor European country. It was a handsome, fleshy Irish face that looked down from these walls—red-cheeked, blue-eyed, smiling. In a fit of discouragement one of his sworn enemies once described his smile as "beautiful." As Alvin Harlow, a chronicler of Bowery life, noted years later, "Perhaps there was never a more perplexing admixture of good and evil in one human character than that of Timothy D. Sullivan."

Sullivan was an inch over six feet, unusually tall in a neighborhood of undernourished immigrants—thus his nicknames of "Big Tim" or "The Big Feller." Born in 1863 and brought up, poor and fatherless, on Clinton Street, he sold newspapers in front of a beanery on Park Row from the time he was seven. By the early eighties he had opened his own saloon at 71 Christie Street, a move that apparently didn't take much capital in that district. A report of an Albany legislative committee not long afterward found in an area six blocks by seven on the East Side five churches and 237 saloons. Big Tim's place was a hangout for the Whyos, the worst of the Irish street gangs that sprang up in the years after the Civil War around the now-vanished conjunction of five narrow streets in lower Manhattan, known as the Five Points. The brawny young Sullivan was a welcome recruit to the Whyos, who took their name from the peculiar cry they gave when they were about to attack. They fought such rival gangs as the Rags and the Boodles with bare fists, brass knuckles, or broken bottles and were particularly adept at eye-gouging. Sometimes they fought to protect their turf, sometimes just for exercise. For walking-around money they robbed, burgled, or hired out as thugs. In the pocket of a Whyo called Piker Ryan the police once found a price list showing that for ten dollars the Whyos would break the jaw of anyone a client specified. Blacking both eyes cost four dollars, breaking an arm or leg twenty, and murder or "doing that big job" a hundred and up. They made their biggest hauls, however, on primary and election days when political leaders paid them to vote several times apiece and to serve as terrorist mercenaries.

Big Tim soon took charge of the Whyos' bookings, especially at election time when he made sure they swung the vote for Tammany Hall, with which he had made a natural alliance. With Sullivan at the head of their guerilla forces, the Whyos not only dragged reluctant Democrats to the polls but in their own inimitable way suppressed Republicans who rashly tried to exercise their franchise. As a result the East Side, which had formerly voted Republican on occasion, became Tammany turf. In 1888 in one district for which Tim had made himself responsible, Grover Cleveland won 368 to 4. Sullivan claimed to be mortified. "Harrison got one more vote than I thought he would," he told Tammany headquarters, "but I'll *get* that feller." Because gangs like the Whyos were so useful to it, Tammany Hall developed a special relationship with local gamblers. To keep gang members in funds between elections, the politicians found jobs for them in the off-season months. Gambling houses, with their steady need for resident thugs—lookouts, steerers, cappers, fowlers, bouncers —offered the ideal solution. Not only the downtown stuss houses but the gambling palaces of the Tenderloin as well found they had a far better chance of staying in business if they enlarged their overhead with retainers to these friends of local democracy, many of whom were no-shows except on payday.

Sullivan's own dedication to the Tammany cause had been rewarded early on with something more impressive than a steerer's post. In 1886 at the age of twenty-three he was elected a state assemblyman. From 1892 on he was a state senator, doing most of his legislating out of the Occidental, an ancient disreputable hotel at the corner of Broome Street and the Bowery. The political hub of the area was the Occidental's bar room with its vast painting of frolicking nudes on the ceiling. Tim's presence in the bar was strictly a matter of conviviality and attention to business. He neither drank nor smoked and, except where his commercial interests were involved, struck a prudish stance on sexual questions. When Elinor Glyn's indecorous *Three Weeks* appeared, his comment was, "Anybody that reads *Three Weeks* should get three months." Though motherhood touched him—tears came to his eyes when the Occidental piano player broke into "Mother Machree"—he didn't care to hear how Mother had got in that fix.

At caucuses in the bar Tim delivered regular lectures to his followers on how to get ahead in politics. The first principle, he said, was not to put on airs. "God and the people hate a chesty man," he often told them. A further precept for a rising politican was to adapt gracefully to a changing constituency. Only a few years after Sullivan had got into politics his Irish province had been transformed into a Jewish ghetto with a large Italian minority in its southwest corner. Tim got along famously with the newcomers, clapping a yarmulke on his big head for weekly Bar Mitzvahs, learning a little strategic Yiddish and Napoli dialect, and arranging to have the legislature declare Columbus Day a state holiday. By the turn of the century Jewish immigrants accounted for nearly 25 per cent of the city's population, most of them concentrated "below the line," as the area south of Fourteenth Street was known. Fortunately, as a later Tammany leader would put it, "The Irish are natural leaders. The strain of Limerick keeps them at the top. The Jews want to be ruled by them." But from the early nineties on Sullivan made sure that many of the runners in his Occidental headquarters were such likely young Jewish boys as Herman Rosenthal.

Tammany headquarters had always been below the line. (For sixty years from 1868 to 1928 it stood on Fourteenth Street between Irving Place and Third Avenue, across from Luchow's, and most major Tammany leaders up through Jimmy Hines were born in the neighborhood of the old Fourth Ward.) From the eighties on Big Tim's guaranteed delivery of the vote of an area then said to be more densely settled than Bombay was the most important single element in Tammany's political strength. In

1902 the East Side overlord moved on to Washington as the district's congressman. But most political assignments outside New York were held in low repute in Tammany circles. When Richard Croker, the boss in the nineties, had been asked to name a young friend as county clerk of Manhattan, his reported answer was: "He's a good boy, but that job requires brains and experience. He'll have to be satisfied with going to Congress." Sullivan won the pinochle championship of the House. Otherwise Washington paid him little attention. In 1907, by his own choice, he was back in Albany—or more often holding forth at the Occidental. In 1911 he was responsible for the passage of New York's Sullivan Law, which makes it a felony to carry a concealed weapon—a move that reflected his distress over the way the character and habits of East Side gangs had deteriorated since his days of good clean fun with the Whyos. The Sullivan Law is one of the few reminders today that the big folk hero ever existed.

When Boss Croker retired to England in 1901 with his ill-gotten gains as Tammany chief, Sullivan could have succeeded him. The administrative chores of the top job didn't appeal to him. Charley Murphy eventually took over while Big Tim kept on raking in money below the line. His loot—said to be in the millions—came from hotels, theaters, burlesque houses, saloons and his part-ownerships in most of the brothels in the Fourth Ward. In his East Side domain he ruled supreme for twenty years, independent even of Tammany Hall. At one point Tammany leaders, noting that some troublesome reformers' committee was running around investigating vice in the city, decided to fend it off by appointing their own tame gumshoes to conduct an independent investigation. Taking no chances, Sullivan announced that, tame or not, those snoops were not to set foot in his territory. They stayed out. "Reform, there's nothin' to it," he often said.

In time Sullivan's commercial interests expanded northward into the Tenderloin. He also controlled all prizefighting in Manhattan. The sport was then illegal in the state outside of private clubs, and it was Big Tim who handed out fight permits to the clubs. A middleweight championship bout was once called off at the last minute because the proper arrangements hadn't been made with Big Tim at the Occidental. When the chief was off answering roll calls the financial negotiations, uptown or down, would be handled by members of his court. Whatever their last names, they were known collectively as "The Sullivans." After Big Tim the most important figures at the tribal gatherings were his brothers, Florence and Patrick, known as Florrie and Paddy; his half-brother Larry Mulligan; Christy Sullivan, a first cousin; a distant cousin also named Tim Sullivan (a lean, taciturn character who eventually became president of the Board of Aldermen and, being only five-ten, was known as Little Tim), and the Considines, George and Jim, who were no blood relation but had extensive commercial ties with the Big Feller. Former Manhattan sheriff Tom Foley was also a card-carrying member of the clan although he kept a few lines out to Big Boss Murphy at Tammany Hall.

From the early nineties on Sullivan was chairman of a three-man board that presided unofficially over gambling in Manhattan. One man of the triumvirate represented the Sullivans, one the big uptown gamblers, and one the top brass at Police Headquarters. By 1912, when the high-level meetings were held at the Metropole, Jim Considine was said to be representing Sullivan. The other two delegates were reportedly Frank Farrell, the bookie czar of Manhattan, and Winfield Sheehan, a former *Evening World* reporter, now chief assistant to Police Commissioner Waldo, who it was understood had no idea what was going on under his nose. A fraction of each application fee for opening a gambling house (ranging up to a thousand dollars for a top spot in the Tenderloin) and of the monthly charges for protection would be earmarked for the neighborhood police captain and inspector. The rest went to the triumvirate for distribution according to an elaborate formula known as the Great Divide. For decades graft collections had been made by the patrolman on the beat, supervised by the local captain and inspector. By 1912, however, many of the collectors were minor gamblers whom the cops got to do the dirty work in return for a percentage. As a precaution, tribute from the fly-by-night stuss houses was exacted every two weeks. The more substantial uptown places paid off monthly, with the real gambling rajahs passing over the money to a high-ranking police official more or less openly at the end of a sumptuous lunch at Delmonico's. Whatever the levy, they could probably afford it. Even after all the payoffs Richard Canfield's profit from his West Forty-fourth Street house in one two-year period at the turn of the century had been a million and a half dollars.

"The long-continued custom of paying the police has made the keepers of disorderly and gambling houses not only willing but eager to pay over such money," former Police Commissioner William McAdoo had written complaisantly in 1906. The payments gave all concerned a sense of security, he suggested. "It is actually, among certain classes, a badge of honor to pay this tribute money to those who represent the law or to politicians who really do, or effect to, control the actions of the police." This was one view of the famous "system" on which local reformers had been concentrating much of their attention for nearly a generation. It was after the shooting down of Rosenthal that the newspapers began to print the word with a capital "S." "Herman Rosenthal," began a *World* editorial the next day, "was murdered in cold blood by the System."

"Stick with gambling. Gambling takes brains, and you're one smart Jew boy," Big Tim was supposed to have told young Herman Rosenthal when he was doing chores around the Occidental in the nineties. (Tim was supposed to have said the same thing a decade later to another of his young hangers-on, Arnold Rothstein—more accurately in the second case.) Herman had taken Tim's advice and was soon running his own crap game. Later he had a string of Second Avenue pool rooms. The stretch of Second between Houston Street and Fourteenth was the Great White Way of the Jewish East Side. A pool room there had nothing to do with billiards but was an off-track bookie joint equipped with a telephone line to the track, blackboards, folding chairs, betting slips, and stacks of the latest *Morning Telegraphs*.

Rosenthal's rooms prospered with the help of Big Tim's influence in warding off overzealous plainclothesmen in the neighborhood. He also showed an aptitude for field bookmaking and had his own betting stalls at the Jerome Park and Belmont tracks. Five years before the murder he bragged that he was worth two hundred thousand dollars. He even moved away from the East Side, taking a suite at a Broadway hotel where he ran up a twenty-five-thousand-dollar annual tab. If you didn't count Sam Paul, a recent graduate from the gangster class, his only close rival among the East Side's high-riding gamblers was Bridgey Webber, who by this time had moved up the ladder from Chinatown and Bridget to Second Avenue above Houston Street and an expensive wife named Pearl. Rosenthal and Webber so detested each other, however, that neither would willingly remain in the same room with the other at the Hesper Club, then the favorite hangout for downtown gamblers.

In 1899 Rosenthal had been one of the minor figures involved in the founding of the Hesper in a brownstone on Second Avenue between Fifth and Sixth Streets. The major figures were all Sullivans. A letter from Big Tim hung in an elaborate gold frame just inside the front entrance, announcing his pride in being a life member and his willingness to help all other Hespers at any time: "A simple word from you will command us." The Sullivans ostensibly had started the club as a social fraternity with political overtones. (No one seems to have left a record of why it was given the poetic name meaning "evening star" or "the western land.") Although most of the original Hespers were Democrats, there were a few ecumenically-minded Republicans. The place had gambling rooms on the parlor floor, and all important East Side gamblers were expected to join up, but at the outset magistrates, assistant district attorneys, and even the city treasurer were also enrolled. Before long the Sullivans were using the club as an ancillary fund-raising operation. In the summer they would sell tickets for monthly parties, usually held at College Point in Queens. Gamblers, liquor dealers, grateful office holders, and upright businessmen who needed the Sullivan cachet for some purpose were all encouraged to buy blocks of tickets. There would be a parade to the chartered steamboat at the Fourteenth Street dock. On board the guests would find roulette wheels, faro boxes, dice, cards, chips, tables, and drinks—all on the house. When the boat docked at College Point there would be more gambling and drinking under the trees, during which festivities the guests would be relieved of even more money.

In the winters the gimmick would be the political ball. It was still sometimes referred to as a "racket" in the sense of its second Webster definition: "social whirl or excitement, reveling, merrymaking, also a large, gay party . . ." The third definition, "a fraudulent scheme," may well have grown out of projects such as Big Tim's. The Sullivans ran other ventures of this sort, setting up "associations" named after various relatives. The associations threw their own rackets and anybody who wanted to prosper in Sullivan territory was expected to buy tickets to each and all of them. (Big Tim and his friends had no corner on the "association" scheme. An East Side saloonkeeper named Biff Ellison, a man with useful underworld connections, formed the Biff Ellison Association whose membership consisted entirely of himself. The B.E.A. would give three annual benefit rackets which then kept Biff in comfort for the rest of the year.)

According to some reformers, another purpose of the Sullivans' benefit balls was to promote their primary commercial interest, prostitution. In *McClure's Magazine* for June 1909 George Kibbee Turner, a charter member of the muckrakers' fraternity, described one of these affairs, an Eve of St. Patrick's Day celebration by the Larry Mulligan Association:

> That night . . . the streets of the Tenderloin lie vacant of its women; the eyes of the city detective force are focused on the great dancing hall—stuffed to the doors with painted women and lean-faced men. In the center box, held in the name of a young Jewish friend, sits "The Big Feller"—clear-skinned, fair-faced and happy. Around him sit the gathering of his business and political lieutenants . . . the rulers of New York: Larry Mulligan . . . Paddy Sullivan, president of the Hesper Club of gamblers; Considine, business associate, owner of the Metropole Hotel, where the "wise ones" gather; Big Tom Foley, and—an exception to the general look of rosy prosperity—Little Tim Sullivan. . . .
>
> The Big Feller smiles gaily upon the frail congregation below him—the tenth short-lived generation of prostitutes he has seen at gatherings like this since, more than twenty years ago, he had started his first Five Points assembly—he himself as fresh now as then. In the rear of the box a judge of the General Sessions Court sits modestly, decently, hat in hand. In the welter on the slippery floor another city judge . . . leads through the happy mazes of the grand march a thousand pimps and prostitutes to the blatant cry of the band: "Sullivan, Sullivan, a damned fine Irishman!"

Possibly Herman Rosenthal was the "young Jewish friend" who paid for the box at this 1909 affair. These, at any rate, were his days of affluence. They were on the wane, as it turned out. From this point on it would also be down hill all the way for Big Tim.

Sam Koenig, the local Republican district leader, an East European Jew, was beginning to attract voters of the same persuasion and to threaten the guaranteed biennial Tammany landslide on the East Side. In the 1909 election—the one in which Charles Whitman was chosen as district attorney and Gaynor as mayor—Tim's cousin Christy Sullivan used up wads of Sullivan money running for sheriff—and lost. The absolute monarchy below the line was beginning to crumble. Soon after this the Hesper Club picnics and balls became so rowdy and so popular among the gang element that respectable officials withdrew. Even the two Tim Sullivans found the club rather *déclassé* for a state senator and a president of the Board of Aldermen. The Hesper was gradually abandoned to the East Side gamblers and their gangster friends. The pretense that it was a social club was also abandoned, and it became simply another downtown gambling house run on a concession basis by Herman Rosenthal, by now widely known as a cop hater.

The beginnings of Rosenthal's bitter feud with the police had closely followed a 1909 vote by spoilsports in the Republican legislature that made it illegal to quote odds or take bets on horses at the track or anywhere else. New York's racing leaders, facing the grim prospect of having to rely on gate receipts, shifted their operations to Canada or Kentucky. Rosenthal's gambling operations were reduced to a couple of Second Avenue stuss houses and the Hesper Club concession. He found the new statute useful in one instance. He declined to pay off on a five-thousand-dollar bet that Charles Kohler, of the piano company, had placed with him. Appealing a judgment against him, he argued that the law could hardly force him to pay off on a bet since betting was against the law. The Court of Appeals agreed, but Rosenthal's fellow Hespers, fearful of earning a group reputation as welshers, persuaded him to pay off Kohler anyhow. They even loaned him the money. Rosenthal then welshed on *that* debt. Some of those who were out of pocket wrote anonymous letters to the mayor reminding him that Rosenthal's stuss houses were operating without interference from the police. Rosenthal was raided the next day. Soon afterward he told the police commissioner that the inspector for the East Side as well as the two cops who had led the raid were persecuting him. He also mentioned "friends in high places." The two policemen were transferred to Staten Island. Rosenthal's long, tiresome, and repetitive series of hollers—as complaints against the police were then known—had begun. The departure of racing, ending his big money days, and the beginning of the decline of the Sullivans, ending his virtual immunity from police interference, had come almost simultaneously. Not a philosophical sort, Rosenthal gambled away what money he had left and spent the rest of his life laying about him, trying to get back at others for the loss of his sinecure.

By late 1910 many former pool room operators on the East Side had begun invading other territories. Among the fliers Rosenthal took—with Big Tim's help as usual—was one in Far Rockaway, Queens. The indigenous gamblers had his place raided and closed. His next stop was southern Harlem, known as "Little Russia" since its middle-class Protestant population had largely fled before a Jewish invasion from the East Side. His partner in this enterprise on West 116 Street was a fellow Hesper, Beansey Rosenfeld. Beansey and Herman quarreled, and Herman had Beansey beaten almost to death by Tough Tony, a member of Spanish Louis' old gang whom he kept on a retainer. The disturbance alerted Police Commissioner William Baker who ordered the place raided and closed. Rosenthal publicly took credit for the fact that a few months later Baker was out of office. He opened up on 116 Street again but Beansey's friends set off a bomb that blew off the front of the house. Again Boob Walker "was reportedly in the neighborhood that night." So were gangsters named Gyp the Blood, Lefty Louie, and Whitey Lewis.

Rosenthal was reduced to his Hesper Club concession and a couple of stuss houses down the block. During the next months his stuss houses were raided several times, with the usual reactions from Rosenthal. Sometimes he complained of "persecution," sometimes of the inflicting of unnecessary damage to "priceless oil paintings." Sometimes he visited the current police commissioner; once he went all the way to the mayor. Sometimes he filed his charges in Magistrate's Court, other times he just hollered to the press, which would make things hot for the cops involved. By now many former Hespers wanted nothing to do with such a troublemaker and were giving their fraternal business instead to a clubhouse around the corner, the Sam Paul Association. One evening in April 1911 fifty policemen arrived at the Hesper, raided it, and smashed its equipment so thoroughly that it never reopened. The next day Rosenthal announced that the outrage would be avenged. A month later Deputy Police Commissioner Driscoll, who had given the raid order, was relieved of duty. "I had been raided at the Hesper Club and that raid . . . cost Driscoll his job in the Police Department . . . Everybody would listen to me in those days," Rosenthal told Swope plaintively in the *World* office in July 1912.

It was an omen, however, that the sacrosanct Hesper Club had been closed; even Big Tim's framed letter of endorsement had been damaged in the scuffle. For some time word had been going around that Big Tim would have to retrench. He could have the East Side gambling graft, but the Murphy contingent at Tammany headquarters was taking over the big bonanza, the Tenderloin. Another rumor was that Bridgey Webber had seen the way things were moving and had shifted his allegiance from the Sullivans to the Murphys. Like other gamblers below the line he was eyeing the opulent uptown territory that had previously been off limits to Hesper types—the exclusive neighborhood of the famous House with the Bronze Door, of Dave Busteed's and Lou Ludlum's and Freeman's, and of other successors to the legendary Richard Canfield, who operated their houses as if they were exclusive private clubs for rich men. As it happened, Webber, the new Murphy man, was the first East Side gambler permitted to invade the Tenderloin. Early in 1911 he set up a faro house at 117 West Forty-fifth Street with a partner known as Jew Brown. About the same time he opened his poker parlor at Forty-second Street and Sixth Avenue and soon afterward, it was said, became a collector of graft for Inspector Hayes.

The second East Sider to open up in the Tenderloin, at Big Tim's insistence, was Webber's old enemy, Herman Rosenthal, who added injury to insult by renting a place directly across the street at 104 West Forty-fifth. He may have explained to Sullivan when he put the bite on once again that this was an economy move, really. Giving up his hotel suite, he took a three-year lease on the Forty-fifth Street brownstone at $250 a month, moved his wife to fourth-floor quarters there, and fitted the rest of the place out as a roulette and faro stand of some elegance: Thirty-five thousand dollars it all cost him, he told Swope. The house opened for business on November 17, 1911. On the nineteenth Inspector Hayes asked Rosenthal to meet him in the backroom of a restaurant. According to Rosenthal's later story—the one he kept trying to sell to the newspapers in the weeks before he died—Hayes demanded a thousand dollars on the side for himself. Rosenthal refused.

"Anyhow, your gambler friend Dan the Dude says you run a crooked wheel," said Hayes, craftily.

"That's a lie! I got straight faro tables and two honest wheels in my house," said Rosenthal who, as suggested, was not one smart Jew boy.

Hayes went to court and got a warrant on the basis of this exchange, "a very unusual action on the part of a man with the rank of inspector," noted the *Sun*, "and indicative of the interest the police have shown in Rosenthal's fortunes." The Forty-fifth Street house was raided by Captain Day of the Forty-seventh Street station and its equipment smashed. Rosenthal did the usual, getting summonses against Hayes and Day and complaining to Mayor Gaynor, but this time got nowhere. The gambling house had been in operation four days.

When Rosenthal tried to see Big Tim for another handout, he found the door barred. In the past two years Tim's brother Florrie and cousin Little Tim had both died after months of mental imbalance. Now the Sullivan survivors were worried about Big Tim, especially the rate at which he was giving away money. While reformers denounced him as a gigantic grafter, many of his constituents thought of him as a philanthropist, a kind of Robin Hood. This gratuitous piece of casting ignored the fact that he took from the poor as well as the rich. Even the pushcart peddlers, toiling through Delancey Street, had to give him a cut of their take. Once the money was paid over, however, Sullivan was often generous with it. Every December for thirty years he handed out eight thousand pairs of shoes and as many Christmas dinners to all East Siders who got in line. Anyone he knew who was down on his luck had a friend at the Occidental. In the last years of his life his fortune was said to have shrunk by seven or eight hundred thousand dollars. Late in 1911 the dispersal rate moved the other Sullivans to establish a round-the-clock watch to make sure he didn't receive visitors who would relieve him of what was left of his hoard. Hard-luck Herman was naturally among the *non grata*. It was in this period while he was scheming to outmaneuver the palace guard that Rosenthal contrived his meeting at the Elks' Club with the most energetic of the strong arm squad lieutenants, Charles Becker.

Sometime in late January 1912 he managed to see Big Tim at last and made another big touch; on March 20 he reopened the Forty-fifth Street house. Becker's squad raided and closed it on April 17. As Mayor Gaynor and Commissioner Waldo would both point out frequently in the months to come, in two tries Rosenthal had been able to operate in the Tenderloin for only thirty-two days in all. Whatever Lieutenant Becker's alliance with Rosenthal had been, the mayor insisted, the gambler's experience proved that in Gaynor's administration a police officer could not deliver protection no matter how much graft was paid.

The Tenderloin gamblers knew better. What worried them most about Rosenthal's noisy performance was the danger that the police would counter his cries of persecution by raiding other uptown houses that were used to more civilized treatment.

"The trouble with Herman is that he don't know the rules," one of the old Canfield crowd told the *Evening Post* the day before the murder. "The rules are, pay your license money . . . lay low, and play like gentlemen. When you get a hint, take it and close down. It's when fighting among the brotherhood is too noisy that the powers step in." "Rosenthal's ruining everything," Dave Busteed said angrily. Thus by July 1912, Rosenthal's powerful enemies included virtually the entire Police Department, the Tenderloin gamblers, and most of his old pals from Second Avenue.

Among the immediate spurs to the April raid, it was reported at Becker's later trial, were several letters to City Hall calling attention to Rosenthal's open flouting of the law. The letters were signed "Henry Williams." The defense would claim that Henry Williams was really Bridgey Webber. It was the same old scenario, really—the anonymous letters to authorities from Herman's enemies, the raid, Rosenthal's complaint to important city figures, the successful threat of revenge on the raiding officer. Only this time, of course, it had ended in murder.

VI

IN the days immediately following the murder Commissioner Dougherty and District Attorney Whitman called in dozens of East Side gamblers for questioning, including Bridgey Webber and Sam Paul. Paul was ex officio president of the Sam Paul Association, the fraternity that had sponsored an excursion to Northport, Long Island, the previous Sunday, the day the *World* had printed Herman Rosenthal's affidavit. This boating party had been attended by all below-the-line gamblers of any consequence. As in the case of the old Hesper Club outings, attendance had not been necessarily voluntary. Discussion on the trip inevitably had centered around what to do about Herman. Numerous remarks said to have been made that afternoon were soon being parceled out to the newspapers by Dougherty and were later repeated at the murder trials. Most of them proposed a rather final solution to the problem, as in "If Herman don't quiet down, we'll get him for keeps," and "If he goes too far with this, he won't have anything left to go anywhere with," and "If Big Jack Zelig hadn't got hisself arrested, Herman would already of been six foot under two months ago." Among the gamblers said to have made ominous observations were Bald Jack Rose, Bridgey Webber, Harry Vallon, and Sam Schepps.

Sam Paul—chunky, smiling, beautifully turned out—arrived in a shiny red Willys for his interview with Dougherty. Paul was ordinarily the silent type, but he had something to say now to reporters on the steps at headquarters. "Herman and I was dear friends," he told them, bowing his head and removing his straw hat. As for the boat excursion the Sunday before, "all of the men on the outing was also dear friends of Herman's and his death come as a great shock to them."

In the newspapers of a decade before Paul had been referred to as a gang leader. "The members are all of the Monk Eastman type," a police description of the Sam Paul Association had said in 1903. (Eastman had been a notorious gang leader of that day, a ferocious-looking, simian figure. Eastman liked to boast that he never used his club on women. When he blacked their eyes it was with his fist "and I always takes off me knucks first.") By 1912 Paul's reference category was "gambler" and in his relationship to gang leaders he was described by the *Times* as "a kind of padrone." Among the gangsters who awarded him a kind of fealty was Big Jack Zelig, who was said to clear all important jobs through Paul. By this year the Association's membership included gamblers, politicians, businessmen, and other comparatively respectable types. Sam Paul's had thus risen in the world as the old Hesper had gone down. There was another difference. When the Hesper crowd transferred their allegiance to Sam's club, they had found that most politicians at their new hangout were Republicans, possibly reflecting the fact that Sam Koenig, the Republican district leader for the East Side, was a pal of Sam Paul's and even, it was said, his backer in some of his gambling enterprises.

Sam Paul's most elaborate stuss house was the Sans Souci on Fourteenth Street east of Luchow's. The Sans Souci had been raided five times in the past few months, with only a slight interruption in the play. Paul had told several people he was sure "that bum Rosenthal" had given the cops the information they needed—that is, the layout of the place, names of dealers and so on, which would support their claim to having played there and result in court warrants. In the months before his death Rosenthal had picked up spare change and simultaneously got back at his East Side enemies by clueing the police in on Second Avenue gambling. Four nights before the murder he had mentioned to a *Sun* reporter that—unlike his place—the Sans Souci had been allowed to open up right after a July 6th raid. Waldo had then ordered the Sans Souci raided and closed on the night of July 15, eight hours before Rosenthal was shot. The story now spreading through the city was that at a council of war at the Sam Paul clubhouse that evening the final solution for Herman had been decided on once and for all.

Asked why he had called in Paul after the murder, Dougherty told the press, "Sammy Paul was a known enemy of the victim." Asked whether Paul had been in the murder car, Dougherty said flatly, "Yes." The Republican district attorney, however, was naturally inclined to treat the reputed business partner of the East Side leader of his party with more respect. "Mr. Samuel Paul appeared voluntarily at the Criminal Courts Building yesterday," he announced, "and gave the state much valuable information."

After his interviews with the police and the D.A., Bridgey Webber was arrested Tuesday afternoon as a material witness. He was released the next day on nominal bail of a hundred dollars, which he paid in a single bill peeled from a roll that dazzled reporters on the scene. He was mighty sorry about poor Herman, he told them. The story that Rosenthal had once hired Spanish Louis' man to kill him was "just gossip." Soon after his departure his part-time employee Boob Walker was released by the police after extensive questioning. Fat Moe Levy and Butch Kitte, Rosenthal's other table companions on his final night, had skipped town. So had Dan the Dude, Beansey Rosenfeld, Abe the Rebbeler, Piggy Schultz, Denny Slyfox, Kid Rags, Spider Rice, Little Doggie, Charley the Jew, Alley Fat, and other leading residents of Second Avenue. Damon Runyon was in town, having arrived the year before from Denver. He was working as a sports writer for the *American* and presumably taking notes for the short stories that eventually became Broadway's *Guys and Dolls*. Possibly it occurred to him that Herman Rosenthal's greatest distinction in this crowd was in his not having had a nickname: he had just been Herman.

If Big Jack Zelig had turned up on Forty-third Street on the night of the murder, he was nowhere around there now. Harry Vallon, Sam Schepps, and Bald Jack Rose were also missing from their usual haunts, even their *most* usual haunt, the Lafayette Baths, an establishment featuring steam rooms and transient hotel accommodations at 476 Lafayette Place near the site of the old Astor family houses. (Bathhouses on the Lower East Side had originally thrived for utilitarian reasons. In the nineties only one tenement flat in ten had a bathtub. By 1912 this situation had improved, but the Lafayette, like similar places in the neighborhood, had become a home away from home where a man could meet his friends or temporarily hide out—a kind of downtown version of the Union League Club.) It was at the Lafayette Baths, the *American* now revealed, that Vallon, Schepps, Rose, Webber, and Paul had slept off their excitement on what was left of the murder night.

Bald Jack Rose and Schepps had not dropped out of sight immediately after their refreshing stay at the baths. About eight o'clock on the morning after the murder Rose had sent Schepps up to the house on Southern Boulevard in the Bronx, where the gunmen were awaiting word of where they could collect the murder payoff. Schepps then had come back downtown to help Jacob Reich keep an appointment. The day before the murder Reich had promised men from the *Sun*, the *American*, and the *Tribune* that he would bring Bald Jack to the Garden Restaurant about 1 P.M. Tuesday to be interviewed about his troubles with Rosenthal. Substituting for Rose, Schepps obliged with considerable background material on the dead man. The reporters thus obliged would be red-faced for months to come about this tête-à-tête with a man who, as they would soon learn, had been about to go on the lam.

A little later that afternoon Schepps and Bald Jack had met two of the gunmen and either Schepps or Rose—according to different stories they would tell at different times—had handed them a thousand dollars in cash. In his first formal testimony Rose would say that the payoff had taken place underneath the baseball scoreboard in Times Square, half a block from the murder scene. Later—possibly believing this sounded too brazen—he thought the money had been paid over at Fiftieth Street and Eighth Avenue. In any case, by the day after the murder Schepps and Rose couldn't be found. But was anyone looking for them? Bald Jack had been mentioned in Rosenthal's affidavit and in the gambler's fuller statement published in Wednesday's *World*. That evening a *Tribune* reporter asked Commissioner Dougherty whether he had men on Rose's trail. "I do not," said Dougherty. "I know of no charge to be preferred against him." In the murder trials that followed, hours of courtroom time would be spent debating whether or not Rose had been the object of a manhunt on that Wednesday evening before he turned himself in.

Meanwhile Libby and Shapiro, the owners of the getaway car, had been arraigned and held without bail on a charge of homicide. Wednesday noon State Assemblyman Aaron Levy turned up at headquarters and identified himself as their counsel. Levy had occasionally acted as attorney for Sam Paul. He was also a close associate of Tammany boss Charles Murphy, who had arranged a few months earlier for him to be chairman of the Judiciary Committee of the New York State Assembly. "Mr. Levy has never been known to disobey orders from Tammany Hall," the *World* had said of him during a 1911 political squabble. The notion that Levy would interest himself in the plight of the two wretched, grease-stained chauffeurs out of the goodness of his heart was considered unacceptable. His appearance was taken as a sign that the Murphy contingent of Tammany was stepping into the case. In view of the uproar about police responsibility for the crime, however, they were firmly separating their interests from those of Centre Street: After all, it was an election year. When Levy emerged from a conference with his clients, he told reporters he was "positive the murder was not done by gamblers or in behalf of gamblers," thus allying himself with the district attorney. He added that from now on he would deal only with Whitman, not police headquarters, and asked that his clients be put in cells in the Tombs next to the Criminal Courts Building, where Whitman had his office. They would be safer there, he announced, than in the cells at headquarters where they had been kept overnight. He admitted that the prisoners had been physically presentable in court, which was more than he had expected.

"With all that, it is perfectly well understood at Police Headquarters," noted the *American*, "that so expert an examiner as Mr. Dougherty was not behind closed doors with the two men for the greater part of ten hours without learning a good deal of what they knew and of what he wanted so much to know." Somehow the deputy commissioner had learned the names of the four gunmen Shapiro had driven away from the crime scene. They were Jacob Seidenschner (alias Whitey Lewis), Harry Horowitz (alias Gyp the Blood), Louis Rosenberg (alias Lefty Louie), and Frank Cirofici (alias Dago Frank).

All four were described in "Wanted" circulars prepared that afternoon as being about twenty-seven years old, five feet six, dark-eyed and dark-haired, and sharply dressed. (Whitey Lewis had got his name because his hair was a shade lighter than was common in their circles, but it was all a matter of degree.) Twenty-seven was the right age for Gyp the Blood, but the others were only twenty-one. Despite their youth, all had served time. Lefty was a convicted pickpocket, the others convicted burglars. All had been arrested in previous gangland shootings but not convicted. From all the evidence presented then or later, they were four young East Side guerillas, guns for hire. Dozens, even hundreds, just like them could be seen lurking in the same shadows off the Five Points where the Whyos had once waited for their victims. Of the four, Gyp the Blood would be the favorite of the feature writers. He had been a bouncer in Bowery dance halls and liked to boast that he could break a man's spine with his two hands. It was even said that he kept in practice by demonstrating his prowess from time to time on some harmless bystander. He had once explained that his favorite assignment was throwing bombs because "I likes to hear da noise." As his lawyer frequently mentioned during his trial for murder, it was unfair to leap to any conclusions on the basis of his unfortunate nickname. He was called "Gyp" because he looked rather like a gypsy, his counsel insisted; "the Blood" referred to his fondness for fancy clothes. One unexplained fact about the quartet of gunmen was how it had come about that three Jewish boys had allied themselves with someone known as Dago.

For the local gang situation had changed notably since the old Whyo days. With the new ethnic distribution below the line the gangs were no longer made up of big, brawling Irish roughnecks but of Italians and Jews, who were likely to be small, quick, and deadly. According to Police Department records, the average gangster in this period weighed 125 pounds. Gangs no longer fought with their fists and broken bottles. First they had graduated to knives and then to guns. Before the passage of the Sullivan Act the year before they had openly worn a pistol on each hip. And with the growing accessibility of automobiles, they no longer kept to their East Side stamping grounds, but were spreading out all over town. Nor were they mere dependents of Tammany now. Gamblers put them on the house manifests for their own purposes—to hold up and intimidate competitors and to protect their businesses from reprisals.

In the gang battles that went on continually between professional assignments it was the Sheenies against the Wops. The major league rivalry until recent years had been between Monk Eastman's gang and the Five Pointers, led by Paul Kelly, whose real name was Paolo Vaccarelli. When these two leaders left the East Side—Eastman for Sing Sing and Kelly for upper Manhattan and a new career as a labor union organizer—their followers had scattered and then regrouped for the same old battle. Only the previous winter Louis the Lump (real name Pioggi) had killed off Kid Twist (real name Max Zweibach). In the months before Rosenthal's murder the bloodiest skirmishes had been between the followers of Jack Sirocco and those of Big Jack Zelig. Gyp the Blood, Lefty Louie, and Whitey Lewis were all members of the Zelig gang. Dago Frank was a free lancer who had pulled a few one-night stands for Kitty Second (real name Decorio). Those who had followed the decades of ethnic warfare weren't surprised when it turned out later that Dago Frank's presence among the gunmen on the murder night had been an afterthought.

Herman Rosenthal, the man this quartet had done in, was buried on Thursday morning from his Forty-fifth Street gambling house. The ceremony was sparsely attended, but in spite of the persisting heat hundreds of the curious gathered in front of the house at the appointed hour. For a while Mrs. Rosenthal, more massive than ever in flowing black crepe, had the impression they were all old friends of Herman's, come to do him honor. The double doors of the front entrance, still bearing scars from the raiders' axes, and the inner peephole door were thrown open. After many sightseers had filed past the coffin in which all that was left of Herman lay in evening dress, his initialed gold cuff links in place, his face marvelously rehabilitated, the widow tumbled to the truth, and the doors swung shut again.

For a man who had been generous with his East Side friends when he was in the money—the *World* described him as "one of the most liberal-handed gamblers the town has ever known"— there were few flowers. None had come from any of the dozens of fraternal organizations to which Rosenthal had belonged. The Exalted Ruler of the Benevolent Protective Society of the Elks formally announced that, in spite of misleading references in the press, Rosenthal was not and had never been an Elk. The widow had appealed to Sam Paul for help with the expenses, and he had obliged. Bridgey Webber had contributed a hundred dollars. Neither man attended the service. The absence of Rosenthal's old friend Big Tim Sullivan was also noted.

No one had cared to have his name listed as a pallbearer for the murdered man, and the undertaker's staff did the honors. There was a brief service by the Rabbi of the Washington Heights Congregation (Reformed) who compared the dead man to King David who had no place to rest his weary head from the darts of his enemies. Herman Rosenthal, he said, had been "cut down at a moment's notice and at the height of his powers." The coffin was then borne out through the peephole door, followed by the handful of mourners: Rosenthal's widow, his brother, his four sisters with their husbands, an actor named Harry Cooper, two pugilists known as Baby Griffo and Kid Betts, and a small delegation from the Hesper Club.

Bald Jack Rose was not at the funeral. About an hour before the ceremony he had driven up to Police Headquarters in a cab, dressed in a Panama hat, a faultless gray suit, a gray silk shirt with a faint green stripe, and a gray tie. He also carried a walking stick. Rose, whose real name was Jacob Rosenzweig, was an extraordinary looking man. He had a long head, a long, sharp nose, narrow amber-colored eyes, chalklike skin, and unusually red lips. His nickname involved no hyperbole. As a result of a childhood illness he had no eyebrows, no eyelashes, and not a hair on his head. One of his subsidiary nicknames was Billiard Ball Jack. To cut down the shine he wore his poll thickly dusted with jasmine-scented talcum powder. On the way from 145 Street where he had been lying low for nearly two days in the apartment of a friend, a vaudeville soft shoe artist named Harry Pollock, he had stopped for a manicure. On each of his soft white hands was a large diamond ring. His usual facial expression ranged from impassive to bored. There was no variation this morning though he had come to turn himself in for questioning in a murder case.

Bald Jack's presence at headquarters was the result of another stop he had made after getting the manicure. He had gone to see a lawyer named James Mark Sullivan. Unlike most of his East Side friends, Rose had spent some time away from lower Second Avenue. In his twenties—he was now thirty-seven—he had worked in gambling houses in northern Connecticut and promoted prize fights and vaudeville shows in that area. He had also managed the Norwich baseball club. The players as a result had been known as the Rosebuds. His off-and-on association with Rosenthal had begun after he'd returned to New York about a decade before. Lawyer Sullivan had been a young free lance press agent when Rose had first met him in Waterbury, Connecticut. A well-fixed cousin had later sent him to Yale Law School. Sullivan's present thriving practice was said to be related to his favorable standing with the Murphy wing of Tammany Hall. The interview between the two men on this Thursday morning two days after the murder had ended with Sullivan's advice to Rose to turn himself in. According to rumor, Sullivan had then made a beeline for Murphy's table at Delmonico's and informed the Tammany leader of the new development.

The lobby at Police Headquarters that morning was crowded, but neither the policemen in charge nor the reporters hanging around hoping for some break in the murder story apparently looked twice at Rose although his name and description were on the front pages of all morning papers. Early the previous evening lawyer Aaron Levy had visited Libby and Shapiro in the Tombs and then released a statement from them explaining how their car had happened to be at the murder scene. Shortly after 10 P.M. that night, they said, Shapiro had had a call to pick up a fare at the saloon on Fourteenth Street run by Tom Sharkey, the former heavyweight contender. At Sharkey's he had picked up several men and driven them way uptown and back down again, ending at Bridgey's place. The passengers had all gone upstairs. Maybe an hour later, maybe fifteen minutes before the murder, some of the same men and a couple of others had got in the car and ordered him to drive around the corner to the Metropole. The man who had hired the car and ridden in it most of the evening, said Shapiro, was one of their regular customers, Bald Jack Rose. "ASSASSINS' AUTO HIRED BY GAMBLER KNOWN TO BECKER" the *Times* headline read that morning.

Perhaps the crowd at headquarters didn't recognize Rose because he had his hat on, making him look less of a spectre, or perhaps they were preoccupied with the latest rumor—that Becker had committed suicide. Approaching the desk, Rose asked for Waldo, but the Police Commissioner was over at City Hall conferring with Mayor Gaynor. "Conferring" was perhaps not the word. According to the *American* the next day, reporters had been able to watch the interview through a window as they stood in City Hall Park.

"When the conference began, the Mayor wore his straw hat," the *American* reported. "He took it off early in the talk, however, and was seen belaboring his Police Commissioner with it. Now on the head, then on the shoulders or chest, as the mood seized him. Toward the end of the talk he contented himself with poking it at the Commissioner."

Bald Jack drove up to headquarters again about half an hour later in another cab. This time he asked no questions but walked up the stairs and sauntered up and down the corridors until he found Waldo's office. Rose gave his name negligently to the sergeant in the outer room and was hustled in to see Dougherty, who was presiding in Waldo's absence. Throughout the forty-five minute interview that followed, Rose insisted the whole afternoon and evening before the murder were very dim in his mind. He had gone to Bridgey's because a friend with him wanted to play poker, he said. He didn't know what had happened to the hired Packard. After that he might have gone to Jack's. Yes, Jack's. Somebody at that cafe, he couldn't remember who, had told him Rosenthal had been murdered. He told Dougherty he knew nothing that would tie Becker to the murder.

At the end of the interview Dougherty arrested him on a charge of acting in concert with others to cause the death of Rosenthal. On his way out Rose told reporters he was astonished at this treatment of a man only trying to be helpful to the authorities. Swinging his cane, he then stepped into the Black Maria for the trip to the Tombs, where he was held without bail. When lawyer Sullivan left there later in the day after a long conference with his client, he took up the popular chant. "The shadow of the police hangs over this crime," he announced.

Several events at Centre Street that morning figured prominently in subsequent trials. While Rose was with the deputy commissioner, Becker arrived at headquarters carrying under his arm the morning *World* with the headline about Rose. He immediately started upstairs to tell Dougherty that he knew where to find Rose, or so he would claim later. (Pollock, the soft shoe artist, had stopped to see him the day before and told him that Rose was staying at his place.) In the corridor Becker ran into

Dougherty's secretary and said he wanted to see the deputy commissioner about the Rose matter. The secretary said that was a coincidence, the commissioner wanted to see Becker on the same matter—and on the double. Outside Dougherty's office Becker got the impression from the secretary that he could go right in, he said later. He opened the door and stopped as if shot when he saw Rose sitting by Dougherty's desk. Two weeks later in a long "confession" that Rose wrote out and that, like all important documents in the case, first appeared in Swope's *World,* Rose described the incident. Dougherty had left him alone in the room, he said.

"I heard something at the door. I don't think I heard anything at all—I just felt it. I looked up and there standing in the door was Becker. I shall never forget that face if I live to be a thousand years. He never moved a muscle. He just stood there and looked. I never had been so scared in all my life. I wanted to go to the electric chair right then—anything to get away from him and his eyes. . . . He disappeared without a word."

Becker's version was less dramatic. When he came to the door Dougherty was sitting talking with Rose, he said, and motioned him to wait outside. His barging into the deputy commissioner's office would be treated by the prosecution at his trial as further proof of his arrogance and of his intent to intimidate Bald Jack. That morning when it didn't seem to make any difference Dougherty supported Becker's version. "By a misunderstanding Becker walked into my office when Rose was there, and I asked him to step out," he told the *Tribune* reporter.

After Rose was taken away, Dougherty called Becker in, removed him from strong arm squad duty, and assigned him to general chores around headquarters. He asked Becker if he had seen Rose since the murder. Becker said he had not, which was true. He mentioned that he had known where Rose was, but he did not add that the previous evening he had sent a lawyer and notary public to Rose to secure an affidavit stating that it was Rose and not himself who had taken the fifteen-hundred-dollar mortgage on Rosenthal's household goods.

As Becker came downstairs from Dougherty's office, reporters crowded around him. "Well, boys, I have committed suicide, as you can see," he told them. His face was grim. Dougherty had told him that the Mayor wanted to see him. He put on his hat and went over to City Hall.

That morning Gaynor had written Waldo a letter and released it to the press even before it reached the police commissioner. "The most brazen crime ever committed in the city," as the *Tribune* had called the murder, did not seem to distress him nearly so much as the charges of graft that the gambler had made before his death. "It is discouraging to have these Rosenthal accusations bandied about," he wrote, "after all we have done." But then Rosenthal was just "a common criminal . . . a miserable outlaw." ("It is easy to knock a corpse," the *World* pointed out the next day.) What upset the mayor most of all, however, was Rosenthal's account of how he and Becker had dined at the same Elks' Club table. "I can't understand why Lieutenant Becker would sit down to dinner with such a scoundrel."

Becker was with the mayor for half an hour during which, he told reporters when he came out, the discussion centered around the New Year's Eve meeting. As for the mayor's complaint that he associated on other occasions with unsavory characters—meaning, presumably, Bald Jack—he said he had vainly tried to explain to Gaynor some of the facts of a policeman's life—the necessity of dealing through stool pigeons, for example, in order to get evidence against gambling houses, which wouldn't let a policeman or a stranger inside.

As Becker left City Hall photographers ran along beside him snapping his picture. Becker shouted at them that he would have them arrested if they didn't cut it out, but the photographers still followed, taking pictures of his back "to the considerable amusement of the crowd." Every few steps Becker would whirl on them, snarling "Arrest that man!" to no one in particular. The *Tribune* was reminded of Lewis Carroll's Red Queen. He must have been happy to be joined in his beleaguered stroll by someone who wanted to help him. It was State Assemblyman John C. Fitzgerald, well known as a cohort of Big Tim's. The two men conferred back at headquarters for some time. When he emerged, Fitzgerald announced that it was obvious Becker would have been far better off if the gambler had lived. What would be his motive for killing Herman? He referred reporters to an editorial judgment of the *Times* on the day after the murder: "The picture of Rosenthal in the public mind has been that of an angry man of

intemperate habits and so evil repute that his unsupported testimony on any matter could not be accepted."

The behavior of Murphy men James Sullivan and Aaron Levy
had suggested that the Murphy branch of Tammany was ready to
hop on the bandwagon and blame the police alone for the crime.
Fitzgerald's public appearance with Becker indicated that Big Tim
was sticking by the major police suspect. But most of the Sullivan
contingent had other ideas, and already that afternoon the rumor
was rife that the overall plan of the politicians was to let Becker
take the brunt of things, to have him "take the splash," to "let him
drop."

VII

Why, down in the courthouse all they talk about is the bad policeman. They call us loafers, thieves, crooks and murderers. The newspapers do the same. Nobody speaks out for us. . . . Go down to the courthouse and look at it—thieves, ex-convicts, prostitutes, procurers, disorderly housekeepers, all received with open arms, coddled and talked softly to and sympathized with while they give their evidence against an honest and innocent man. . . . The newspapers and all the well-known enemies of the police are on the trail. Now, Commissioner, you know it to be a fact yourself that if any man, no matter who he is, gets up and calls the police grafters, thieves, crooks and murderers, he gets applause . . .

As for grafting, I know some men connected with other businesses, in politics, the newspapers, and at the bar, who would take anything from five cents to a hot stove and no questions asked. And what's the difference between what they call a system for collecting graft on the police force and the systems in the insurance companies at the City Hall and at Albany?

Go down tomorrow and tell the District Attorney that you have a charge against a policeman, and every assistant will be fighting to see which will get you to his room. Go down to the newspaper offices tomorrow and tell them

you know something to the credit of the police and watch
the janitor getting you into the elevator as quick as he
can. . . .

Thus ran the complaint of "a New York City policeman," anony-
mously quoted in former Police Commissioner McAdoo's *Guard-
ing a Great City*, published in 1906.

It is almost impossible to understand the Rosenthal murder
case without knowing something about the concern over crooked
policemen that obsessed New Yorkers and many other American
city dwellers for over two decades beginning in the early 1890s.
The philosopher G. M. Young once remarked that the central
theme of an era is often not what happened but what people
thought was happening at the time. Sweat shops, child labor,
yellow dog contracts, the political and industrial exploitation of
the vast new immigrant population and the cruel gap between
their lives and those of the gilded few, the open purchase of
public office, gross corruption involving municipal contracts, and
a brazen collaboration in such abuses between the later waves of
robber barons and the tin horns at City Hall, all of them prosper-
ing mightily at the expense of the ordinary citizen—these are the
blots on the historical landscape that are usually dealt with now
in any account of urban life in the decades before the First World
War. All these civic evils were properly deplored from time to
time during these years, but there were intervals when it seemed
that the most hideous sin of all in the minds of many Americans—what seemed to them to be happening—was the greasing
of the palms of city policemen by prostitutes, gamblers, and other
small-time local criminals. Any serious crying of havoc over
examples of venality in other circles could often be upstaged by
the launching of an investigation into police graft, like a diver-
sionary striptease set off from the opposite wing to take the play
away from a dramatic offering that raises more fundamental and
troublesome questions.

Inquests into the sins of the men in blue were held every couple
of years and were always sensationally covered by the press,
which naturally found crimes involving payoffs by hard-bitten
gambling house proprietors and blousy madams more fun to
write about than watered-stock sales and dubious corporate
mergers. In the last years of the nineteenth century the index of

the New York *Times,* still a rather abecedarian affair, lumped under the heading of "New York City" all official municipal concerns and many unofficial ones, from local architecture to the rise of street gangs. There were usually only two separate subcategories under "New York City." One of these was "Politics," the other "Police Abuses," a phrase that nearly always meant the taking of graft. Listings under the second heading normally ran far longer than those under "Politics," even allowing for cross references.

The chief instigators of the biennial exposés of police graft were very wealthy men—J. Pierpont Morgan, George F. Baker, Robert Fulton Cutting, James Speyer, and Gustav Schwab, for example, along with numerous Astor and Vanderbilt sons-in-law with such names as Webb and Schieffelin. Usually Republican and Protestant, except for a few Schiffs, Seligmans, and other delegates from the great Jewish merchant-banking families, they personified the Establishment and the power structure long before these terms were invented. Many of them could afford not only the money but also the time to crusade for moral reform. And inevitably they identified reform as having to do with redressing the behavior of certain members of the lower and lower middle classes such as petty criminals and minor civil servants rather than, for example, improving the morality of the financial and industrial trusts whose dividends made it possible for them to practice their civic philanthropy.

Over the years these sincerely public-spirited individuals launched a staggering number of fraternities devoted to civic improvement. These groups, which had interlocking directorates, bore such names as the City Reform Club, the City Vigilance League, the Society for the Prevention of Crime, the Bureau for Civic Betterment, the Bureau for Municipal Research, and two that survive, the City Club and the Citizen's Union. There were also many *ad hoc* spin-offs—the Committee of Fourteen, the Committee of Fifteen, the Committee of One Hundred—and, for a time, subsidiaries called Good Government Clubs, which gave their opponents a chance to dismiss the members of all these benevolent societies as "The Goo-Goos." Other jaundiced observers dubbed them the "Simon Pures" or the "Gold-Plated Holies" or sometimes just "The Holies." "Silk hats and silk socks and nothing in between," Big Tim Sullivan described them sourly. Many of the Holies thought they were pious "whereas they are only bilious," said Mayor Gaynor, another Tammany man, though one of an unorthodox—and certainly bilious—type. He added that some of these Holies seemed to be too good for this world and the sooner they were translated the better.

All of these unofficial reform groups dedicated to the purification of the New York political scene were convinced that such purification would follow the moment they succeeded in banishing the Tammany Irishman from public life. There was one sure way to do this. Over and over, they found that the single corruption issue that moved the public to rise up and throw the rascals out was police graft. The only instances when the anti-Tammany forces succeeded in putting their men in office during these two decades were when the committees had just concluded a dramatic exposé of corruption in the New York Police Department and then, before the public clamor subsided, had thrown a fusionist slate against the Tammany candidates. Virtually every important anti-Tammany politican during these years—and all those involved in the Becker murder case—came to prominence as the result of publicly going after greedy cops.

The exercise of this magic political principle had begun in February 1892, twenty years before the Rosenthal murder, when Dr. Charles Parkhurst, a peppery, bearded gentleman who was pastor of the Madison Square Presbyterian Church and head of the Simon Pure's Society for the Prevention of Crime, had preached a sermon denouncing the leaders of Tammany as "a lying, perjured, rum-soaked, and libidinous lot" and "polluted harpies that, under the pretense of governing this city, are feeding day and night on its quivering vitals." That Tammany's methods of government could be described as polluted was hardly news to New Yorkers; in every election campaign they heard this story from the opposition candidates—and generally disregarded it at the polls. Still, it had been over twenty years since they had risen up in their wrath and evicted Boss Tweed, and another rising-up was about due. A *World* reporter was at the church by invitation of the publicity-minded Parkhurst. When the Tammany leaders blandly asked for proof of the charges, Parkhurst had none, but he immediately set out to collect it, starting with evidence of dirty work at the police precincts.

Though the New York Police Department was more or less a branch office of Tammany's Fourteenth Street headquarters, the local Democrats' alliance with the men in blue was only a small part of their wide-ranging depredations. But proving graft in the awarding of municipal contracts, the prime source of Tammany's boodle, would have been a tedious procedure. Complacent cops with fat bank books in their back pockets were on every corner, however, and on the side streets were flourishing brothels, gambling dens, and after-hours saloons. The headline-hunting Parkhurst shrewdly concentrated his attention on the first of these. Proof that the cops were being paid off by any particular madam was mostly hearsay, but his researches into the entertainment available in such establishments was thorough. On one occasion he went so far as to join a group of young whores in a game of leapfrog while one of his associate investigators served as the frog. You can't beat that kind of political news.

Every Sunday Dr. Parkhurst offered his congregation new installments in the sensational story of his high-minded researches, and in January 1894, when a Republican legislature took over in Albany, it voted to conduct a formal inquiry. Rural upstate Republicans were always happy to oblige the reformers by arranging for revelations that would embarrass downstate Democrats. The appropriation for the investigation was vetoed by the Democratic governor, but the well-fixed Holies simply subsidized the state hearings themselves until the governor thought better of his move. Although Parkhurst's original sermon had denounced Tammany's corrupt alliances in general, the official title of the inquiring body was "The Senate Committee Appointed to Investigate the Police Department of New York City." It was popularly known as the Lexow Committee in honor of its nominal head, Clarence Lexow, state senator from Yonkers, but Lexow hardly got a word in edgewise. The year-long hearings were produced and directed by three Parkhurst nominees: John Goff, who at Parkhurst's request was named counsel to the committee, and William Travers Jerome and Frank Moss, his two assistants. All three (who would meet again at the Becker trial) had previously done legal chores for Parkhurst's Society for the Prevention of Crime and other crusading brigades of Holies.

"Mr. Goff was suddenly an uncanny prestidigitator in a dingy room thronged with reporters, evoking strange beasts from a bottomless hat," wrote Thomas Beer of the Lexow hearings in *The Mauve Decade*, his dissertation on the nineties. "He summoned the Irish patrolmen who bullied contribution from bawds and gamblers or took it from wretched immigrants in unlawful business. . . . The hog's share of this income passed upward from official glove to glove and vanished in a political haze over Tammany Hall. The scandal was superbly handled by the press. Harvey Scott sent a reporter hurrying clear from the misty slope of Portland to whip back news to the *Oregonian*. New York, the hussy, was taken in sin again. . . . The writhings of vice before the Lexow Committee had their place in the news all summer even with the great [Pullman] strike gripping the midlands and Altgeld hardily pitching his epigrams. . . ."

Prestidigitator Goff's assistants Jerome and Moss were also capable and resourceful men. Most of the effective witnesses they persuaded to testify before the committee were criminals of some sort—counterfeiters, policy men, pimps, madams. By coming forward to bear witness against the police they showed courage that, from the committee point of view, made their own sins irrelevant. "At issue, after all, are not their sordid characters and ways of life," the committee's final report noted, but the fact that "the members of the police force . . . have gone for years unpunished and unwhipped for those offenses which, if committed by citizens, would have resulted in fact in sentences to the penitentiary." The Police Department of the City of New York, added the report written by counsel Goff, was "not only corrupt . . . it was oppressive and repulsive to a degree beyond endurance. The members of the Police Department were bound together by the bond which Burke so eloquently described as 'the cohesion of public plunder.' " Before the hearings Goff said, "The police force of New York had become an established caste. They were not of the people. . . . They regarded themselves as separate and apart from the people. They regarded themselves as the possessors of powers and privileges away above and beyond the people. They were the violators of the peace and the oppressors of society. They recognized that any man who merited the infamous title of 'squealer' could not exist. . . ."

John Goff, author of this report, would be the judge at Charles Becker's first trial for murder. Emotions, deep convictions, and recourse to legal procedures that had vast effect on the policeman's fate could be traced back to what had gone on in the hearings of a legislative committee nearly twenty years earlier.

The Lexow hearings which, as Beer noted, seemed to have lost sight of the fact that New York policemen were "in general dull, underpaid creatures and, frequently, fathers," resulted in six thousand pages of testimony, all those headlines, and the election of a reform mayor, William L. Strong, in the fall of 1894. In the same election John Goff was chosen for a fourteen-year term as the chief judge of the Court of General Sessions. Soon afterward Jerome was appointed to the Court of Special Sessions. The man the reform government picked as its new chairman of the Board of Police Commissioners—this was before the city had a single police commissioner—was Theodore Roosevelt, who thus, as Beer saw it, "came bouncing back from obscurity to the bright, noisy center of things, where he remained until flags were lowered for him." Years after the Lexow hearings, said Beer, someone wondered what the current President of the United States might have been doing if it hadn't been for the wicked New York cops.

That reform regime lasted but one term. "The people can't stand all this police corruption, but they can't stand reform either," Tammany Boss Croker cannily remarked, and on the night the reformers were overturned thousands of New Yorkers stomped through Madison Square to the exultant shout of "Well! Well! Well! Reform has gone to hell!" Goff and Jerome's long-term appointments were not affected, however, and when Roosevelt moved on to a national role Dr. Parkhurst's other protégé, Frank Moss, succeeded him as head of the Board of Police Commissioners. Parkhurst and his Goo-Goo friends would continue to be forces to reckon with.

A number of prominent policemen had hastily resigned during and after the Lexow hearings and a few had been dismissed, but criminal prosecutions did not come to much. When Moss took over as presiding police commissioner, he discovered to his chagrin that, although the reformers were now officially in charge, corruption was still rampant in the Police Department. A couple of years after that when Tammany had recaptured City Hall, the Holies got Moss appointed as counsel to still another legislative investigation into the misdeeds of New York police. This exploratory operation was informally known as the Mazet Committee. Where the Lexow hearings had dealt largely with police involvement with prostitution, the Mazet hearings worried about illegal gambling graft. The resulting criminal convictions were about the same, or zero. The political consequence was that once more a reform mayor was elected in November 1901 and once more lasted a single term.

And so it went for the reformers through the first years of the century—out again, in again and out again, without much purification to show for it. In each succeeding investigation of the police there was great harking back to the original Lexow researches that had made such a satisfactory splash, and the word "Lexow" became a common verb: "LEGISLATURE MAY LEXOW AGAIN," read a 1909 headline when the reformers had been sidelined for several years. The legislature didn't Lexow; instead there was a rousing grand jury investigation of police involvement in the white slave trade, the jury foreman being a new Simon Pure recruit, John D. Rockefeller, Jr. That did it. In the fall election the reformers took five of the six major city offices, and although the Tammany candidate won the top post at City Hall, even there the victor was William Gaynor who was famous for having made trouble for the police in his long stretch on the local Supreme Court bench.

Few mayors of large cities have had a formal philosophy of government. As in so many respects, the eccentric, articulate, and splenetic Gaynor was the exception. The dignified-looking Irishman with the Van Dyke beard and the cold blue eyes was a live-and-let-live man. "You elect men from among yourselves not to do as they like, not to trample on you, not to club you, not to wrong you, not to put a hand on you . . . except in so far as you have allowed it . . . in those laws which you have made," he said in a 1910 Fourth of July speech. "He was a primitive American and really believed in the Bill of Rights," the *Globe* would write after his death. "These things did not represent sentimental nonsense to him nor did he regard them as impractical abstractions." The presumptuous representative of the state whom Gaynor had especially reviled and thwarted at every opportunity in his years as a judge was the arrogant policeman who wielded his stout club on the defenseless and smashed down doors as he pleased—the same cop who would provide the negative image of police power in the convulsive national debate that would divide Americans much later in the century. From the bench Gaynor had handed down a long line of decisions relegating policemen to their place as servants of the community. "To be plain about it . . . as the citizens do not want to be doing police duty, they hire policemen for that purpose, but do not thereby make them their masters." Police oppression was particularly deplorable, he added, in the case of those whose rights and liberties ought to be jealously guarded, namely, the weak, uninfluential and friendless whose protection should be the chief aim of government."

When a special committee of the New York Board of Aldermen was set up to investigate the Police Department in the furor that followed Rosenthal's murder, Gaynor would list for the committee a long string of his victories over Centre Street, concluding proudly, "The police do not club boys and defenseless people in this town, not after the first month I was Mayor, nor break into houses without warrants, either." The aldermen, mostly Republicans that year, would nod absently. They were not used to construing police reforms in terms of protecting heads and complying with due process. After all the noisy legislative investigations, what they wanted from Gaynor was the admission that his narrow view of police power had encouraged gambling and prostitution—and grafting—in the city. For in his most famous judicial decision Gaynor had held that the primary duty of the police "is to be in the streets preserving outward order and decency. The law does not commit the supreme folly of making them the custodians or guardians of the private morals of the community. . . . So long as a house on my block is so decorous and orderly in the windows and on the stoops that I am not able to see a single thing wrong with it, I am willing to go by and leave it alone, and I want the police to do the same thing." Such a house should be entered only with a warrant obtained on evidence, Judge Gaynor had ruled, and "if a place is so decorous that no evidence against it can be obtained, then leave it alone."

With this brand of philosopher taking over City Hall in 1910 some of the big-time gambling house proprietors who had left for Saratoga under previous, less permissive regimes moved back to town, and others still in residence bearishly moved in more tables. Taking note, unfriendly politicians began blaming the mayor's decade-old "outward order and decency" dictum for all kinds of city crime. Early in 1911 a bumptious young magistrate named Corrigan charged that the city had never been as wide open.

("Corrigan's mind is full of vice and crime," Gaynor had snapped, "and if you wonder how come his mind is full of vice and crime, just follow him around at night.") The *Times* would claim later that certain local newspapers had deliberately manufactured a crime wave to liven things up in a slack news period. "You cannot prevent the proprietors of the ragbag newspapers from inventing a crime wave whenever they feel disposed to do so," Gaynor wrote his police commissioner consolingly. "They would be willing to bring any infamy on the city for the sake of increasing their circulation."

But eventually he did go after the gamblers. Running the show was different from fulminating on the sidelines. Moreover, Gaynor's sympathy for beleaguered outlaws had been reduced somewhat by the fact that in his new role at the center of things he had come face to face with some of the gamblers who were operating behind those decorous doors. Specifically he had encountered Herman Rosenthal and some of his associates who had come to him to complain of police "oppression." Gaynor later called them "the worst gang of men I ever saw."

Half a dozen years before, a Committee of Nine (Robert Cutting, Isaac Seligman, and Jacob Schiff had been among the familiar reformers' names on the roster) had delegated itself to advise the legislature on how to reorganize the city's Police Department. They proposed that control of gambling, among other social evils, be taken away from the precincts and put under the jurisdiction of a special central office squad. In June 1911— after running through two police commissioners and just swearing in a third, Rhinelander Waldo—Gaynor decided to try the scheme with his own variations. In order to reduce the chance of pay-offs, there would be not one but several squads, which would gather evidence independently. Raids would be made only on order of the commissioner, who would make sure warrants were properly issued. Thus no one squad leader would be in a position to promise protection. In the fall of 1911 three antigambling squads, including one headed by Lieutenant Charles Becker, were raiding gambling houses at the rate of one every other night.

Those who favored the notion that crime was raging unchecked in the city would not pipe down, however. A grand jury investigation of general police laxity in law enforcement was convened in February 1912 and adjourned without any particular result. In July of that year another grand jury—the one Rosenthal would be ready to testify before—was empaneled to consider the relationship between the police and gambling graft. District Attorney Whitman was prepared to be cooperative.

The Simon Pures had been hammering away at the Police Department for twenty years now. Enormous amounts of time, energy, earnest thought, and public and private money had been expended in the cause. Yet nobody of much importance had gone to jail, and the situation down at headquarters was said to be grafting as usual. There was a feeling among the reformers that year—and among a good many bystanders—that the time had come for them to really get some of these boys or turn their efforts elsewhere. In the early spring of 1912 about a dozen directors of the Citizen's Union, the City Club, and the Bureau of Municipal Research met at the home of Mr. and Mrs. William Jay Schieffelin with this aim in mind. Schieffelin, the great-grandson of John Jay, first chief justice of the United States, was the head of the prosperous, family-owned Schieffelin and Company, international dealers in chemicals and had married a great-granddaughter of Commodore Vanderbilt. When he was still in his twenties, he had been among those who had subsidized the Lexow investigation, and ever since he had rejected the inane frivolities of the Newport and Palm Beach crowds in favor of working vigorously to improve conditions in his city.

Schieffelin suggested to his guests that if they wanted to expose once and for all the grip the Sullivan dynasty and its corrupt police henchmen had on the city the reformers should hire a private detective agency to get the goods on them. Not by coincidence, William J. Burns himself, of the Burns Detective Agency, was awaiting Schieffelin's call. When the group reaction to his proposal was favorable, Schieffelin telephoned Burns, who came right over and reportedly told the assembled company that such an investigation might cost as much as two hundred thousand dollars. No one boggled at this price. Without further ado Burns was given a fifteen-thousand-dollar retainer and put on the job with orders to spare no necessary expense in the cause of "getting some of these boys at last." Not in their most sanguine dreams, of course, did the reformers think that what they would get one of them for was murder.

VIII

"THE police are too busy going after Rosenthal's killer to pay attention to the newspaper stories that take up so much of Mr. Whitman's time," Deputy Police Commissioner Dougherty remarked three days after the crime. But the ex-Pinkerton man's ties to bluecoats were new and easily loosed, and although he thereafter worked hard to keep his own reputation burnished he soon stopped protecting Becker. The Saturday after the murder he meekly came to call on Whitman at the Criminal Courts Building, "the first time a police commissioner in the course of a great crime has ever called on the District Attorney in person," declared the *Tribune*. Dougherty asked Whitman what he thought should be done next. The colloquy between the two men appeared in the right-hand column of the front page of several New York newspapers the next day.

> DOUGHERTY: Do you want me to arrest Lieutenant Becker?
> WHITMAN: Not yet.
> DOUGHERTY: All right. I see we agree as to who is back of this killing.

Apostasy got him nowhere, however. When Becker was finally arrested eight days later, Whitman made sure the deputy police commissioner had no part in it. The *Sun* had been reminding its readers of who was the probable major defendant in the case by printing on its front page a daily box headed: "WHAT BECKER DID

YESTERDAY." Meanwhile runners-up for the title were being locked up, one by one, in the Tombs. Of the two men first jailed and charged with the murder, chauffeur Libby had proved to be a disappointment. Five people swore that he never left his rooming house that night. Nevertheless, he would remain behind bars for another month. His partner, Shapiro, was beginning to remember more details of the evening's events. Harry Vallon had been one of his passengers when he had sped away from the Metropole. Sam Schepps was another, he now recalled. "Wanted" circulars went out for these two men. By this time District Attorney Whitman had an independent police force to help him track down the fugitives.

What, if anything, the William J. Burns agency had accomplished for the reformers who had hired it at such a large financial outlay many months before the murder was never revealed. Part of Burns' scheme for undoing the System had involved the infiltration of the Metropole. During the months before the murder transients at the hotel often had their beds turned down or their bags carried by a Burns operative. But if any such ringer was on duty on the night of July 15 he never reported anything usable in court. Hope sprang eternal, apparently. On the Saturday after the murder the *American* announced that "for the first time in the history of the Police Department a private detective agency was put to work yesterday by the District Attorney's office on an official murder mystery." In spite of the heat, William Schieffelin had made a special trip down from his summer home, Tranquillity Farm, at Ashford, Maine. A conference had followed with other civic-minded and well-heeled New Yorkers who had been horrified at the revelations in the Rosenthal case. Theodore Roosevelt had been among those on hand. Schieffelin appeared the next day at Whitman's office and made a formal statement.

"I have come to tell you," he said, "that a committee of citizens, among whom are several of the most prominent bankers in New York, have authorized me to place at your disposal any amount of money that may be needed to employ aid independent of the Police Department to carry your investigation to a definite and thorough conclusion." The score of Burns detectives already at work would simply be turned over to Whitman to augment the dozen so-called county detectives regularly assigned to the D.A.'s

office. If he needed more, all he had to do was holler. The reformers were ready to foot the bills. Their purpose, said Schieffelin, was to help Whitman not only solve the Rosenthal crime but
to expose the connection of the Police Department with it. The
names of the men said to have chipped in for this project were
again familiar: Morgan, Speyer, Seligman, Cutting, Rockefeller,
as well as Elbert Gary of U.S. Steel and railroad tycoon Arthur
Curtiss James.

"I am immensely gratified," Whitman told Schieffelin, pump-
ing his hand. The next day he let it be known that he could hardly
expose the connection of the police with the murder while working out of an office only a few blocks from Police Headquarters.
At the reformers' expense he took over a large suite at the
Waldorf, then at Thirty-fourth Street and Fifth Avenue. He
wouldn't feel it was safe to move back to his shabby office in the
Criminal Courts Building until after Thanksgiving that year. A
former member of his staff recalled much later in the century
that from that July afternoon on, "Whenever we had any problems, Whitman would just pick up the phone and make a call and
a couple of hours later Schieffelin would come in with a bundle of
money. Those Simon Pure fellows were really generous. They
were so grateful to have someone working hard to clean up the
city."

A few minutes after Schieffelin left that first afternoon Whitman announced he was dispatching half a dozen Burns agents to
the Catskills where Vallon and Schepps were said to be hiding.
The next arrests were made closer to home, however—and by the
police. Bridgey Webber and Sam Paul had been questioned at
headquarters every day since the murder. On Sunday, July 21,
they were both arrested there for being "implicated in the murder"
of Herman Rosenthal. Webber was so unprepared for this development that he had told his taxicab to wait. Late the next
evening Harry Vallon, reportedly summoned by Bridgey to come
share his misery, also rode up to the Centre Street building in a
taxi and strolled inside. As in the case of Bald Jack a few days
earlier, the cops on duty paid him no attention. The *Evening Post*
man finally directed Vallon to the detective bureau. There he was
hastily arrested, charged also with being implicated in the murder. Vallon, who had a face like a hatchet, said his real name was
Harry Vallinsky. He had changed it, he said, so as not to seem to

be trading on the fame of his brother, the well-known pickpocket Sheeny Mike Vallinsky. The *Tribune* now ran a cartoon showing Waldo and Gaynor looking prim and fatuous under a sign that read: "Criminals Will Not Be Received Unless Properly Introduced." Still, by Tuesday, July 23, a week after the shooting six men were being held without bail in the Tombs on the murder charge. In order of appearance they were Libby, Shapiro, Rose, Paul, Webber, and Vallon.

So far the mayor of the city had made no move at all in the case except to publish a letter deploring Becker's choice of dinner companion. He now did some further corpse-knocking in a letter responding to Commissioner Waldo's question of whether he should suspend Becker from the force.

"Do not bend a single bit to clamor and especially to clamor chiefly created by hired press agents of the gamblers with whom you are at war and those corrupt newspapers which have been all along and are now at the service of such gamblers and against you," he told Waldo. He reviewed the case against the police lieutenant: that, "acting under your orders," Becker had raided Rosenthal's gambling house and kept a guard there afterward and that, having tried to evict the police in numerous ways and made charges against other public figures, Rosenthal had finally announced that Becker had been his business partner.

"It is possible that this may turn out to be so," Gaynor wrote of Rosenthal's claim. "But until you obtain some evidence you have no ground for suspending and trying Lt. Becker on that charge. If this outlaw and scoundrel Rosenthal were alive, the case would be the same," he went on. "His word would not suffice. No honorable man in the world would accept it to the injury of a beast, let alone a man. No court would tolerate it for an instant." Possibly there was some corruption among members of the force "for they are fearfully tempted." There had always been gambling: "The police cannot eradicate vice from the hearts of men." But the number of gamblers in the city was comparatively small. As for the charge that Becker had "instigated the degenerate outlaws who killed Rosenthal . . . this is possible, but thus far there is no evidence to support such a charge. . . . No doubt the complicity of Lt. Becker will be revealed if it exists. Let us proceed in order."

The next day the *American* cartoon showed Gaynor telling Waldo: "Everything is all right. Becker is all right. You're all right. I'm all right. There is no gambling. Rosenthal isn't even dead. Everything is all right except the blackleg newspapers." The *Evening Mail* took a sterner view. "We wonder if Mayor Gaynor appreciates the importance of this venal crisis in the life of our city," read the day's editorial. "Is he aware that New York is fighting a kind of Gettysburg battle against a form of treason infinitely baser than anything which assailed the nation in 1863?"

The mayor's letter to Waldo did not stop with his directive about fair play for policeman Becker. It went on to blame most of the city's current troubles on the members of one ethnic group— or so most Jewish New Yorkers would interpret it. Gaynor had not before this been a baiter of those who were then often called "our Hebrew friends." But in his fury at the charges being thrown at his administration as a result of the murder he pointed out that New York had the largest foreign-born population of any city "and a large number of these are degenerates and criminals. The gambling of the city is almost all in their hands, not to mention other vices and crimes. The published names of everyone connected nearly or remotely with Rosenthal and his murder shows them to be of this same class of lawless foreigners to which he belonged." Rabbi Stephen S. Wise of the Free Synagogue jumped into the fight, declaring that Gaynor was trying to divert attention from his own sins by "inflaming the public mind against the Jews."

"I have not said so much as one word about Jews in connection with the Rosenthal murder," Gaynor snarled back. "I said that those whose names have been published in connection with the gambling murder . . . showed them to be 'degenerate foreigners' . . . and if you look at the list of those names you will see that they are not all Jews, although it contains . . . many Jews. A degenerate outlaw is the same to me, Jew or gentile," he finished grandly.

Before Gaynor's letter appeared the old, millionaire German-Jewish families in the city, who had long added their luster and support to the gold-plated Holies, had naturally been appalled at the accounts of criminal antics below Fourteenth Street that filled the headlines after the Rosenthal shooting, but without any thought of being defensive about the revelations. What did these dregs from Eastern Europe have to do with them? They had viewed the Second Avenue Jews in the case as no less remote and alien than did the other affluent and respectable citizens of the town. Within a few hours after the mayor's contemptuous remarks were published, however, Adolph Lewisohn, Jacob Schiff, Felix Warburg, Cyrus Sulzberger, and other members of the executive committee of the Kehillah, or Jewish Community, a kind of holding company for seven hundred Jewish educational and charitable societies, had met in emergency session and issued a statement deploring the crimes "in which individuals reputed to be Jews are implicated," but pointing out that such "practices and vices . . . have up to very recent years been proverbially unknown among our people." All the individuals mentioned, they added, had come to New York at an early age and grown up there. What had been exposed by the Rosenthal murder was not the corruption of a race but "the moral and political degeneracy of this city."

More than the usual number of prominent Jews would, by their own request, be on the committee that was formed after the rally in Cooper Union to assist Whitman and others in their fight to stamp out this degeneracy and particularly to see that the man who had become its most flagrant symbol, police grafter Becker, was brought to book. Presumably leading Jews were also unusually well represented among financial contributors to the cause. The fact that Whitman's captive witnesses in the trials that followed would frequently quote Charles Becker as having made derogatory remarks about their race ("Becker said to me, 'Nobody gives a damn about that dirty Jew cur,'" said Sam Schepps) possibly loosened their purse strings further. With the addition of the spectre of anti-Semitism to a case already heavily charged with emotion, the lines were drawn more sharply than ever. On one side, it would seem to many, were high-minded citizens, fighters for a better world, and on the other were crooked or morally indifferent Irishmen, Tammany riff-raff, incorrigible police grafters, and people with an irrational hatred for all members of the Jewish religion.

In response to the first part of Mayor Gaynor's otherwise reckless and damaging letter, Commissioner Waldo did not suspend Becker from the force. In one of his final statements Becker would recall that this decision led to rumors—untrue, he said— that he must know something shameful about either the mayor or the commissioner. Instead of suspending him, Waldo now transferred Becker to the Bathgate station house in the Bronx. A dozen newspapermen gathered around his desk on the first floor at headquarters as the lieutenant packed up his belongings the next day. They asked him if he thought the transfer meant that higher police officials were no longer standing by him. "Are they going to 'let you splash'?" one of them asked him.

"I'm not even supposed to talk to you characters," Becker told them as he tied up a shoe box full of papers. Swope was there and suddenly asked him about the details of his divorce from his second wife. Becker was "plainly astonished." "Tell the New York *World* I don't give a damn what it says about me," he told Swope.

The press had discovered that at the time of the murder Becker had been about to move from his four-room apartment to a two-story Tudor-style house he had bought on Olinville Avenue in the Bronx. This area was one where a number of high-ranking policemen had recently established themselves in a style to which their salaries could not have accustomed them. Becker's house was said to have set him back over nine thousand dollars and, most damning of all, it included a *garage*, proving that he even had an automobile in his future plans. Becker's explanation was that he had borrowed some money from his bachelor brother John. Moreover, since he had been on the force for nineteen years and his wife had been teaching school for seventeen it would have been surprising if they hadn't had some savings to fall back on, he said. This remark encouraged the press to dig around and discover that his wife's long years of teaching were beside the point since they had only been married since 1905, which led in turn to a look at his total marital record. His first wife, Mary, had died in October, 1895, eight months after their marriage. The case of his second wife, Letitia, turned out to be more interesting. Married in 1898, they had had a son named Harold two years later. In 1905 she had divorced him on the ground that he had been caught in a room with another woman at the Eagle Hotel on Cooper Square. The news stories mentioned that soon afterward the second Mrs. Becker had married Charles Becker's younger brother, Paul, and had migrated with her new husband and child to western Colorado. None of them pointed out that adultery—staged or not— was the only grounds for divorce in the state. They did observe reasonably that a man who paid eight dollars a week in child support out of forty-three dollars in wages was not a promising customer for an automobile salesman.

A group of Bronx civic leaders protested Becker's new assignment as an insult to their borough. More cheerful news for Becker was the attempt of another long-time crony of Big Tim's to throw doubt on Rosenthal's *World* affidavit. Sullivan's friend, who had been Rosenthal's lawyer, insisted it had been Inspector Hayes' treatment of him that the gambler had been bitter about in his last months. He didn't understand how Becker had got to be so important in the case.

Late in the second week after the murder Dougherty received an anonymous phone call, and that afternoon Dago Frank was arrested in a rooming house on West 138 Street. With him was a girl named Rose and a warm opium pipe. He was still in a daze when he arrived at the Tombs. Five days later there occurred what keepers of the necrology in the case always considered the second murder in the Rosenthal affair. Three men strode into the Cafe Dante on West Thirty-fourth Street and emptied their revolvers into the man behind the bar, one Giacomo Verella. Verella was known to be a police tipster and was suspected of having made the anonymous call to headquarters that had led to Dago Frank's arrest.

Not only Dago Frank but also Jacob Reich now swelled the numbers of East Siders in the Tombs. At the coroner's hearing earlier that week Louis Krause, the Coney Island waiter who had been on Forty-third Street on the murder night, was on the stand when he suddenly waved a hand at Reich—who was in the audience, hanging around the press box as usual—and said he recognized him as a man he had seen in front of the Metropole before the shooting. (Reich, of course, claimed he'd arrived some minutes afterward.) The *Times* mentioned that an assistant district attorney had been seen pointing Reich out to Krause before the hearing. Krause was questioned about how he had happened to offer his testimony to the district attorney's office. His lawyer, James Mark Sullivan, had sent him there, he said. The coroner leaned down from the bench. Was this the same man who was Bald Jack Rose's lawyer, he asked, astonished. A mere coincidence, Krause explained. He had simply got Sullivan's name out of the newspapers. (The defense would claim at Becker's later trial that the day after the murder Krause had told a fellow worker in Coney Island that he had been too far away to see anything at the murder scene. His Coney Island friend had said that was too bad, that no doubt there would be money in it for him otherwise. Krause had thought things over and then consulted Sullivan. Unfortunately for Reich, the fellow worker who reported this conversation was an ex-policeman, and the credibility of cops—even ex-cops—was at its nadir.) Whether or not the D.A.'s office had reminded or persuaded the eager-to-oblige waiter that he had seen Reich, Becker's late-evening companion, on Forty-third Street before the murder, Krause's testimony at the coroner's hearing was reported as a new Whitman triumph. On Krause's word Reich was arrested as a material witness.

Webber, Rose, and Vallon, whom Reich now joined on the first tier of the Tombs, had been visited by the district attorney nearly every morning since their arrests, and assistant district attorneys came by even more often to see if the East Siders could recall anything "more interesting to the prosecution." Whitman's office wasn't getting much satisfaction, however. For example, in the crucial matter of the Rosenthal mortgage, Rose still supported Becker's version: Rosenthal had been willing to do business with Rose "so I got part of the game, but I had to put up fifteen hundred dollars to get it. I took the mortgage because I wanted to be sure I wouldn't be bilked out of my money." Was this a crime? he demanded.

The jail where the gamblers were being held was across the street from the Criminal Courts Building and connected to it by a second-story roofed corridor, inevitably known as the Bridge of Sighs. The jail had got its name because the prison it had replaced in 1878 had been modeled on an Egyptian tomb. The second Tombs, a gray, brooding, chateau-like structure, was built on piles on the site of the old Collect Pond of New York's colonial days. The pond had never been properly drained and the cells constantly dripped with moisture; the lower tiers were often ankle deep in water forced back through the pipes, and it was generally believed, recalled Arthur Train, then an assistant district attorney, that the building rose and fell with the tide. The cells, as he described them, "had no windows and were about seven feet by three-and-a-half with barely enough room for the prisoners to stand between their iron cots and the opposite walls. There was no running water, no sanitation except for tin pails and no ventilation save through small chutes like chimney flues which pierced the massive walls to the roof above. The only light came through the bars of the heavy iron doors from the windows on the opposite side of the corridor. "The Tombs," Train concluded, "came near to convincing me of man's inhumanity to man." It didn't help that in late July 1912 the weather continued to be in the nineties and very humid. It was a place a man might say almost anything to get out of.

So far no indictments had been handed down against any of the imprisoned men although the coroner held daily hearings in the case. These were attended by vast crowds that spilled out into the corridors and even into the street. An indictment could result from either grand jury action or a hearing before a magistrate. The coroner was sitting as a magistrate in this case, and indictments were expected; nevertheless the hearings were adjourned day after day without any formal action. Rose, Webber, and Vallon testified at colorful length but denied they had been at the Metropole at the time of the murder or that they had anything but friendly feelings for poor Herman, so why would they have killed him? They also denied they had known Lieutenant Becker to speak of. None of this seriously interfered with the case against them: A number of witnesses could place them on the scene and connect them with the getaway car.

In spite of the crowds clamoring to get in the hearing room, most of the passes unaccountably seemed to be held by evil-looking East Siders. ("You could pave Broadway with those faces," said Inspector Hughes during one session.) Several witnesses who had agreed they had seen the gamblers in the neighborhood on the fatal night changed their minds on the stand after a quick look around the room. Whitman did not consider this a problem, however. He simply had the nervous deponents arrested as material witnesses and held in the Tombs until they reconsidered. A man known as John the Barber got this treatment. Back on the stand a few days later he explained with tears in his eyes that he had suddenly lost his memory because he was fearful of what might happen to his six children. "Mr. Whitman laughed heartily at this excuse," reported the *World*. John the Barber then agreed that after all he *had* seen Bridgey running away from the Metropole after the murder.

Also in session that day in the Criminal Courts Building was a hearing of the grand jury investigating police graft. After the murder the three heads of the police strong arm squads had received formal letters asking them to come before the grand jury. Two of them, lieutenants Costigan and Riley, had complied, and Becker had also agreed to do so. (He had asked Waldo if he had to waive immunity and Waldo had told him he damn well did). On Friday, July 26, Becker spent the afternoon cooling his heels in a corridor outside the grand jury room, waiting to be called. Whitman, however, asked for an early adjournment. Becker, he announced, would be heard at the next session on Tuesday morning.

Probably Becker had no intention of telling the truth about the sources of his suddenly amplified net worth. There is no question, however, that the fact that he had testified before the investigating grand jury, without a subpoena, waiving immunity, would have marred the later prosecution picture of him as a policeman willing to do anything to conceal his grafting gains, a man who thought of himself as answerable to no one, above the law.

"I am sorry I did not have a chance to go before the grand jury," he told a reporter for the *Evening Post* as he left the courthouse. "I want to clear myself. I am the victim of circumstances. It is an outrage that I should be the unfortunate man to be singled out to bear the brunt of all this scandal."

Meanwhile, across the street in the Tombs, chauffeur Shapiro's memory was getting keener each day. The district attorney's office now issued a statement reporting that not only had Shapiro seen Bald Jack on Forty-third Street just before the murder but also that Vallon, driving off afterward in the Packard, had held a smoking gun in his hands and rapped Shapiro on the head with it, telling him to "step on it." Shapiro had not seen the actual murder, he still insisted, because "I must have dozed off just at that moment."

Although the case against the gamblers was shaping up nicely, Whitman showed little interest in it. Lawyer Levy offered to have Shapiro testify to everything he knew against them, even perhaps decide he hadn't taken a nap at the critical moment, in return for immunity. The district attorney turned the offer down. "We're after the big fellows, not the small fry," he said.

By the evening of Monday, July 29, two weeks after the night of the murder, the various behind-the-scenes power ploys, deals and secret maneuvers came to a dramatic conclusion that solved the problems of most of the principals in the case. On that evening Rose, Webber, and Vallon suddenly were released from the threat of an indictment for murder. Sam Paul was released from the Tombs and the homicide charge against him dismissed. And Charles Becker was under arrest for murder.

Becker, on duty in the Bathgate station, was busy cleaning a typewriter when two county detectives from Whitman's office arrived about half past eight. He stood up when he saw them and slowly began wiping the ink from his fingers.

"Welcome to the Bronx," he said. They thought afterward that his face might have been pale, but his voice was calm enough. It was the last moment of his life out of custody.

Told that he was under arrest, Becker asked for permission to telephone for a replacement and to change into civilian clothes: He preferred not to shame the department by being arraigned in his uniform. When the replacement arrived, he shook hands all around with the men in the precinct house and then walked with the detectives to the el station. There was no conversation on the long ride down, the district attorney's men reported. When they got to the Canal Street stop, Becker led the way off. He was taken in a side entrance of the Criminal Courts Building.

Becker now learned that only twenty minutes earlier the grand jury, sitting in extraordinary session, had indicted him for first-degree murder. They had taken this action on the testimony of Rose, Webber, and Vallon, who had all turned state's witness. The three gamblers had sworn that they had made arrangements with Big Jack Zelig, the East Side gang leader, to hire the four gunmen, bailing Zelig out of jail for that purpose, that they had assembled the killers at the Webber poker rooms, had then located Rosenthal, and had sent the gunmen to murder him. The day after the shooting Webber had given Rose a thousand dollars, and Rose had given it to Sam Schepps, who had paid off the killers in Times Square. They had done all this, they had testified, out of terror of Lieutenant Becker, because he had told them to, because he had told them if they did not he would plant guns in all their pockets and send them up for seven years, the penalty under the Sullivan Law. "I had no choice but to do what Becker said. I had to make a living," Bald Jack had said to the grand jury, according to excerpts from his testimony that were released later.

Becker, arraigned at once, pleaded not guilty. His lawyer, John Hart, was in the room but was not permitted to speak to him. Bald Jack's lawyer, James Sullivan, was there; so was Max Steuer, the attorney since noon that day for Bridgey Webber and Harry Vallon. "They looked seriously pleased with themselves," reported the *Herald* of Steuer and Sullivan. A number of the grand jurors had stayed in their seats to see the rest of the evening's performance. About two dozen newspapermen were on hand. Becker stopped and raised his hat to the reporters as he was being led out of the courtroom.

"Good-bye, boys," he said. He was smiling, but his eyes were "cold and cynical." Flanked by two keepers, he walked over the Bridge of Sighs. About eleven-fifteen he was locked up in Cell 112 on the lowest tier of the Tombs, his home until he left it for Sing Sing.

IX

A policeman is not a natural object of sympathy. On a dark night when a citizen is in trouble there is no more welcome sight than that of a man in blue plunging around a corner, gun drawn. But such dramatic need and such on-the-spot response seldom occur in an ordinary life. The policeman by informal definition is not a brave rescuer but an ominous lumbering figure, chewing other citizens out over traffic tickets or over nothing at all, throwing his weight around, clubbing and even shooting people unnecessarily, and raking in graft.

The forces that brought Lieutenant Becker to a cell in the Tombs owed much of their strength to this public mistrust of the man in blue, intensified by the special passions that the mention of police graft set off in America early in the century. But Charles Becker was not a blameless, victimized hero. He was a brutal and corrupt man.

Like District Attorney Whitman, he was a poor boy who had come to the big city and made good. His German-born parents had settled on a farm near Callicoon Center in New York's Sullivan County, where Becker was born on July 26, 1870. Arriving in the city in his late teens, he worked at odd jobs—as a bouncer in German beer gardens off the Bowery, a baker's assistant, a door-to-door clothing salesman. His older brother John joined the police force in 1891. Becker waited another two years, perhaps until he had saved up the $250 fee that Tammany Hall then exacted from all police candidates—nearly a third of a new recruit's annual salary. A few years earlier a department historian had defended this arrangement. "It is safe to say that nearly every appointment is made through personal or political influence," he wrote. "Those who cavil at this should remember that this almost invariably secures for the department men who have lived long enough in the city to know it, for politicians and friends of Police Commissioners are not disposed to interest themselves in strangers." Becker's political leanings were Republican, but probably all it took to establish himself as no stranger to Tammany was money in hand. The date of his swearing in was November 1, 1893.

The most famous policeman then on the force was Inspector Alexander Williams. Reminiscing later in the nineties, the *Tribune* recalled that in his days of glory Williams "was an object of so much interest that people would stop in their tracks and stare at him as he strode along the street." In 1893 he was the inspector for the district that included the Tenderloin, formally the Twenty-ninth Precinct, an area lying roughly between Twenty-third and Forty-second streets and Fourth and Seventh avenues that contained most of New York's expensive theaters, hotels, gambling houses, and brothels and was thus the richest grafting territory in the city. It was appropriate for Williams to be presiding over the Twenty-ninth. In the mid-seventies he had been briefly transferred there after a stretch in a West Side precinct where the pickings were meager. "I been living on chuck steak for a long time," he told a newspaperman. "Now I'm going to get me a little of the tenderloin"—thus giving the Twenty-ninth the name by which it would be known for a generation. (By the year of the Rosenthal murder the city's rich gaming preserve had shifted northward, and it was the Sixteenth Precinct lying between Forty-second and Fifty-second streets west of Fifth that was generally called the Tenderloin or sometimes the New Tenderloin.) For being so free with his billy Williams had a nickname of his own, "The Clubber." Such was his influence on the force, the *Tribune* claimed, that in his heyday "it was hardly safe to ask a lordly policeman a plain question. He was inclined to make reply by a stiff punch with the end of his big night stick." "Boys, just remember," Williams once told some impressionable young recruits, "there's more justice in the end of this night stick than there is in all the courts in the land." Reporter Lincoln Steffens noted in his autobiography that it was the spectacle of Williams enthusiastically breaking the heads of the poor and helpless that led him to join the reformers perennially fighting to wrest the city from Tammany and its Police Department allies.

The Lexow hearings began three months after Becker joined the force. A number of police officers turned contrite, even tearful, on the witness stand. But Williams, bigger and broader than anyone in the hearing room, was a bold and defiant witness. Counsel John Goff asked if it were not true that he had been charged with clubbing more people than any other man on the force. Williams said it was. Goff said he supposed there had been no man in the department charged with as much corruption.

"If so I have not heard of it," answered Williams complacently.

He denied the charge that he was worth half a million dollars but admitted owning such amenities as a seventeen-room house at Cos Cob and a seventeen-thousand-dollar yacht. His affluence, he said, was the result of a gratifying increase in the value of some building lots he had bought in Japan in his seagoing years before he joined the department. When he was accused of consorting with criminals, his answer was: "You don't catch murderers and burglars by hanging around the YMCA."

"I haven't any doubt that there is nothing under the sun that is outrageous and unlawful that you would not do," Goff said reflectively.

"I suppose not," said Williams, shrugging his shoulders. Goff added that he didn't want to get into any personal altercation with the witness.

"You better not, either," said the inspector.

Charles Becker, then a brash and brawny young recruit, naturally identified himself with the outrageous Williams rather than with the meeker Lexow witnesses, especially Captain Max Schmittberger, who did Williams in. For Williams was summarily retired in January 1895 by the new reform administration's Police Commissioner Roosevelt. Though Williams was never indicted, enough had come out at the Lexow hearings to force his retirement. Most of this adverse information had been supplied by Schmittberger, a stout, somber man who had worked under Williams in the Tenderloin and who testified that he had turned over to the inspector a fat portion of the graft. When he was first summoned before the Lexow committee Schmittberger had been almost as unco-operative a witness as The Clubber, but when the committee got him indicted as a grafter, Schmittberger decided to bare not only all his own sins but also those of his fellow officers. A number of prominent policemen were indicted as a result. Most of them were eventually reinstated, but in the case of Williams, the department hero, the separation was permanent.

Before Schmittberger told all, counsel Goff—as it would be relevant to recall eighteen years later when he was the judge at Becker's first trial—had arranged to give him a guarantee of "immunity from prosecution of the indictment then pending against him and for all acts of an incriminating nature which he in his testimony might admit he had committed." Of Goff's two legal assistants on the Lexow staff, Frank Moss, who would become one of Becker's prosecutors, had welcomed this arrangement. William Travers Jerome had been against saving a brazen grafter from prison. Schmittberger avoided not only prison but removal from the force. Reporter Steffens persuaded Roosevelt that the captain was truly a reformed man and would remain so if he were permitted to stay in uniform. But Williams and other peached-on colleagues saw to it that he was treated as a pariah. He was not even permitted to march in the annual policemen's parade.

From his early days in the department, Becker had faithfully molded himself in The Clubber's image. After the Rosenthal murder it was often said that it had been the sight of Charles Becker manhandling a young prostitute that had driven Stephen Crane to write *Maggie: a Girl of the Streets*. In fact, *Maggie* was published nine months before Becker put on the uniform. But a crusader against the evils of a certain profession rarely has trouble locating a live practitioner of the trade who represents all he most detests about it. As it happened, it *was* Charles Becker whom Crane eventually found.

The Red Badge of Courage had been published in 1895 and by the next summer Crane was a well-known literary figure in town. He didn't care for tea parties in the staid offices of the *Century* magazine however and spent his time instead with more disreputable New Yorkers—pimps, dead beats, Bowery bums. From his first days in the city their natural enemy, the police, had also been his enemy. In August 1896 he was so exercised about the overbearing behavior of the New York cops that he wrote to a new acquaintance, Commissioner Roosevelt, protesting their reckless use of night sticks. The September 1896 issue of *Book News* reported that he was at work on a series of short stories about a metropolitan police officer. They were not expected to give a favorable picture of men in that line of work.

On the night of September 15 Crane, who had been assigned by the New York *Journal* to write a series of sketches on low life in the Tenderloin, was at the Broadway Gardens, a music hall on Thirty-second Street, with two young women he had picked up. Shortly after midnight they were joined by Dora Clark, an auburn-haired young prostitute whom Crane had never seen before. About two o'clock, as he told the story later in court, he led his three companions out to the street and helped one of the women on a cable car. When he stepped back to the sidewalk he found a policeman putting the other two women under arrest. The policeman was Charles Becker. Crane later described him as "picturesque as a wolf." The young novelist rescued one of the women by insisting she was his wife. Becker then took a firm grip on Dora Clark and hauled her off to Magistrate's Court, charging that she had solicited two men in the previous five minutes. Crane went to the Tenderloin station house and got Becker's name and number. "Whatever her character, the arrest was an outrage," he told reporters later. "The policeman flatly lied."

When Dora Clark was tried, Crane appeared at the Jefferson Market Court to testify for her. She complained that she had been arrested repeatedly during the past month by members of the precinct who were persecuting her because she had spurned the advances of one of their fellow officers. Actually, she admitted, it hadn't been as simple as that. Rosenberg, the policeman who had approached her, was rather swarthy, and she had taken him for a Negro. (There were no Negroes then on the force.) "I said to him, 'How dare you speak to a decent white woman?'" Dora Clark testified. The station house fraternity had set out to avenge this insult, and Becker had not shirked his part. Considering the questions that arose later about his attitude toward Jews, it was ironic that in his first appearance in the local press he was allied with a man named Rosenberg. At Dora Clark's hearing he stuck to his story that he had seen her soliciting just before her arrest. The magistrate, whom Crane had had the foresight to write up favorably for the *Journal* during the intervening week, declared that he believed Crane's version of the incident and dismissed the charges.

Crane's willingness to challenge "the buttons" was hailed up and down the Eastern seaboard. The headline in the *Journal* was "STEPHEN CRANE AS BRAVE AS HIS HERO/SHOWS THE 'BADGE OF COURAGE,'" but he was not satisfied. He telegraphed Commissioner Roosevelt suggesting that a departmental trial of Becker was in order, that the policeman was going around town arresting innocent bystanders because he was "bucking for a record." Becker's ambition to get ahead in the department was already apparent. In mid-October Dora Clark ("She bids fair to become as famous as Trilby," said a Boston paper) charged that Becker had seized her by the throat and knocked her down when he met her in the street. Crane agreed to appear for her again and repeat the story of the earlier arrest.

Becker's departmental trial, the longest up to that time in Police Department history, began on the afternoon of October 15 and lasted till nearly three o'clock the next morning. Becker arrived for the ordeal surrounded by an intimidating phalanx made up of every member of the precinct not on duty. His lawyer asked the twenty-four-year-old Crane a series of questions implying that he was an opium addict and that he lived off the earnings of women of the streets. The presiding police official reserved decision. The evening's events proved what decent people had known all along, wrote the *Brooklyn Eagle,* that the New York Police Department was "one of the most corrupt, brutal, incompetent organizations in the world."

The eventual ruling was that Becker, though possibly overzealous, had made an honest mistake in the course of duty. Soon afterward Commissioner Roosevelt turned up at the station house, commended Becker for his generally efficient record, and advised the Tenderloin force to be more considerate of the rights of "unfortunate women"—well, all citizens, come to that. Disregarding this order, one of Crane's roommates reported later, "an aroused and resentful police department bent all its unscrupulous energies to discrediting Crane and making New York too hot for him to live in." By the end of October the prospect of being in the midst of a mere shooting war was a welcome one to the young novelist. He left for the Cuban front. In the three and a half years that remained of his uncommon life he prudently stayed out of the jurisdiction of "New York's Finest" except for a brief stopover in 1898. Becker's friends had long memories. During this stay a policeman, hearing his name, suddenly tried to arrest him in a crowded theater lobby and referred to his companion, the mother of a college friend, as a "whore." In *Active Service*, published the next year, Crane described being caught between the lines in the Graeco-Turkish war and terror so sharp that he would even have been willing to trade his situation for one in which he was at the mercy of members of a metropolitan police force.

In 1896 the New York force numbered about five thousand men, but few below the commissioner's rank received as much local press attention that fall as ordinary policeman Charles Becker. On September 20, while the Dora Clark matter was still pending, he played a role in what was the lead story of the day in most papers. At dawn he and a fellow policeman named Carey had given chase when they saw three men carry a sackful of loot out of a tobacco store. One escaped, Becker brought another down with a night stick to the head, and Carey shot the third man through the heart. The official story stated that the dead man had been identified as "a notorious fanlight operator." To show the kind of villain the boys had done in, the report added that the fingers of the dead man's right hand were bright yellow, proving that he was a habitual cigarette smoker.

The two policemen were hailed as heroes. The sketch of Becker in the *World* showed him sporting a full constabulary moustache and looking very dashing in a tall bobby's helmet. Two days later, however, it was announced that the dead man was not a "notorious fanlight operator" but a nineteen-year-old plumber's assistant. The boy's family claimed he had been a bystander accidentally shot in the course of the chase and hastily given a bad character to build the policemen up as heroes instead of gun-happy killers. Although in time he was exonerated (again) it was an unlucky break for Becker, especially since he hadn't fired the fatal shot. His early career on the force continued to be a series of unfortunate misunderstandings. In December 1896 a respectable New Jersey matron dared to ask him a plain question—directions to the subway. When she didn't understand him the first time and repeated her question, he arrested her as a common drunk. The lady was released with apologies the next morning. (Everybody looks sober the next morning, Becker pointed out.) A few months later a teen-age boy charged that for no reason Becker had beaten him up in a theater lobby. Again it was put down to overzealousness. In his first years on the force Charles Becker was the very epitome of the arrogant, club-swinging policeman then being reviled from the bench by Judge William Gaynor.

About the time of the Crane incident ex-Inspector Williams took notice that Becker was his kind of cop, and they became good friends. Becker was soon campaigning for Williams who had been nominated for the State Senate. To the consternation of the Simon Pures his sponsors were not Tammany members but local Republicans. Justice Goff took time out to denounce Williams, and Dr. Parkhurst was fit to be tied. "Throughout the whole world," he declared from his Madison Square pulpit, "the name of Williams is a synonym for all that is profane, brutal and cowardly." The inspector (who fortunately lost the election) was "the perfected flower of the most corrupt police system that ever prevailed outside of Turkey or Madagascar."

Discord was inevitable when Becker was transferred early in 1901 to the Upper West Side precinct where his friend Williams' old enemy, Max Schmittberger, was the captain in charge. Though Lincoln Steffens always believed Schmittberger stayed clean, others were not so sure. When Becker, still bucking for a record, hauled in some saloonkeepers for violating the liquor laws and didn't clear things first with Schmittberger, the captain had him transferred out of the precinct. Egged on perhaps by Williams, Becker filed various malfeasance charges against Schmittberger, who filed counter charges. All were withdrawn, but Becker had established himself as a man with a special grudge against the turncoat captain.

For all his early conformity to the public notion of the brute-fisted, conscienceless cop favored by Centre Street, Becker was not rewarded with a promotion until ten years after he was sworn in. In November 1903 he finally moved up to the rank of roundsman. By this time he had apparently concluded that, The Clubber to the contrary, knocking citizens around was not the way to get ahead in the department. For half a dozen years there had been no civilian complaint against him. In 1904 he had even been awarded the department's highest medal for heroism. According to the citation he had seen one James Butler struggling in the

Hudson and had jumped in fully clothed and saved the man's life.

Soon after this event Becker had his second run-in with Schmittberger. For years the sulkers at headquarters had prevented the famous squealer's promotion to inspector. Faced with another rebuff, Schmittberger decided to make a public issue of it. Jerome helped fight the promotion, inquiring whether Schmittberger's supporters would name an acknowledged embezzler as cashier of a bank. The supporters included many members of the reform element, still grateful to him for his contributions to the Lexow exposé. Parkhurst hailed Schmittberger for having "left the old gang behind." Goff called the department criminally prejudiced. Lincoln Steffens wrote a letter of endorsement. Schmittberger finally got his promotion and was assigned to the Third Inspection District, which included the New Tenderloin. By the summer of 1906 the graft situation was worse than ever there. Deputy Police Commissioner Rhinelander Waldo, lately back from the Philippines, was put in charge of getting evidence against Schmittberger. To be sure the men on the job had their hearts in the project he set up a special shoo-fly detail headed by a sergeant and two roundsmen who were known to feel that Schmittberger had done them wrong at some point in their police careers. One of the roundsmen was Charles Becker.

"Years ago . . . I wanted to land a certain inspector. I put Becker on the job and he delivered the goods," Waldo would say in 1912 when he had moved up to the police commissioner's post and Becker was the man being investigated. For several weeks the raiding squad made up of the three grudge-bearers and fifteen supporting policemen conducted surprise raids on gambling and disorderly houses to get evidence of suspicious negligence on Schmittberger's part. As a result of these maneuvers Schmittberger went on departmental trial in September 1906.

Whether or not he was again raking in graft, Schmittberger managed to be represented by the town's most expensive lawyer, Martin Littleton. "The greatest American jury lawyer of his generation," as Lloyd Paul Stryker described him in *The Art of Advocacy*, Littleton had been known to charge seventy-five thousand dollars for a routine case. Possibly the reformers persuaded him to defend Schmittberger *pro bono publico*. Littleton's strategy was to prove that all three policemen testifying against Schmittberger were themselves "far more reprehensible characters than the defendant himself." One of the shoo-fly cops had once tried to cash a forged racing ticket; the second had been involved in a bad check charge. In the case of Becker, Littleton succeeded in making him look not only corrupt but ridiculous. He produced an affidavit from Butler, the man Becker had saved in the Hudson, saying that Becker had promised him fifteen dollars for staging the scene. The affidavit added that Butler was a good swimmer and strongly intimated that it was he who had saved *Becker's* life. At the next session of the trial, however, Butler showed up in person to swear that members of Littleton's staff had offered him two hundred dollars for his affidavit, that they had then got him drunk and he didn't know what he'd signed. Becker *had* saved his life, he insisted. The prosecution put in evidence a letter to Butler from Littleton's office discussing payment for his revised version of the rescue and charged Schmittberger with helping to engineer a frame-up. But the damage had been done, the inspector was acquitted, and once again Becker had been branded a fake hero.

The policeman who complained to Commissioner McAdoo about the antipolice bias of the press would not have been surprised to learn that Becker's alleged heroic rescue had not been reported in the newspapers. Butler's later report that it had all been staged received extensive coverage. But his return to his original story was barely mentioned. Thus when roundups of Becker's career appeared in newspapers after his arrest for the Rosenthal murder, they followed the old clips in reporting the fake hero story without any suggestion that there was a possibility of funny business on the other side. Most of the 1912 biographies also added that some years earlier Becker had killed a plumber's helper in cold blood and tried to cover it up.

The long-run consequences of the Schmittberger trial were even more serious. Among those publicly offering Schmittberger congratulations on his acquittal was Justice John Goff. Thus when Goff presided over Becker's first trial for murder he had a reason other than his hatred of the police department to be disinclined to give Becker the benefit of any doubt.

Back in 1905 Becker's immediate superiors had recommended his promotion to sergeant. It fell through when McAdoo, then the commissioner, announced after a look into Becker's bulging folder in the Bureau of Complaints office that he was clearly unfit for promotion. But in January 1907 Theodore Bingham, McAdoo's successor and the man who had ordered the drive to get Schmittberger, stated publicly that henceforth positive achievements would be the primary consideration in departmental advancement. It was a simple matter, he said, for a patrolman assigned to guard the office of some charitable institution to maintain a clean record. It was the policeman in the thick of things, said Bingham, who was the object of charges "by characters of dubious probity to whom such a policeman's actions might have proved inconvenient." Presumably on this basis and certainly for services rendered in the Schmittberger matter, Bingham the next day skipped over two other eligible roundsmen to promote Becker to sergeant.

It was Charles Becker's last promotion. A year or two later one of the recurrent reorganizations at headquarters involved nomenclature. The rank of roundsman was abolished, with all roundsmen automatically becoming sergeants and all sergeants lieutenants—the rank, of course, that Becker still held on the night of the Rosenthal murder, when he was one of over six hundred lieutenants on the roster.

Four and a half years after this last promotion when Waldo was setting up a squad to break up street gangs, he remembered Becker from the Schmittberger shoo-fly days. If Mayor Gaynor had had a look at his early record, the appointment might have fallen through and Becker might have lived to a ripe old age. Instead, Waldo brought him up to headquarters from his job as desk lieutenant at the Madison Street station. In the fall of 1911 Becker was ordered to enlarge the duties of his squad and to join the two competitive strong arm squads in Gaynor's special scheme for going after the city's gamblers.

Although in earlier assignments Becker had no doubt picked up five, ten, or even fifty dollars here and there, this antigambling detail was apparently his first real chance to grab some of the lush graft that successive legislative investigations had assured the public was there for the taking. ("I got to hand it to you, feller," Big Bill Devery, the chief of police in the 1890s had told one of the Holies with a straight face. "Honest, I never knew it was so good till you showed it all up in black and white.") During the nine months before the murder he banked a small fortune. After the murder his explanations of where it had all come from varied from interview to interview: generous friends of the family, a dead sister's secret cache, a doting uncle of his wife's. Although the Court of Appeals would rule it a procedural error, the district attorney's description of him as a grafting policeman in the opening statement at his first trial was undoubtedly accurate. The other two strong arm squad leaders, lieutenants Costigan and Riley, had the same power in the gambling world that Becker had, a fact not gone into by the prosecution or by newspapers of the time. "Becker *was* the System. Like Caesar all things were rendered unto Becker in the underworld. Like Briareus he had a hundred arms . . . and more power than any person in the Department but the Commissioner," Swope would write of him in the *World*. Actual tables of organization make dull reading.

Some of this misapprehension was Becker's own fault. All three gambling squad lieutenants were bucking for captain, and the competition between them was fierce. Becker soon took the lead. Waldo had picked Becker for the squad, one of his fellow policemen told the *American* after the murder, "because he would raid his own crippled grandmother if he thought it would make him look good at Headquarters." Becker made his first raid on October 15, 1911, two days after Waldo enlarged his assignment. Between then and the next July his squad took part in over half the raids recorded at Centre Street instead of the third expected. This performance not only showed up the other two squads but made the district inspectors look bad. "I can say that Becker knows he is very unpopular in the Police Department," John Hart would say in an interview after the murder. "He . . . has been an ambitious man."

In addition, the gambling houses Becker got evidence against included several of the grander uptown establishments that were used to immunity from this kind of inconvenience. When he raided Freeman's roulette palace on West Thirty-eighth Street in February 1912, it was the first such indignity the place had suffered in eighteen years. Lawyer Hart claimed later that the real charge against Becker was "the too efficient performance of his duties." Becker was also too clever by far in another respect. He cultivated the press, making friends with such reporters as Hawley and Terry. He took on press agent Charles Plitt to keep reporters informed of his daily triumphs. The resulting newspaper stories could hardly have increased his popularity among his fellow policemen at Centre Street. But, worst of all, they made Becker sound much more important than he was, a colossus astride the Tenderloin as one cartoon depicted him after the murder.

How could Becker rack up a spectacular record as a raider and at the same time get rich collecting graft from gamblers for protection from raids? After the murder Waldo released figures on the record of his strong arm squads for the previous year. There had been 203 raids, resulting in 898 arrests—and 103 convictions. Most of the sentences had been suspended. Fines had averaged fifty dollars apiece, and some had been as low as two dollars. And most of the raided houses had been back in business a few days after the police dropped in. Waldo blamed all this on judicial corruption. Others blamed the police. Having gotten a raid on his record, Becker, for example, apparently often arranged for his men to be afflicted with almost total amnesia as to evidence when the case reached court. Corrupt or not, the judge would have no choice but to acquit all around.

Becker didn't worry his head over the fact that when a gambling house was closed even briefly the owner lost money, that nervous customers would stay away for some time afterward. Meanwhile the fat weekly payoffs were to go on as usual. Becker's zealous attitude eventually got to be an expensive bore in the Tenderloin, in Hesper Club territory, and among the gamblers' friends in high places. Like Herman Rosenthal he went too far.

Becker finally realized that his position was perilous. A Hearst newspaperman warned him as early as Thanksgiving 1911 that there was a plot afoot to frame him, he said later. Sometime the next spring when he had a tidy amount of loot squirreled away, he went to Waldo and asked for some other assignment. As Waldo reported later, he had suggested that Becker's notion of a frame-up was highly imaginative, assured him he was doing a fine job, and ordered him to keep up the good work.

Late in March 1912 the letters to Waldo from "Henry Williams" about Rosenthal's extralegal operation on West Forty-fifth Street showed an enlarged interest. On March 27 Waldo got a letter that read: "I would like to have you investigate quietly Lieutenant Becker. He is now collecting more money than Devery, and it is well-known to everyone at Police Headquarters. Please do this and you will be surprised at the result." When such a missive arrived, it was Waldo's quaint custom (perhaps in some prep school spirit of fair play) to forward it to the policeman complained about for investigation. He was not put off by the fact that the accused person invariably found no basis for the complaint. He followed this practice with Becker, and during the weeks after the murder was often taunted about it. But nearly a year later when the special aldermen's committee investigating police graft handed down its final report, it noted that Becker had been the only police officer to commit what they called "the creditable display of delicacy" of sending the letter back to Waldo with a note saying that he did not believe he was the appropriate person to conduct such an investigation. Perhaps Becker knew this was a safe risk. Whoever Waldo sent the letter on to came to the usual conclusion: nothing to it.

The letter—and several others that followed—must have given Becker a further notion of the danger he was in. Again he asked for reassignment, and again Waldo turned him down. Becker went on playing the role of demon raider. One place Waldo ordered him to raid early in June was the Lincoln Hotel on Columbus Circle, suspected of being a high-class call house. Becker captured a number of girls and their customers but refused to be put off when told that no manager or representative of the owner was on the premises. He went through the place kicking down doors until he found several favorite henchmen of the owner, Sam Paul. By the night of the murder Becker was—like Herman Rosenthal—a man with a formidable array of enemies. He had two staunch supporters he knew he could count on in any weather, however. One was old Alexander Williams. The other was his wife, Helen Becker.

If Helen Becker had not existed, it would have been impossible to invent her. She was too perfect. The tough, arm-twisting, corrupt cop was married to a sweet-faced, ladylike schoolteacher. Inevitably, sentimentalists among his defenders, noticing the absence of brutality charges on his record during his later years on the force, would credit the love of a good woman.

"I was born Helen Lynch, one of ten children, and my husband, Charles Becker, was also one of ten children," began an article in the September 1914 issue of *McClure's* magazine that she sold to raise funds for his legal defense. "I grew up like hundreds of New York girls in moderate circumstances, going to the public school, then to the high school, and completing my studies at the Normal College, after which I became a public schoolteacher and have remained so ever since . . . I met my husband when he was a roundsman on the New York police force, and after a brief courtship we were engaged and married; and I will say now that, in spite of all our sorrows, I have never regretted it and I would do it all over again. I often wonder though why this trouble could not have come to people who did not love each other as we do. Charley and I were everything to each other. We were together whenever it was possible. Until I met him I had been very much alone . . . I never had a woman friend that I confided in very much. My only friend was my husband."

The daughter of a saloonkeeper, Helen Lynch was born in 1874 and started her career as a teacher in the fall of 1895. She was assigned to P.S. 41 in Greenwich Village at a time when Becker was posted to the Charles Street station nearby. Becker's second wife began divorce proceedings in the fall of 1904, and they were married soon after his divorce became final the following year (a sequence she omitted from her rundown of events). By 1912 she had been teaching for six years at P.S. 90 on West 147 Street near Seventh Avenue at a salary of $1,820 a year.

In *McClure's* Helen Becker discussed the rumors of their vast wealth "which did us much harm. I wish to say that, during our seven years of married life before our trouble came, I did all the housework, the cooking, the cleaning, everything except the washing, and I taught school besides. That does not look as if we were very rich. I always got up at six o'clock in the morning; and for three years, after a long day's work, I went out again in the evening and taught night school . . . in the evening school for women at the corner of Houston and Essex Streets . . . Up to the time of Mr. Becker's imprisonment we almost never had a servant, and our rent never exceeded forty dollars a month."

Her special responsibility at P.S. 90, she went on, was "the overage graduating class." ("These backward pupils have always appealed to me.") Her husband took great interest in her schoolwork, she said. "He would often collect papers for me or write out report cards, and he knew the name of every girl in my class. Each day I would tell him everything that happened." As for recreation, "Mr. Becker was very fond of horses, and we used to drive a good deal in the parks and out in the country. . . . We always went away together on Charley's vacation. We have been to Maine several times and to Mount Clemons. My husband likes hunting and trout fishing. He does not care for lake fishing. He likes ball games, but I don't think he followed the ball games as much as the fights."

His greatest interest in the months before his arrest, she said, was the new house, which was near the Botanical Gardens. Country-born, he had always wanted a place "where we might have trees and green things about us." He had done the repair work on the house himself, she reported, "and had made it attractive with piazzas and window seats and hardwood floors, and there was a garden back of it where my husband expected to spend his spare hours raising vegetables . . ." ("MURDERER CHARLEY JUST A COUNTRY BOY AT HEART" read one headline after the article appeared).

"On the very day of his arrest he had been up at our new house and had given the last finishing touch by fastening on the number over the front door," Helen Becker went on. "Everything was ready for us to move into, and three days later I did move in, but I was alone." She had been out marketing when Becker was arrested, having "no idea of any such trouble." The superintendent of the apartment house had told her the news. "A little later some lawyers came, and a friend of my husband, a newspaperman, who brought Charley's revolver and his keys that had been taken from him. I could not believe that Charley was in any serious difficulty." The next day the reporter had taken her down to the Tombs.

"When I went inside, I saw a woman crying, an Italian woman; and right then I made up my mind that I would never get hysterical and cry and annoy my husband," Helen Becker said later. "It does no good and it distresses people. I have made many visits since then to my husband in prison, but I have never broken down or cried before him, although I have felt like it. I have never seen Charley break down or cry," she added.

Probably it would have been far better for the prisoner if he had publicly broken down from time to time. As Big Tim always said, God and the people hate a chesty man.

X

BIG Tim Sullivan liked to say, thankfully, that so far as political
scandal was concerned, New York was a nine-days town. After
that the public got tired of reading about a subject, and the crowd
on the griddle could relax. It did not work that way for Becker.
Never in their history had New York newspapers found room for
as relentless coverage of a story as they did for the Rosenthal
murder, the trials that followed, and the numerous investigations
that flourished because the murder happened and that kept the
evils of police graft before the public eye. In the six months after
the publication of Rosenthal's affidavit the running story was on
the front page of the *World* 136 out of 186 days, and three-
quarters of this time it occupied the right-hand lead column. On
half a dozen occasions it took up the *whole* front page, and there
were often two and sometimes as many as five full pages of carry-
over inside. The city's other high-circulation paper, Hearst's *American,* was even more attentive, giving it page-one treatment in
over eighty per cent of its editions during this period when it also
had to make room for news of a local World Series, the attempted
assassination of Theodore Roosevelt, and state and national elections. Even the *Times,* inclined at the outset to view the show as a
shoddy skirmish among East Siders, got into the spirit of the
thing and had the story on its front pages nearly three-quarters of
the time in these months. Someone once calculated that the
World devoted more space to the testimony of one witness at

Becker's first trial—Bald Jack Rose—than it had to the sinking of
the *Titanic* the previous April. Over at *Collier's* the celebrated Mr.
Dooley complained that there was so much in the papers about
the case that when he read debates in the Senate they seemed to
be between characters named Bridgey Webber and Sam Schepps.
Even in Europe there were complaints that news of the fifth
modern Olympic games in Stockholm was being slighted in favor
of the latest word on the Rosenthal murder from the Criminal
Courts Building in New York.

Many European readers of this period must have had the impression that New York *was* America. "All the newspaper correspondents of the European press without, so far as I know, a
single exception, cable from New York," W. H. Stead, editor of
the London *Review of Reviews* had written a few years earlier.
"Not a single British newspaper has a correspondent at Boston,
Philadelphia, Chicago or Washington. New York . . . is the only
window through which the old world peeps into the new." It didn't
surprise most local citizens that New York news was world news.
The period between the Spanish-American War and the First
World War, the author of *The Fabulous Mizners* once noted, "was
a time when America had not yet learned that Europe existed.
Washington was a secondary news center. . . . New Yorkers
were almost exclusively concerned with the events of the village
stretching from Yonkers to the sea." The author was Alva Johnston, who served as the *Times* leg man on the Rosenthal case in
its later stages. Americans outside New York were far more involved with what was going on in that city than they would be a
decade later. The Associated Press and other agencies had comparatively few bureaus in the hinterlands, but every major small-
city newspaper had "Our New York Correspondent." The story
that dazzled and horrified New Yorkers one day would be setting
off little cries of disbelief all over the country a day or two
afterward. For the New York journalist of the period, wrote Alva
Johnston, "it was the golden age of newspaper reporting."

In the Rosenthal case the New York journalist was often not
only a paid observer but also a crucial witness, a carrier of
diplomatic messages between the principals, even something
close to a principal himself. As he described it in later years,
Herbert Bayard Swope's role in the case was overall producer and
director. Among the achievements he took credit for at dinner

parties was having arranged for Rose, Webber, and Vallon to turn state's evidence. But this master coup for the prosecution was almost certainly negotiated below the line in dim back rooms inaccessible to a brash young reporter.

About an hour after Becker was locked up in the Tombs, reporters interviewed Jack Rose's lawyer whom they found at Shanley's across Broadway from the Metropole. James Mark Sullivan, a big, noisy man, was in an expansive mood. How come Becker had been scheduled to testify before the grand jury about graft on Tuesday morning if the plan was to arrest him on Monday night? Oh, Whitman hadn't ever intended to have Becker go before the grand jury, said Sullivan. It had all been a stall. By Friday, Sullivan had already been negotiating with Whitman to win immunity for Rose, promising, as he told the reporters, that "Rose's testimony would put the murder squarely up to Police Lieutenant Becker."

They had still been working out the details, said Sullivan, but this morning, Monday, July 29, ten hours before the arrest, Bald Jack had learned that Webber had hired Max Steuer as his lawyer and was frantic for fear Webber would confess first and get out from under, leaving Rose to rot in the Tombs. He'd begged to see Whitman fast. As soon as Rose left the district attorney, Steuer had arrived and talked to Whitman for a couple of hours. Then Steuer had talked to Webber, reported Sullivan, explaining to Bridgey all the bad things that might happen to him if he didn't confess to Becker's part in the murder as Rose had done. When Steuer took Webber to the district attorney's office poor Bridgey was practically babbling, Sullivan said. Vallon had tagged along, of course, and added his bit. There had been a five-hour conference among the eight of them—the three witnesses, their two lawyers (Sullivan and Steuer), Shapiro's lawyer Aaron Levy, and Whitman, joined by the assistant district attorney, Frank Moss. Then had come the parade before the grand jury and the indictment. Altogether it had been a good day's work, said Sullivan, ordering another Scotch all around.

"It was a good day's work," Whitman, by coincidence, had told the reporters at the Criminal Courts Building an hour earlier.

In his opening statement at Becker's second trial Whitman would give his version of how the mutually satisfactory arrangement had come about, "the sudden conversion of the three gamblers from roles of innocence verging on defiance," as the *Evening Post* described it on the day after the indictment, "to contrite and humble witnesses for the state." "I pounded and pounded and pounded at Vallon, Webber and Rose," said Whitman, "and held them in jail day after day . . ." At the time he also gave credit to Max Steuer. Without Steuer, he told reporters as Becker was led away, Webber and Vallon might not have confessed and Rose's unsupported testimony would have been worthless.

Steuer "has been called by some the greatest criminal lawyer of his time," reported the *Times* after his death in 1940. In 1912 he was already well known as a successful attorney whose appearance in a case was the signal that a client's case was critical and that all kinds of dubious measures might be in order. He was not known for his squeamishness about the character of his clients. Breach of promise actions were a specialty of his. Earlier in 1912 he had won an acquittal for the owners of the building involved in the Triangle fire, proving that the deaths of 145 young garment workers were all their own fault. Steuer was an important figure in Tammany circles, being allied with the Sullivan rather than the Murphy wing. Mrs. Bridgey Webber would say later that she had gone to him because he was famous for being Big Tim's lawyer. He was another East Side newsboy who had found his way to the Sullivan clubhouse early in life.

Steuer's first official appearance in the Rosenthal matter took place just before noon on the day of Becker's indictment. On the front steps of the Criminal Courts Building he met Pearl Webber, a handsome blonde wearing an ostrich feather hat and a diamond as big as, say, the Occidental. In front of half a dozen watching newspapermen, Steuer accepted a retainer from her in the form of a roll of bills. One sharp-eyed reporter insisted that the denomination of the bill on the outside of the Webber roll was a thousand dollars. Steuer had thus established as publicly as possible his reason for being on hand. The negotiations in Whitman's office that James Sullivan had told reporters about had lasted until five o'clock in the afternoon. By that hour the members of the grand jury had gone home for the day. Telegrams were sent out requesting them to double back, and by ten minutes after seven a quorum had been assembled.

The indictment of Becker, based on the testimony of the three now co-operative gamblers, had been handed down just before nine. It was the first time in county history that a grand jury had been reconvened for a night session. Asked why the matter couldn't have waited until the next morning, Whitman at first said that he was afraid the gamblers would change their minds. Perhaps he felt this implied a rather infirm basis for an indictment for first-degree murder. "The District Attorney had reason to believe that Becker was about to flee the country" was the story his office put out the next day.

Despite the charade on the courthouse steps Steuer was not in the neighborhood primarily as a lawyer for Bridgey Webber and his employee, Vallon. Discussing his taking the case, the *World* said the next day: "It is known he was unwilling to take it up, but yielded to the persuasion of some friends who said they would not feel that the interests of a man whose name has not been mentioned in the matter would be safe unless a lawyer of Steuer's ability was there to look after him. So Steuer, out of motives of friendship, consented." Actually, he had been seen going into the district attorney's office several times during the previous week. The Sullivan tribe, in a panic for fear Big Tim's playing some part in the murder preliminaries would become the subject of official investigation, had called in Steuer. He had worked out the agreement by which the three gamblers would help convict Becker of the murder. As a reward for his efforts Steuer apparently exacted from Whitman a promise that Big Tim's name would be kept out of the trial. (In fact Whitman would be even more obliging. On the chance that he might need Tammany support at some juncture he would denounce the System in court day after day without suggesting that politicians had ever been involved in the payoffs. The old Lexow strategy of getting at Tammany Hall indirectly by going after the police was no part of his plan.)

Another item in the good day's work of Whitman, Sullivan, and Steuer was the agreement to drop the murder charge against Sam Paul, who had many influential friends in both parties. Although he had taken part in the last-minute planning in Bridgey Webber's poker rooms and probably had delivered three of the gunmen there, he was never to be put to the embarrassment of being called as a witness. The ideal solution had been found— besides the actual gunmen there was to be but one villain, policeman Becker.

In none of Whitman's announcements about the gamblers'
change of heart did he mention the word immunity. They had
confessed, he said, in a great outpouring of truth when they
understood that the district attorney would protect them from
Becker's terrible wrath. When he was later on the stand as a
witness Whitman would deny that there had been any special
immunity agreement. The men had merely signed "the usual legal
stipulation," he said vaguely. What they had signed was the
following:

> Whereas [Rose, Webber, Vallon] has made a statement
> to the District Attorney of New York County to the effect
> that Charles Becker was a principal in the murder of
> Herman Rosenthal and that his testimony should show
> that fact [Rose, Webber, Vallon] does hereby consent to
> appear before the Grand Jury for the month of July, 1912,
> and to testify and produce any evidence, documentary or
> otherwise, which may be in his possession, and hereby
> waives any immunity and privilege to which he may be
> entitled on account of Sections 584 and 996 of the penal
> law, and any other provision of law for any and all
> transactions, matters and things concerning which he
> may testify or produce evidence and for which he may
> hereafter be prosecuted on the charges of conspiracy,
> gambling, bribery, extortion, and murder. . . .
> He signs this consent and waiver, knowing full well the
> provisions of the law herein referred to and after con-
> sulting with counsel and signs the same voluntarily and
> not by reason of any threats or undue influence on the
> part of any person or persons whatsoever, and it being
> agreed that the same [Rose, Webber, Vallon] will imme-
> diately be called before the Grand Jury and fully and
> truthfully give his evidence concerning the murder of
> Herman Rosenthal, and the criminal liability therefor of
> the said Charles Becker, the District Attorney, with the
> knowledge and consent of the Court, agrees that the said
> [Rose, Webber, Vallon] shall not be prosecuted for said
> crime of murder or any crime which may be included
> within the testimony which he shall give. Upon these con-
> ditions, however:

That the same [Rose, Webber, Vallon] did not fire any of the shots at the body of Herman Rosenthal and provided also that the said [Rose, Webber, Vallon] will remain in City Prison or any other prison in the County of New York which may be agreeable to the District Attorney until said Charles Becker shall have been tried for said murder and the indictment shall be disposed of.

Each of the chief witnesses for the prosecution was thus being let off a murder charge and all related criminal charges only because he had made statements "to the effect that Charles Becker was a principal in the murder of Herman Rosenthal and that his testimony would show that fact." He would continue to be let off only if he gave evidence "concerning the murder of Herman Rosenthal, and the criminal liability therefor of the said Charles Becker." It wasn't enough to testify in a general way for the prosecution. There could be no wavering, no second thoughts. The gamblers would go on trial for murder themselves unless they were willing to hang Becker in any and all trials "until . . . the indictment shall be disposed of." Although this was surely pertinent courtroom information, the defense would have great difficulty getting the agreements in the record. When it was finally arranged late in the first trial there was no great public ado over the revelations. The general view seemed to be that the arrangement might be a bit startling, but anything went if it meant bringing to justice the man responsible for a crime reflecting a moral crisis "infinitely worse than the one that confronted the nation at Gettysburg."

There was one tiresome development for the district attorney on the day after Becker's arrest. Harford Marshall, Bridgey Webber's first attorney of record, announced that he had resigned from the case and recommended Steuer as his successor "because I couldn't stand for certain things that were going on." On the same day most local papers carried a statement by "a former lawyer for one of the confessing gamblers"—years later Marshall dropped the anonymity—declaring that on the Sunday night before Becker's arrest Bridgey had said to him in the Tombs: "Look here, just how bad does Whitman want Becker? Why, the way things are going I could go to the electric chair. If what he wants is Becker, we'll give him to him on a platter." Whitman dismissed the story as the unreliable tattle of a discharged counsel.

That same day it was widely noted that not only had the New York police played no part in Becker's arrest but they hadn't even known it was about to come off. Rhinelander Waldo had been given the news by reporters while having a late snack at his club and immediately had looked ten years older, the *Tribune* observed. It was also a newspaperman who informed Deputy Commissioner Dougherty in a late evening telephone call. "Very interesting," he said glumly. "Thanks very much, Swope."

In the days following the Becker indictment James Sullivan continued to hold court for the press at his favorite table at Shanley's, gossiping, prognosticating, playing his own angles, or perhaps Tammany boss Charley Murphy's. Lawyer Sullivan's part in the case to date had been no small one although Whitman had never publicly acknowledged it as he had that of Steuer. It was Sullivan who had advised Bald Jack to turn himself in. He had sent Whitman witness Krause who had obligingly placed Reich at the crime scene and led to Reich's arrest. And it would soon develop that two days after the murder, a few hours after he advised Jack Rose to surrender, Sullivan had suggested to Bald Jack's hanger-on, Sam Schepps—now being referred to in the headlines as "The Murder Paymaster" and "The Missing Witness" —the advantages of shaking loose from the other implicated gamblers and getting out of town fast, an arrangement that later would be of great procedural value to Whitman.

"The Tombs," Sullivan told his tablemates at Shanley's, "is well named. The Tombs did it. The place is a hole of depression. It got Rose. It will get Becker, too. Forty-eight hours in the Tombs is usually enough." If Becker should decide to tell what he knew about gambling in the city, Sullivan added, it would be "in spite of strong urging and whatever influence can be brought to bear on the lieutenant to keep his mouth shut and thereby save others." He did not doubt, he said, "that Becker will be told that if he will only stop the scandal from going further, he himself will be in no danger."

Whether or not the Tombs had done it, part of Rose, Webber, and Vallon's deal with the district attorney was that they were not to spend another night in the hole of depression. Reporting that the three confessed stagers of the murder were in a state of "pitiable terror" at the prospect of being under the same roof with Lieutenant Becker, Whitman let them camp overnight in his outer office, ostentatiously guarded by Burns men, and the following morning transferred them to the small jail attached to the West Side Prison on Fifty-third Street "where the keeper is a man I have much confidence in." (The word "keeper" was still in general use for tenders of human as well as animal prisoners.) There they passed "a very entertaining first day," reported the *American* the following morning, "seeing the D.A., their own lawyers, and their wives and other friends. Every comfort that money can provide has been arranged for them." Food was regularly sent in from nearby restaurants. Tailors and pressers were in attendance, as their sartorial splendor in court would show. Toward the end of the second week Mrs. Pearl Webber threw "a very jolly party" for the group in the jail corridor. Naturally Becker's lawyer was overstating the case when he later described their new way of life to the press: "All the delicacies of the season make up their repast. Chiropodists are furnished to treat their feet and manicurists to cut and highly polish their fingernails. Tutors are provided to instruct them in the modern classics. American Beauty roses adorn their cells each day. . . ."

But for Bald Jack Rose, especially, life was not all American Beauty roses. Immediately after Becker's indictment the district attorney began releasing daily excerpts from the grand jury testimony that had led to the arrest. It was apparent that most of the adverse evidence had come from Bald Jack, the mission of the other two being to nod their well-barbered heads vigorously. The grand jury investigating police graft continued to sit, and Rose appeared before it daily. At one point, Rose estimated that he and other collectors had taken in $640,000 in graft for Becker. Much of this, he agreed, had been passed on to Becker's superiors. Rose named them—Inspectors Hayes and Hughes, Deputy Commissioner Dougherty, Waldo's secretary, Winfield Sheehan. All these men instituted suits for libel against the newspapers printing the testimony, suits that were later quietly dropped. Beside these courtroom excursions Rose was made available for a daily exclusive interview with reporter Swope, cashing in in spades for his hunch that Rosenthal would prove to be a useful figure. On August 15 Swope's *World* published Rose's so-called confession, a thirty-eight-page document that gave the public its first detailed account of how Lieutenant Becker had arranged the murder. It described a villain so bizarre and evil and outside the normal experience that no defense attorney was afterward able to counter its stunning effect.

"I want Rosenthal murdered, shot, his throat cut, any way that will take him off the earth," Becker had told him early in May, according to Rose's confession. If Zelig's gunmen didn't go along, "I will find out where they hang out and frame every one of them and send them up the river for carrying concealed weapons"— and that went for Webber, Vallon, and Rose, too. "Why isn't he dead yet?" he had kept asking Rose when there was some delay. "Why isn't he croaked? You're all a bunch of damned cowards." On the evening of the murder he had called Dora Gilbert's and told Rose over and over "if only that s.o.b. would get croaked that night how happy he would be, how lovely it would be." "All that's necessary is to walk right up to where he is and blaze away at him and leave the rest to me. Nothing will happen to anybody that does it. . . . Walk up and shoot him before a policeman if you want to. . . ."

Soon after the killing, Rose declared, Becker had met the gamblers on Forty-second Street below Bridgey's after first visiting the Forty-seventh Street station and had told them that if they hadn't come through he would have done it himself. "I told (the chauffeur) to drive by the Metropole and slow down without stopping," Rose quoted Becker as saying. "I intended to take out my gun and blaze away at him if Rosenthal was there, but he wasn't there. It was a pleasing sight to me," Rose said Becker had added, reporting on his trip to the back room of the station house, "to see that squealing Jew lying there, and if it had not been for the presence of Whitman I would have cut out his tongue and hung it on the Times Building as a warning to future squealers."

Feeling a bit diffident, perhaps, over the fact that the three major documents in the case—Rosenthal's original affidavit, his expanded statement, and Rose's confession—had all reached the public by way of the front page of the New York *World* in articles written by Swope, Whitman pointed out that Rose's confession was not only entirely handwritten but contained no punctuation whatever, a lapse that presumably absolved any professional newspaperman of the suspicion of collaboration. Rose would later deny on the stand that he had received two thousand dollars from the *World* for the right to publish his story.

Second to Becker in importance in the murder plot, as Rose's confession described matters, was the gang leader Big Jack Zelig. Zelig, a baby-faced man with a long record as a master pickpocket, had been arrested early in May 1912 for carrying a concealed gun, his second violation of the Sullivan law, which had turned out to be a wonderful convenience for the Police Department in keeping small-time criminals in line. After his earlier arrest Zelig had had all his pockets sewn up and arranged to have one of his henchmen follow behind him carrying his money, keys and weapon, so it is probably true that he was framed this time. The arrest was made by a trio of cops under orders from Inspector Hughes at headquarters. It was Becker's bad luck that two of the policemen had been transferred a few weeks later to his strong arm squad, giving Whitman a basis for charging at the trial that it was Becker's men who had brought Zelig in, which strengthened his argument that there had been a sinister tie-up between the gangster and Becker.

Bridgey Webber, who found it useful to have Zelig and his gang at the ready, had furnished Zelig's fifteen-hundred-dollars bail after the May arrest. Unfortunately almost as soon as he was sprung, Zelig tried to shoot up a cafe run by his rival Jack Sirocco and was arrested again. This time the bail was higher—ten thousand dollars. A group of concerned East Siders, including Webber, Rose, Vallon, and Sam Paul, finally arranged another release on the second of July. It was Rose who made several pilgrimages to the Upper West Side apartment where members of the Zelig gang were hanging out, to explain how things were going. He was especially anxious to carry the word since—as he would mention in court in Becker's second trial—Herman Rosenthal had falsely spread the word that it was Rose who had put the finger on Zelig in the May arrest, a charge the gangster's followers would not have taken lightly.

From the beginning the major problem of those prosecuting Becker would be the establishment of some connection between the lieutenant and the actual murderers. The prosecution would not claim that he had ever laid eyes on the gunmen or on their leader Zelig. Rose helped immeasurably by reporting in his *World* confession that in his dealings with Zelig he had acted only as

Becker's agent. When Becker was after him to kill Rosenthal, the policeman had sent him to Zelig in jail to find out if the gangster would do the job in return for his release. Zelig said no, according to Rose. When Becker kept hounding Rose, the gambler asked some of Zelig's boys—Gyp the Blood and the rest—to help him out. When they stalled, Becker had insisted, according to Rose, that Bridgey be brought in to use his influence on the gunmen. Perhaps Whitman felt that the Zelig-Becker connection remained uncomfortably tenuous. In mid-August at least two newspapers printed the information that the district attorney knew for a fact that it was Becker who had put up the money to get Zelig out of jail early in July in time to order his boys to take on the murder. A few days later a reporter for another paper consulted the record of the surety company and found that the major security for the bail had been a piece of real estate put up by Nathan Paul, Sam Paul's brother. Whitman immediately issued a statement. "I cannot understand how the story about Becker's furnishing bail ever got started," he said.

After the arrest and indictment of the principal suspect, even in a sensational murder case, there is usually a lull while the opposing legal sides gather their forces. Often it isn't until the trial begins months later that the case again hits the headlines. But in the matter of the People vs. Becker just the tracking down of the three missing gunmen would have kept the case on the front pages. By the first week in August there were eight men in jail for complicity in the murder (Libby, Shapiro, Rose, Webber, Vallon, Frank, Becker, and Lewis) and one (Jacob Reich) still being held as a material witness. The most recent arrival at the Tombs was Whitey Lewis, the second gunman captured. Burns agents had been scouring the eastern seaboard for him, but it was two of Commissioner Dougherty's men who picked him up in the Catskills. Dougherty went upstate to fetch the gangster back personally and exhibited him to the press like a trophy. Whitman's only comment was that obviously the police had known where Lewis was all along. As for Gyp the Blood and Lefty Louie, still out of custody, Whitman announced that Becker was keeping them in a safe place nearby, having them coached to testify as surprise witnesses for the defense. Paying no attention, Williams Burns men made one headline after another during the next month as they chased down leads to the missing gunmen in other parts of the country. Squads of agents were vainly dispatched to Denver, Boston, Tallahassee, Fargo, South Dakota, and half a dozen other far-flung sites. Another fugitive who continued to elude them—and Dougherty's men as well—was the still-missing murder paymaster, Sam Schepps.

When the manhunt stories faltered, the press and District Attorney Whitman could always fall back on their running exposé of Becker's bank deposits. Three days after the indictment, Whitman had announced that he was investigating a report that Becker had accumulated one million dollars in the nine-month period after his strong arm squad had assumed their antigambling duties, a large estimate for one man's take since the most inflated figure Whitman's captive expert, Bald Jack Rose, had cited for the overall annual gambling take in the city was about two and a half million dollars.

By mid-August Whitman was saying he expected to prove that Becker's cash on hand amounted to at least two hundred thousand dollars "and he wasn't speculating in Japanese lots." All during that month his office issued seriatim reports of Becker's bank deposits beginning in November 1911. From then through the next July, according to varying figures issued by the district attorney's office, Becker had banked either $68,000, $58,000, or $48,000 and change. Becker's friends would claim that even the smallest sum was an overstatement since it counted twice about eighteen thousand dollars that Helen Becker had withdrawn from several other banks on the day after her husband's arrest and consolidated in one Corn Exchange account. Whitman continued to refer informally to Becker's take as "upwards of a hundred thousand." Whatever the total, it was a sum far too large for a man making $2,150 a year to explain away. None of the financial reports ever had to be documented since Becker did not take the stand and thus could not be cross-examined about his financial circumstances. At one point when someone questioned the figures Whitman was putting out, the district attorney said, oddly, not to ask *him* about them, that he had just got them from a newspaperman.

The eagerness of the city's civic betterment groups to call attention to the apocalyptic nature of recent developments also kept the story from slipping to the back pages. Their expressions of shock and horror over the murder had an undercurrent of repressed exhilaration. One "leading citizen interested in municipal reform" was quoted by the *Sun* as saying: "Rosenthal was killed in a good cause. This town had to have a man like Rosenthal turn informer and then be killed to wake it up." Nothing else, including the arduous efforts of the reformers over the years, had had the slightest effect on the terrible problem of police graft, he pointed out.

On August 8 "a large delegation associated with municipal righteousness" issued a call for a mass meeting of indignant citizens at Cooper Union. The names of the chief ralliers included J. P. Morgan as well as other familiar Simon Pure names and a few new ones—Joseph Choate, Jr., Elihu Root, Jacob Schiff, Arthur Curtiss James (the railroad millionaire had been an Amherst classmate of Whitman's and was his frequent host at Newport), John Auchincloss, Clarence Mackay, Eugene Seligman, and William Schieffelin. A ladies auxiliary, headed by Mrs. J. Borden Harriman, joined in the call. Schieffelin, the informal treasurer, announced that large sums were already pouring in to help Whitman in his fight for the city's soul. At the mass meeting a week later the old Astor Place hall was packed. The demonstration for Whitman lasted five minutes.

"Three cheers for our next governor," someone cried in the audience, and at the words, according to the *Times*, "a bedlam of sound shook the hall."

"We need you in New York," another voice shouted.

"Yes, and we need you in Albany, too," cried someone at the rear of the platform.

"You don't need me half as much as I need you," Whitman shouted back. The killing of Herman Rosenthal, he went on to tell them, "was a murder, of course, an awful murder, but it was more than that. In the light of all the circumstances connected with it, it was "a challenge to our very civilization itself." When the applause died down, he concluded: "I appreciate tonight, ladies and gentlemen, that you have accepted that challenge. I knew you would."

Other politicians had not been slow to grasp the political possibilities of the situation, and among those with whom Whitman had to share the limelight at Cooper Union were two fellow Republicans, Henry Curran and Emory Buckner. A member of the Board of Aldermen, Curran had just persuaded the Board to appropriate twenty-five thousand dollars to conduct its own investigation of police graft and to put him in charge. Buckner, a young ex-Nebraskan, had resigned from Whitman's staff to be chief counsel to Curran's committee. The new enterprise infuriated Mayor Gaynor who announced his own independent investigation of Police Department corruption.

But of all the convolutions that kept the furor over the Rosenthal murder at white heat through the summer, none was relied on more by the press than the still continuing grand jury investigation of police graft, which heard a dozen witnesses a day through these hot weeks. At the Cooper Union meeting a resolution endorsing the need for Curran's special police graft committee pointed out that "the proceedings before the Aldermanic Committee are published and . . . have as one of their greatest utilities the germicidal effect of publicity with its consequent enlightened public opinion," a valuable circumstance since "the proceedings of the Grand Jury are secret and cannot be known." The members of a grand jury and all witnesses before it swear an oath at the outset never to reveal what went on in the courtroom. Nevertheless, on the days after the more interesting witnesses appeared before this particular body, nuggets from their testimony would be reflected in headlines in newspapers across the country. In this way the prosecution was able to fix firmly in the minds of readers, including prospective jurors, evidence against Becker (his alleged enormous take in graft, for example) that it could not legally get into the record in his later murder trial. Whitman denied that he was responsible for these leaks. Later he simply told a *Times* reporter with a shrug of his shoulders: "There is nothing illegal about a District Attorney releasing reports of grand jury testimony."

It was not long before some people began to suspect that the version of grand jury testimony given out by Whitman might not always reflect the official record. One problem for a witness the district attorney had misquoted was that he could not repeat what he had said on the stand without violating his oath of secrecy. Denials were possible, however. One of the strong arm squad leaders, Lieutenant Costigan, denied on twelve basic points Whitman's press release which had him accusing Waldo of condoning vice and Becker of obstructing justice. Whitman dismissed the policeman's version as amounting to "mere differences in phraseology." The denials never caught up with the headlines, and in any case the credibility of strong arm squad leaders was by this time almost nonexistent. In a trial early in August of a Harlem gambling house owner arrested by the strong armers the judge polled the jury ahead of time over whether they could bring themselves to believe the testimony of any member of the squad. They said no, and rapidly acquitted the defendant. The gambling house was just west of Seventh Avenue on 124 Street. The raid had taken place late in the evening of June 27. The chief witness was a small, graceful black stool pigeon named James Marshall. It was a raid that Becker would later have reason to wish that he had never made.

At one point during the grand jury proceedings, however, Whitman's headline-feeding tactics offended a witness in a position to give him some real trouble. He had called the president of the Corn Exchange Bank to testify about Becker's deposits. The testimony was available to the press even before adjournment. When the banker read the next day's headlines, he indicated that a considerable part of Whitman's account was untrue, wanted to know what ever had happened to grand jury secrecy, and accused the district attorney of indiscretion. ("This is the first time Whitman has been held directly responsible for the leakage of grand jury secrets," noted the *Evening Post*.) But the fuss didn't last long. Whitman was now a public hero and could do no serious wrong.

In time Whitman got in the habit of giving out witnesses' testimony *before* they took the stand. ("It is known on the very highest authority that what the witness will say is . . .") One important deponent crossed him up in this maneuver—Big Jack Zelig. The gang leader had stayed out of sight since the murder, but about two weeks after Becker's indictment he was reported in Providence. At Whitman's request police there picked him up on suspicion of being a pickpocket, and a day later the D.A. scheduled Zelig to go before the grand jury.

Zelig's testimony, newspapers reported "on the highest authority," would certify that Rose had told him that Becker had demanded that Rosenthal be murdered and had later warned him that Becker was getting impatient, that everyone was in danger. Zelig would state, said the *World*, that "he was so afraid of Becker and believed so implicitly in the lieutenant's power that he had no alternative but to hire the quartet of murderers and had then fled the city in terror of the policeman." Further: "It is known that Zelig will say" that it was Becker who had framed him on the Sullivan Act violation in May and who, for his own purposes, had then bailed him out.

When Big Jack came swaggering from the grand jury room, however, the remarks he made to waiting reporters indicated that his testimony had not been like that at all. He didn't know a thing about Rosenthal's murder, he said. And the man he was in a rage at was not Becker but Bald Jack Rose. "I know he framed me and I don't believe Becker knew anything about the frame-up of me," he said, one long-fingered hand reaching ominously toward his sewed-up pocket. "It was Jack Rose that had me bailed out . . . He was scared. If I had been sent to prison as it looked at one time I might be, Rose knew my friends would kill him. . . ."

"Would avenge you, you mean," his lawyer broke in hastily.

"That's what I said, would avenge me," said Zelig, grinning.

"Never in the history of the country has such a spectacle been witnessed," said Becker's lawyer. "Day after day that which trans- pires in the grand jury room is spread broadcast . . . to so prejudice the public mind that the accused will be denied a fair and impartial trial." His client, he said, was being "tried and con- victed every day so that there was left "only the perfunctory act of passing sentence." In addition, he said, "as soon as someone gives an indication that he will testify for the defendant, he is brought to the grand jury room and grilled by the District Attorney." The purpose, said the lawyer, was to give the prosecution a preview of the defense case and "to menace and intimidate prospective witnesses."

The strategy was often successful. Having worked out their deal to keep Big Tim Sullivan's name out of the case, the Sullivan Protective League, from all reports, had explained to their leader, who was growing more irrational each day, that all he had to do now was lie low, that Becker would surely be acquitted. But Sul- livan kept confusing matters by trying to help the defense. In mid- August, James March, East Side district leader and one of Tim's close friends, announced that he would be glad to appear as a character witness for Becker and explain the bank hoard. He had helped the policeman make a number of lucky investments, he said. That afternoon March was subpoenaed to appear before the

grand jury. On the stand, according to the D.A.'s routine afternoon press release of grand jury proceedings, his story had been
cut to ribbons. He emerged from the ordeal looking very pale. His
name did not appear on the eventual list of defense witnesses at
the murder trial.

While these power ploys were going on, defendant Becker remained in the Tombs. His wife was allowed to see him for an
hour every day but Sunday. The Tombs had apparently not gotten
to him, as lawyer Sullivan had predicted. The only complaint he
made was about the lack of a chance to exercise. He took full
advantage of the two short periods a day when he was allowed to
run around a small track in an areaway. Most of his inactive
hours were spent reading local newspapers. He was upset at press
reports that he was not eating well, that he was looking haggard.
"I haven't missed a meal," he said. "A guilty man would look
haggard about now—that's what they're trying to say."

By choice Becker saw only two newspapermen during his first
month in the Tombs—Hawley from the *Sun* and a man from the
Times. He looked more massive than ever, they reported, in his
tiny cell with its low ceiling. He was smoking a cigar. His hand
through the bars "had the grip of a bear." For public consumption, at least, he took a detached view of his predicament.

"I have no fear of its not turning out right, but it's inconvenient
for the present," he told Hawley. "There is such a thing as law
and the rules of evidence. . . . The whole thing will be tried and
it won't be tried in the papers, either. There is a lot that the public
does not understand," he added. "It is largely a political squabble."

The loquacious James Sullivan turned up again one afternoon
at Shanley's and passed out to reporters a letter he had just
written to Becker's lawyer, urging him to persuade Becker to tell
the truth about gambling graft and corruption among the higher-
ups in the Police Department. "It hardly seems fair to stop with
Becker. After all he was just a notch above Rose in the setup."
Becker, he wrote the lawyer, could take advantage of "a unique
opportunity to do a public service that seldom comes in the way of
any man to perform and thus save himself "from a disaster that
seems inevitable." Whoever had inspired Sullivan's open letter, it
clearly relayed a promise of reward. If Becker would talk, wrote
Sullivan, the county, through the district attorney, was willing

"that extraordinary and marvelous concessions (I use the word advisedly and conservatively) shall be offered."

After Sullivan's letter was published, newspapermen sent notes in to Becker asking if he cared to comment on the Irishman's advice. "Tell them I'm no Schmittberger," was the word he sent out.

Whitman now had a new plan for the Rosenthal murder defendants, and another indictment was prepared. Before Becker was arraigned again, Whitman mentioned pointedly that what he was really after was the policeman's help in catching "the big fish." According to one of Becker's last letters, an offer of immunity was brought to him in the Tombs. "I feel sure . . . that you know the man who brought me the message of immunity on August 23, 1912," he wrote cryptically to Deacon Terry. According to an affidavit sworn to much later by Jacob Reich, the courier was Terry himself.

He was with Becker in the Tombs, Reich swore, when Terry had come in with a message from Whitman. "Terry said to Becker that . . . if Becker would give up Winfield Sheehan or Dougherty or Inspector Hughes that Becker would be turned out." Becker refused the offer "in impolite language." Terry told him he did not want to go back to Whitman with such a message.

"I would not give that rat anything," were Becker's parting words.

That same week he was rearraigned under a new blanket indictment that charged seven men with the murder of Herman Rosenthal: Charles Becker, Gyp the Blood, Dago Frank, Whitey Lewis, Lefty Louie, William Shapiro, and Jacob Reich. Reich was an addition to the list, promoted from material witness. Shapiro's partner Libby had finally been released.

Reporters asked Waldo that afternoon how he felt about having one of his trusted men about to go on trial for murder. They found Whitman's former luncheon companion in his office, studying a plan to enlarge the pockets of policemen's uniforms.

"Just tell Charles Whitman for me," he said, "that he can't get to be Governor by lying."

XI

As various public figures scolded from time to time, the handsome, shrewd, energetic Lieutenant Becker was exactly the sort of man who might have risen naturally to the top of his chosen profession if his talents had not been perverted by excessive ambition and greed. Charles Whitman was also handsome, shrewd, energetic, and ambitious, and he had not blown it. Although by late that summer the two men were being portrayed in song, story, and cartoon as melodramatic opposites—absolute hero versus total villain, public service above and beyond the call of duty versus criminal betrayal of public trust—they had several things in common besides their first names. Both were in their early forties, had been brought up in small towns in the East, were restless and intent on a life beyond the backwater, had first hit the big city a little over two decades before. Both were Protestant and Republican and had fought their way upward in fields— politics and the Police Department—then dominated locally by Tammany Irish Catholics. Unlike Charles Becker, however, Charles Whitman had all his life been counted among those on the side of goodness and virtue.

Becker's higher education had taken place in the back rooms of station houses. Charles Seymour Whitman, however, had gone to Williams for a year and then to Amherst, graduating in 1890. Born in 1868, he had grown up in genteel penury in Hanover, Connecticut, where his father was the pastor at the Presbyterian church. Though he had to work at odd jobs to get through Amherst, he made Phi Beta Kappa. He then moved to New York and taught Latin and Greek for a year at Adelphi Academy in Brooklyn. For three more years he continued to teach part-time while he went through New York University Law School. In 1894 when he passed the bar exams he was twenty-six years old.

During the next eight years Whitman and a partner eked out a small living in private practice. As he reached his mid-thirties he must occasionally have wondered whether this was all there was going to be to his life. The term "late bloomer" had not been invented. He had not married and in the long evenings began hanging around the nearby Republican district headquarters as much for the social life, perhaps, as with an eye out for professional or political advancement. After a time the leader, Abe Gruber, made him a district captain in the Forties west of Fifth Avenue, then still a somewhat fashionable residential neighborhood. (Herman Rosenthal was at this same time district captain in Tim Sullivan's Fourth Ward on the other side of town, but the social connections there would not have interested Charles Whitman.) Early in 1902 his political activities finally led to the break he was waiting for.

The Mazet Committee had recently raised big headlines about police corruption in the city, and the electorate, in familiar Pavlovian style, had thrown Tammany out. The man elected mayor by the reformers was the sober-sided Seth Low, former head of Columbia University, whom a member of the Tammany opposition had once described as "my friend, the human turnip." But it was widely agreed that the candidate who had actually brought off the Fusionists' victory over Tammany—and who thus, indirectly, gave Whitman his chance—was the aggressive and flamboyant William Travers Jerome. Jerome, nine years older than Whitman, had made the most of his 1895 appointment as a judge on the Court of Special Sessions, his reward for his leading part in the Lexow investigation. Still bearing down on the problem of Centre Street graft, he had pointed out not long after he went on the bench that New York policemen continued to be suspiciously ineffective against the city's flourishing gambling industry. Soon afterward he had approached some of the prominent reformers with whom he had worked so congenially on the Lexow investigation. As they would for Whitman later, they had gladly raised a kitty to put a private strong arm squad at his disposal.

Armed with search warrants issued by Justice Jerome, members of the special squad—Pinkerton men in this case—would break into gambling houses without warning and make citizens' arrests. Directly behind them would come Jerome, a swashbuckling type who would leap on top of the green felt tables and hold court hearings on the spot, surrounded by the incriminating wheels of fortune and by crowds of newspapermen. During his six years on the bench, Jerome's demonstrations of moral indignation on the rampage were so compelling that, in the words of his 1934 obituary in the *Times*, "No one who lived through those fighting days of Mr. Jerome's can forget the sort of a thrill which ran through this city and indeed spread to other cities throughout the land." In January 1902 after a noisy and well-publicized campaign featuring further moral indignation, Jerome became district attorney. Among the very minor figures that his spirited campaigning had helped sweep into office was young Samuel Seabury who, after being defeated two years earlier in a try for the same post, had finally been elected a justice in the City Court.

Most of the winners on Mayor Low's Fusionist slate were independents or anti-Tammany Democrats, who rapidly parceled out jobs on the municipal rolls to workers of the same persuasion. Finally Mayor Low, a Republican, asked fretfully if it would be possible to find room for some members of *his* party. A spot was still available in the office of the city's corporation counsel, and, casting about for a Republican, someone thought of Whitman from Gruber's district. For the next two years he served creditably in the city's legal office. On the last day of December 1903 the departing Seth Low—for the human turnip had not been re-elected as Tammany bounced back again—named Whitman to the magistrate's bench. A magistrate presided over police courts of first jurisdiction and was the lowest ranking of all the city's judicial offices. Not only was such a post light on prestige, but it was generally thought of as a consignment to the political graveyard.

"While the police court is not the most dignified tribunal in the city, it is the court where the American people get their notions of justice at first hand," Magistrate Whitman sturdily reminded an *Evening Post* reporter a year after he took office. From January

1904 to July 1907 Whitman was the magistrate usually assigned to the Jefferson Market Court at Sixth Avenue and Tenth Street, a local landmark whose red brick tower and clock were then visible from all over Greenwich Village. According to the judicial division of labor, most of the defendants at Jefferson Market were street-walkers. (It was there that policeman Becker had taken Dora Clark.)

Even the satisfaction of an assignment that allowed him to jail or fine a class of offenders whom he had once labeled collectively "the most dangerous factor in the spread of crime" soon palled with Whitman, but he labored faithfully on. He had been on the magistrate's bench three years when he made the first move that brought him some public attention. Many of the offenders who came before him each morning had been arrested after court hours the night before, often on mere suspicion. The next day the arresting policeman would offer so little evidence that the case would be dismissed. Whitman discovered that to avoid a night in jail most of those arrested had done business with a bail bonds-man and that the bail money would be split three ways: For every five dollars paid over, two went to the bondsman and three to the policeman who in turn would split his with the captain at the precinct house and the collector for Tammany, usually a relative of Big Tim's. Whitman gathered evidence of four hundred such cases and presented it to a legislative committee in Albany, pro-posing the establishment of night courts so that defendants could be arraigned at once and do the bail bondsmen and cops out of their squalid sideline. During his visit to the capital he paid a call on Republican Governor Charles Evans Hughes. The night court matter was still pending when Whitman's life was changed through a happy political accident.

Early in March 1907 the city's twenty-six magistrates met at Delmonico's to choose a presiding officer, or president of the Board of Magistrates. Though the jurists were overwhelmingly Democratic, they were split at that moment in two acrimonious factions. The shrill argument and inconclusive balloting went on into the night. About 3 A.M. someone suggested settling on a compromise candidate. The grudging solution was to give the job to the mild-mannered and apparently harmless Whitman, and everyone went home to bed.

Whitman then lived in a modest floor-through apartment at 16 West Forty-fifth Street with his father, a widower. Each night he played a dutiful game of chess with the old man, but this was not the extent of his after-hours amusements. He was no longer dependent on Republican block parties for fun, and in a modest way had become what was then a recognizable social species, a clubman. Besides making the rounds of his clubs each night he had found himself, as an attractive bachelor, much in demand as an extra man at parties given by hostesses on the fringes of the Fifth Avenue and Newport crowd—all of which must have been a welcome change from daytimes spent in the company of young drabs, with a few old lags for variety.

Late one night, two weeks after his unexpected elevation to the presidency of the Board of Magistrates, Whitman was making his way down Broadway in evening clothes after a party that had ended in a few hands of whist. All his life Whitman was inclined to drink more than was good for him, and he was feeling no pain. He decided to stop in a bar for a nightcap. The time, Whitman discovered when he had drunk up, was twenty-three minutes after one. The legal closing hour of 1 A.M. went notoriously unobserved in those days, especially in this Tenderloin area where Whitman had lived—and had patronized the bars—for a dozen years. His imposing new title had apparently given him a new sense of responsibility, however, and he asked if it wasn't late for the saloon to be open. The barkeep rashly explained that it was all right, things had been fixed at headquarters. Whitman made another call at a bar half a block down Broadway. "Oh, we own this precinct," the bartender there told him. "The captain at Forty-seventh Street is a damn good fellow." Whitman made several more stops, having an illegal drink at each one, and a short while afterward reeled into the Forty-seventh Street station, heady with incriminating evidence.

"I am the president of the Board of Magistrates," he announced in a ringing voice to the astonished sergeant in charge, and ordered him to send a policeman out to arrest the offending saloonkeepers. When the lawbreakers were brought in, they found that the new president of the Board of Magistrates had taken over the desk in the captain's room, the same room in which he would later confront Charles Becker on the night of Rosenthal's murder. Whitman held court on the spot and fixed bail, stopping at intervals to denounce the police for having failed for their own corrupt reasons to enforce the law.

"Isn't this an awful thing?" he asked the newspapermen who soon appeared on the scene. "I'm going to smash this thing or go out of business." At one point in the proceedings the desk sergeant asked Whitman if he was sure it had been whiskey he had been drinking, a question that reporters, observing Whitman's condition, thought must have been meant ironically. ("The fellow that should have been arrested was that magistrate, on a charge of intoxication," the precinct captain commented sourly a few days later.)

Delighted with the press coverage the next morning ("DREAD GRAFT HUNT/POLICE SCARED BY/MAGISTRATE'S SALOON RAIDS") Whitman repeated the after-hours procedure several times during the following weeks, accompanied by plainclothesmen and reporters, to whom he delivered lectures on the subject of police graft. Several papers were happily reminded of "the old Jerome days." One of Whitman's after-hours stops was at a place named Healy's at Sixty-sixth Street and Columbus Avenue, which he got into by banging on the door and bamboozling the unwary proprietor. ("Who are you?" "I am a private citizen with a terrible thirst.") Once he had satisfied his terrible thirst, he arrested the four other people sitting around a table in the back room. "We were just cleaning up," said the owner. "You were doing business," said Whitman coldly. He added that he meant to continue making such rounds until every saloon in the city closed at the proper time.

There are worse ways for a drinking man to spend his evenings, but Whitman soon had to retire briefly from the barroom circuit to see his night court bill through the state legislature. (Apparently its provisions were not entirely effective as finally passed; five years later during the Aldermanic Committee hearings on police graft a brothel keeper testified that the cops would simply wait to make their raids until after the night courts closed at midnight—Whitman's bill had not specified any hours—and that the bail bond racket was as much of a bonanza as ever.) The Republicans, whose rolls were recurrently short of personable young crusaders, recognized a political find in this magistrate with the public relations touch and the intensely moral program. Closing down the saloons on time and seeing that they stayed locked on the Lord's Day was a perennial concern of the more militant Simon Pures. It was also one that caused them to be regarded with special bitterness by the city's poorer drinking citizens, especially the Irish, who were aware that many a campaign to keep the saloons in line was mapped out in private clubs where whiskey was available any time, any day.

A few weeks later, in July 1907, Governor Hughes plucked Whitman from the limbo of Magistrate's Court and named him to fill out a term on the Court of General Sessions, which dealt with more important—and generally more newsworthy—cases. Unfortunately, when Whitman had to run for reelection four months later it was not the reformers' year, and although he proved to be an effective campaigner and was compared again to Jerome, he lost. He returned to private practice for two years, but he had had a taste of the political limelight and would be back. Meanwhile, in December 1908, at the age of forty, he married Miss Olive Hitchcock, a Colonial Dame, a Colonial Daughter, and a Daughter of the American Revolution, which group would elect her its vice-president general some years later. ("This will be the only wedding of importance in town during Christmas week," reported the *Times* society editor.) In the Fusion slate that the anti-Tammany crowd pieced together for the city election in November 1909, Whitman was the candidate for district attorney. This time it was the reformers' year, and he took office the following January.

Jerome, whom he succeeded, proved to be a hard act to follow for many reasons. After he had taken over the district attorney's office, Jerome, a first cousin of Jennie Jerome, Winston Churchill's mother, had continued to display the dramatic instincts that would also distinguish his younger relative. He laid siege to the great gambling halls of the Tenderloin, which gradually closed down. Some of their owners, including the fabled Canfield, left the city for good. But most of his time was taken up with a number of sensational criminal trials that kept him in the public eye during the middle years of his eight-year regime that began in 1902. These included the *Town Topics* blackmail affair, the jailing of the famous criminal lawyer Abe Hummel, and the Nan Patterson, Molineux, and Harry K. Thaw murder cases. Jerome was a warm-hearted, genial man and an object of hero worship not only to his staff but to local newspapermen. "Everything

Jerome did was news, and the reporters never left his heels," recalled Arthur Train, an assistant district attorney under both Jerome and Whitman. The press maintained a permanent encampment outside Jerome's office and wrote of him as if he were a combination of Savonarola, St. George, and D'Artagnan.

In his early days as district attorney he was "one of the three best-known men in America," the other two being Roosevelt and Bryan. It was with reason that Jerome was said to have had both eyes on the governorship and at least one on the White House.

But in the last years of his second term his dreams had faded. "He was aggressively honest," Arthur Train recalled. "If there was an inopportune occasion for speaking the truth, it seems as if Jerome always selected it." It was entirely acceptable to his Simon Pure supporters for him to attack Tammany Hall or, safest of all, grafting policemen. But he had also gone after distinguished Republicans ("When I say a senator is unfit, I mean Chauncey Depew"), eminent members of the judiciary ("I have not reverence . . . not even common everyday respect for the judges of the Appellate Court"), and, most dangerously of all, the city's newspaper publishers ("Every paper in New York, almost without exception, is run from the counting room"). Word went out from the publishers' offices that Jerome's tergiversations in the name of righteousness should be reviewed less admiringly and sometimes not covered at all. The habit caught on. "Now there is scarcely one journal left to do him reverence," noted the *Literary Digest*, late in 1908. "The press giveth, and the press taketh away." The next Fusionist nomination for district attorney had gone to Charles Whitman.

Studying the debacle of his predecessor Whitman possibly made notes on advisable deportment if a man wants to stay in the political arena. To judge from his later conduct, the items had to do with ends justifying means; with the necessity of compromise even in the case of political virtue's traditional enemy, Tammany Hall; with the sure-fire nature of the gambling graft issue, and with the importance of cultivating the press. The last precept must have been much in his mind during his first months in office as he tried to lure back reporters who had got out of the habit of dogging the district attorney's heels in the period of Jerome's decline. To complicate matters further, most of them seemed content to stay over at City Hall taking down the words of the city's colorful new mayor, William Gaynor. But in the end Whitman would find ways and means.

One very unfriendly glimpse of the way he ran the D.A.'s office survives. Whitman's first staff had a number of holdovers from Jerome days, including John Hart, Lloyd Paul Stryker, and George Whiteside, all of whom would eventually turn up as defense lawyers for Becker. His chief assistant was the bearded Frank Moss, a hymn-singing evangelical type whose career as a leading reformer and denouncer of grafting policemen dated back, of course, to the Lexow days. There was also young Emory Buckner. Buckner's Harvard Law School classmate, Felix Frankfurter, was working in Washington. In their frequent letters back and forth Whitman came off poorly. Buckner wrote Frankfurter that from the moment of taking office Whitman had been running for governor. Since he was off most of the time making speeches on how to fight crime, he knew almost nothing about the criminal cases in the office, claimed Buckner, whose term for Whitman was "the hog." Nevertheless, he said, "the hog" always made sure he delivered the opening and closing statements in important cases "which is all the papers will notice."

"Absolutely under the belt," Buckner had written Frankfurter in October 1911, "I am informed that he is working night and day for the nomination. He has Abe Gruber absolutely backing him (in the dark), and I do not see why he can't get it. He makes a splendid wooden horse because he has so many people fooled including your friend Schieffelin, etc. etc. *ad glorificandum* . . . It makes me put my lunch."

One of Whitman's problems in garnering the publicity necessary to a rising politician was that during his first years in office little that was especially newsworthy turned up on his calendar. For some reason he did not attack illegal gambling directly as Jerome had done. Former Police Commissioner McAdoo had pointed out that the police had no subpoena power, no chance to resort to John Doe proceedings and other legal gimmicks. "The gambling situation is to a very large extent in the hands of the district attorney." Instead Whitman launched an investigation into the high cost of living. He denounced the tainted meat in butcher shops. He tried leaders of the poultry trust. His biggest chance for headlines came with the arrest for malfeasance of Charles Hyde, the city chamberlain in charge of investing municipal funds. Hyde was a collateral relative of Mayor Gaynor, who lunged to his defense. It was probably the Hyde matter more than anything else that set Gaynor against Whitman, ready to uphold the virtue of any group the district attorney attacked, an attitude that played so neatly into Whitman's hands in the Rosenthal case. As the uneventful months went by Whitman did the best he could with the material at hand. In *Felix Frankfurter Reminisces*, the justice gave one view of how this process worked, quoting a letter from Buckner that described the scene in the D.A.'s office after the Triangle fire in 1911.

> Whitman came in this morning mad as fury, and he called in the head of the homicide division and said, "What's happening in the Triangle case?"
> This was only a few days after it happened. "Well, boss, we're not finished with the investigation, but very soon we'll have the case before the grand jury."
> "Well, get an indictment! We can always *nol pros* it." [That is, decide later not to prosecute on the ground that there wasn't enough evidence after all.] "Here, look at it!" and he held up an editorial in the Hearst New York *American*. "You go and get an indictment. We can *nol pros* if we can't maintain it. You can always *nol pros.*"

"Whitman was getting indictments because Hearst's *American* was yelling blue murder," Frankfurter concluded wrathfully. He cited Whitman as his prime example of "the politically-minded D.A.—one of the great curses of America."

Thus it was not only *World* press directives that Whitman was paying attention to around the time of the Triangle fire. ("I think this is what the D.A. should say about the fire for the morning papers.") But sometime before this Whitman had formed the special alliance with young Herbert Bayard Swope that would take them both a long way.

Swope had come to New York from St. Louis in 1901 when he was nineteen. Although he went to work for the *Herald,* in his first eight years in the city he seemed to feel that the newspaper business was hardly worth his time. The *Herald* soon fired him, hired him again for a brief period, and fired him once more. The editors' major complaint was that Swope was covering too many fires between rounds of open-end crap games or from the race track. For a while he worked for the racing sheet, the *Morning Telegraph*, which temporarily simplified his leg work. It didn't bother him if he didn't have a steady job. He could always pick up spare change at the faro tables or sign a chit if he lost. Even in his early twenties Swope had a self-possession and an authoritative air about him that can't be accounted for by anything in his rather plodding middle-class background or by his slight encounter with formal education, which amounted to a high school diploma, reluctantly granted.

Soon after he got to New York Swope began to pay close attention to the life style of the most famous journalist of the day, Richard Harding Davis. Davis was the handsome reporter who had arrived in the city a decade earlier and who had soon made journalism seem a romantic and adventurous calling rather than a rather disreputable trade followed by drunks and misfits. Van Wyck Brooks described him as "one of those magnetic types, often otherwise second-rate, who establish patterns of living for others of their kind." Even Mencken called him "the hero of all our dreams," and Frank Norris mentioned that one of his characters was suffering from "an almost fatal attack of Harding Davis." Swope seemed to thrive on the malady. Davis was famous for dressing fashionably, carrying a walking stick, wearing spats and yellow chamois gloves. Fresh from a theater opening, he often turned up in white tie and tails to cover an East Side murder. Swope was soon doing the same. Beneath the new tailoring he was, like Davis, a superb and hardworking newspaperman (although a rival, Frank Ward O'Malley of the *Sun* once said, "If Swope should say, 'I've bought a new pair of shoes,' I'd want to see those shoes"). Like Davis, Swope was soon moving easily in influential social and sporting circles where journalists had not always been well received. Whatever made Davis a welcome figure wherever he went, Swope was strident, noisy, aggressively brilliant, often obnoxious, and the secret of *his* success seems to have been that he simply overpowered most of the more diffident sorts whom he met during his long life.

In the fall of 1909 when he finally got a job on the *World*, the equivalent of arriving at the promised land for reporters of the day, Swope decided to cut the comedy and settle down to full-time newspaper work. He had been technically unemployed for nearly two years, but almost immediately was dazzling the *World* city desk with exclusive stories, many of them based on tips given him by people he had met while shooting the breeze at Shanley's or Jack's. Over the gaming tables he had gotten to know many of the major news sources of the city. He had also got to know many of the men who ran the games. He had been far too grand to have anything to do with the East Side stuss houses, but when Bridgey Webber and Herman Rosenthal invaded the uptown scene from Second Avenue, he had a close-up view of the resident Tenderloin gamblers' fury over the development. His view was not entirely detached. For some years one of his closest friends had been a Tenderloin gambler named Arnold Rothstein.

Although he had been born on Henry Street on the East Side, had hung around Sullivan's Occidental headquarters as a boy (some time after Herman Rosenthal who was a decade older), and had found Big Tim's sponsorship invaluable in the gambling world, Rothstein was never part of the Hesper crowd. Quiet-spoken and socially well behaved, he dressed like a Wall Street broker. His Russian-immigrant father had prospered in the cotton-converting business and long before Rothstein was grown had exchanged his ghetto flat for an apartment in the West Eighties. Rothstein, much like Swope, had turned his back on his bourgeois home life in favor of a more adventurous world. By the time he was in his early twenties he had the upstairs poker concession at Big Tim's Metropole. He was particularly congenial with Tim's first deputy, Tom Foley, who was said to consult him frequently about the scuttlebutt of the Tenderloin gambling world. In 1909 Rothstein opened his own elaborate faro house in a double brown-stone at 108 West Forty-sixth Street.

Swope treated Rothstein's place as his midtown *pied-à-terre*. He also began the practice of treating Rothstein as his occasional, and generous, banker. There may have been other convenient financial understandings between members of the New York press and local gamblers at this time. Some of them may even have played a role in the Rosenthal case in which inventive news coverage was so influential. A few weeks after the murder Commissioner Waldo issued a statement saying, "The systematic circulation of false rumors against the police administration cannot be attributed entirely to malevolence. . . . For months prior to the publication of Rosenthal's affidavit it was common rumor that local gamblers had raised a fund to employ young newspapermen

as press agents for the purpose of discrediting the police administration which had caused the gamblers to close their doors." And
about the same time an editorial in the *American* reported that
some of the leading figures maligned in the case were "threatening to make public a list of newspapermen who, it is alleged, have
been recipients of graft from the same source which paid tribute
to Becker and his guilty associates."

Whether or not Swope's name was on the reputed list, his
relationship with Rothstein, like his alliance with Whitman, was
that of two people who found each other useful. Beyond this,
Swope seemed truly to enjoy the company of the gambler. The
two young men, who were the same age, often made the rounds
of the Eastern casinos together. When Rothstein was married to a
showgirl playing in Saratoga in the summer of 1909, the only
attendants were Herbert Bayard Swope and Margaret Powell,
who not long afterward became Mrs. Swope.

Rothstein's Forty-sixth Street place prospered from the first. It
was not a small-time operation. On one occasion Rothstein took
Percival Hill of the American Tobacco Company for a quarter of a
million dollars. By 1912 he knew many important people in town
and wasn't relying entirely on Big Tim for protection. Early that
spring, however, his house was raided by a squad headed by that
go-getting cop, Lieutenant Becker. After certain formalities and
some repairs Rothstein was back in business within a week. But
he did not care for being raided. Like Swope, he was also in close
touch with Freeman, Ludlum, and the other proprietors of first-
class gambling houses in the Tenderloin who were in a rage at
Becker.

Until shortly before the murder Herman Rosenthal's targets on
the police force were Inspector Hayes and Captain Day, whose
practice it had been not to inconvenience the important Tenderloin gamblers any more than was absolutely necessary. It was
only in his *World* affidavit and other statements that went
through Swope's hands that Rosenthal turned his full fury on
Charles Becker. Rosenthal had reason to be angry at the police
lieutenant, and perhaps he shifted villains on his own. Still the
question remains: If Becker hadn't made enemies of Swope's
gambling friends, especially Arnold Rothstein, would he have died
in the electric chair?

XII

"WHY, he looks like a criminal of the lowest type!" exclaimed Sam Schepps. A reporter in Hot Springs, Arkansas, had just showed him a mug shot of Gyp the Blood. Gyp, of course, was one of the men with whom Schepps had sat drinking at Bridgey's place until a few minutes before the murder, and for whom he'd reportedly held the door of the getaway car conveniently open while the dirty deed was done. Inevitably the murder paymaster of recent headlines became a favorite of the press after he was discovered in his southern hideout early in August, 1912. To official embarrassment he had been tracked down neither by Dougherty's men nor by Burns agents but by reporters from the New York *American*.

An hour after the story appeared in the Hearst paper, Schepps' lawyer, Bernard Sandler, sent him a telegram saying "DON'T TALK TO ANY PERSON UNTIL YOU REACH NEW YORK AND SEE WHITMAN WITH WHOM SATISFACTORY ARRANGEMENTS HAVE BEEN MADE IN YOUR BEHALF." Although the telegram was duly delivered, Schepps evidently did not get the message. When *American* reporters mentioned Becker to him the next day in the steamroom of Hot Springs' Buckstaff Baths, where they found him taking his ease, the gambler remarked (according to the reporters' later courtroom depositions): "Becker—the man that I scarcely know? Why, I don't believe Becker would know me if he saw me. I had no dealings with Becker. I never spoke three words to him in my life. . . . How can I tell anything about a man I scarcely know?"

As soon as the *American* revealed Schepps' dilatory domicile, Whitman had sent a telegram of his own to the mayor of Hot Springs, warning him not to make the mistake of turning the natty little gambler over to a member of the New York Police Department any of whom, he implied, would almost certainly kill Schepps. In the national furor over the crimes of the New York police no one seems to have questioned this assumption for a moment. During the week before Whitman was able to dispatch an assistant D.A., two county detectives assigned to his office, and several of the now-widely-traveled Burns agents to claim him. Schepps talked steadily to leading citizens of Hot Springs and to newspapermen who flocked to the town from all over the country.

Schepps' assessment of Herman Rosenthal's character differed from that of the D.A.'s office, which now presented him as a hapless, public-spirited victim. With "a more powerful bunch of gunmen at his command then any other man in New York," Schepps assured his eager listeners, Rosenthal "could get a man assassinated for a five-dollar bill. That gave him a lot of confidence." Asked about Whitman, he said he hadn't yet made up his mind about the fellow. "He wants to be governor, and then it is only a step to the White House," he observed.

According to a later affidavit sworn to by the manager of the Hot Springs hotel where he was staying, Schepps agreed when the hotel man said to him, "Looks as if you've got something to sell."

"It's up to me to make the best bargain I can," Schepps said, according to the affidavit. "One man confesses, another man corroborates, but it takes a third man to make the case against a fourth man. I'm the third man."

Schepps didn't have the legal situation quite straight, but he was right that he had something to sell. New York state law holds that the testimony of accomplices to a crime is insufficient for a conviction unless such testimony is corroborated by a witness who is not an accomplice. Whitman now planned to use Schepps as this nonaccomplice corroborator. Schepps told his new friends in Hot Springs, however, that he hadn't decided how he would testify in court.

"They haven't got me to say Becker ordered the killing of Rosenthal," he remarked at one point. Still, he added thoughtfully, "I think I will look better as a witness than as a prisoner."

Whitman himself finally put a stop to Schepps' talkativeness. In Albany he boarded the train bringing the gambler back and presumably explained certain facts to him during the trip into the city. There was an unseemly scene at Grand Central in which Dougherty's men tried to wrestle the prisoner away from Whitman's mercenaries, but the latter won out and Schepps landed not in the Tombs but in what the press was beginning to call "Whitman's Ritz" on West Fifty-third Street. From that moment on the D.A. kept his gabby corroborative witness out of public circulation by the simple expedient of having Schepps arrested as a common vagrant and then postponing hearings on the charge until the trials of both Becker and the four gunmen were over. During this period, which lasted over three months, Schepps stayed locked up with Rose, Webber, and Vallon on the first tier of the West Side Prison.

It wasn't too bad a life. The men, according to later testimony in court, did not have to be in their cells except at night and spent as much time as they liked playing cards (and, the defense would contend, getting their stories straight) in the jail's counsel room. Friends and relatives visited them constantly. Bridgey Webber insisted many months later that during his entire time in prison Schepps had been paid a weekly salary through a lawyer and that he had also helped himself regularly to money from Bridgey's wallet. A few days after Schepps' arrival a reporter claimed he had intercepted an order from Schepps to a Fifth Avenue store for an eiderdown, two feather pillows, a large rug, two folding chairs, and six pairs of white silk socks at $2.50 a pair. Soon afterward Schepps appeared in court for a vagrancy hearing (postponed, of course). He was "the Beau Brummel of vagrants," reported the *Tribune,* "whose faultlessly cut clothes of a modish pattern showed never a disfiguring wrinkle. His white silk shirt with narrow black stripes was clearly a tailored product."

As soon as he got to town Schepps had signed an immunity agreement almost identical with that signed by Rose, Webber, and Vallon, freeing him from all criminal charges (except, temporarily, vagrancy) if he testified against Becker. From then on, in public at least, Schepps had no doubt that the policeman was responsible for the murder.

There was one sticky matter that had to be straightened out. In his testimony before the grand jury and in his *World* confession

Rose had stated that on the morning after the murder he had sent
Schepps uptown to talk to the gunmen and make arrangements
for paying them off. He had then got a thousand dollars from
Webber, he said, had given it to Schepps, and Schepps had
handed it over to Lefty Louie and Gyp. Thus: the murder paymaster. Now that Schepps was to be the nonaccomplice corroborator of the other gamblers' testimony against Becker, this story
would no longer do. He was to testify as a figure constantly
present during the planning of the crime but totally unaware of
what was going on and not implicated in it in any way. Rose now
announced that he had misremembered. What had happened
was, he, Jack Rose, had given the money to Lefty Louie. The
earlier account had been the result of "too hasty recollection."
And it came to him now, for good measure, that at the meeting
they had all had with Lieutenant Becker at daybreak after the
murder, Becker had ordered Webber to put up the money, saying
he would pay him back later. ("That's a thousand I owe you,
Bridgey.")

   Which of the town's leading criminal lawyers would defend
Becker? John Hart hoped it would be his old chief at the district
attorney's office, Jerome, but negotiations fell through when
Jerome insisted that if he took the case on Becker must admit his
guilt as a grafter. He declined to complicate the defense against
the murder charge with the pretense that Becker had never taken
a dishonest dollar. The defendant didn't want to play that way.
Becker thought—had been encouraged to think, perhaps, by
Tammany leaders who wanted him to keep his mouth shut—that
he would come out of the trial unscathed and, if there were no
admission of grafting, could go back to his job in the Police
Department. (One of the reasons why many citizens found it
hard to feel for Becker the sense of identification often felt for a
man under siege was that he had *enjoyed* being a policeman.)
Martin Littleton was said to be the first choice for defense attorney among Becker's advisors, and that wily operator with his
steely, understated style would probably have done well by him.
But Littleton, remembering the old encounter with Becker at the
departmental trial when he had represented Schmittberger, was
not interested. ("I knew he would never have anything to do with

me," Becker told reporters.) The feud with Schmittberger had cast its shadow again.

John F. McIntyre, the man who got the job, was an old-style Tammany lawyer, fifty-seven years old, who fancied himself as a great orator and liked to boast that he had taken part in more trials than any other criminal lawyer in the city. Most of these dated back to the eighties and nineties when he had been in the district attorney's office under Delancey Nicholl and had prosecuted 614 cases of murder and manslaughter and won 580 convictions. His credentials with the local Irish establishment were impeccable. His grandfather had taken part in the Irish Rebellion and been exiled to the United States in 1878. Eighteen years later McIntyre himself had been summoned to London to conduct the defense of Edward Ivory, the Fenian who was on trial for plotting to blow up the Houses of Parliament and kill the Queen, and had won an acquittal. Possibly Helen Becker, who was said to have chosen McIntyre, had favored him in the hope that he could pull the same trick for Becker in a similarly hostile atmosphere. On the other hand, according to a rumor popular in later years (supported by a sworn affidavit or two), the negotiations with McIntyre had been conducted by Tom Foley, who was beginning to take over Tim Sullivan's duchy. According to this tale, McIntyre's cut-rate fee of thirteen thousand dollars had been paid by a check drawn on the Tammany Hall account, part of the deal being the understanding that the defense, like the prosecution, would leave Big Tim out of it. The rest of the defense team consisted of John Hart, a comparative veteran, and Lloyd Paul Stryker and George Whiteside, who were both still in their twenties and had practiced for only a year or two since leaving the district attorney's office.

Probably the worst news McIntyre brought Becker in mid-August 1912 was the rumor that the judge in his case was likely to be Justice John W. Goff, famous as a cop hater since his work on the Lexow investigation. He had served his fourteen-year term on the General Sessions Court, his reward for his Lexow work, and since 1906 had been dispensing his erratic brand of justice on the state Supreme Court (which, despite its name, is a court of original jurisdiction in New York). Although he professed to hate publicity, Goff nevertheless had displayed a special fondness for the more sensational trials and had shown much skill at juggling docket assignments so that he had presided over more than his share of spectacular cases. These had included many of the noted murder trials in which the prosecutor had been his old Lexow colleague, William Travers Jerome, with whom he had long since ceased to be on speaking terms.

Goff's appointment as judge in the Becker case came about oddly. In the third week of August Whitman put in a formal request to Governor Dix to call an extraordinary session of the criminal branch of the State Supreme Court of New York County that would be empowered to try all cases growing out of the Rosenthal murder investigation. (Regular sessions of the court were not scheduled until later in the fall.) Dix announced that he had acceded to every one of Whitman's requests for co-operation and named as the presiding judge Justice Goff whom the district attorney's office had noted earlier in the week was known to be willing to interrupt his summer recess to take on the demanding assignment. If Whitman had not requested the court shift, Becker and the gunmen would have been tried in the city's Court of General Sessions, where none of the judges was considered as totally reliable on the police issue as Goff. Whitman's argument to Dix had been that such judges could not be impartial in local police matters. From the start of the trial Goff was thus beholden to Whitman for having arranged things so he could preside over the kind of headline-making case he was partial to and for his chance to deal with a capital charge against a member of the municipal department he most distrusted.

However, Goff's orneriness had dealt rude surprises in court in the past to prosecutors who had thought they could count on him. Perhaps to cinch matters, Whitman was back in the governor's office a few days later, successfully petitioning for an extraordinary grand jury to be empaneled simultaneously with the extraordinary session of the Supreme Court. Although the July grand jury that had indicted Becker was still sitting, he argued that this new special grand jury was needed to investigate all aspects of New York police corruption that had been revealed since the murder. With this move Whitman made certain that a grand jury would be available to convene in a hurry to subpoena, hear, and automatically grant immunity to witnesses whose position in the case might otherwise be somewhat anomalous. Whitman then requested Governor Dix to name Goff to preside also over this new special grand jury, an arrangement that would make it necessary throughout the Becker trial for the prosecutor to be in frequent consultation with the judge on separate, though not entirely unrelated, matters.

Indeed, right after his second trip to Albany, the Whitmans sent their regrets to Mrs. Belmont and joined Goff at his country place for a weekend to hash over questions having to do with the future special grand jury inquiry and, as Whitman described it, to "iron out a few kinks in the Becker case." The following Tuesday McIntyre and Whitman appeared before Goff to present various opposing motions. One of Whitman's motions formally requested that Becker be tried separately from the other six men cited in the blanket indictment—and be tried first. This avoided the awkwardness of having to deal with the denial by the two captured gunmen that Becker had had anything to do with the murder. If they were tried first, this would become vital evidence for Becker's defense. Goff granted every single major motion put by Whitman and turned down every one, without exception, offered by the defense.

Goff also foiled a move by McIntyre to have Becker refuse to enter a routine plea of not guilty until a certain matter had been cleared up. Becker's first lawyer, John Hart, had been subpoenaed to testify before the July grand jury about having got the affidavit concerning the mortgage from Bald Jack Rose. Since this amounted to being forced to testify against his client, the defense claimed, and might invalidate Becker's indictment (which was based on evidence presented to the same grand jury) McIntyre announced that his client would not plead guilty or not guilty to the indictment. Goff had no trouble with that one. "In the charge of murder against Charles Becker," he said in his shrill whisper, "the court directs a plea of not guilty to be entered."

There was some talk in legal circles that, in view of his long history of bias against the police, Goff should disqualify himself in the Becker case. The defense also considered asking for a change of venue, but Whitman said Governor Dix had assured him that no matter where the case was tried Goff would be the presiding justice since the crime had been committed in New York County. After weighing the danger of antagonizing the old man further, McIntyre denied to the press that he thought his long-time friend Justice Goff should yield to another judge. Nothing, he said, could be further from his thoughts.

Becker's counsel did protest when Goff set the trial date as September 12, exactly one week after the arraignment, probably the shortest allotment of time in history for the preparation of a major criminal case. McIntyre pointed out that hundreds of men indicted long before Becker in New York County had not yet been brought to trial. Moreover, McIntyre insisted, Becker should not be forced to go to trial in the midst of clamor and hysteria and at a time when someone—he would not say it was the district attorney, he would *hope* it was not the district attorney—was deluging the public prints day after day with information of what had happened in the grand jury room and prejudicing the public mind with "diabolical and infamous lies." Goff's answer was to bang down his gavel and declare the court adjourned.

In a move that apparently took Whitman by surprise (and that presumably underlined for him the danger of entrusting the case to a judge other than Goff) McIntyre then went before another Supreme Court justice, George Bischoff, and asked that the opening date of Becker's trial be postponed until October 7. The motion was granted as was another defense request that a special commission be sent to Hot Springs to take depositions on what Sam Schepps had said during his garrulous days before he signed on the dotted line with the district attorney's office. Too late, Assistant District Attorney Frank Moss came hotfooting downstairs and tried to get both motions transferred before Judge Goff, arguing that Bischoff should allow this as a matter of courtesy to a fellow justice. "It is not a matter of courtesy to another justice which is in question," Bischoff told him sternly. "It is a matter of justice to an accused man being tried on a charge for which the penalty is death."

McIntyre was soon complaining that before the official commission could get to Hot Springs Whitman had made a quick trip down there himself and—contrary to all legal ethics, said the defense counsel—had interviewed all prospective witnesses before they gave their formal testimony. Nevertheless the prosecution would not be happy with many of the sworn statements quoting their important nonaccomplice witness. Possibly some of Whitman's influence was counteracted by Bat Masterson. The famous former westerner made a special trip to Arkansas to talk to folks there about what a raw deal his friend Charley Becker was getting and stood encouragingly by at every interview Becker's lawyer had with Hot Springs residents.

Early in September Mayor Gaynor and Commissioner Waldo had a bit of fun at the expense of their tormentors. They released an official Police Department study of the Sam Paul Association that described the standard bearer as "a notorious criminal" and its membership as "a company of criminals and Republican politicians." Paid-up members on the rolls, the report said, included not only Gyp the Blood, Harry Vallon, Jack Rose, Boob Walker, and Big Jack Zelig, but also two members of Whitman's staff, one of them Assistant District Attorney Morris Koenig, the younger brother of the Republican County Chairman. Waldo was also very obliging about furnishing the newspapers with a picture taken at Jacob Reich's wedding party at the Cafe Boulevard two years earlier, showing Herman Rosenthal as best man and Morris Koenig among the grinning guests.

Although this information may have been disconcerting for Whitman, who planned to spend considerable time during the trial denouncing Becker for hobnobbing with these same criminal types, he swiftly took the spotlight off his associates' social life by releasing the information that a supporting witness had been found who had overheard Charles Becker confess the murder. A Sing Sing prisoner named James Hallen was ready to swear that on August 12, while he was in a Tombs cell awaiting sentencing, he had heard Becker talking to a member of his strong arm squad.

"They have no one to testify against us but criminals," he swore Becker had told his fellow policeman. "No jury on earth is going to believe them . . . After this is passed over the public will give me a pension for killing that dirty crook."

A disbarred lawyer with a long record of convictions for forgery, Hallen was currently serving a sentence on that charge. He had apparently followed the Becker case closely enough to have an idea of who was running things. When he had written his letter from Sing Sing offering to testify about the overheard conversation, he had directed it not to the D.A. but to "a prominent member of the reporting staff of the New York *World*." A day later Hallen was brought down from Sing Sing and lodged in the Tombs not far from Becker.

When the policeman learned of what Hallen had sworn to, he lost his formidable poise for the first time, according to the *Times.* As he and Hallen took their exercise in the corridor he was overheard berating the other man.

"Why would you make up a story like this? What's wrong with you that you want to do such a terrible thing to a man that never did you any harm?" (Eavesdropping on conversations in the Tombs seemed in danger of becoming a recognized job category.)

About the same time a half-forgotten name provided another diversion that was good for a few days' headlines. Whitman discovered that Thomas Coupe, the British desk clerk at the Elks' Club, was among the passengers aboard the *Lusitania* that had sailed the day before. Lead stories immediately announced that Coupe, distraught over his key role in the murder case and in terror of his life, was decamping to where he had come from. Whitman announced also that he had it on good authority that the System—or possibly Becker himself—had paid Coupe ten thousand dollars to leave the country. Statements by the Elks' Club that Coupe had been fired by them for persistent absentee-ism made the deep inside pages.

Docking in Liverpool, Coupe denied that he had been bribed to leave New York, and indeed it was hard to see why anyone would have bothered. He had caught the license number of the car which both sides had already agreed to stipulate was the one involved in the murder. His only other contribution to the case had been his insistence that chauffeur Libby—exonerated by the time he sailed—had been the single murderer. His departure however, gave Whitman a chance to stir up a little more righteous indignation, charging the powerful System with tampering with a state witness. Within a few days he had dispatched Assistant District Attorney Billy De Ford to England to persuade Coupe to return.

De Ford and Coupe were discovered some time later at London's Savoy Hotel where they had been living for several weeks while they labored, more or less arduously, over the terms on which Coupe would agree to return. Eventually the desk clerk accepted a check for five hundred dollars and a round-trip first-class ticket good on any Cunard liner. The two men would arrive back in New York too late for Becker's trial but in time for that of the four gunmen. For the next few weeks Coupe was put up at the Hotel Westbury, sharing an elaborate suite with two Burns detectives. In the end he was never called to testify in the gunmen's case either, and eventually used the other half of his round-trip ticket to go back to Liverpool where he reportedly invested his five-hundred-dollar payoff in a thriving pub. The Coupe caper was later found to be the single most costly item among the district attorney's expense vouchers in the case.

Throughout the month of August and into September, at great cost to Schieffelin and his friends, Burns men were still fanning out through the country in search of Gyp the Blood and Lefty Louie, the two missing gunmen. A detachment of Burns agents even took off for Panama City, declaring they had information that the gangsters were spending a leisurely month going from New York to California by way of the canal. But on September 14 when Gyp and Lefty were captured at last they were sitting in their underwear in an apartment in Brooklyn where they had been living with two girl friends since the last week in July. The arrest of the two suspects, who were described in the *Times* account as being "of the gangster type developed by the Gaynor administration," was made by Deputy Commissioner Dougherty who pointed out that, in spite of all the slanders they had been subjected to, it had been the New York police who had captured all four gunmen.

Whitman, who may have been growing disillusioned over the performance of the highly touted Burns agents, said sourly that there was something fishy about the gunmen's capture. How about the rumor that letters from Becker to the gunmen had been found and concealed by his policemen friends? Nothing loath, Justice Goff set off another rash of headlines by instituting a special judicial investigation of the department's handling of the arrests.

Thus as the day approached for Becker's trial to begin, various aspects of criminal behavior by New York city policemen were being noisily investigated by the regular grand jury, by the mayor's special committee, and by the Aldermanic Committee to Investigate Police Graft. The newspapers were also filled with stories of the upcoming special grand jury investigation to be presided over by Goff. Now came this additional *ad hoc* inquiry into possible police malpractice. Although Goff eventually would come to the grudging conclusion that there had been no Becker letters to conceal, this judgment would get no farther than page fourteen or so in the papers, and by then Becker's trial would already be under way.

By September the Aldermanic Committee was giving Whitman competition for headlines. This committee, according to Martin Mayer's biography of its counsel, Emory Buckner, had "arranged for the members of the City Club and the Citizens' Union, the financial heart and lungs of the reform movement, to supply it with additional, unpaid investigators—unpaid, that is, by the City." These were "young businessmen and lawyers whose employers would volunteer their services for the tedious work of plowing through the Police Department files." They came on loan, for example, from the House of Morgan, from E. H. Seligman and Company, from Kuhn, Loeb, and from the law offices of Elihu Root and Joseph Choate. Commissioner Waldo soon complained that the committee was "employing a large number of young men who are not in city service and are not responsible . . . to me, to the committee, or to anybody else, and who are changing continuously." Such individuals had no business being allowed to rummage through police files, he said. Buckner saw no virtue in his position. "Well, of course, they are drawing a good deal bigger salary than we could afford to pay, or the city could afford to pay, and they are answerable to the committee."

One of Buckner's first formal actions was to subpoena Mayor Gaynor to defend himself against the charge that, as the *American* had put it a few days earlier, "the policies of the Gaynor administration led directly to the Rosenthal murder." Gaynor had been anything but a popular candidate for the chief post at City Hall in the election of 1909, either with the reformers or the press, even though his relationship with Tammany, under whose banner he was running, was known to be an uneasy one. Only the *World* and the *Press* had supported him, and the *Times*, for one, had described his nomination as "a scandal." He was the only Tammany candidate who was elected that fall. (Someone asked the laconic Charley Murphy why his party had lost all the other races. "We didn't get enough votes," he said.) Once Gaynor had moved into City Hall he announced that all his life he had been "thinking and building up what I could do in such an office" and, heedless of all grim predictions from political savants, had put Tammany on a starvation diet so far as patronage was concerned.

"What do we have for Charley Murphy?" a colleague asked Gaynor at one point. "Maybe a kind word?" said the mayor tentatively.

Gaynor drastically pared the city payroll and so streamlined muddled municipal affairs that at the beginning of 1912 Robert Fulton Cutting, founder of the Citizens' Union and one of the presiding chairmen of the gold-plated Holies, listed seventy-four worthy achievements of the new administration. The *Times,* dramatically changing its tune, commented editorially that his first year in office had been "an epoch in the history of the city," adding that "new standards of administration have been established which it would take years of misrule to eradicate." Only Hearst's papers continued to berate him ("Mentally cross-eyed! Incapable of telling the truth!"), and Hearst had been one of the candidates for mayor whom Gaynor had beaten in 1909. It was asking a bit much of a newspaper publisher to encourage his employees to write admiringly of a man who had said during the campaign: "Hearst's face almost makes me want to puke."

The *Times,* besides awarding Gaynor's administration high marks, had had some affectionate words for Gaynor himself. "His vigorous and original personality . . . the native wit and stored learning at his instant command, the delightful tangents from the usual orbit in which he indulges, his impatience with fools, and the strain of kindliness that shows in incalculable ways have made the chronicling of his daily life an exceedingly pleasant relief from the routine of newspaper work," read a *Times* editorial in January 1911. The long, colorful letters that he regularly fired off for public consumption were enlivened by citations from such varied authorities as Don Quixote, Robert Burton, Benjamin Franklin, Frederick the Great, Macaulay, Cato, Homer, Rabelais, Emerson, Gil Blas, the Bishop of Toledo, and Epictetus. The spectacle of a Tammany man quoting Epictetus so staggered the press that cartoonists regularly depicted Gaynor crouched at his City Hall desk under a portrait of that comparatively obscure Latin philosopher.

The delight the public and the newspapers took in their uncommon new mayor must have been a trial to the ambitious Whitman during his first two years as district attorney. Gaynor was frequently described in that period as the next governor of the state. The Gaynor phenomenon attracted national interest, and early in 1912 Colonel Edward House, nosing out likely Democratic candidates for the presidency, paid a few visits to City Hall. Gaynor, however, was in a bad mood that week and treated the Texan with great rudeness. House eventually "wiped Gaynor from my political slate, for I saw he was impossible." But "there was no reason why, if he had been sensible, we wouldn't have elected Gaynor," he said on another occasion. "He was actually better known than Wilson."

The mayor's eccentric and self-destructive treatment of House was of a piece with much of his behavior during the last years of his regime, behavior that was almost certainly the result of the attempt on his life. The bullet was never removed from his throat, and he coughed constantly and spoke only in a harsh whisper. As the discomfort continued, his temper curdled further, and his control over it and his vindictive tongue—never very firm—all but disappeared. He began to treat all who disagreed with him as subversive and publicly blamed Hearst's inflammatory editorials for the shooting. When the would-be assassin turned out to be an inveterate reader of the *Times,* Gaynor enlarged his attack to include all the press, which gradually lost patience with him as it had only a few years earlier with Jerome. Gaynor grew more and more convinced that the 1912 crime wave featured in the press did not exist. He seemed to consider the Rosenthal murder a personal affront, staged just to prove the enemy's argument that crime was rampant in his administration. When the storm of wild charges broke after it, he was not in a sufficiently balanced mental state to assess the political realities.

"GAYNOR DROPPED AS SUCCESSOR TO DIX. MAYOR'S STAND ON POLICE QUESTION TOO MUCH EVEN FOR MURPHY" read the headline in the *American* a few weeks after the murder. "Murphy is disappointed greatly over the Mayor's failure to realize the importance of existing conditions in the Police Department," the story went on. "He has told several friends that if the Mayor had taken a firm stand and directed Waldo to spare no effort to get those responsible for Rosenthal's death, whether in or out of the Police Department, he would have become the strongest man available for the gubernatorial nomination."

"He failed to seize the greatest opportunity of his life," Murphy was quoted as telling other Tammany leaders. If the mayor, with his matchless talent for publicity, had taken charge of the situation, the district attorney's performance would necessarily have been secondary. As it was, the cantankerous old Irishman's decision to sulk in his tent had given Whitman the big opportunity of *his* life.

Early in September 1912, Gaynor finally agreed to appear before the Aldermanic Committee with the stipulation that he would answer only questions that suited him and none on the Becker case. This latter reservation suited Emory Buckner. Becker, he wrote Frankfurter late that month, "is on trial for his life and is entitled to a fair jury, and one of the worst things in the whole case is the newspaper campaign which has been waged undoubtedly at the inspiration of the District Attorney, which has resulted in a very inflamed feeling against Becker. On the merits I do not wish to add to this, no matter how bad Becker may be."

Sitting ramrod straight on the witness stand, dressed like a London banker and carrying his familiar top hat (which he kept to himself this time), the mayor gave the kind of performance that had caused newspaper writers of the day to use his name as a useful verb, as in "He is inclined to gaynor," meaning to lay about him irascibly. He reminded the committee that policeman in his administration no longer bashed in heads "as Clubber Williams used to do." Clearly dismayed by Whitman's sudden vault upward, Gaynor dragged in the Becker case himself. The notion that the New York police were under orders not to capture the Rosenthal murderers "is baseless in the sight of every sensible man . . . a cruel accusation emanating, like all the principal falsehoods in the case, from the district attorney's office." The police should not be distressed but consider the source from which it came. "What degenerates think of us is of no concern."

Someone—and he had a good idea who it was, said Gaynor— was spreading the word that the police had done nothing and the district attorney everything in the case—another lie. One grafter had turned up in Waldo's department and "now every dog in town is at his throat." If one cashier absconded did people lose faith in banks? There had been grafting forty years earlier when he had first come to New York. There had been grafting since the beginning of history. Gaynor had done his best to root out grafting through his strong arm squads. "But I suppose it is impossible to get a hundred and fifty men and three lieutenants without getting a certain percentage of grafters among them. Of course when this turned out to be so, I was terribly hurt."

"When it happened that Becker turned out to be a grafter," he went on to the committee, "I immediately surmised that he was the head and front of all the grafting in the department." Counsel Buckner quickly interposed that it had been not the committee but the mayor who had mentioned Becker's name. "His name!" snarled the mayor. "I hate the sound of his name, and I hope I shall never hear it again."

Next day the *Evening Post* reminded its readers that only a few weeks earlier the mayor had refused to recommend that Becker be dismissed without evidence. ("Let us take things in order.") "Now that the man has been indicted, however, Gaynor chooses to be injudicious. . . . In Becker the Mayor now discerns the man solely responsible for the conditions that led to the Rosenthal murder. Against a man awaiting trial by due process of the law, Mr. Gaynor brings forward charges with a recklessness that even 'ex-convicts and newspaper proprietors' [two groups that Gaynor frequently equated in his public statements] are seldom guilty of."

Shortly before his death Charles Becker would write in a letter to a policeman friend that he believed the mayor's testimony that he was "the head and front" of all police graft had made the difference in his fate. Coming, as it had, so close to the beginning of his trial, he felt it had established him irrevocably in the public mind as a powerful and vicious criminal and had put the jurors in a frame of mind to convict him.

XIII

"It is one of the gloomiest structures in the world . . . Tier on tier it rises above a huge central rotunda, rimmed by dim mezzanines and corridors upon which the courtrooms open, and crowned by a . . . glass roof encrusted with soot, through which filters a soiled and viscous light. The air is rancid with garlic, stale cigar smoke, sweat, and the odor of prisoners' lunch. The corridors swarm with Negroes, Italians, blue-bloused Chinese, black-bearded rabbis, policemen, shyster lawyers and their runners, and politicians, big and little." This, in the words of Arthur Train, was the Criminal Courts building where Charles Becker went on trial. The walls of the building had started to buckle soon after it was completed in 1885. City officials periodically announced that it should be condemned as a menace to human life and left it at that.

The first-floor courtroom of the criminal branch of the Supreme Court where the principals in the case convened on Monday morning, October 7, had been the scene of most of the dramatic New York trials earlier in the century. In the witness chair where Bald Jack Rose would sit, former Floradora girl Evelyn Thaw had described her alleged deflowering by architect Stanford White. In the same chair another former Floradora girl, Nan Patterson, had tearfully told how it had come about that her lover, traveling downtown with her in a hanson cab, had committed suicide by shooting himself in the back. There were no

Floradora girls in the Becker case. As Richard Harding Davis pointed out a few weeks later in *Collier's,* one of its most unusual features was the fact that "in no place, from first to last, does a woman appear. There is no single hint of love or passion. None of the conspirators can plead 'the woman tempted me.' " Still, the Becker drama had its fascinated observers.

Unexpectedly, the show was preceded by a curtain raiser. A few weeks earlier a reporter had unearthed a program for a dance given on Second Avenue the previous April. It carried a large ad for Libby and Shapiro's "gray Packard taxicab service (Cafe Boulevard main stand)," and among the listed floor directors were East Siders familiar by now to newspaper readers from Perth Amboy to Puget Sound, including Lefty Louie, Sam Paul, and Big Jack Zelig, the honored beneficiary of the evening's gate receipts. Zelig was generally given credit for having killed three men, all Italians, in the months preceding the dance. His most recent victim, Julie Morell of the old Paul Kelly gang, had hit the floor just as the band had swung into "Home Sweet Home" at a ball much like this one and Morrell's successor, Jack Sirocco, had resolved to do the same for Big Jack. The dance program had therefore ended on a note of earnest hope: "In conclusion we trust that nothing occurs to disturb the peace and happiness that we assume will prevail among us. . . ." Peace had prevailed that April night. When they finally got Big Jack, no band was playing.

On the evening of October 5, two days before Becker's trial began, Zelig left an East Side cafe and stepped on a northbound Second Avenue street car at Fifth Street. At the next stop a man known as "Red Phil" Davidson hopped aboard. Just before the car reached Fourteenth Street he moved up behind Zelig and killed him with a single bullet through the head. In the coat pocket on the body when it arrived at the nearest station house were several objects of interest to students of the Rosenthal murder: the calling card of the common law wife of Gyp the Blood; an "advertising contract" requiring Libby and Shapiro to pay Zelig a hundred dollars a month tribute from their taxi receipts; a slip of paper reading "Harry Klemperer, night telephone operator, Elks' Club" (Klemperer had been outside getting a breath of air at the moment of the murder and before dawn had left for Florida for a long vacation); a card bearing the name of a man who'd been an overnight guest at the Elks' Club the same night, and another listing the address of Bernard Sandler, Sam Schepps' lawyer. There were also letters to Zelig from each of the four gunmen, assuring him that, though stuck in the Tombs, they were in good health and confident of the future ("Dear old pal, we will have a good time at Mother's house as soon as we all get out," ran one line in the note from Dago Frank) as well as a letter Zelig had been about to mail to Gyp the Blood asking him to assure Frank that Zelig didn't hold it against him that he was a "dago." This letter reinforced the impression that it is hard to tell a hoodlum by his literary style. "Yours received," it began, "and it was more than pleasant to hear from you. . . ."

Davidson, Zelig's killer, was captured in a matter of minutes. Dago Frank's acceptance by the Zelig crowd wasn't the only evidence that ethnic lines were beginning to blur in gangland. Although a Russian Jew, Davidson was loosely affiliated with the Sirocco bunch. But the only reason he had shot Big Jack, he said, was because Zelig had robbed him of four hundred dollars during a fight earlier in the day. By the next morning the hoots and hollers from the East Side at the notion of Red Phil's having four hundred dollars to his name had reached the Tombs. What he'd meant to say, Red Phil amended hastily, was that Big Jack had robbed him of *eighteen* dollars. Though he insisted this was his only motive, it was inevitable that the killing would seem to have something to do with the Becker case. The defense kept pointing out the curious fact that Davidson had lived next door to the Sam Paul Association. But the British correspondent of the *Times* reported on October 7 that every paper in London was convinced that Becker's friends among the police had done the job.

The theory that the cops had killed Zelig to prevent his appearance at Becker's trial was given its most powerful impetus by Whitman's reaction to the murder. He announced at once that Zelig would have been one of the most important witnesses— some reporters understood him to say *the* most important witness—for the prosecution. "DEATH OF ZELIG. D.A.'S STATEMENT: PRINCIPAL WITNESS FOR THE STATE," was the headline in the *American* the next day. The subhead in the *World* read: "Zelig's Death Held Blow to Prosecution. . . . Would Have Testified Rose and Vallon Told Him Becker Wanted Rosenthal Killed and that He Must Supply Gunmen." The *Times* described Whitman's reaction to the news, given to him by reporters who had waited

for him in the lobby of his Madison Avenue apartment until he
returned from a dinner at the Waldorf.

"The news staggered the District Attorney as a physical blow
might have done. He threw up his hands and exclaimed: 'My
God, what next? What next? I don't know what to do.' Mr.
Whitman evidently realized," the *Times* went on, "that the death
of no one man could have resulted in such tremendous benefit to
Becker as the death of Zelig."

A difference of opinion existed between the *Times'* news and
editorial departments. Without calling Whitman a liar, the latter
expressed serious doubts that Zelig could have been intended as
an important witness for the state, that "if Whitman's case is as
overwhelming as he has described it, he would have relied on the
word of a notorious criminal." If that *was* the plan, said the
Times, it seemed incredible that Zelig had not been under lock
and key (or even, as it turned out, under prosecution subpoena).
No major paper recalled Zelig's statement outside the grand jury
room the previous August in which he denied that Becker had
either framed him or bailed him out and put the finger on Bald
Jack Rose instead. The next day far down in the news columns of
only a few papers, it was reported that what the district attorney
had really meant to say was that he had hoped to make effective
use of Zelig on cross-examination if Zelig were called as a *defense*
witness.

Defense attorney McIntyre's apoplectic response to what he
called Whitman's "contemptible ruse" was reported on the first
day of the trial. As soon as court opened McIntyre rose to declare
for the record that because of the district attorney's "falsehood"
the defendant was being forced to trial under circumstances in
which he could not expect to get a fair and impartial hearing. The
district attorney had "clutched Big Jack Zelig to him as a witness
when Zelig was no longer of this earth. He stooped to the lowest
depths to prejudice the case of a man who . . . is entitled to a
fair trial. He never subpoenaed Zelig, and he knows in his heart
that Zelig told him he would not corroborate the story of Rose and
Webber about hiring the gunmen . . . The fact is that Zelig had
been subpoenaed as a witness for the defense. It was our intention to call him to refute the statements by Rose that Becker had
requested Zelig to furnish the gunmen who were to slay Rosen-

thal. Zelig was to have testified to that effect and thus show that the statements made by Rose were false."

At this point Justice Goff ordered McIntyre to sit down. "Your honor," said McIntyre, putting his hand on his heart, "I have a human life in my custody."

"This is a court of justice," snapped Goff. "It is not a place for the display of eloquence. . . . If you continue, I shall be under the unpleasant necessity of directing the court officer to remove you out of the court." As the later reversal by the Court of Appeals pointed out, this was the jury panel's first view of the degree of respect the presiding judge felt was due the counsel for the defense.

Goff had not been in line to be the presiding judge when McIntyre was hired as defense counsel early in August. Possibly if Whitman's intentions had been suspected, Becker's advisors would have chosen another lawyer. Both men were devout Irishmen, members of the revolutionary Clan-N-Gael. But it was not enough. McIntyre's old chief, Delancey Nicholl, had fought and scorned the work of the Lexow Committee, and Goff, its counsel, had not forgotten. What counted even more was that McIntyre was the kind of man Goff couldn't stand to be in the same room with. Where Goff's manner was pianissimo, darting, mercurial, McIntyre's style was ponderous, overblown, stentorian, and often maddening even to those who were on his side.

At first glance the sixty-four-year-old Goff did not seem the dragon of courtroom legend. His aureole of silky hair, his full beard, and his dense brows were all a brilliant white and his deep-set eyes a piercing blue. Some who saw him for the first time were reminded of a stained glass window or of one of Giotto's medieval saints. Few of the attorneys who had come before him saw him with a halo. Abraham Levy, a leading criminal lawyer at the turn of the century, called him "that saint-like son-of-a-bitch." Goff was a tiny man whose voice was also tiny—and deadly. Distinguished members of the bar at the height of their careers confessed to waking up in their beds in a cold sweat, having heard in nightmares the sound of that low, sibilant voice saying "Buzz, buzz, buzz, buzz, *guilty!*"—a verdict he pronounced, it seemed to them, with joy. Levy's son Newman described him as "the cruelest, most sadistic judge we have had in New York in this century." Each time he entered the courtroom where Becker was on trial, Lloyd

Paul Stryker wrote years later, "I felt like some four-footed deni-
zen of the jungle that suddenly stares into the cold visage of a
python . . . [Goff] had a cold heart and a sadistic joy in suffering." Stryker was reminded of Macaulay's description of Jeffreys,
London's seventeenth-century "hanging judge": "He had the most
odious vice which is incident to human nature, a delight in misery
merely as misery."

Reporters covering the trial could not have described Goff in
this fashion without risking contempt of court charges. No such
consideration—or pretensions of impartiality—inhibited them in
their descriptions of the defendant as he sat among his lawyers at
a small table on the left side of the courtroom.

"The personality of Becker is not a pleasing one," declared
Hearst's *American*. He was "powerful of physique, his heavy body
topped by a bullet-like head." There is no hint of the finer things
of life in his make-up. His hands were "hairy, sinewy"; his black
hair had not a touch of gray in it. (The writer seemed to find this
ominous.) "His large nose . . . reveals to the student of physiognomy the fact that arrogance and relentless pursuit of any
object desired are the strongest features of his being. Charles
Becker is steeped in the memory of the power that was his. His
gaze is brilliant, sardonic, menacing. I am very glad," the *American* reporter concluded, "that someone dear to me will not sit on
that jury and hold the life of Charles Becker in his hands."

The trial's opening had been delayed for the swearing-in of
members of Goff's special grand jury inquiry into police graft.
This proceeding was temporarily adjourned, but Whitman and
Goff were frequently observed consulting about it before, after
and during the recesses of the Becker trial. The *Post* ran an
appreciative account of the rapport between the two men and the
pleasant picture they made conferring on the bench with Whitman's brown head bent close to Goff's silvery one.

If the selection of the jury in Becker's trial was a long, tiresome
procedure it was no fault of the D.A. A special blue ribbon list of
250 names had been prepared by the commissioner of jurors.
"Any twelve representative business men or men of affairs will
prove as satisfactory as any other twelve," Whitman said, confidently. Disagreeing, McIntyre insisted on asking each prospective
juror a formidable series of questions about his social and professional friends. (Did the candidate know, for example, Inspector

Schmittberger?) At the end of the first day a single juror had been chosen. Goff, who had a reputation for being willing to sacrifice almost any legal nicety to get proceedings over and done with, had set the outside limit of the time he could spare for the case at two weeks which, he announced, would break the speed record for a major murder case. He put the court on night and day sessions until the jury was chosen.

By the end of the third day, even with sessions running until nearly midnight, the jury was still not complete, and the first panel was exhausted as were the principals in the courtroom. McIntyre had used up most of the thirty-five peremptory challenges allowed him in an effort to make sure that all selections conformed as closely as possible to his concept of ideal jurymen. To begin with, he explained, they should be married ("Married men approach their responsibilities with the necessary gravity"). Like the *American* writer he put great faith in physiognomy. Jurors must be tall ("Men of shorter stature are inclined to be grouchy and cantankerous and bear a grudge against the world") and blue-eyed ("All great thinkers throughout history have been blue-eyed"). When the twelfth member of the jury was chosen at last from a second panel on the fourth day of the trial, the press noted with amusement that the majority of the twelve bore a noticeable resemblance to McIntyre himself—big, stout, red-faced, blue-eyed, middle-aged men with, in ten out of a possible twelve cases, thick gray moustaches like that of the chief defense counsel.

By trade the jurors were all substantial white-collar types— real estate dealers, bankers, engineers, an auditor, an architect. McIntyre had reservations about at least one of the final twelve. He had rejected this candidate as obviously biased: The man had testified he was a friend of Emory Buckner, the counsel to the Aldermanic Committee, and also of Assistant District Attorney Frank Moss, who would carry the burden of the Becker prosecution. Goff, in a snit over McIntyre's long-winded tactics, had ordered the man seated anyhow.

The delay had not been entirely McIntyre's fault. Thirteen of the first fourteen prospective jurors, for example, had had to be dismissed because they said they had been reading the papers and had already made up their minds. Thanks, perhaps, to Becker's menacing gaze and certainly to the sinister character attributed to his fellow policemen, word had got about that it might not be a healthy thing to serve on the jury. All kinds of professional and domestic crises had afflicted the candidates. One of them successfully pleaded that he was in the undertaking business and October was his busy season.

Swope reported in the *World* that Becker himself had given orders that there were to be no Jews on the jury. As he was brought into court the next day Becker leaned over the rail and told several reporters from other papers that the story was a damned lie. In the end there were two men on the jury with Jewish names. Whitman had rejected one with a Jewish name for an unusual reason. The candidate had been accepted by both sides and was about to take his seat when he mentioned that he could hardly be prejudiced since he had been out of the country from mid-July till early September and hadn't read a single newspaper account of the case. Instantly Whitman stepped forward, used one of his peremptory challenges, and got the uninformed fellow out of there fast.

The reference to his proscription of Jews on the jury wasn't the only time the *World* portrayed Becker as anti-Semitic. As he was leaving the courtroom on the trial's opening day Becker passed a group of newspapermen clustered by the door leading to the Bridge of Sighs. "What do you think my chances are?" he asked. He was looking remarkably cheerful, they noticed. His dimple was showing. One of the reporters said there was speculation around town of disagreement, a hung jury. In all major papers but the *World* the next day Becker was quoted as responding with small variations: "Disagreement? How could any juror vote to convict on the testimony of known criminals like that? They're the scum of the earth." There were no references to "racial slurs" or the euphemism "East Siders" in the other papers. In the *World*, the quotation from Becker ran:

"Why, you don't mean to say that any decent man is going to give any credit to the testimony of such dirty Jews as that crew?" And where the encounter was little more than a footnote in other papers, in the *World* it moved into the headline: "BECKER SAYS HE IS SATISFIED I'LL NEVER BE CONVICTED OF ANYTHING ON THE TESTIMONY OF THIS BUNCH OF DIRTY JEWS.'"

Presumably Becker had the standard prejudices of a second-generation German brought up in rural New York who had spent most of his adult life among city cops, reputed to be as down on nongentiles in 1912 as they would be on nonwhites fifty or sixty years later. In testimony before the aldermen's committee a few weeks later an informer reported that an inspector named Sweeney wouldn't touch any graft money that had come directly from Jewish sources, insisting on having it exchanged for other bills before including it in his graft hoard. And in the Lexow hearings a man named Morris Rosenfeld had testified that when he had complained to Becker's good friend Alexander Williams of being falsely arrested, Williams' answer had been: "You people killed Jesus Christ for the sake of a few pieces of silver. Get out of here. I will not take any complaints from sheenies at all."

In the privacy of his Tombs cell Becker presumably called the gambler witnesses ranged against him much worse names than "dirty Jews." But there is some question whether he would have used the phrase in public—deliberately, not in the heat of argument—to a dozen representatives of the press at a time when the jury was not yet chosen and, whatever his specifications, might well include Jews. He must have had some sense of needing public support in a city then close to 30 per cent Jewish. Becker hotly denied the *World*'s version of what he had said. "He declared," reported the New York *Globe* two days later, "that if this denial did not suffice he proposed to stand up in court and protest to the judge that he had made no such statement." "That alleged quotation," Becker told the *Globe*, "was absolutely without any basis of truth. It was a vicious and unjust act to place such words in my mouth."

At the trial's start several of the staider newspapers made an attempt to refer to the principal figures in the case by their correct names. But by the time they got through reporting the first days of testimony, clotted with references to Jacob Rosenzweig, Harry Vallinsky, Harry Horowitz, Jacob Seidenschner, and Louis Rosenberg, the built-in implications seemed to make them uneasy. There was also the problem of sorting out characters named Rosenthal, Rosenzweig, and Rosenberg, not to mention Beansey Rosenfeld, in paragraph after paragraph. (One reporter called the case the Second War of the Roses.) Like the other papers in town, they soon settled down to a cast of Jack Rose, Harry Vallon, Gyp the Blood, Lefty Louie, and the rest. This change simplified matters since throughout the trial the district attorney and Judge

Goff used the jazzier names. "Surely it must be a wonderful aid to the conviction of a man, presumed to be innocent, to have him described by the trial justice as 'Gyp the Blood,'" Gyp's defense attorney would protest in appealing the verdict of the following month that found all four gunmen guilty. He also took offense at having his clients referred to as "gunmen"—a word not even in the dictionaries, a word made up by the newspapers, he said. During the first full day of testimony at Becker's trial Lefty Louie grabbed the rail and complained of the use of his nickname, "stuck on me by them reporters." After court some of the reporters sought out the girl who had been captured with him in Queens. What was *her* name for him? "I always called him Mr. Rosenberg," she told them primly.

In his freshman quarters at Yale that week a young man named Lewis, later the world's greatest Horace Walpole scholar, brooded about *his* first name, Wilmarth, which he considered sissy. In New Haven as everywhere else the Becker trial was Topic A, and within a few days campus wags were calling him "Lefty." He didn't agree with his namesake about the degradation of the thing and was known as "Lefty Lewis" for the last fifty-seven years of his life. In his autobiography he wrote, "I am much in Lefty Louie's debt because the possession of a nickname is a gift beyond rubies."

District Attorney Whitman's hour-long opening statement was delivered on Thursday afternoon after the selection of the final member of the jury. In it he called Rosenthal's murder "the most cunning and atrocious of any time and in any country." "We will prove," he concluded, "that . . . the real murderer, the most desperate criminal of all, was the cool, calculating, scheming, grafting police officer." Becker, wearing a dark gray suit that hung on him loosely—he had thinned down in the Tombs—sat leaning back in his chair as he listened, his right arm over the chairback, his head slightly on one side. When it was over he turned and smiled across the room at his wife.

Helen Becker had on a blue silk suit with a white lace collar and cuffs and a beaver turban and looked "small, charmingly feminine, cheery," noted the *Tribune*. (The *World* thought her outfit looked more expensive than it should have.) "Most people who meet me are surprised after seeing my pictures in the papers," she told a reporter many months later. "They expect to find a great big woman, and often say: 'You are so different from what I thought you were.' And they take me for younger than I am. I have often been told that I look young. It must be my coloring and because I am slender, but I am not so terribly young." On this first day of trial testimony she was seated in a chair inside the rail leading to the judge's chambers. After Whitman's speech Judge Goff noticed she was in full view of the jury and ordered her to move to the other side of the room where they could not see her.

"In the courtroom I managed to control my feelings, although it was very hard at times," Helen Becker wrote later. "There was one day when I thought I should lose my strength and sink to the floor. It was when the judge called on me to change my seat so that the jury could not see me, and I had to walk across the room with everyone staring at me." At the age of thirty-eight after seven years of marriage, she was about five-and-a-half months pregnant with her first child. This fact, rather sad in view of the circumstances, had not become general knowledge. The newspapers never referred to it in their most detailed accounts of Becker's situation and constantly described her as "trim" and "slender."

Late in the afternoon Chief Inspector Schmittberger, fingering his large constabulary moustache, took the stand as a prosecution witness. As he gave his testimony about routine disbursals for gambling raid expenses he never once looked in the direction of his old enemy. When reporters asked him afterward how he felt about the reversal of their positions as witness and defendant, he "smiled enigmatically." Besides reporting this event as well as the testimony of the doctor and the cops at the scene of the murder, proving that a man had died violently, the newspapers were full of sidelights. Big Jack Zelig's funeral had been attended by 150 members of the Sam Paul Association wearing black sateen arm bands. A special background article in the *Times* discussed the urge to gamble and offered Carl Jung's thesis that to the American male gambling took the place of what in other countries was satisfied by—as the *Times* put it—"love of woman," at which the American male was not very good, Jung suggested. (The same article mentioned Sigmund Freud and his new theories, which the writer managed to describe without using the word "sex.") And in case New Yorkers thought they were the only folks preoccupied by the trial, the British correspondent of the *American* reported that "next to the war in the Balkans," the London press was now devoting its leading space to the Becker case.

Four times on Friday, the second day of testimony, the four gunmen, snarling and handcuffed together, followed Charles Whitman Indian file through the door from the Bridge of Sighs and lined up in front of the courtroom. The brilliant overhead lights came on and witnesses were asked to say whether these men were the ones who had killed Rosenthal. They were then led back to the Tombs, handcuffs clanking, until their next summons. The first of the identifying witnesses was Louis Krause, the hawk-nosed Hungarian waiter who had been on Forty-third Street on the murder night. He had testified at the coroner's hearing that he couldn't identify any of the gunmen. Now he was sure of all of them with maybe the exception of Dago Frank. How was it, McIntyre asked sarcastically, that he could now remember the gunmen's faces so well?

"I am a waiter. It is my business to remember faces," said Krause, scoring smartly. The *Times* congratulated him the next day on having put the defense counsel in his place. Krause testified again that Jacob Reich had been on the scene at the time of the shooting. Records of the D.A.'s office later revealed that the living expenses of Krause and his family were paid from the opening day of the first Becker trial until a week after the second, nineteen months later, and that for two years, beginning in late July 1912, he was on salary as a "research man" for Dr. Parkhurst's Society for the Prevention of Crime of which Assistant District Attorney Frank Moss was the current president. During most of the same period he was also on the district attorney's payroll as a process server.

Apparently suitable arrangements hadn't been made with the second identifying witness, Thomas Ryan, the taxicab driver who had hung around the Metropole to see what happened next. He agreed that he had promised Whitman he would identify at least one of the killers, but now he hesitated—and little wonder. A moment before, Lefty Louie had protested to Judge Goff over being dragged back and forth into the courtroom. He spoke, reported the *World*, "with lips drawn back until the white strong teeth glistened savagely . . . like some wild animal at bay."

"I don't want to identify the wrong man," said Ryan, backing away. "Everything happened very fast." For his sudden scruples the *World* described him as "yellow." Goff called him "obstreperous" and threatened to hold him in contempt of court.

The third identifying witness was Giovanni Stanich, an Austrian of uncertain means of livelihood but elegant bearing who had been talking to a prostitute a few steps from the corner of Forty-third Street and Broadway at the moment of the murder. Although the defense was later able to point out that this spot was over a hundred feet from Rosenthal, and Stanich admitted he hadn't been wearing his glasses and couldn't see well without them, he identified Whitey Lewis without the slightest trouble. When McIntyre asked if it were true that he had been given a check for twenty-five hundred dollars for testifying, the court properly had the question struck from the record.

The fourth identifying witness, Morris Luban, a small, beady-eyed young man who gave his occupation as "manufacturer of artificial flowers" and who would turn out to be the most obliging of all these early deponents for the state, unhesitatingly picked Dago Frank, Gyp the Blood, and Lefty Louie out of the four-man lineup. As Whitman questioned him further, the *Sun* noted that testimony had been taken for nearly a day and a half and the name of the actual defendant in the case had not yet been mentioned by a single witness.

The parading of the gunmen in and out of the courtroom was most likely done to establish the evil nature of the characters involved in the murder and, by showing them off within a few feet of Becker, to encourage the jury to think of him as part of the gang. The gunmen were an ugly looking crew and had not been favored with the special attentions of the tailors, barbers, and manicurists said to be in regular attendance on Bald Jack Rose and his fellow gamblers. The question before the court, however, was not whether the gunmen had killed Rosenthal but whether Becker had had a hand in it. McIntyre wasted endless time cross-examining the witnesses about their identification of the gunmen. He also protested loudly each time the gunmen were put on parade. "I'm afraid counsel is becoming trivial," Goff said to him. Finally he told McIntyre, "You may consider in each instance that you have made an exception and that I have overruled it. That will expedite matters." From the beginning of the testimony Goff alternately upheld Whitman's objections and overruled those of McIntyre. As he spoke to the defense counsel, reported the *Globe*, "he kind of dripped each word on McIntyre so that it foamed up a little before the next one fell."

Apparently it didn't occur to anyone that Whitman's reliance on the charade of the gunmen and other witnesses, whose only purpose was to identify them, suggested he was desperate for witnesses against Becker. The district attorney had stated several times that Rose, Webber, and Vallon's testimony before the grand jury had been supported by ten other witnesses. Certainly Morris Luban, the first witness to mention Becker's name at the trial, had not been one of the ten. He had arrived in the city in handcuffs only twenty-four hours before he took the stand.

Luban had a respectable brother in the artificial flower business, but his own line was actually somewhat different. He and another brother Jacob were members of a small-time gang of swindlers, and in the past half-dozen years had been arrested for fraud, check-kiting, and robbing apartment house mail boxes. In August 1912 they had been arrested and locked in the same jail cell in Newark on a forgery charge. A few weeks later Jacob Luban had sent the first of four letters to Becker in the Tombs. It just happened, wrote Jacob Luban, that early on the evening before the murder he had been at Sam Paul's place. Sam, Nathan Paul, his brother, and a few others were joined there by Jack Rose, Vallon, and Schepps, and before long Rose had said that Rosenthal ought to be croaked and immediately the others had said "they could all frame up Becker for it." (The verb "frame" took a preposition in 1912.) Luban would now be glad to testify to this effect, he wrote, if the defense could find some way to get him out of jail.

Becker's lawyers had turned Jacob Luban's proposition down on the theory that no jury would believe such a story from a man with his record, especially if he had been released from jail to testify. A few days before the trial started Luban tried again, this time sending a keeper at the prison to McIntyre's office to renew the offer. The lawyer showed him the door. Luban had then gotten in touch with Whitman. The district attorney had more—or less—faith in juries. He grabbed him.

The day before Morris Luban went on the stand, Whitman had sent a member of his staff, a boy just out of law school, over to the Essex County Jail to see what was up with this Luban. The young man talked to both brothers. "They were the very worst looking men I ever saw," he recalled when he was in his eighties. "They were abominable. They told me their awful stories, and I believed every word of them. How could I have believed such things? I went back and told Whitman. He was older and I think now he should have known better, but he seemed to believe them, too. Looking back on it now, it all seems incredible."

The evening before Morris Luban testified, he and his brother had been brought to New York where their jail cell was exchanged for a comfortable suite of rooms at the Broadway Central hotel. Unfortunately for Jacob Luban, all those letters were inconveniently in the hands of the defense (which eventually was allowed to mark them "for identification" though not to put them in evidence). Younger brother Morris therefore got the job of witness. When McIntyre later asked him in court whether he had been present when his brother had written to Becker offering to give evidence incriminating Bald Jack and the other prosecution witnesses, Justice Goff disallowed the question.

Morris Luban's testimony was wondrously helpful to the prosecution. He could easily identify the gunmen, he said, since he had happened to be standing just two feet behind Rosenthal when he was shot. He had been at the Metropole because he had taken a girl named Annie to Hammerstein's Victoria Theater that night and had stopped at the hotel afterward. (Annie would prove to be untraceable, Hammerstein's had been closed on the night of July 15, and the respectable artificial-flower-manufacturer brother would testify for the defense that Morris had spent the whole evening at a family gathering in Brooklyn. Asked what his brother's reputation was, he said, "Bad.")

But identifying the gunmen was only one of Morris Luban's contributions. Sometime before the murder, he said, he had happened to come into the steam room at the Lafayette Baths where he had found Lieutenant Becker and Bald Jack Rose sitting together on a bench, naked. Although the steam was dense, he had recognized Becker, having seen him once about ten months before during a raid on Denny Slyfox's stuss house. (The matter of identification was not complicated in those days by the prevalence of newspaper photographs. Few were printed, and those that appeared were so fuzzy they were hardly recognizable.) The naked policeman had greeted him politely, he said, and then had turned to Bald Jack and said: "If that bastard Rosenthal is not croaked, I will croak him myself." Five or six other men were nearby in the steam room and must also have heard the remark, Luban added.

The question of whether a veteran police officer would have so incriminated himself before so many total strangers did not seem to worry the prosecution. Their point about Becker was not that he was looney or that he was stupid. In Luban's account and in much of the prosecution testimony that followed the favorite theme was that the policeman had been drunk with power and had believed he could get away with anything.

McIntyre's cross-examination started with his pointed extraction of the fact that the little forger had been born in Odessa. He then inquired whether there had been any arrangement that the New Jersey charges against Luban were to be dropped in return for his testimony. (They were dismissed a few weeks later "because of assistance accorded the District Attorney of New York.") "When I came over here, I expected some favors," Luban agreed amiably. McIntyre tried to fix the date of the Lafayette Baths meeting. Luban said it could have been any time in June or maybe May or early July. The defense had its spies, and McIntyre asked if it weren't true that before Luban went on the stand he had been allowed to confer with Bald Jack Rose for several hours. The purpose, the defense attorney suggested, was to rehearse their stories and be sure there were no conflicts. (In fact there was a small slip-up. Luban testified he had known Jack Rose for twelve years. Rose said the next day that he'd never seen Luban before in his life.) Luban told McIntyre he hadn't been alone with Bald Jack for long: The district attorney had been with them much of the time.

"Mr. McIntyre, of course, could not accuse the District Attorney of having entered into a plot with Luban by which Luban was to testify falsely," noted the *Times* the next morning. A few minutes after Luban's remark about the district attorney, although McIntyre protested that he was not finished with the questioning, Justice Goff declared the cross-examination at an end and adjourned the court until the next day when the scheduled prosecution witness was Bald Jack Rose.

XIV

A sufferer from ulcers, John Goff made do with a bowl of milk and crackers and a swig of Irish whiskey at mealtimes, in court and out. He saw no reason to make allowances for others whose stomachs and appetites were stronger than his own. On Friday, the first full day of testimony, he had limited the noon recess to fifteen minutes. His personal thermostat was also less sensitive than that of ordinary men. All through the middle weeks of that October the weather was unseasonably warm. On Saturday, October 12, the day Bald Jack Rose was scheduled to testify for the prosecution, the temperature outdoors was in the high seventies. The courtroom was even more crowded than usual. People had been standing in line since 4 A.M. to have a chance at the few seats that weren't reserved for the prosecution, the defense, the press, and special friends of McIntyre, Goff, and the district attorney. Mrs. Whitman, a pleasant looking woman, was on hand, wearing a large picture hat and accompanied by Mrs. O. H. P. Belmont.

Some years earlier young Winston Churchill had attended a trial in this courtroom during a visit to New York. As a house guest of Bourke Cockran, the well-known Tammany Hall figure, he was seated on a special bench just below the judge. "Quite a strange experience and one which would be impossible in England," he wrote to his brother Jack. "The Judge discussing the evidence as it was given with me and generally making himself socially agreeable—& all the while a pale, miserable man was fighting for his life. This is a very great country, my dear Jack. Not pretty or romantic but great and utilitarian. . . . Take for instance the Courthouse. No robes or wigs or uniformed ushers. Nothing but a lot of men in black coats & tweed suits. Judge, prisoner, jury, counsel and warders all indiscriminately mixed. But they manage to hang a man all the same and that after all is the great thing."

There were electric fans now in the steamy chamber, but its acoustics were so poor the jurors had complained the day before of being unable to hear the witnesses, and Goff had ordered the fans cut off. When the sounds of horses' hoofs on the cobblestones and of children roller-skating had then drifted through the open windows, Goff had ordered them closed. This morning McIntyre asked whether the windows might be opened again. Goff refused. A moment later he gave a further order. "Have the shades drawn low," he said to one of Whitman's young assistants. When the man looked bewildered, Goff offered an excuse that would define his grotesque character to a generation of trial lawyers. "Have the shades drawn low," he said in his fierce whisper. "There is not enough gloom in the courtroom."

In his passion to move ahead Goff had insisted that the court meet this Columbus Day morning although, thanks to Big Tim Sullivan, it was a legal holiday. Bald Jack Rose took the stand, a symphony in medium dark blue, perfectly groomed, his head lightly powdered. Guided by Assistant District Attorney Frank Moss, he set about at once on an arraignment of Becker such as, said the *Times* the next day, "perhaps no other man on trial for murder or any other crime ever before was compelled to hear." With an occasional glance at the defendant, the gambler recounted how off and on during the weeks before the shooting (throughout the testimony Rose was very vague about dates) Becker had made numerous remarks to him about the need to get rid of Rosenthal. He had said, "The fellow is getting dangerous. . . . He ought to be put off the earth. . . . *There* is a fellow I would like to have croaked. . . ." A bit later he had told Rose, "Have him murdered, cut his throat, dynamite him, or anything. . . . Tell Zelig to issue an order from the Tombs to kill Rosenthal tonight and tomorrow [Zelig] will be out on the street." When the gang leader had balked, said Rose, Becker's line had been, "It begins to look like I will have to do the job myself." After that, said the gamblers, Becker had sent him to the gunmen directly to get them to pull the murder without orders from Zelig. "Don't be particular when you do it. . . . Break into his house and get him if you want. . . . Kill him anywhere. . . ."

"We doubt if there has ever been heard in an American court a story of such deadly greed, of such unconcern for human life," the *World* proclaimed the next day. Every few moments there would be a rhythmic interruption in the courtroom. McIntyre: "Objection." Goff: "Objection overruled." McIntyre: "Exception for the record."

Rose's brief affiliation with show business during his Connecticut years had not been wasted. When he quoted Becker, he played the part to the hilt—successively commanding, querulous, angry, hysterical, vicious. In quoting his own responses, however, Rose had no need for varied histrionics. By his own account he had always been the even voice of sanity. "Don't excite yourself, Charley" . . . "Why, I wouldn't do that, Charley" . . . "Why that is awfully dangerous, Charley."

Back in his Lexow days when Goff had had Harry Hill, proprietor of the notorious Haymarket dance hall, on the stand the witness had suddenly let his voice trail off as he described the wickedness of the New York police. "There is so much to tell. It takes too long," he said. "We will be patient," Goff had put in quickly. "You are holding the audience." There was no more rapt spectator than Justice Goff at Jack Rose's performance in the courtroom now as the imperturbable East Sider told the story of his relations with Rosenthal (always his good friend, he now insisted), of his urging Becker not to meet Rosenthal at the Elks' Club or go into business with him ("That's a dangerous thing, Charley"), of the long negotiations for the murder ("It's not a nice thing to murder someone, Charley").

Goff was half on his feet, craning his neck down from the podium as Rose described the evening before the murder: Rose's trip uptown with Vallon and Schepps in the hired gray touring car; the stop at the house where the gunmen lived and the discovery that only Dago Frank was there, the other gunmen having already been called downtown; the spur-of-the-moment decision to include Dago Frank in the shooting party; the trip back down to Forty-second Street with Frank now among the passengers; the arrival at Bridgey's where, on the sidewalk in the shadow of the Sixth Avenue el, the other three gunmen had stood talking with Sam Paul (who, it was generally assumed, had delivered them there); the adjournment upstairs where they had all had more drinks while Bridgey went looking for Herman. . . .

At one stage when Frank Moss broke into Rose's testimony and suggested that he get on to the next point, the judge turned on him with something like a snarl.

"Let the witness proceed," he said, leaning even further forward. Rose was holding his audience.

Yet all these details were irrelevent unless the prosecution could prove that Becker was responsible for the murder, however indirectly. He had never dealt with the actual murderers or even known when and where the murder was to take place, as the prosecution admitted. He had met at times with Rose but could claim this was on police business. He had had little to do with Webber, even less with Vallon, and may never have knowingly met Schepps in his life, as Schepps had suggested in his Hot Springs phase. Rose could report various hair-raising conversations with the policeman; the other gamblers could say they'd heard some of them. But this evidence was not enough to send a man to the chair. What had to be found (or constructed) was a meeting between Becker and the four gamblers (Schepps would have to be there to corroborate the admitted accomplices) at which the murder had been formally plotted. On the stand Bald Jack Rose now described such a meeting at the corner of 124 Street and Seventh Avenue. From then on it was known as "the Harlem conference."

Harlem had been almost rural up to the last quarter of the nineteenth century when it was annexed to the city. It had then been famous for harboring "hundred per cent Americans," citizens, that is, whose ancestors had shipped over from northern Europe a few generations before the Irish and the Jews had arrived at the great melting pot downtown. But after the subway was extended to Harlem in the nineties, its southern reaches had begun to fill up with Hester and Rivington Street Jews who were a little flusher than their old ghetto neighbors. It was this migration that had lured Herman Rosenthal and Beansey Rosenfeld to set up their gambling house in Harlem. Meanwhile members of New York's small Negro community had leapfrogged up from the West

Forties and were occupying Harlem's northern section. In 1915 Jewish leaders would hold a formal meeting with a Negro delegation and propose that a permanent line be drawn, that no black man thereafter should set up housekeeping south of 130 Street. The suggestion was poorly received and soon afterward the Jews would pull out in the direction of the Bronx. Already in 1912, followers of the Becker trial would learn, there was at least one Negro gambling house on West 124 Street. As they also learned, nothing but a vacant lot stood at the northeast corner of 124 Street and Seventh Avenue, which before long would be part of the Times Square of black Harlem.

Sometime in mid-June, or possibly early July, Rose testified, Becker had phoned one night and asked Rose to meet him half a block from the colored gambling house on West 124 Street, which his strong arm squad was about to raid. Rose was to bring along Webber, who, Rose had assured the lieutenant, had considerable influence over the gunmen. Nothing wrong with bringing Vallon too, said Becker (according to Rose). Rose and Vallon had hired a car and driven up to Harlem about 9:30 P.M. Webber came along in another hired car a few minutes later, bringing Schepps, whose presence allegedly didn't bother Becker either.

"We all stood at the vacant lot, sat on a board across the vacant lot, talking about Rosenthal," Rose testified. "Becker said to Webber, 'Bridgey, why don't you help Rose in that thing and have that fellow croaked.'" But Webber had said he didn't want to "lay himself liable" to the gunmen. "There is no laying liable to anybody or anything," was Becker's reply to Webber. "There is nothing going to happen to anybody that has any hand in the croaking of Rosenthal," he continued. "See that this thing is done for me, will you?" And, according to Rose, Webber had answered, "Leave it to me now. The job will be done and done quick." Their conference over, the gamblers had then all got into their cars and driven back downtown, leaving the "cool, calculating, scheming . . . police officer" perhaps to ponder the fact that he had just laid himself liable to four of the most unprincipled thugs in town.

"Nobody connected with the prosecution or trial of the defendant has doubted that this conference was the very foundation upon which was built the theory of defendant's guilt," read the Court of Appeals decision in the case sixteen months later, "for there it was that he, as claimed, definitely enlisted the aid of

Rose, Webber, and Vallon in the plan for the murder of Rosenthal, and in accordance with which such murder was finally consummated. It would be idle to discuss for a moment the guilt of defendant under the present prosecution unless this conference did take place."

Bald Jack insisted on the stand that Becker had also conferred with his murder agents after the crime, that he'd turned up "all smiles" and talked to Rose and Webber in front of the Murray Hill Baths, just a few steps west of Bridgey's pool parlor on Forty-second Street. He had just come from the Forty-seventh Street station, he told them. With relish Bald Jack repeated on the stand the lieutenant's remark about how he had felt as he viewed Rosenthal's body. "It was pleasant for me to look and to see that squealing Jew bastard there and if it was not for the presence of District Attorney Whitman I would have reached down and cut his tongue out and hung it on the Times building as a warning to future squealers."

The Murray Hill Baths meeting had posed special problems for the prosecution. When Rose first described it for the grand jury (according to the excerpts from his testimony released by Whitman) and when he was interviewed by Swope a few days after Becker's indictment, he described Becker as saying on his apartment phone that he would come right down and meet the boys below Bridgey's place. He had met them maybe half an hour later, Rose reported, and had then left, saying he was going to the station house. But soon after he told the story this way Rose had remembered—or someone had suggested to him—the ghoulish remark about the dead man's tongue. This meant that Becker would have had to visit the station house *before* meeting the gamblers. The time schedule had been hastily amended. Rose now swore, as he had stated in his *World* confession, that Becker had arrived in front of the Murray Hill Baths several hours after the murder, "about daybreak," that is when he would have been even more visible to passersby.

Another problem Whitman had with the Murray Hill Baths meeting was that no one but Bald Jack seemed to have it clearly in mind. Jacob Reich, whom Rose had at first named as a witness to the scene and who had admittedly been with Webber in the hours after the murder, denied from first to last that Becker had appeared on Forty-second Street that morning, early or late. Rose explained this lack of corroboration by saying that at the moment Becker strolled up Reich had happened to turn away to talk to an East Side acquaintance who happened to be passing by. What threatened to be even more troublesome for the prosecution was the fact that back in August a reporter from the *Times* who was allowed to talk to the gamblers in their cells (an interview that caused Whitman once again to ban the press from the West Side Prison, except, of course, for Swope) had found Bridgey Webber extremely unreliable on the subject. Rose kept mentioning the meeting on Forty-second Street, wrote the *Times* man, and Webber kept forgetting about it. Finally Bridgey had said, "Keep me out of this. I can't remember being there at all." "Then, after a talk with Rose," said the reporter, "Webber recollected the meeting. He forgot again on several occasions . . . but each time the bald-headed gambler cut short his protestations and each time Webber's memory returned to him." Fortunately for the prosecution, when Webber took the stand the day after Rose, he would recall the meeting letter perfectly.

Rose was on the stand from ten in the morning till adjournment for lunch about one-thirty. At half past two (Goff had been more generous than usual) court reconvened for McIntyre's cross-examination, which continued without a break for nearly six and a half hours.

In the view of Lloyd Paul Stryker, the young defense counsel who sat beside Becker throughout the trial and wrote about the case four decades later in *The Art of Advocacy*, McIntyre's examination, as he had mapped it out, was brilliantly designed to discredit the witness by his own deeds and words. Each question, as he had planned it, "searched some dark chamber of this rascal's life, reached into the putrid cesspool of his past, turned the light upon his meanness, his depravity and his crimes." But Justice Goff, fawning upon Rose as Stryker described it, constantly interfered with the blocked-out scenario. When McIntyre's questions turned the light on Rose's murky past as a part-time embezzler and full-time pimp (his current wife was said to be one of his former clients) the judge leaned down and suggested that the witness might well plead the Fifth Amendment to this kind of thing, and Rose shook off all such questions from then on. Goff also declined to allow the gambler's *World* confession and other earlier statements to be put into evidence so significant variations in his account of Becker's part in the crime could be brought to the jury's attention.

Not everyone, however, agreed with Stryker that McIntyre's performance had been so brilliant or that Rose had seemed much in need of rescue. The defense attorney, his fat thumbs in his galluses, declaiming in his florid style, haggled endlessly with Rose in an effort to disprove the statement that the gambler had called Becker on the phone soon after the murder although, as the Court of Appeals later pointed out, why wouldn't he have called him—Becker would naturally have found the news of interest. (What *was* significant was the fact that Rose had deliberately made the call not to Becker's unlisted number, which the lieutenant agreed he had given him for his stool pigeon reports, but to the switchboard in Becker's apartment house, thus making sure he left a record.) McIntyre also wasted his usual quarter of an hour getting the witness to admit that he had been born in Poland. After that "Mr. McIntyre became very dramatic and talked about the value of a human life and tried to make the witness feel that he had done a dreadful thing in helping along the work of taking a life," reported the *Times* without admiration. "But Rose, unmovable as a Chinese god, gave no sign that the picture touched him in the least."

Had the witness felt the slightest remorse when he saw the gunmen leave Webber's to take a human life? Rose: "I guess not." Why at some stage in the plot had he not gone running through the streets crying "Murder! Foul murder!" Rose, shrugging his shoulders: "Not in that part of the world I frequented is there anybody that would have paid any attention to me." When Becker had said it looked as if he would have to do the murder himself, why had Rose not simply let him do it? Rose, shrugging again: "I did not try to stop him." It was not really a pertinent answer, but McIntyre couldn't seem to find a way to point this out. He did score in one instance. The existence of the immunity agreements was not yet general knowledge, and Goff had not allowed the defense to put them in the record. Rose denied that he had been given any immunity. But he remarked in answer to one question that he had often tried to get into a respectable business "and I will do the same again." McIntyre looked at him for a long moment.

"Then you expect to get out of jail?" he asked. Over at the defense table Charles Becker smiled for the only time that afternoon. The jury looked confused. Goff disallowed the question.

"He continued without a break or a request for an indulgence until six in the evening," Stryker wrote of McIntyre. "I shall never forget that afternoon. It was a steaming day and in a stifling courtroom, hour after hour, our chief counsel relentlessly pressed on. His collar wilted and sweat streamed down his face as he confronted one of the worst men who ever lived." At six o'clock McIntyre requested an adjournment. Goff told him to proceed. He plodded on for another two and a half hours. "Cold, calculated, deliberate oppression," Stryker called it.

One of Justice Goff's curious attributes was that he had the continence of a camel. McIntyre did not. He had been forced to stay on his feet in the courtroom since two-thirty in the afternoon without a chance to go to the men's room and was beginning noticeably to fidget. Possibly distracted, he seemed unable to depart from his script and in the long, long session never got around to asking Rose a single question about the most crucial point of all, the Harlem conference. He spent twenty valuable minutes, for example, battling with the witness to get him to define the word "lobbygow," in order to suggest that Schepps, the corroborator—generally known as Rose's lobbygow or errand boy—would have done or said anything Rose told him to. At ten minutes to nine McIntyre leaned heavily on the counsel table and told Goff he could not go on.

"Nonsense, you are stronger than you were this morning," Goff jeered. The court would stay in session for as long as McIntyre needed, he said. He could cross-examine for another three hours if he liked. Nothing could be fairer than that.

"I am physically exhausted. . . . I have had to go without my dinner. I have been on my feet six hours. It is against the interest of justice for me to go on," McIntyre told him in a strangled voice. John Hart jumped to his feet and offered to take over.

"Sit down, young man," said Goff, waving him aside.

"I cannot ask another question. My mind will not work as it should," McIntyre told him.

"If there are no more questions, the witness is dismissed," said Goff and declared the cross-examination at an end.

The Rosenthal murder case, and particularly Bald Jack Rose's revelations at various stages of it, gave the American public its first glimpse of a criminal underworld whose existence would be a commonplace assumption a few years later. The day after Bald Jack testified the *Evening Post* declared that what had to be faced was the fact that "murder is a trade in this city." Where in Rose's testimony, they asked, was "the sacred horror which, according to tradition, besets the most perverted soul at the thought of taking human life? Where . . . was the aftermath of remorse? The fact seems to be that the people of this city and state must deal with a class in which the intuitive horror of shedding blood does not function." The *Times* devoted half its front page and all of three inside pages to Rose's testimony. More than anything else, they said, Rose's picture of Becker "gloating over the body of the dead Rosenthal in the back of the West Forty-seventh Street station delivered a smashing blow to the battlements of the defense."

The same observers were openly disappointed in the next prosecution witness, who took the stand the following Monday. "Webber in many ways failed to achieve the standard as a witness set by Jack Rose," ran the *Times* review. Like most of the local press, their commitment to the reliability of the chief prosecution witnesses was by now shameless. Krause, the Hungarian waiter, had testified he had seen Webber running away from the crime scene. Bridgey denied that he had been anywhere near there. "Perhaps Krause was mistaken," commented the *Times*. Or, they suggested tolerantly, Webber "must have forgotten his presence at the tragedy in his excitement. . . . In any case, it was a trivial point."

Like Rose, Webber claimed to have played the part of the gentle dissuader. ("It's a pretty hard thing, Charley, to have a man murdered.") But he mentioned without prompting that about an hour after the murder he had hired a barouche and driven to the Forty-seventh Street station where he had had a look at Rosenthal's body. Although he was apparently on hand before Becker, the defense made no more of this pilgrimage than Whitman had in the station that night just before he came to the positive conclusion that Becker's appearance there proved his guilt. Nor did McIntyre belabor Webber for his remark on the stand that he'd never been afraid of Becker. The witness also "must have forgotten" that the only reason the gamblers presumably had for commissioning the murder was their terror of the police lieutenant. As for the Harlem conference, Webber said it had taken place about eleven o'clock one night (he had looked at his watch at the time) but he couldn't even give a guess as to the date.

Unlike the press, Goff had been so fascinated by Webber's performance that he proposed to have the court sit right through the luncheon recess. The jury showed spunk and insisted on some respite, but Goff then kept them in their seats till nearly seven-thirty that evening, by which time the third gambler-witness, Harry Vallon, had finished testifying.

Vallon was small, furtive-eyed, and nattily dressed like Webber, for whom he'd worked most of his life. There was a rumor around town that Vallon had fired one of the shots at Rosenthal, even that he had started the shooting. The gamblers' plan, the story went, had been not to kill Rosenthal on the spot but to kidnap him and then decide what to do with him. Hence the failure to cover the license plate: in "the part of the world they frequented" abduction wasn't a crime to skulk around about. Vallon had been drunk, some said, and had changed the plot on his own. The day he was arrested Vallon had told reporters in the district attorney's presence that he had been very drunk that night. On the stand he was sure he had been sober. He had been on Forty-third Street but nowhere near the Metropole at the moment of the murder. He had met Becker perhaps four times before the Harlem conference. He had no idea of either the hour or the date of the Harlem meeting.

Vallon's testimony was dismissed at the time as having added nothing to that of Rose and Webber. Although, like Webber, he swore the three of them had never discussed their testimony, the *Evening Post* observed the next day that "the mechanical similarity of their stories was so marked that it inevitably suggested rehearsal." But Vallon added one hardly noticed remark that would be enough to send Charles Becker to the chair. While he had stood in the Harlem lot talking to Rose and Becker and waiting for Bridgey to arrive in another car, he said, "Becker was telling us he was going to raid a crap game. There was a little colored boy on the other side of the street, and he called him over and spoke to him."

Each day of the trial the crowds of people unable to get into the courtroom were so large that special police reserves were assigned to keep order. After each day's adjournment the crowds would surge outside and wait beneath the Bridge of Sighs to catch a glimpse of Becker on his way to the Tombs. Helen Becker sat in court every day, well out of sight of the jury. Sometimes she was allowed to exchange a few words with her husband as he moved toward the door to the Tombs, but Goff specified that this could not happen until the jury had filed out.

When Sam Schepps took the stand, he looked startlingly respectable. He was wearing a new pair of rimless glasses on a black ribbon that made him look more like a prosperous department store auditor than a man recurrently dependent on Bald Jack for sandwich money. On cross-examination Schepps admitted he had done some opium smuggling in his time, seeming rather pleased at this indication of his versatility. McIntyre also brought out that he had been born in Austria. (Webber and Vallon had been born in New York, but the defense counsel had got them to admit that their parents were from southeastern Europe.) Schepps' performance was cool, shrewd, and smart-alecky. (McIntyre: "Where did you stop?" Schepps: "We didn't stop, the car stopped.") The district attorney and the court were so protective of him that at one point when Whitman objected to McIntyre's tone, Goff sharply reprimanded McIntyre for being impertinent to the prosecution witness.

But what counted was whether Schepps qualified as the necessary corroborator, the witness who had heard and seen enough to prove that the other gamblers were telling the truth without hearing and seeing so much that he could be branded an accomplice. Bobbing and weaving deftly, Schepps swore that he had never heard any of the discussion about Rosenthal on the Sam Paul outing, being too busy shooting craps. Later that Sunday evening he had had supper at Luchow's with Vallon and Rose, but when they'd started to talk about the Rosenthal thing he had gone out and stood on the sidewalk. Although he had spent the evening before the murder traveling around the city with Vallon and Rose, had made the call summoning the murder car, and had rung the bell at Dago Frank's, Schepps had never heard any discussion of murder in all that time. What had they all talked about then, as the gamblers and later Dago Frank drove about the city? "Oh, the sun came up and the clouds were in the sky and things like that," said Schepps airily. At Bridgey's later the only discussion had been over what to have to drink. Hadn't he been in the least suspicious when Webber came back and said, "Herman's at the Metropole," and the gunmen went lunging out?

"No, why should I be suspicious?" asked Schepps, with a bored look around the room.

For three months before the murder he had carried money and messages from Rose to the gunmen, but he'd never wondered what they did for a living. It was true that he had gone uptown to see them in the early morning after the murder and had made an appointment to have them paid off later in the day, but he hadn't carried the money—Bald Jack had done that. At the Harlem conference he had stood a block away—on second thought more like half a block—so he could see who was there but not hear what they said. On the trip downtown, although Webber and Vallon had presumably just heard a murder proposed for the first time, nobody mentioned it. It was the sun coming up and the clouds in the sky again and "maybe the topics of the day." As for when the meeting had occurred, it might have been in June. Or May. "There is no use in asking me questions about time. . . . Time means nothing to me. I don't keep track of days, months, years."

Justice Goff did not permit McIntyre to put into the record for the purpose of cross-examination the court depositions taken from Hot Springs citizens quoting Schepps' unfortunate remarks in the days before the prosecution had set him straight. He was not allowed to ask about Schepps' statement that he'd probably said three words to Becker in his life (on the stand he testified he'd visited Becker at his office and even his home numerous times) or his remarks to the Hot Springs postmaster that "I don't want you to think of me as a common murderer," that, after all, Rosenthal had been only "a dirty cur," that all would have gone well but "the great mistake that was made was in not covering the license number of the car." (Days later, when the crucial moment had passed, Goff suddenly admitted the depositions to the record.)

A witness Whitman sent in after Schepps was too much even for Goff. He was a young man named Max Margolies, a newspaper tipster and part-time stool pigeon whose testimony was not about the murder itself but Becker's familiarity with Rosenthal's gambling house. Cross-examination about his past career brought the admission that he had committed perjury in his stool pigeon days "but Becker made me do it." When the defense offered some documents to discredit Margolies, Goff brushed them aside. "The witness has discredited himself," he said contemptuously.

Except for Morris Luban, allegedly present at the remarkable scene between Rose and Becker in the Lafayette steam room, the only prosecution witness other than the four gamblers who gave testimony linking Becker to the murder in either word or deed was James Hallen, the Sing Sing prisoner who claimed to have overheard the self-incriminating conversation between Becker and a member of his strong arm squad in the Tombs. It did not add to Hallen's credibility that on the stand he read Becker's supposed statement from a piece of legal foolscap on which, he insisted, he just happened to have jotted the words down at the time.

In February 1914 the New York Court of Appeals would reject Luban and Hallen's testimony out of hand. ". . . Luban . . . was produced for the purpose of the trial by the criminal authorities of a neighboring state where he was confined in jail. . . . After being brought to New York and before going on the stand this witness, in a manner which we cannot but regard as significant, was given an opportunity for conference with Rose, the chief witness for the prosecution, and who was immediately to follow him upon the stand. Their evidence was entirely harmonious. Another witness, Hallen, was a degenerate lawyer and convict who also was temporarily delivered from jail to be a witness. In addition to the impeachment of their evidence furnished by their character and by the direct contradiction of other witnesses, much of the testimony of these men is, as it seems to us, inherently improbable and subject to suspicion."

XV

"I have absolutely no fear that Jerome's testimony will discredit Rose," Whitman announced the day before the defense began to present its case. *Someone* was worried, however. On Whitman's motion, the former district attorney's testimony was cut short before he'd done much more than give his name. When he started to protest, Justice Goff snarled, "Not another word!" and ordered his old Lexow comrade to leave the stand. Jerome stepped down, his eyes blazing.

At first glance Jerome's role in the case seemed highly peripheral. During the two days before the murder John Hart, Becker's lawyer, had called his old chief several times for advice about how the policeman should respond to Rosenthal's statements in the *World*. A libel suit was an enormous expense. Did Jerome think the thing could be handled by getting affidavits that would refute Rosenthal's story? Jerome thought it might. On Wednesday, the day after the murder, Hart asked Jerome if he would talk to Becker directly, and Jerome said all right.

The two lawyers had dinner at Delmonico's, then strolled west on Forty-fourth Street to the Bar Association building where Becker joined them in a private conference room. The murder was barely mentioned that evening, according to the three men. What worried Becker was the graft charge that threatened his police career. Obviously a statement from Bald Jack Rose admitting his part in the mortgage deal would be helpful. In the affidavit sworn to later that evening before a notary public and John Hart, Rose stated that during February 1912 he had given Rosenthal several thousand dollars in return for 25 per cent of the profits on the Forty-fifth Street house, that in March Rosenthal had asked for another fifteen hundred and Rose had also provided this sum. However, he'd been nervous about the last investment, he said, and had done it through a dummy, explaining to Rosenthal that the fellow he'd got to put up the cash had insisted on a chattel mortgage as security. Rose's affidavit added that he'd heard Rosenthal say he'd break Becker for raiding him as he'd broken cops before. When McIntyre later cross-examined Rose about this sworn statement, the gambler said it was all lies, perjury if McIntyre insisted. He had signed whatever he'd signed, only because Becker had made him sign.

Jerome agreed later that at the Bar Association conference, learning what kind of a fellow Rose was, he'd advised Becker to get the affidavit fast before someone else got to him. Sitting at Jerome's elbow, the policeman had lifted the receiver in the room and called the number vaudeville hoofer Pollack had given him earlier that day. When a woman's voice answered, Becker asked for Rose and, as the other men listened, greeted him by name when he came on. He explained about the affidavit, and the man on the other end agreed to the project. Becker told him his lawyer, Hart, would be up later that evening with a notary public, and the conversation was over. Jerome was ready to testify that it had taken two minutes at most.

In his *World* confession and later on the witness stand, however, Rose had reported quite another conversation, following the arrangement about the affidavit. Not knowing that a former district attorney had been present at the other end, he had described a long, significant exchange that the defense estimated would have taken fifteen or twenty minutes. In the course of it, according to Rose, Becker had told him, "Why, there's two hundred policemen looking for you." This contradicted the defense contention that Rose had not been on the police "Wanted" list at the time as far as Becker knew. Rose's account therefore accused a police officer as well as Hart, a member of the bar, of being in clandestine touch with a known fugitive. The defense would argue that Hart and Becker had unsuccessfully scoured the nearby Harvard Club for a notary public and that Hart had finally gone to the rendezvous accompanied by a notary who was a total stranger he and Becker had found in a West Side cigar store—a move they would hardly have made if they had been contemplating an action they knew to be criminally chargeable.

Bald Jack's version of Becker's end of the conversation also included a series of incriminating remarks advising Rose to lie low, promising him he would be protected, and other lines suitable to the leader in a murder conspiracy. Jerome's testimony that the conversation had never taken place would have cast suspicion on all of Rose's accusations against Becker, most of which were based on accounts of conversations reported only by Rose and his confederates. Goff ruled Jerome's testimony out on the ground that, although the former district attorney had listened while the policeman asked for Rose and a man answered, he could not swear that the other man's voice had been that of Bald Jack.

The next defense witness, also a prominent New Yorker, was also made to feel unwanted. As he explained later, Rhinelander Waldo took the stand to testify that Becker had had nothing to do with stationing the police guard in Rosenthal's house, that he himself had ordered Inspector Hayes to do this. Waldo had other information to contribute. Faced with the reiteration by the defense that it would have been madness for Becker to plot to kill Rosenthal just when the gambler had so sensationally attacked him, when suspicion would be bound to fall on him, Whitman had relied on the motive of greed. Becker, he explained, was in a panic that Rosenthal's carrying-on would ruin gambling in New York and thus cut down his ill-gotten gains on the strong arm squad. But Waldo was ready to testify that, far from being comfortable in his assignment in the weeks before the murder, Becker had twice come to him, mentioned that he seemed to be in a spot where people were trying to get him into trouble and asked to be assigned elsewhere. Waldo's appearance ended abruptly. Goff ruled that all such testimony was irrelevant to the murder charge.

McIntyre had announced that he had no intention of giving out his list of defense witnesses since the district attorney would immediately call them in and threaten them with some trumped-up indictment, "and I've lost too many witnesses that way." Whitman was plainly taken by surprise by the next man who took the stand for the defense. In cross-examining, noted the *Post*, the district attorney's voice "shook throughout the first question. It was the most dramatic incident of the trial."

The witness who caused this distress was Frederick Hawley, the young police reporter for the *Sun* who had called Becker on the phone on the night of the murder. He now testified that he had been with the policeman steadily from about three-thirty till eight o'clock that morning, which meant, if true, that Becker could not have met Rose and Webber at Sixth Avenue and Forty-second Street to congratulate them on a job well done. In cross-examination Hawley said he had told his city editor of this fact but had not gone to anyone in authority. "I did not care to have the District Attorney know what I was going to testify to," he said, looking Whitman in the eye.

"That is the most insulting statement ever made in an American court," said Whitman. In a rage, he asked to be sworn in himself and declared on the stand that he had seen Becker in the station house at 3:30 A.M. and had not seen him there after four so that Becker had had plenty of time to meet with the gamblers. The prosecution's summing up would simply brush aside the reporter's account. Before Whitman stepped down from the stand, however, McIntyre took advantage of the unusual fact that he had the district attorney under oath.

"Did you promise Jack Rose immunity from prosecution if he would testify against Becker?" he asked.

"I did not," said Whitman. Rose had only signed "the usual legal stipulation."

There was a penalty for testifying for the defense in the Becker case. The following day Hawley's employers inserted a short notice in their publication. "Frederick M. Hawley," it read, "is no longer a member of the staff of the *Sun*." The same afternoon Whitman told the press he planned a grand jury investigation of Hawley's testimony and confidently expected an indictment for perjury. That was the last heard of the matter.

Hours of the defense case were given over to testimonials by character witnesses for Becker including, ostentatiously, a number with Jewish names. Members of the police force upheld the defense version of various incidents (and were denounced in the closing prosecution statement as officers who had thereby betrayed the public trust). No defense witnesses refuted the story of the Harlem conference. The vagueness of the prosecution witnesses about when it had taken place prevented the defense from offering any countering evidence—which presumably was the reason for their vagueness. But several East Side witnesses were ready to cite remarks Rose, Webber, or Vallon had made long before the murder about their hatred of Rosenthal and their plans to put him six feet under. "It would have strained credulity to the breaking point to believe that those involved in the present case went about public streets telling comparative strangers that they were about to kill Rosenthal," was the comment of the *World*, whose credulity had been more flexible in the case of similar remarks by Charles Becker.

The most important witness for the defense was Jacob Reich or, as he was still usually referred to, Jack Sullivan. There was a recurrent problem of sorting out not only the Roses in the case but the Sullivans—Jack, lawyer James, as well as Big Tim, who, though unmentioned at the trial, was not out of the minds of many of the principals. Reich was a short, burly man with the face of a bulldog and two odd bald spots at the front of his head that, even before he opened his mouth to testify for Becker, reminded the *Times* reporter of "two little red horns." He and the other East Siders in the case, including Rosenthal and Sam Paul, were all in their late thirties and had known each other in grammar school and, in most cases, reform school. Unlike the others, Reich had not gone into gambling. His line, as he was forever boasting, was newspapers. As a young man, he had hired on as a bodyguard for William Randolph Hearst. Later he had worked in the circulation departments of several city newspapers and then set up a central system for distributing the papers to the newsboys who in 1912 hawked their wares on every busy corner. In 1905 he had raised money to found a local shelter called the Home for Newsboys. "Are you sometimes referred to in the newspapers as the King of the Newsboys?" McIntyre asked him on the stand. "That is the truth. I am the Founder. I am the King," said Reich, beaming. Moving in and out of newspaper circulation rooms he had met many reporters who then used him as a point of contact with the East Side, where he had kept in touch with his boyhood friends. He had then bragged to the latter about his newspaper connections and his inside knowledge of what was going on in important places such as the D.A.'s office and Police

Headquarters. Like the best man at his wedding, Herman Rosenthal, Reich was a talker and a self-important busybody.

The major difference between him and his old Second Avenue buddies, as he told it, was a small foible: He did not hold with murder. In the spring of 1912 he had gone to several of his newspaper friends with a story that Bridgey Webber had quarreled with his uptown gambling partner, Jew Brown, and was planning to have him waylaid and killed. The reporters came nosing around, which gave Reich time to hustle Jew Brown onto a transatlantic steamer, so he said. (Jew Brown *had* left for Europe in some haste that spring.) As Reich told it, his intervention was the reason that Webber and the other gamblers in the case had made sure not to let him in on their plan to murder Rosenthal. "I stopped one murder, and I wish I could of stopped this one," he said fervently on the stand.

Sometime in late June, he went on to testify, Rosenthal had come to him and asked for help in persuading newspapers to print stories about his problems with the police, especially Inspector Hayes. The gambler wasn't satisfied with Reich's results and had eventually gone to Swope. Reich had seen Rosenthal after the *World* statement appeared and tried to persuade him to take back what he'd said about Becker. Reich had known Becker maybe seven years though never well enough to call him by his first name, he said. He had gone back and forth between the two men several times but Herman had been stubborn. What had made Bald Jack Rose a specially vindictive enemy of Herman's, he further testified, were Mrs. Rosenthal's frequent references to his wife's having formerly been a prostitute ("Why doesn't Hattie go back to her old business?").

Reich was not only the most important witness for the defense but also the most enthusiastic. He had many things stored up to say and was so indignant when Judge Goff repeatedly refused to let him say most of them that, as the *Post* put it, "Goff would probably have committed Sullivan for contempt if it didn't seem foolish to commit for contempt a man already in jail, charged with murder in the first degree." Unlike the rhythmic interruptions in the prosecution phase of the case, those in the defense's behalf consisted of Whitman's "Objection!" and Goff's swift, hissing "Objection *sustained*." At one point he disallowed eighteen successive questions put to Reich by McIntyre. Toward the end of the case, however, Whitman or Goff apparently began to worry about the look of the record for appeal purposes—the enormous leeway given Rose, Webber *et al.* and the virtual muzzling of Reich, often in testimony about the same conversations and events. On the last day of the trial Goff called Reich back to the stand and ordered McIntyre to ask the questions Goff had previously excluded. But momentum and cumulative effect in courtroom examination are believed to be crucial, and McIntyre said this last-minute addendum wouldn't be the same thing at all. Goff then directed the prosecution to put the questions for the defense. In this backhanded way some of Reich's frustration was relieved, and the audience in the courtroom got a startling glimpse of life among the state's witnesses in the People vs. Becker.

Reich testified that he had been in the Tombs, held then only as a material witness, on July 29, the day of Becker's indictment. He had seen Rose, Vallon, Webber, and their lawyers conferring "like a big bargain and sale," and had himself been approached by an assistant district attorney offering him immunity if he would testify against Becker. The morning after the indictment he had bawled Rose out. Rose had defended himself, saying that he was facing the electric chair, "that the newspapers were yelling for Becker, that Whitman wants Becker, that giving them Becker was the only way to beat it." "Leave me alone, my head is busting. I would frame Waldo, the Mayor, anybody to get out of here," Reich said Rose had told him as he packed up to move from the Tombs to the West Side Prison.

Early in August Reich had been shifted suddenly from the Tombs to the comparative luxury of Whitman's Ritz where Rose, Vallon, and Webber were taking their ease. "He was transferred . . . probably to permit Rose and Webber to persuade him that the best course lay in telling all he knew to Mr. Whitman," the *Times* had suggested the day after the transfer. What the district attorney had badly needed was corroboration for the Murray Hill Baths meeting with Becker, and the gamblers had promised Whitman they would talk him into providing this. They went after him, Reich now testified, in marathon sessions in the general rumpus room, otherwise known as the prison counsel chamber. Webber told him, Reich said, that the word from Whitman was "if I corroborated the story of Becker meeting the crowd I would go free. I said to him sure, perjure myself and go free. I tell the truth and get soused in jail." Webber had reminded him over and over, "We're all Jews, stick with us. Becker is a Dutch bastard," Reich testified. But he had held out.

"Unless Jack Sullivan concludes to be a witness for the state, I do not see how it would be possible to withhold an indictment against him," Whitman had announced the week he sent Reich to join the other East Siders, although the only evidence against Reich ever made public was waiter Krause's testimony that he had been among the thirty or forty men in front of the Metropole immediately after the crime. ("He had to say that—how else could he frame me?" was Reich's comment on the stand.)

On August 12, as Reich continued to resist the D.A.'s suggestion, a formal letter from Whitman's office, signed by Frank Moss, was delivered to him in his cell. It did not refer to his recalcitrance, but began: "I deem it my duty to inform you that the evidence already submitted to the grand jury would justify that body in indicting you for the Rosenthal murder." The jury would make its decision the next day, said the letter. When he read it, Reich said, he told Rose and Webber, "I wouldn't swear a man's life away . . . I'll rot in jail first."

The D.A. gave him his chance to do so. The following day Reich was transferred back to the Tombs. He was one of the seven men in the case indicted a week later for first-degree murder. He would remain in his Tombs cell until May 1913. When he was released Whitman's office announced that his murder trial would begin shortly. He was never tried, but the murder indictment against him stayed on the books for twenty-five years. Reich's motives in the case were never clear. Would a successful businessman by East Side standards have spent ten months in the Tombs out of loyalty to a man he knew only slightly? If he was paid off, who put up the money? After Reich was released he went to work as a distributor for the *Saturday Evening Post*, showing no signs of unexplained affluence. It is possible that the reason for his dogged support of Becker at the expense of a ruined year of his life was no more or less than the one he gave on the stand: "I couldn't stand to see any man get such a raw deal from those lying bums." Whoever was lying, Reich, at any rate, had not testified as he had in return for favors at the disposal of the district attorney.

The most dramatic event of the last day of testimony was the appearance of Shapiro, the murder-car chauffeur. Scheduled as a defense witness, he was expected to testify that, as he had often said in the weeks after the crime, both Vallon and Schepps had been riding in the car as it sped away from the Metropole. This testimony would have been particularly inconvenient in view of the prosecution's claim that Schepps was a certified nonaccomplice. In the late morning of the final trial day, court adjourned early on Whitman's motion. When everyone returned, it developed that in the interim Shapiro had been granted immunity by the grand jury, convened by Justice Goff. Now, transformed into a rebuttal witness for the prosecution, Shapiro denied that the two important state witnesses had been anywhere near the murder car after the crime. Since his lawyer, Aaron Levy, had been on hand for the final negotiations that had ended with Becker's indictment, it seems probable that his conversion had been plotted months before. *Five* formal immunity agreements might have seemed rather much, and this present maneuver took care of the matter nicely. Speculation immediately spread that the first-degree murder indictment against Shapiro would now be dismissed, and it eventually was.

From his Tombs cell Becker had sent word the day before that he looked forward to taking the stand. McIntyre now told the press, however, that he had decided this move wasn't necessary. The state's case had failed. Who would believe three self-confessed murderers and two convicts (Luban and Hallen)? Besides, he admitted to reporters, if he put the police officer on the stand there would be questions about grafting. When the jury was being chosen, McIntyre had remarked that he needed intelligent men, men who would differentiate between grafting and homicide. Now he said that if the grafting question came up in open court, the jury would be prejudiced against Becker from the beginning of its deliberations.

In his summing-up McIntyre brought to a climax the theme he had strummed in the background throughout the trial. "I am defending an American!" he shouted, stomping up and down the narrow pen in front of the court and thrusting his big hand in the face of one juryman after another. "His accusers are vile creatures, not lovers of the flag or the institutions under which we live but a lawless and degenerate lot. . . ." Were the members of the

jury, "twelve good *Americans*, loving home and the flag," willing
to believe their damnable, lying story? And if these words
sounded as if he were against "people of foreign blood," he added
at the top of his lungs, the fact was that some of his best friends
were people of foreign blood.

Justice Goff's icy blue eyes looked colder than ever during this
turn. McIntyre could have discovered from Goff's formal report of
the work of the Lexow Committee that Goff might be particularly
sympathetic with foreign-born citizens when an arrogant policeman was accused of pushing them around. "Those who fled from
oppression abroad have come here to be doubly oppressed in a
professedly free and liberal country," he had written. "The poor,
ignorant foreigner residing on the great East Side of the city has
been especially subjected to the brutal and infamous rule of the
police." A few months after the trial Goff would mention in an
address at Yale Law School that many a case had been lost before
him through the asininity of lawyers who thought themselves
great orators.

McIntyre's speech went on for four hours. He confused the
spectators by spending considerable time arguing that the gunmen—who were not on trial—had not killed Rosenthal. He accused Whitman of having been misled by ambition to "debauch
his great office." "As McIntyre ranted on," reported the *Evening
Post*, "Becker became manifestly nervous." He moved about in his
chair. He broke into a sweat. When the lawyer finished at last, he
looked greatly relieved.

Frank Moss then summed up for the prosecution. No one knew
better than the counsel for the defense, he said, that the state's
chief witnesses would never walk free on Broadway. "The friends
of the gunmen would take care of them if they did." Engaging in
a little double-think of a variety that was not unheard of in the
case, Moss made fun of Reich's testimony, arguing that the
gamblers would hardly have put themselves in Reich's power by
talking to him so indiscreetly about their roles in the murder ("I
ask you to consider the improbability of that—is Rose a fool?").
He described Becker as "the most hideous criminal ever brought
to the bar in New York" and—two could play at this game—asked
the jury to find him guilty in the name of God and country.

In charging the jury Justice Goff simply outlined for them the
case against Becker as Whitman had presented it, offering each

prosecution contention as a fact. He referred three times, for example, to the postmurder conference on Forty-second Street as if there were no possible doubt that it had occurred as Rose and Webber had described it. Schepps, he said, did not appear to be an accomplice. He read at some length and with apparent interest and pleasure from Rose's testimony. "If it be true that Becker gave Rose such instructions," he said, "I instruct you that Becker constituted Rose his agent and that anything Rose did Becker did. . . . Becker, in law, must be held responsible for the account of everyone who acted in pursuance of his request or instructions." It was not necessary to settle upon a motive "where proof of crime is direct," and, besides, the defendant had "an all-engrossing motive." Though the jury should not hold it against Becker that he had not testified in the case, they should nevertheless "remember he was at liberty to take the stand."

When the jury had filed out, reporters asked Becker how he felt about the judge's charge. "Well, I don't feel very good about it," said Becker. He was sweating again. "It was virtually a direction to the jury to find me guilty."

XVI

BEFORE Justice Goff's charge the defense had confidently expected an acquittal or, at the very worst, a hung jury. Becker had told his wife to wear her best dress for the celebration afterward. Because of the character of the witnesses against him, the prosecution also was not counting on a conviction. One of the assistant district attorneys admitted the next day that not five men on Whitman's staff had expected anything but an acquittal.

Justice Goff had not quite made his two-week deadline. His frequent goadings—"Time is precious, now!" "Get on with it, now!"—had their effect, however, and even with two days given over to final statements and the charge to the jury the case had run only seventeen days. Still, these had been long days, many of them extending into the dinner hour. There had been ninety-nine witnesses. There were 3,754 pages of testimony. At the start the *Times* had described it as "this simple case that in all decency should be got over with as quickly as possible," but it was not a simple case. The jury filed out at 4:21 P.M. and were still out long after nightfall.

Charles Becker and his wife and a number of their relatives and friends were allowed to wait for the verdict in the office of Sheriff Harburger, who was one of Big Tim's boys. In their two large families each of them was closest to a brother named John. Police Lieutenant John Becker was there, as was John Lynch. Former Inspector Alexander Williams was in the room also, no longer a terrifying figure but grizzled now and tonight a little drunk. Also on hand was Louis Grant, the police lawyer who sixteen years earlier had given Stephen Crane such rough handling for daring to complain about Becker's treatment of Dora Clark, another defendant who claimed to have been lied about by witnesses for the state—but that had been long ago and in another precinct.

"I never had the slightest doubt that my husband would be acquitted," Helen Becker wrote later. "Lawyers and everyone else had kept reassuring me right along. But while we were waiting for the jury to come in I was nervous and did not feel like talking to people. Charley and I sat . . . hour after hour, waiting. Some food was brought in, but I could not eat. Neither one of us ate; we just waited." From time to time visitors poked their heads in the door and relayed rumors about the jury vote. Some of the rumors may have been true. The tall inner door of the jury room had a transom, and assistant district attorneys had been known to pull up a step ladder and get a line on how things were going inside.

While they waited for the verdict Frank Moss led some of the younger members of the prosecution staff in a hymn fest. Sitting in the sheriff's office Charles and Helen Becker could hear, from far off, the rousing strains of "Bringing in the Sheaves" and "Will There Be Any Stars (Any Stars) in My Crown When My Trophies at Last I Lay Down (I Lay Down)."

After a pull on the bottle of Irish whiskey that he kept under the bench, Justice Goff had gone to the Museum of Natural History to attend a lecture on "The Last Great Indian Council." Sometime after eleven he got a message saying the jury was ready and started downtown. When word reached the sheriff's office that the moment had come, Becker was led down an inside passage to the courtroom. Newspapers and cigar butts, debris of the seven-and-a-half-hour wait, littered the floor. The gloom that Goff had specified throughout the trial was gone, and spectators blinked in the garish electric light.

After her husband was led away Helen Becker stopped to put on her turban hat and then started down the main staircase. "I ran as fast as I could," she reported later, "but when I reached the courtroom door it was closed and they would not open it. An attendant gave me a chair, and I sat down, with a crowd of people pressing about me—for they all knew who I was. I waited three or four minutes—it seemed a long time—and then the door flew open and a reporter rushed out shouting 'Guilty!' He saw me just as he spoke and felt sorry for me—he told me so afterward. But he could not stop the word or alter the fact."

"The former Master of the Tenderloin, the virtual czar of the White Light District," as the *World* described Becker retrospectively the next day, had nodded his head once when he heard the verdict: guilty of murder in the first degree. A few moments later, in accordance with a court routine which he must have observed hundreds of time in his life, a court clerk stepped before him, and, with a set smile on his face, Becker raised his right hand and gave his pedigree: name, age, nationality, birthplace of parents. He stated that he could read and write, that his religion was Protestant, that his habits were temperate. "Have you ever been convicted of a crime?" asked the clerk. Becker started to answer, then stopped, looking startled. "I have never been convicted of a crime *before*," he said.

The following day Commissioner Waldo announced that under Section 302 of the police regulations Lieutenant Becker had been dropped from the force. Waldo then submitted his own resignation to Mayor Gaynor, who refused it.

McIntyre now announced his retirement from the case. Young Whiteside and Stryker also withdrew, and John Hart left town almost immediately to practice law in California. Newspapers reported that defense costs had already passed the twenty-five-thousand-dollar mark. McIntyre would not say what his fee had been, "but I was not backed by a tremendous sum of money, either of Becker's or anyone else's." Whoever had paid him, McIntyre had clearly worked hard to get Becker off. Whether it was the unpopularity of the defendant, Becker's apparent lack of further large financial resources in spite of the wilder tales of his graft booty, or the impression that his only political supporters, the Tim Sullivan crowd, were no longer interested in the case, there was no stampede of applicants now for the job of appealing to a higher court. It would finally be taken over by Joseph Shay, who had done little criminal trial work and had once been temporarily suspended from practice as a chronic ambulance chaser. Possibly he wanted to prove he was capable of more respectable legal achievement. Becker's remaining supporters naturally thought Shay was off to a good start when he immediately compared his client's plight to that of Captain Dreyfus, who, he noted, had been found innocent when the public came to its senses. An hour after Becker's conviction McIntyre had expressed a similar view. "He was tried in a time of great public clamor," he said. "Had the conditions been normal no American jury would have convicted him on the evidence. . . . The alleged grafting was constantly in the minds of the people."

Asked for a comment on McIntyre's statement, Charles Whitman said only that the verdict spoke for itself. "He took his victory quietly, gravely," reported the *World*. He had no comment either on the remark of Emory Buckner, who had been on hand to witness his rival's triumph. "Well, that does it," Buckner had said on his way out. "That makes Whitman the next Mayor of New York!"

The reaction around the country was highly favorable. The verdict was hailed editorially in, for example, the Philadelphia *Times*, the Los Angeles *News*, the Cleveland *Plain Dealer* ("If there were more Goffs on the bench, American judicial procedure would cease to be a thing of reproach . . ."), the Springfield, Massachusetts, *Union*, the Peoria *Herald-Transcript* ("It is well to give credit to . . . the jurymen who placed their own lives more or less in jeopardy . . ."), the Milwaukee *Sentinel*. The La Crosse, Wisconsin, *Tribune* did express regret that the gamblers would go free ("However, it is probably true that were informants refused immunity, it would become impossible to convict the ringleaders of criminal cliques anywhere"). The Sioux Falls, South Dakota, *Argus*, pronounced it "a great trial . . . a model trial." The Ogden, Utah, *Standard* declared that though it was against capital punishment on principle "in this case we would not raise the slightest protest if Becker and the gunmen were sent heavenward. . . . New York State has our permission to assemble the entire police force of New York and, in the presence of officers and men, blow Becker and his gang of cutthroats to Jericho." *The Nation* struck a more moderate note of quiet jubilation. Obviously the verdict had been a surprise. "This did not mean that Becker was not generally believed guilty . . . it was the legal proof that was called in question." The verdict therefore had brought "an unmistakable feeling of relief. It must be regarded as a most tonic event . . . a signal and heartening vindication of justice."

Now that holding his tongue both in and out of court had gone so badly for Becker, he turned downright garrulous for publication. If he had plotted to commit the murder through other people, would he then have been such a pinhead as to drive within a few hundred feet of the crime scene just before it happened, he asked reporters. He speculated that the gamblers had planned the murder for weeks and then had kept in touch with him so they could blame it on him. All they'd had to do to keep from being framed on any Sullivan charge was to mention Becker's alleged threat to Waldo. The commissioner wouldn't have stood for their gun-rap arrest after that. Webber, especially, had friends in the political picture he could have complained to, Becker told his visitors. Had the jury really believed that Rose and Webber, who knew their way around the underworld, would have committed murder because a mere police lieutenant told them to? Still he had faith in American justice, Becker insisted. There were certain rules of evidence. The appeals court would put it right. But for the moment, "what I have been through knocks hope dead."

Although Goff's insistence on keeping Helen Becker out of the sight of the jury suggests that the defense could have used her as a valuable asset, could at least have capitalized on any sympathy her pregnancy might arouse, they had not done so. She and her husband had wanted it that way, she said later. But in an interview on the day after the verdict Becker mentioned for the first time that his wife was going to have a child in January. And at the conclusion of visiting hours that same day Helen Becker seated herself in a chair in the entrance room of the Tombs and talked at length to reporters she had always snubbed before. What made her change her mind, she told them, was the story in all the newspapers that she had fainted after the verdict. The *World* had had her fainting three times in the space of an hour.

"Now wasn't that ridiculous?" she asked, her eyes flashing. "I have courage. Every Irish woman has that. I never fainted in my life, and I will not faint, no matter what happens."

Of course her husband—who, she assured them, she loved more this day than ever before—was innocent of the murder, and she ought to know. "I know Charley Becker better than anyone . . . and no man could be a murderer at heart and conceal it from the woman who could read his inmost thoughts." Mrs. Becker, who may never have heard of W. C. Fields, added that she knew her husband couldn't be a murderer because he was so fond of children.

"Maybe sometimes in performing his duties as a policeman, he *was* rough," she told the reporters. "He is big and very strong and maybe he did use force when dealing with men who interfered with the performance of police duty. But I know that he was not a man who could sit down and calmly direct the taking of a human life."

How was it that she could remain so composed, so strong through all this, asked a woman reporter. "My mind has helped," said Helen Becker firmly. "In the great crisis of her life, a woman must use her mind."

On October 29, the day Becker was sentenced, another reunion of family and friends occurred in Sheriff Harburger's office. The former policeman was brought over from the Tombs half an hour before he was to go into court. Several of his brothers and sisters were there as well as farmers from his home town and members of the Police Department. "Everybody was crying but us two," Helen Becker said later. The uproar in the courthouse rotunda sounded to one reporter "as if a mob were thirsting for the life of the doomed man." The trial of Red Phil Davidson for killing Big Jack Zelig had been interrupted for the sentencing. (For shooting Zelig in the back of the head Davidson was sentenced to twenty years and released after twelve.) Judge Goff, whose asceticism did not exclude "love of woman," had issued a special invitation to a dozen young society women to come and see the show. Wearing bright-colored gowns and large hats, they sat in an enclosure just below the judge's bench. John Hart waited for his client by the door. "The only word for Charley Becker is grim," Hart had told the press a few days earlier. "All his old chestiness is gone."

But Becker now walked in briskly as if—so someone complained—he were about to have a good conduct medal pinned on him. Swope insisted that he turned and "gave the *World* reporter a single piercing glance." The courtroom had been noisy, but after Goff pronounced the mandatory sentence of death it was suddenly so quiet that everyone plainly heard the snap of the handcuffs as the sheriff fixed them to the prisoner's right wrist.

The fact that the law had beaten him after all made Becker eligible for some of the sob sister treatment withheld up to now. "He thought of the little woman waiting outside the courtroom, of the babe soon to come into the world fatherless—and kept his nerve," wrote a lady on the *Globe*. After he was led away "a woman inside the judge's railing in silks and diamonds . . . clenched her fists and tears rolled down her cheeks. 'What if he is innocent!' she cried."

Helen Becker was allowed to travel with him on the train to Sing Sing along with reporters and guards from the sheriff's office. The party took over the smoking car for the journey. "I was the only woman there," Helen Becker recalled. "They let me sit on the seat beside my husband, and they took off his handcuffs. . . . The newspapermen pressed all about us so that we could have no private conversation. One reporter leaned over so close to us that his head was almost between Mr. Becker and me." (The reporter insisted later that in this fix the two had spent much of their time discussing women's suffrage. They were for it, he said.)

"At every station the platform was lined with people waiting to stare at us," Helen Becker said, and a big crowd followed as Becker walked the three-quarters of a mile to the prison from the Ossining station. The cell the warden led him to was even smaller than the one he had had in the Tombs—seven feet long, three feet four inches wide, and six and a half feet high. It was just large enough to hold a bucketful of drinking water, a tall slop pail, and a cot. The cot was two feet wide and six feet long, several inches too short for Becker. In those days the cellhouses were built directly on the ground near the Hudson River, only a few feet from tidewater, and an investigating grand jury found it was possible "to wet one's hand by drawing it over the cell walls." The windowless cells had walls of thick stone that made them look as if they had been hollowed out of solid rock. "A prisoner confined in one of them," reported the chief prison doctor at that time, "invariably suffers an impression of crushing weight closing in from all sides."

Helen Becker was taken down to see Becker about half an hour after he arrived. "We went through a long stone passage with iron doors and little iron windows where people peek out at you, and when we passed the punishment cells I had a feeling I almost wished Charley had died before he came here. Finally we stopped before a cell, and there was my husband. I never saw such a look of agony on anybody's face—a gray look. He did not say any-thing—he could not talk—and they told me to come back the next day. I did come back, and this was the beginning of many visits to the death house."

Within a few weeks Becker was joined at Sing Sing by Gyp the Blood, Lefty Louie, Whitey Lewis, and Dago Frank, though they were put in a different cell block. After the Becker verdict *The Nation* had congratulated Whitman on having had "the true in-stinct for all demands of the situation when he arranged to try Becker first of all." McIntyre had taunted him earlier with the possibility that Becker might be convicted of having committed murder through the gunmen who would then be acquitted of having murdered anybody. Whitman was willing to take this chance. According to the arrangement he had worked out with Governor Dix, the same man was to preside over all the cases arising out of the Rosenthal shooting, which meant that the judge in the gunmen's trial was again Justice Goff. This time the trial, which began on November 13, lasted only seven days. At one point when a witness who was there to identify the de-fendants individually became confused, Goff ordered them there-after to sit in a row in the order they were listed in the indict-ment, thus simplifying any identification problem. The jury took half an hour to find all four men guilty. Each of them had con-tinued to insist that as far as he knew Lieutenant Becker had had nothing to do with the murder.

A few days later a meeting of the reformers' Committee of Fourteen passed a resolution acclaiming Whitman as "one of the great heroes of the age" for his contribution to the city's moral regeneration, which they counted on to follow the two trials. But an embarrassing development had clouded the reformers' earnest attempt to help Whitman by giving him his own private police force. Whitman had discovered that the men hired to trail police grafters had very soon got on very cozy terms with their assigned prey. The reformers had had to hire a new set of private detec-tives to trail the first crowd. Eventually the whole thing had got so out of hand that Whitman had sacked the lot and thereafter relied on the ordinary cops routinely assigned to his office. To what extent the Burns agency had collected the two-hundred-thousand-dollar fee William J. Burns had estimated as the cost of running down Police Department grafters was never cited for public consumption.

The day after the verdict in the gunmen's trial the four gamblers were released from the West Side jail at the insistence of Webber's lawyer, Max Steuer, and Bernard Sandler, Schepps' attorney, who was now also representing Vallon and Rose. There was a festival air in the prison. Bridgey Webber had had a case of champagne sent in. Newspapermen wandered up and down the cell blocks interviewing keepers and other inmates about the habits of the four celebrities. Schepps, the most famous vagrant in town, was set free first. Just before noon, after the vagrancy charge was formally dismissed in court, he hurried back to the third tier to pack up.

"That's not fair," said Webber, according to the *American*. "How come you get the special privileges and get out before the rest of us?"

"That's because you aren't the corroborator. I got pulled in last and got to be the corroborator," said Schepps.

"I wish I'd of been pulled in last. Then I could of been the corroborator," said Bridgey Webber plaintively.

Webber and Rose and Vallon were released about three that afternoon. The *Evening Mail* complained that the Turks had just surrendered in the war in the Balkans but that no one in town seemed to be paying the slightest attention. Fifteen hundred people clogged Fifty-third Street, however, to watch the departure of the three gamblers. A large touring car—not a Packard—awaited them outside the door. Beautifully pressed, smelling of lavender water, and each swinging a cane, Bridgey, Vallon, and Bald Jack climbed in. "I will be at the office of my lawyer, Mr. Sandler, to meet any gangsters who might care to see me," Rose shouted out the window as the car started up, and they rode off toward Second Avenue in fits of laughter.

Early in December Whitman was guest of honor at a dinner at the Hotel Astor attended by a thousand people. The chief toastmaster was Republican Senator William Borah of Montana. Sam Koenig was on hand along with other prominent local Republicans. Mrs. Whitman sat in a box with Mrs. Elbert Gary, wife of the head of U.S. Steel. "Well done, thou good and faithful servant," Borah's toast to Whitman concluded. "You have been faithful over a few things, we will make you ruler over many."

Police Lieutenant Charles Becker

Herman Rosenthal

Helen Becker

Herbert Bayard Swope

District Attorney Charles Whitman

Big Tim Sullivan

Mayor William Jay Gaynor (center, with beard), reviewing police parade

Gunmen and friends: Gyp the Blood, Lefty Louie, Dago Frank,
standing from left to right: Whitey Lewis, seated at right

Justice John W. Goff

Bald Jack Rose

Sam Schepps

Bridgey Webber, front left

Harry Vallon

Charles Becker, returning to Sing Sing, 1914

XVII

"I'D like to be Governor," Whitman told a reporter for the *Evening Post* in September 1912, with "a snap of his broad powerful jaws and a glint in his choleric hazel eyes. . . . They say that Charles Seymour Whitman is ambitious," the *Post* added accusingly, as if this were a quality not usually found in politicians. He didn't get the Republican nomination for governor that fall. In any case, the Democratic candidate (William Sulzer, a local man of the Sullivan persuasion) won in November. Whitman's next important chance to "rule over many" was the mayoralty election of 1913. He embarked on the peripatetic routine required of prospective candidates for higher office. Among his club dates was a banquet of the Horse Owners' Protective Association, formed to combat East Side gangs whose specialty was poisoning horses. Presumably this was the last New York campaign in which a horse owners' protective association was considered a significant political stop. Another of his stops was the Jewish Institute, a social and educational center set up on lower Second Avenue as a result of the revelations of criminal activity among young East Side Jews in the Rosenthal case. "Shall the race remain stained and blotted in reputation or rise to new heights?" the head of the Jewish community had asked, and prominent members of "Our Crowd" had founded the Institute, hoping there would be fewer Gyp the Bloods in the future. Wherever Whitman made speeches that spring, the crimes of the police grafters were invariably his topic, though grafters had threatened his life, he reported, "by steel, poison, bombs, cords and suffocation." His accounts of the wickedness of the System were so impressive that at one meeting the audience broke into startled laughter when he concluded his talk by describing New York as "the brightest, noblest, best, and purest city in the world."

The kickoff dinner for Whitman's campaign was held at the Cafe Boulevard. Libby and Shapiro were not at their accustomed stand in front of the cafe that evening. They had a new limousine now. The gray Packard had been sold to a sightseeing outfit. Thrill-seeking tourists kept it busy making the rounds of the spots recently made famous—the Metropole, the Forty-seventh Street station house, the Lafayette Baths. At the dinner the counsel for the Hearst papers mentioned what he called "Whitman's stuck-out chin," which he said symbolized the district attorney's "grit, simple honesty, tireless energy, and perseverance." Whitman took the opportunity to defend himself against the charge of being ambitious, quoting the politician's indispensable *vademecum, The Collected Sayings of Abraham Lincoln:* "Every man is said to have his peculiar ambition," Lincoln had once said. *His* only ambition, said Whitman, was to be mayor of New York so he could transform the Police Department into "an effective agency for the protection of property and the security of life within this city." At the moment, he said, it was "a menace (and a grave one) to both." It would be a civic calamity "if another man were elected who might divert the attention of the electorate to questions more or less abstract from the evil which threatens the existence of civilized society. Beside it, all other questions seem to be of minor importance."

"Can it be possible that the sentimental wave initiated by the trigger that caused a gambler's death will sweep the ambitious D.A. to the Mayor's chair?" demanded an angry letter-writer to the *Times.* As it turned out, no. Whitman had the backing of local Republicans, but in that Democratic city, then as now, no Republican could win except as part of a Fusion movement. To that end Republicans and independents were courting Teddy Roosevelt's Progressive Party, and Roosevelt had no use for Whitman. Whitman's prime rival for the nomination was John Purroy Mitchel. As chairman of the Board of Aldermen, Mitchel had taken over briefly for Mayor Gaynor after the attempted assassination and had seized the opportunity to conduct a crusade against police grafters in Coney Island, thereby establishing his locally indispensable credentials for higher public office. A committee delegated by the various factions to select a Fusion slate met in July 1913 and chose Mitchel as their candidate. The vote was forty-four to forty-three. At thirty-four Mitchel was the youngest man ever nominated for mayor of the city. Whitman, eleven years older, was put on the slate for another term as district attorney. A few weeks earlier, commenting on some Tammany overtures in his direction, he had said, "I could not under any circumstances accept the nomination of any organization whose political tenets are so different from my own," but now he accepted the nomination for district attorney on the Tammany as well as the Fusion line. Nothing in the record of the Becker case had made him objectionable to leader Murphy, and his presence on the ticket would allow Tammany to imply throughout the campaign that the graft scandals were entirely the work of Mayor Gaynor and the cops.

About the time the mayoralty campaign moved into high gear, a grand jury inquiry into conditions at Sing Sing reported that the cells there "are unfit for the housing of animals, let alone human beings." In the death house prisoner number 62,499 was bearing up better than might have been expected. Warden James Clancy reported that the former policeman had given him no trouble and that he seemed philosophical about his plight. Perhaps he would have been more troublesome if his new lawyer hadn't kept assuring him that his stay at Sing Sing was temporary, that the higher courts would recognize his conviction as a gross miscarriage of justice. As in the Tombs, Becker's major complaint was of the limited opportunity for exercise. He was allowed out in the narrow, cinder-floored yard for only half an hour each morning. He would run around it at full speed a dozen times and spend the rest of his recess slamming a handball against a wall. In the evenings a keeper or even the warden himself sometimes played a game of cards with him. Otherwise in his first months there he had nothing to do but read, write letters to his lawyers and his wife, clip the New York City papers that one of the chaplains brought him each day, and meditate on the grim drama as at intervals a fellow citizen of the death house walked or was dragged past his cell on the way to the execution chamber. Little was left

to the imagination of those scheduled to follow. In this respect the
interior arrangements of the death house were particularly bar-
barous. The entrance to the execution chamber was only a few
feet from many of the cells, including Becker's, and a man in
death row could plainly hear not only what went on in the electric
chair but what happened afterward in the adjacent autopsy room.
The Sing Sing doctor in Becker's time wrote that the sound the
prisoners told him they dreaded most was the rasping noise as he
sawed off the top of the dead man's skull to examine the brain.

A favorite plot in the old nineteenth-century plot books starts
out with two characters, a good man and a bad man. Gradually
the good man's character deteriorates and that of the bad man
improves until at the end of the story their roles are to a degree
reversed. The alternatives to becoming a better person are not
extensive on death row. Confined alone in a room hardly larger
than a coffin a man can either subside into apathy or madness or
decide to play a positive role in the tiny enclave of human existence that is left to him. Since the age of twenty-three Becker had
never tried to make his way in a strange group without his billy
club at the ready or its symbolic equivalent—the power to arrest,
humiliate, or even ruin. Apparently he discovered qualities in
himself that he had not drawn on before. No formal social life
was permitted among the men in the death house, but every
sound carried. Becker organized games in which men called out
moves on imaginary checker boards. He began to read aloud in
the evenings. Western stories were especially popular among the
prisoners, he said later. As he built up seniority Becker became a
kind of counselor to the other condemned men on the block, who
had probably never dreamed they would be baring their souls to a
cop. Warden Clancy and the chaplains were soon treating Becker
as an unofficial spokesman for the men on death row. In a small,
grotesque world he had reached the top at last.

During his first months in Sing Sing, Becker, a Lutheran, had
sometimes seen the Protestant chaplain. Later he began to receive
visits from Father James Curry, the venerable priest from St.
James Catholic Church on Oliver Street on the East Side. Becker's
wife had been raised in the St. James parish, and although she
would say later, "I have never been very religious," presumably
Father Curry first came to Sing Sing at her suggestion. Sometime
in the summer of 1913 Becker joined the Catholic Church. Each

Saturday Helen Becker made the trip up the river and was allowed to spend an hour and a half with him, sitting on a chair four feet out from his cell, separated by a thick wire grille, with a keeper at each end of the corridor to make sure that nothing passed between them. She also wrote him a letter every day of the two and a half years he was in the death house except for three days at the beginning of February 1913, immediately following the birth of her child.

In the house on Olinville Avenue that she had moved into a few days after Becker's arrest nothing had gone well. "I cannot call it our home, for my husband never lived there," she once said. Its dark gray stucco walls gave it a sinister air, she thought. The neighborhood was heavily wooded and lonely. There were occasional prowlers who rattled the door knobs and peered at her through windows as she bent over the legal papers she regularly carried back and forth from Becker to the lawyers. She got a watchdog, an Airedale named Bum. Bum immediately bit the milkman and had to be shot. After that a young hired girl named Lena stayed with her. One afternoon Lena killed herself by taking poison in the dining room of the house. Helen Becker bought a canary bird for company. It died too.

When she answered the telephone, it was often a stranger denouncing her husband or abusing her for living off the fruits of graft. The mail was similarly abusive. There were also begging letters from people who had read the stories of Becker's enormous haul, asking her to pay off their mortgages, to buy them artificial legs, to send them ten thousand dollars by return mail or suffer painful consequences.

But not all the communications were unfriendly. In the months after Becker was sentenced many of the ladies around the city— and from places as distant as Seattle and Phoenix—were sorry for her in her predicament, far advanced in pregnancy, not at all young, alone, with her husband in the death house. Encouraging letters and little hand-knit sweaters and shawls arrived in the mail every few days, accompanied by cards reading "The Mothers of 16th Street" or "Three Mothers and a Grandmother from Jackson Heights." The bounty grew larger and the letters even more sympathetic after it was learned that there were complications in her pregnancy. Early in January she entered Woman's Hospital on West 110 Street where she stayed for four weeks until her child was born on February 1. The worst part about this, she said later, was not being able to make her weekly visits to her husband in Sing Sing. Her single-minded allegiance to him had its consequences.

"It was a little girl, just what I wanted," she wrote later, "and very pretty, not red like most babies, and quite large. She was alive then, and I thought she was all right. But that afternoon she died, and they told me the next morning."

Inevitably there was a considerable outpouring of sympathy for her and even for Becker, who was described as weeping in his cell when he heard the news. In a few days, however, the story leaked out of the hospital that the child's death had been the result of a decision made in the delivery room by Helen Becker. She had been given the choice of saving her life or the child's and had chosen her own. She did not deny this.

"The birth of my baby was delayed," she said later, "and the long wait was terrible. At the last moment I had to decide whether to take the chance on my life or the baby's life. I was alone. . . . The doctor said I must decide. I thought of the position my husband was in, there in prison under sentence of death, and I knew that my life would be more help to him than the baby's. So I decided that if there had to be a choice my life was to be saved. Then they gave me ether, and I did not know anything more until I found myself on my cot again."

That really did it. Letters denouncing her as a betrayer of the eternal noble instincts of her sex replaced the earlier friendly mail. One correspondent pointed out that now there were two cold-blooded murderers in the family. Another mentioned Lady Macbeth.

By the end of February Helen Becker had resumed her weekly visits to Sing Sing. She was still on maternity leave from her school and was working actively with the lawyers on the motion for a new trial to be brought on the ground of newly discovered evidence. Shay, the former ambulance chaser, had had the good sense to call in several young legal scholars to help him with the Becker appeals. The new-trial motion was argued before Justice Goff in May. Becker's side offered sixteen affidavits that threw doubt on the testimony of the state's witnesses against him. The most important of these came from three men known as Moe, Itch, and Muttle.

In cross-examining Schepps about the Harlem conference Mc-Intyre had asked the names of the chauffeurs who had driven the gamblers there in two hired cars, the men with whom, according to Schepps' testimony, he had stood talking for half an hour as the other gamblers plotted the murder with Becker, a block away. At first Schepps said he'd never seen the chauffeurs before. Finally he said he'd known them as Moe and Itch, but these weren't their real names. McIntyre didn't pursue the matter, but Shay was more enterprising. Operators of limousines for hire weren't so numerous in 1912 that two such East Side tradesmen couldn't be traced. Moe and Itch, partners in a taxi business, had been frequent drivers for Rose, Webber, and Schepps. Itch was really Isadore Schoenhaus. Moe's real name was Harry Cohen. Now, in May 1913, the chauffeurs had given the defense affidavits saying they had never in their lives driven the gamblers to 124 Street and Seventh Avenue. They also swore they had been called to Whitman's office sometime before Becker's trial and had told the D.A.'s men this fact. Muttle's real name was Max Brescher. He had been identified by Rose and Webber as the man Reich had veered off and talked to in front of the Murray Hill Baths at the moment Becker had turned up after the murder to congratulate them. Muttle swore he hadn't been in front of the baths that night. He had seen Rose, Webber, and Reich in the neighborhood, but certainly not Becker. Before the trial, he said, an assistant district attorney had asked him if he'd seen Becker on Forty-second Street with the others. He had said no. He had then been left alone with Bridgey Webber, he said, and Webber had told him he "wanted me to remember, had begged me to remember." When he still couldn't remember anything of the kind, the district attorney's office had let him go, saying he wouldn't be needed as a witness. To the surprise of few Justice Goff turned down Becker's appeal on the ground that the so-called new evidence was merely cumulative and not such "as would probably change the result if a new trial were granted." Becker's last hope was the highest court in the state, the Court of Appeals.

When interviewed from time to time, the four main witnesses against Becker showed little interest in these legal maneuvers. Before the verdict Bald Jack had said he might return to the theater, but first would complete a book about his twenty years in the underworld. Sam Schepps insisted he would spend his remaining years meditating on Spinoza and the Talmud, which he had been poring over in his cell. Webber—"our pal Bridgey, the rich one," as Schepps called him—thought he might take Mrs. Webber on a little trip around the world. Harry Vallon said Buenos Aires had always kind of appealed to him.

Jack Rose never finished his book, but he did turn out a series of articles on his one-time criminal life for various publications. He also became the darling of the church lecture circuit. High Episcopal churches were his speciality. Confessions of a reformed sinner were apparently as surefire among Anglicans as among Southern Baptists during revival season, and Rose's tales of his wicked life before he had been saved were a rousing success. Six hundred people were on hand at a church in East Norwalk, Connecticut, for his sermon. When Grace Church in Brooklyn heard the same address on "Life in the Underworld" a few weeks later, not only the regular minister, but the minister emeritus, was there to introduce Rose—now dressed in black from head to foot—to a packed house. The minister emeritus thanked God for the gambler's salvation, and hundreds of parishioners stood in line to wring his manicured hand as they filed out of the church.

Soon after leaving the West Side Prison Harry Vallon had quarreled with his old employer and after a sojourn in the Catskills was rumored to be back at work as a lookout for one of Bridgey's competitors. When asked, he gave his profession as "chandelier salesman." For Sam Schepps the life of meditation had palled rapidly. A few weeks after his release he had invested his cash resources—it seemed that he had some—in the production of a movie called *The Wages of Sin*. It covered about the same ground as Jack Rose's standard lecture, but the general public was not as fascinated by the subject as the average suburban churchgoer. After a turn in vaudeville on the West Coast ("Sam Schepps Himself! Will Answer Questions from the Audience about Becker, the Murdering Policeman!") Schepps departed for Paris. Some months later Helen Becker received a cable from him reading "HAVE IMPORTANT REVELATIONS MAY SAVE CHARLES." Her answer was "WHAT HAVE YOU TO SAY?" Schepps' reply to that was to advise her to come to France herself, that what he had to suggest could not be handled by mail or cable. She did not go, but word soon reached her indirectly that for ten thousand dollars Schepps would be willing to give evidence that

Becker had had nothing to do with the murder. Although she did not meet his terms, Becker's lawyers were soon mentioning to the press that there was a good chance that in Becker's second trial, which they confidently expected to follow the Court of Appeals decision, Schepps would be testifying for the defense. Someone from the district attorney's office immediately brought up the immunity agreement and predicted that if he did any such thing Schepps would find himself in the dock on a charge of murder. Nothing further was heard of his proposition.

Bridgey Webber gave evidence for Becker in a more informal fashion. Instead of setting off around the world, he and Mrs. Webber had gone only as far as Cuba on a Caribbean cruise. Half a dozen reporters were on hand to meet him as he got off the boat.

"I get sick every time I think of those fellows up in the death house," Webber told them, squatting on his set of fancy new luggage. "It's an awful thing to think of sending five men to the electric chair. I'll feel like dying myself the day they are killed."

"I cheer him up all the time by telling him they are sure to get new trials," said Mrs. Webber, patting his arm. Poor Bridgey couldn't sleep nights, she went on, for worrying about those men in Sing Sing.

"We never expected to have Rosenthal killed," Webber told the reporters. "If two of the gunmen hadn't got drunk there wouldn't have been any shooting. All we wanted then was to scare Herman . . . the idea was to buy him off or scare him away." As for the gunmen, "Rose had been stringing them along telling them how powerful Becker was in the Police Department, that if Becker was behind them they could do anything. . . ." He was now at odds with all the other gamblers involved, Webber said. Sam Schepps was "a rat." He also took out after Jacob Reich "and his gabby mouth," which had stirred up much of the trouble before the murder, he said. He complained about the ten-thousand-dollar fee to Max Steuer. "That was an awful fee to have to pay when Jack Rose turned around that very afternoon and confessed. After that there was nothing to it but do the best you could, to get in line when the death chair was staring you in the face."

Asked about his future plans, Webber said he was moving out on the gambling business and moving out on New York, too. He was going into a legitimate business in New Jersey with his wife's brother. Was he leaving New York because he was terrified that the friends of the gunmen would get him? Bridgey smiled for the first time that afternoon.

"Don't make me laugh," he said. "If you knew those fellows like I do you'd laugh your head off at the idea of anyone being afraid of them."

When he saw the interview in print the next day, Webber retreated rapidly. He hadn't said a single bit of it, he insisted, although, declared the *World*, "newspapermen present all agreed that he was underquoted rather than overquoted."

Becker's lawyer, Shay, was jubilant. If the newspapermen would give affidavits about the interview, he said, they would virtually assure a new trial. (Three of them did so, their affidavits being included in the "new evidence" rejected by Justice Goff.) If Rosenthal had really not been murdered according to a premeditated plan, "if there was no contract in advance to commit murder, Becker was not rightfully convicted," Shay told the press.

Helen Becker was more cautious. His story, if true, was "good news." But "since Webber has lied before, it is difficult to say whether he is telling the truth now." Whitman was not similarly retrospective. Webber, he said, "would say anything now if he thought it would help his own interests."

The various crusades against police grafters continued to hog the headlines, especially the hearings of the aldermen's committee. In line with Buckner's insistence on fair play for Becker, the inquiry had gone into hibernation during his trial, but it made up for lost time in the sessions that followed. By early 1913 revelations before the committee had led to the arrest and indictment of several inspectors on the force, none of them close associates of Becker. Their headlined trials were presided over by State Supreme Court Justice Samuel Seabury. None spent more than a few months behind bars, which presumably would have been the worst that could have happened to Becker if the charge against him had been grafting—and if he hadn't tangled with Herman Rosenthal.

Justice Goff meanwhile found it necessary to be in constant consultation with the D.A. concerning his special grand jury inquiry into bluecoat grafting. Their twin press releases attracted respectful attention although the results of their prolonged investigation seems to have been a large goose egg. Buckner, who was now frequently referred to as "our next District Attorney," was not above pointing out that the only evidence that had resulted in indictments in the drive against grafters had been the work of his committee, to which Whitman should be beholden. Whitman's natural resentment of this suggestion from another ambitious prosecutor was not allayed by the rumor, widespread among members of his staff, that Buckner had left the D.A.'s office the previous July because he thought Becker was getting a bad deal and might even be innocent of the murder.

The squabbling between the competing committees over witnesses and over credit for exposing police scandals got to be what the *Globe* described as "a continuous shindy." But shindies make even more headlines. Very rarely, a voice in the newspaper columns would suggest that there might be other evils in the contemporary world. The columnist known as F.P.A., posing as the modern Pepys for the *Evening Mail*, complete with tortured olde English, observed at one point: "All the town is full of the talk of the great turpitude now abroad in it and of its causes, and I am not one to set myself above them that have given deep study to such matters, but meseems that where children must labour and girls do hard tasks for too small wage there too must be great misery."

But the new Democratic legislature in Albany wasn't frittering away its advantage investigating child labor. One of its first acts was to establish a joint legislative committee to consider the police scandals in the city. Among those appointed to consider this unneglected field were two young state senators, Robert F. Wagner and Franklin D. Roosevelt. Nothing came of their survey except useful publicity for the young politicians involved. In all these investigations the name of Becker was constantly invoked. A few months later a state senator who had introduced a bill to ban capital punishment in the state had an implication pointed out to him. His duty was clear, he then announced. Since there was a slight possibility that it might be used to save Lieutenant Becker from the chair, he had no choice but to withdraw the bill.

XVIII

THE antagonisms stirred up by the Becker case brought about an odd exchange of roles in the summer of 1913. The same citizens who had accused Mayor Gaynor of cosseting police grafters, those preyers on criminals, were accusing him of cosseting criminals by ordering the police not to use their nightsticks unnecessarily or to break into houses without warrants. In an article in *McClure's* that could have been written later in the century, Gaynor's old enemy, magistrate Corrigan, complained: "The criminal classes have 'the drop' on the police. . . . Instead of being used, as formerly, to anticipate and prevent the commission of crime, they must wait until a crime is actually committed or themselves run the risk of having some charge preferred. . . . The staring danger of the present is not that liberty will be unduly interfered with but that society will be unable to protect itself. . . ." If Becker hadn't shifted to grafting but had stuck to his old style of clubbing down citizens in the name of law enforcement he apparently would have had more defenders.

Gaynor became more and more enraged by the charge that he was soft on criminals and at ten minutes after the one o'clock closing time one August night dispatched fifty cops to Healy's Cafe at Sixty-sixth Street and Columbus Avenue—the same Healy's where, six years earlier, Whitman had personally had the owner arrested for staying open after the legal closing hour. Gaynor announced that he had ordered the raid on the principle that decent people "could guzzle wine and dance enough before one o'clock" (or, as a later saloonkeeper, Toots Shor, would put it, "Anybody that ain't drunk by midnight ain't tryin' ").

The following night when the raiders again arrived at Healy's a few minutes after one they were greeted not by a few stragglers but by a whole saloonful of defiant customers. Standing in the doorway was the former advocate of enforcing lawful closing hours to the hilt, Charles Whitman, striking, Gaynor later charged, "heroic attitudes" for the photographers. The district attorney and his elegant companion, Richard Harding Davis, were shoved aside and the raid carried out, with much flailing of the clubs that Gaynor had bragged were no longer recklessly used in his administration. Whitman arranged to have a Republican magistrate pal of his issue a warrant for the arrest of the inspector who had directed the raid, charging him with oppression. Gaynor, turning the tables, denounced Whitman as "the champion of criminal and lewd persons. *I* do not work as Mayor through press agents and writers who can easily be persuaded to falsify . . ." he added. The inspector was arrested. But when the case finally came to court a few weeks later, it was dismissed. The fun had gone out of the game: Gaynor was dead.

On September 4 the mayor had boarded the White Star liner *Baltic* for a trip to Europe. He was hoarser than ever and very low in spirits over his political prospects. "I have given them four lean and hungry years," he had said earlier when word had come that Tammany would not renominate him because of his handling of the Rosenthal murder. "I have had a pretty hard time for four years to hold my own against all comers and against every corrupt influence, but *I have been Mayor.*" The circumstances surrounding the murder were still on his mind. A short time before the *Baltic* sailed, Gaynor mentioned to a friend the harm the case had done the police commissioner. Did the friend know that Big Tim Sullivan had tried to bribe Waldo to protect the dive run by Rosenthal "the scoundrel whose murder was procured by Lieutenant Becker"? When he got back, said Gaynor, he was going to make public "the whole damnable story." Five days later as the *Baltic* approached the coast of Ireland he was found dead in his deck chair. "It may be doubted if any other man in New York's checkered history ever escaped greatness by so narrow a margin," declared the *World*. "In a long line of commonplace and slate-colored Mayors of New York he towers as a giant among pygmies."

Many of the mayor's obituaries speculated that if only Gaynor had been willing to fire Waldo over the Becker affair he could easily have weathered the political storm. He had not done this either out of plain obstinacy or because he had been largely his own police commissioner and knew it was unfair to throw Waldo to the lions. After Gaynor's death Waldo was fired by the interim mayor, who cited his "childish behavior," and retired from public life. The rank and file at Centre Street remembered him kindly as the commissioner who had put man-sized pockets in patrolmen's overcoats and as the "red-blooded fellow" that "stood by Charley Becker in his trouble," as he was described in *Our Police Guardians,* a bluecoat history of the department published in 1925. What with the Rosenthal murder and "the killing of poor innocent Becker," this history went on, the years when Waldo was commissioner had been "the toughest years old New York has seen since the days of the Know Nothings and the Dead Rabbits . . . times so tough they killed Mayor Gaynor."

Before Gaynor's body was returned to the city there was another enormous funeral in New York. Big Tim Sullivan had had irrational spells during the late summer and fall of 1912, but his mind had not begun to go entirely until sometime in October or, insiders said, soon after he heard the news that Becker had been convicted. It was obvious to East Side leaders that Big Tim would not be in shape to take his customary seat in the State Senate. Someone else was drafted in his place. Not knowing what else to do with Sullivan, perhaps, they nominated him as congressman from the Sixteenth District. (He had to be satisfied with going to Congress.) Sullivan did not appear in public once during the campaign, but he was elected anyway. At the time of his death ten months later he was still on the congressional rolls, though he had never got to Washington. In January 1913 a court had formally judged him incompetent to manage his personal and business affairs, but the affairs of the United States government were not mentioned. Sullivan now spoke entirely in whispers, one doctor testified, believing there were dictagraphs in the walls around him. "He has the face and bearing of a man living in constant terror." Rumors that his distress had something to do with the Becker case flourished as the months passed.

The Sullivan clan took him to Europe for a while and then established him with a pair of keepers in his brother Paddy's house in the Eastchester section of the Bronx. Early in August he evaded his guards and turned up at his old stamping ground below Fourteenth Street where he received the faithful in his hotel suite. The doctor stated later that he was on his way to recovering his sanity, that he was beginning to remember everything. He had been about to tell what he knew about the Rosenthal case, legend would have it, when a body suddenly turned up on the New Haven railroad tracks below the Pelham Parkway. Although it had been hit by a train that had just gone by, the body—said the legend—was unaccountably cold when yardmen reached it.

The body on the tracks was taken from one morgue to another, ending up at Bellevue, a few blocks north of the empire where Sullivan had reigned supreme for a quarter of a century. It remained unidentified for thirteen days. Finally an Orchard Street policeman, hearing a rumor that the old boy was on the loose again, took another look and began to charge around the morgue shouting "It's Big Tim! Lord of God, it's Big Tim!" He had "typified in the highest degree a fast-vanishing side of the life of New York," said the obituaries. The Rosenthal case had "come very close to him. . . . His name was bandied about freely in connection with it." "It is consoling to think the audacious and domineering grafter of the Sullivan type has passed into history."

The funeral of the man hailed as the last of the big-time grafters was said to be the largest in New York up to that time. In one day an estimated twenty thousand people filed past the body as it lay in state on the lower Bowery. Thousands more than this followed the cortege the next morning. There were five U.S. senators and fifteen representatives in the company. Al Smith was there of course, and so were Assemblyman Jimmy Walker and a young Tammany helper named Jimmy Hines. Also noted in the crowd were Tom Sharkey, Paul Kelly, and Beansy Rosenfeld. The vast procession, winding its way from the Bowery to Old Saint Patrick's Cathedral, brought all other activity on the East Side to a standstill. "There must have been something large and strong in him," said the *Times* next day, sounding a little puzzled, "some sincere symmetry with human ills and misfortunes—else would he have been able to make an appeal so long and so effectively to his enormous following?"

During the mayoralty campaign that fall Whitman pained some of the reformers by praising the Tammany candidate as "an honest man" and saying nothing about Mitchel, whom he hadn't forgiven for beating him out for the nomination on the Fusionist ticket. By the time Mitchel was elected, Whitman was already running full speed ahead for the governorship. A few months earlier, the *American* had noted with a journalistic shrug that the contest for the Fusionist nomination for mayor was hardly a life or death political matter for either candidate—whichever of the two men lost this fight would no doubt run the following year for governor. But two votes cast the other way on the last Fusionist ballot would have made a great difference to one man. To Charles Becker it may have been a matter of life and death. For if Whitman had become mayor in January 1914, as he certainly would have had he gotten the nomination, the district attorney of Manhattan that spring and the governor of the state a year later would not have been a man to whom Becker's guilt, proven and punished to the full measure of the law, represented the single compelling achievement of his political career, an achievement the office holder was ready to go to almost any lengths to preserve.

During all these political maneuvers the legal fight for Charles Becker's life was proceeding at the traditional tortuous pace. The delay infuriated many amateur criminologists. "Becker has the advantage of a system in which every trifling technicality in this state seems to work to the advantage of the criminal and against society," fretted the *World*. That newspaper had been incensed to discover that in the previous decade in the nation's sixty largest cities there had not been a single murder case in which the execution of the murderer had taken place in the same calendar year as the crime. "What blindness afflicts the American people that they permit this blot on their government to remain uncleansed?" cried the *World*.

Becker had been in the death house over thirteen months when his lawyers argued his case before the Court of Appeals. The decision came down a little less than three months later on February 24, 1914. On February 22 Helen Becker's mother had died. As she left Gimbels, where she had been buying mourning

clothes, Mrs. Becker heard the newsboys shouting out the headlines of the extra editions. Her husband's lawyers had been right
this time. He had been granted a new trial. The gunmen, on the
other hand, had lost their appeal and were scheduled to die the
week of April 9. That afternoon in Shay's office Helen Becker
found a crowd of reporters waiting to interview her. Although her
mother had died so recently, she said, she could truly say this was
the happiest day of her life.

Becker had no clothes to wear during his brief interval in the
outside world—the train trip from Sing Sing to the Tombs where
he would await the new trial—and because of her mother's
funeral Helen Becker was unable to bring him any until the
second day after the favorable decision was handed down. The
afternoon before she came, however, there was such a clamor
from newspapermen for interviews with Becker that Warden
Clancy scheduled a press conference in his office. The prisoner
came striding in, said the news stories the next day, "the same
jaunty Becker, erect, smiling, fearless . . . swinging his arms
. . . exuding an air of physical—almost brute—force." Thanks
to his program of daily calisthenics in his cell, Becker "was physically as fit yesterday as in the days when he took delight in felling
rioters and street car rowdies without the aid of a night stick."

After the prisoner had shaken hands all around, the warden
offered him one of his favorite long black cigars. Puffing away,
Becker then told the reporters that he had been the victim "of
such a deal as I hope no man shall ever get again. The murderer
of Rosenthal is still at large," he said, "and when I am free, as I
sincerely think I shall be, it will be my first duty to run the
assassin down. It can be done, just as my lawyer Shay proved me
innocent after I had been convicted on perjured testimony. I think
Harry Vallon killed Rosenthal. . . ." Incidentally, Becker added,
"I never saw Jack Zelig in my life."

He was reassured about American justice. "This proves that no
frame-up can go to a finish." On the other hand, it didn't seem fair
about the gunmen. "There's no crueler place on earth than the
death house." Father Cashin, the Catholic chaplain, leaned forward and mentioned that Becker had helped him conduct the
nightly Bible classes there. "He said that Becker had been of the
greatest assistance in comforting and preparing men who were
going to die and that he had done much good in that part of the

prison," said the *Sun*. Remembering the old Becker, some of the reporters looked dubious.

"Look here, I don't want to be made a white angel or anything of that kind," Becker told them hastily. "They say Jack Rose has adopted religion for a calling and is preaching in churches. Leave that to him."

One thing he had learned in prison, Becker said, was the pleasure of reading. He had even read Shakespeare, he said. "I liked *Measure for Measure* best. . . . There is so much in it that fitted my case. There are some terrific passages on death in it, too, that I pondered over. . . ." The book he had been reading just the day before when the good news came, he said, was the diary of Robert Scott, the polar explorer. "One thing I would like to do after I clean up the Rosenthal case is go to the North Pole. That diary of Scott's is one of the greatest things ever printed."

Clancy and Cashin then began to rag Becker about being such a literary type. "Give us a little Latin," said Clancy.

"Well, I will," said Becker. "*Cum grano salis* (with a grain of salt). That is a Latin quotation that you reporters ought to study. I think that will be all the Latin for today," he added and was taken back to his cell.

Early the next afternoon Helen Becker arrived at Sing Sing with his going-away clothes. Before reporters were allowed to see Becker again, the warden cleared out his office except for one keeper and brought Helen Becker in to have a moment almost alone with her husband. "For more than a year I have not even touched his hand," she had said in Shay's office after she heard the news. What happened now could hardly be described as a conjugal visit, but it was probably as close to it as Clancy felt he could go. "I was allowed to see him in a room—really to see him, not through steel netting and iron bars, but to sit beside him and kiss him," she recalled later. "It was the first time I had kissed my husband in sixteen months."

Becker then put on the sack suit and overcoat and black derby that his wife had brought and asked permission to say good-bye to some of his friends in the prison. After he had visited the death house, he thanked the warden for his kindness and went around shaking hands with all the keepers. "Becker is very popular," Clancy explained to the press. "We judge prisoners by the way they act here, not what happened before in their lives." Father

Cashin stepped forward with further enlightenment. "Sometimes tribulations are necessary to bring a man to look on things differently," he said, portentously. "St. Paul was a sort of a cop, too, you know, and needed a knock on the head to bring him around to righteousness."

There had been a massive snowfall two days before, and the trip to the Ossining station had to be made by sleigh. Becker, his wife (although she was in mourning, her cheeks were "scarlet with happiness"), and the two guards from the New York sheriff's office climbed into the first sleigh. Nine other sleighs filled with reporters and photographers followed behind, sleigh bells jangling in the clear, cold air. As the long caravan moved past the front row of cell blocks, "from a hundred slitted windows," reported the *Sun's* man on the scene, "came a roar of cheering as convicts yelled their good wishes to a man who had got another chance . . . an uncanny sound of gladness wafting out of the grim buildings."

The train trip to the city was shorter than expected. The sheriff sent a car to take Becker off at the 125 Street station in order to avoid the thousands of New Yorkers who had thronged Grand Central waiting for him to arrive there. It was not believed to be a friendly crowd. Thus the reporters who had made the Sing Sing trip and been impressed by the new Becker were reminded that, however the prisoners might regard him, to the world outside he was an evil man and one who, to widespread indignation, might even be going to beat the rap. Late that evening Becker was locked up in Cell 120 in the Tombs, three cells away from the one where he had spent the months after his arrest in 1912. Within a few days both prosecution and defense forces were hard at work getting ready for his second murder trial.

On the afternoon the Court of Appeals decision was handed down, long before the other newspapermen saw Becker, Warden Clancy had had a call from Herbert Bayard Swope. In the year and a half since the murder the *World* man had not become quite the mahatma he would turn into later in his life, but he was on his way. He had made so much money on the Rosenthal case at space rates that he was outdrawing the publisher, who hastily put him on salary. There was no question thereafter that he was *the* reporter on the *World*. His assignments had become more and more important, and his name was beginning to be known all over the country. He always explained, as he would throughout his life, that it all went back to the Rosenthal murder case, the story that had really got him started.

Now the famous Swope had no trouble getting Clancy on the phone or persuading the Sing Sing warden to do a little chore for him. Clancy was to ask Becker for a special message for Swope on how the prisoner had taken the news.

"Do you have any special message for Swope?" Clancy asked the happy man in his cell.

"Sure," said Becker. "Tell him to look at verses one through seventeen of the fifty-first chapter of Ecclesiasticus." As the *World* story described it the next day, the fifty-first chapter of Ecclesiasticus (which appears only in the Roman Catholic Bible) "indeed contains verses strikingly applicable to his situation." In this passage the writer, a priest, gives thanks to God:

> Thou hast preserved my body from destruction, from the snare of the unjust tongue and from the lips of them that forge lies, and in the sight of them that stood by. And Thou hast delivered me . . . from them that did roar, prepared to devour . . . They compassed me on every side, and there was no one that would help me . . . And Thou hast saved me from destruction and hast delivered me from the evil time.

"No other message for Swope, just the Bible reference?" Clancy asked him.

"That's all," said Becker. "He'll know what I mean."

XIX

SECTION 528 of the New York State Code of Criminal Procedure reads: "When the judgment is of death, the court of appeals may order a new trial, if it be satisfied that the verdict was against the weight of evidence or against law, or that justice requires a new trial. . . ."

The six-to-one decision of the Court of Appeals after Becker's first trial took up seventy-seven printed pages and was one of the longest handed down by the court in a decade. It began with a description of the murder and took judicial notice that public interest in and excitement about it "were sustained and stimulated by daily newspaper reports, apparently emanating from authoritative sources, that members of the police force were . . . implicated and that the clues were being followed which would lead to one 'higher-up' in the police force." Soon these rumors had been directed specifically at the defendant, who in short order was indicted and convicted. The prosecution had never suggested that the defendant had directly participated in the killing "but the claim is that the defendant accomplished the murder by proxy, twice removed."

The court noted that "absolutely no testimony was given in the trial directly tending to connect the defendant with the murder by other than six witnesses. Without their support the People's case utterly fails." Dismissing two of these witnesses, ex-lawyer Hallen and "feathers merchant" Luban, as "convicts or persons charged with crime who were temporarily released from jail in order to be witnesses" and their stories as "inherently improbable and subject to suspicion," the court then considered the cases of Rose, Webber, and Vallon. "Indisputably they were guilty of the murder and . . . subject to the punishment of death," from which they had been saved by agreements in writing "giving immunity to them, conceded murderers, if they would furnish evidence tending to convict Becker." Schepps, the court indicated, was probably in the same boat, some of the members of the court believing that although "the presiding justice permitted the jury to find that Schepps was not an accomplice," this finding was "opposed to the overwhelming weight of evidence." Having negotiated the immunity agreements, the court added, the four major witnesses against Becker were then confined in a place where "ample opportunities existed for collaboration on the evidence they were to give under their life-saving agreement to convict Becker."

On the question of the police lieutenant's motives, the court observed that until the publication of Rosenthal's story in the *World* on July 13, 1912, the gambler had been unsuccessful in persuading any public official to show the slightest interest in his charges and that Becker, according to several prosecution witnesses, had "expressed himself as quite indifferent to Rosenthal's efforts." Yet the prosecution claimed that at some point several weeks before the *World* story appeared Becker had met with the gambler witnesses in Harlem and commissioned Rosenthal's murder. The murder project had then "somehow languished" until the expedition of the Sam Paul Association less than forty-eight hours before the shooting. The court mentioned as a possible explanation for this languishment the defense argument that "if the exact truth could be known it would be found that the plan to murder Rosenthal was not formulated by Becker in a vacant lot in Harlem in June but on the excursion of an enraged gambling fraternity a few hours before the killing occurred." Also, "it does make one somewhat wonder," added the court, why Becker should have been engaged in such strenuous efforts to discredit Rosenthal in the hours before the murder if he had already made arrangements to put him out of the way permanently.

As for the rendezvous in Harlem, "if the existence of the conference is not established the case against the defendant falls in utter collapse." Yet the four witnesses had not seemed able to remember when it had taken place. "If the Harlem conference ever occurred, as claimed by the People, it is urged that two other witnesses could have testified to it." The court then went into the cases of Moe and Itch, noting their affidavits that they had never driven the gamblers on such a trip and the fact that during the trial the district attorney's office had been aware of their denials and had not called them as witnesses. "Thus Becker stands condemned without any opportunity for a jury to hear these persons. . . . It is urged that the mind of an appellate court should recoil from the proposition to take the defendant's life without hearing this testimony, which should go so far toward settling the question whether the primary event in the People's theory ever occurred."

A new trial was not formally granted on the ground that the verdict was against the weight of evidence. Some members of the court thought this should be done, noted the justice who wrote the prevailing opinion, but since this feeling was not unanimous among those voting to reverse, they had decided to rely instead on a ground "on which there will and can be no difference of opinion." Considering "all the conditions attending and surrounding this case" and the fact that only "dangerous and degenerate witnesses" gave significant testimony against the defendant he "certainly was entitled to a scrupulously fair and impartial trial. . . . We do not think the defendant had such a trial."

Defense counsel Stryker once described the proceedings that led to Becker's first conviction as "a shambles of justice," and the Court of Appeals seemed to agree. It began by citing the near-eviction of the leading defense counsel from the court before the jury had even been chosen and went on to complain that the district attorney in his opening statement had "committed the serious error of making many statements either in words or to the effect that Becker was a 'grafter' and was collecting blackmail and protection from gambling houses . . . that he was a 'cool, calm, calculating, grafting police officer.' . . . There can be no doubt about the very prejudicial character of these statements." The repeated charge that Becker was a grafter had "inflamed the minds of the jury." This was the court's only overt criticism of Whitman's conduct during the trial. In the matter of Justice Goff it was far less restrained.

"It may be stated very briefly but accurately that repeatedly without any objection, complaint or request by the very able and alert district attorney, the court on its own motion criticized the defendant's counsel for some little peculiarity in the form of his questions which was utterly innocuous; intervened to protect the People's witnesses on cross-examination; objected to and excluded questions asked by defendant's counsel and on one occasion when such counsel asked if the district attorney would concede a fact about which apparently there was no dispute, the court ruled for the district attorney, 'No, I will not let him concede it.' "

The opinion mentioned that "at other times haste seems to become the essence of the trial," and took further note of Goff's bias in favor of the prosecution: "With one exception . . . every appeal by defendant's counsel to the discretion of the court for an adjournment, for the very common leave to reopen the examination of a witness in order to correct some inadvertent omission or utilize on cross-examination of a hostile witness some newly acquired information . . . was denied, whereas applications of a similar character on the part of the People were quite uniformly granted." The court cited one occasion when McIntyre begged for adjournment during the cross-examination of Schepps because he was exhausted from the long day on his feet. He was refused, forcing him to terminate the questioning. Immediately afterward when Whitman asked for an adjournment because his witness— Mrs. Rosenthal—was "exhausted" (she had been sitting on a bench for a couple of hours waiting to be called), Goff granted it instantly.

Goff's rulings, the court held, were often erroneous not as a matter of discretion but as a matter of law. Among these rulings were Goff's refusal to allow the introduction of the immunity agreements, Rose's contradictory "confession," and the Hot Springs Commission reports on Schepps' erratic testimony in time for them to be used in cross-examination by the defense. Goff had often treated such defense witnesses as Reich as if "they were committing or were liable at any moment to commit perjury." On the other hand he had acted toward a prosecution witness like Schepps with great deference and permissiveness although "there can be no possible question concerning the character of this man or concerning the extent to which the truthfulness of his evidence as a whole was impeached." Goff had also erred as a matter of law in not allowing McIntyre to show that the gamblers "were in constant communication with each other in prison engaged in the common undertaking of attempting to save their own lives by placing in forfeit that of Becker." The court also censured him for cutting short the cross-examination of numerous prosecution witnesses, the worst example of this being, it said, the case of Bald Jack Rose.

Rose was "concededly the most important witness of the People," his testimony was "a corner stone" of the People's case, on which the prosecution especially relied to "fasten the charge of murder on the defendant." The court then described at length the debacle of McIntyre's cross-examination of Rose during the afternoon and evening of Columbus Day. The only beneficiary of Goff's insistence that both direct examination and cross-examination of Rose be completed in one session was clearly the prosecution, noted the court. Given sleep, sustenance, and an opportunity to examine the witness' testimony on direct examination for signs of weakness and inconsistency, the defense counsel would have had a good chance of discrediting Rose. In the view of the court, this was the outcome that Goff's ruling had been intended to prevent. "We do not think that it was the duty of the trial justice to protect the prosecution against this danger. . . ." And, finally, the court held that in his charge to the jury Goff had outlined "most effectively" the claims of the prosecution, ignoring "any arguments or evidence in behalf of the defendant."

Taken altogether, the court held, the actions of the trial judge constituted grounds for reversal "in a case where proof even of a distant connection by the defense with the actual homicide rests upon the testimony of criminals and degenerates in whose characters nobody has at any time claimed to discover any trace of such conscience or moral sense as would be any more bounden by their oaths as witnesses than by the blowing of the wind." Becker, the opinion concluded, "never had a fair chance to defend his life and it would be a lasting reproach to the state if under those circumstances it should exact its forfeiture."

The prevailing opinion, one of the most slashing in the history of the Appeals Court, was written by Frank Hiscock, a Republican from Syracuse. There was a written dissent by Justice William Werner. Werner, also a member of Whitman's party, declared that the judgment of the facts should be left to the jury. He then

outlined the facts almost exactly as they had been presented by
the prosecution. The trial justice, he declared, was entitled to use
his discretion in all rulings, and it was not the business of the
Appeals Court to speculate as to his motives. There had never
been any connection between the gamblers and the gunmen until
Becker entered the scene, said Werner. The immunity agreements
were "a collateral matter." This dissent so angered another of the
justices, Nathan Miller, that he entered his own concurring
opinion in answer to it, a document that dealt even more severely
with the trial judge and the prosecution than had the prevailing
opinion. If Werner virtually repeated the prosecution's case,
Miller admittedly adopted a large share of the arguments offered
by Shay in his plea for a new trial for the defendant.

The verdict, said Miller, had been produced "by the compelling
influence of a forceful judge, whose prejudgment of the case had
unconsciously created a determination to convict the defendant."
As for leaving the facts to the jury, "I emphatically deny that we
are obliged to sign the defendant's death warrant simply because
a jury has believed an improbable tale told by four vile criminals
to shift the death penalty from themselves to another." Becker, he
declared, not only had had no adequate motive to plot Rosenthal's
murder at the time of the alleged Harlem conference, as the main
opinion had suggested, but no motive thereafter. "In view of his
rise to the position of lieutenant of police, he must be credited
with at least a grain of sense and with some knowledge of how
crimes are detected." The moment Rosenthal's charges against
him appeared in the *World* "he certainly had less to fear from the
uncorroborated charge of being interested in a gambling place
made by a discredited gambler than he had from a charge of
murder committed with the aid of eight of the worst criminals to
be found anywhere, which was sure to be laid at his door." From
that time on he had "the strongest motives of self-preservation"
not to commit the murder. "Rose makes the defendant say to him
in the last telephone conversation before the murder: 'Now . . .
tonight is the time and it will just fit. It will look like the
gamblers did it on account of his threatened squeal.' Imagine the
defendant telling the men whom he had employed to commit
murder that the time was ripe because they would be suspected!"
wrote Miller.

He insisted that the story of the Harlem conference was "a pure fabrication" for which the witnesses had "studied and rehearsed their parts." Going over the details of his constant presence at all the crucial moments leading up to the crime, Miller declared flatly that Schepps was an accomplice. The meeting afterward in front of the Murray Hill Baths was another fabrication. ("They evidently thought it expedient to connect the defendant with the payment of the $1,000 to the 'gunmen.' . . . I shall not discuss the likelihood that the defendant, if guilty, would hold a consultation with two of the murderers on the sidewalk on Forty-second Street within two blocks of the scene of the murder two or three hours after its commission.") "In my opinion," Miller concluded, "a new trial should be granted because the newly-discovered evidence imperatively demands it in the interest of justice, because the verdict is shockingly against the weight of evidence, and because the trial was so conducted as to insure a verdict of guilty regardless of the evidence."

There was widespread sympathy for Charles Whitman, whose best-known achievement in public life had been dealt such a crushing blow. He responded with dignity. "It is not the province of the District Attorney of New York County to comment on the decisions of the Court of Appeals," he announced. "The District Attorney is the last man in the world who should want a conviction to stand that is not justified in law."

Not all statements on the subject were so temperate. Judge Edward Swann, of the Court of General Sessions, a long-time admirer of Whitman's, pointed out that if the British found one trial enough for the wife-murdering Dr. Crippen, Lieutenant Becker should certainly be entitled to no more. "The one indisputable fact is that the reversal in the Becker case is a scandal," fumed the *Times*, "that it brings our administration of criminal law into deep and deserved contempt." The editors there were also reminded of the British system of justice. In that country, by contrast, "there would be no new trial for Becker." By this time, the *Times* pointed out with apparent approval, "he would already be dead." Rereading the decision later in the week the *Times* decided that what it found most regrettable in Hiscock's opinion was his reference to "the atmosphere of the trial, the atmosphere of prejudice." Although the court had not emphasized this point, it was one not commonly made and would be heavily relied on by Becker's lawyers in his second trial.

Over at the *World* the editors acknowledged glumly that Americans would have to accept the decision as final in law "although Becker is one of the most cold-blooded scoundrels that ever lived and had more to gain from the death of Rosenthal than any man." But how did it happen, the editors asked, reasonably enough, that the Court of Appeals by a vote of six to one found so many errors in Goff's conduct of Becker's trial and, by unanimous decision, none at all in that of the gunmen? The next day the *World* ran a cartoon entitled "We Who Are About to Die Salute You," showing the gunmen watching tearfully as Becker, in full uniform, strode out of Sing Sing carrying a satchelful of cash marked "Police Graft."

By the middle of March when it was time for the dinner that the New York County Lawyers Association annually tendered to the members of the Court of Appeals, public indignation over the decision had reached such a point that a far larger percentage than usual of the Appeals bench judges turned up for the occasion to defend themselves and their court. The presiding justice of the Appellate Division of the State Supreme Court, who almost never attended such gatherings, made a long speech complaining that "citizens of the whole continent of America from Canada to Patagonia have been treated to criticism of decisions of the Court of Appeals of this state as though these decisions were the enunciation of some monstrous doctrine." A former chief judge of the Court of Appeals declared that the decision ought to be a source of congratulation, that the people should be gratified that the court had refused to consign a man to the grave without ample evidence. Nevertheless, noted the *Times*, most of the six hundred lawyers present "gave evidence that the people are growing very restless about judicial procedure."

Even the usually urbane F.P.A., now writing his latter-day Pepys diary for the *Tribune*, was wrathful over Becker's second chance: "Dreadful things, methought, and not destined to give lawbreakers great respect for the law." In *Harper's Weekly* a few weeks later Raymond B. Fosdick, a former New York commissioner of accounts, who had just returned from a trip abroad, insisted that all of Europe was laughing at the outcome. Perhaps Americans didn't realize how closely Europeans had followed the

Becker case. Before the decision, in every country he visited, he had been greeted with the question, "What about Becker? Will the 'System' save him?" Now, said Fosdick, all of Europe believed that it had.

The gross arrogance that allegedly had led Becker to plot Rosenthal's murder was the most typical theme in his conversations, as reported by the state's witnesses in his first trial. "What do you think I am in this department? I can do what I damn please." Or, in reference to the gamblers' taking the stand against him: "No jury on earth is ever going to believe them." To the great advantage—and surely not entirely to the surprise—of the prosecution, the response of the average contrary-minded newspaper reader and particularly of the average juryman to this kind of boast seems to have been something like: "Oh you can, can you?" Or "Oh, they won't, won't they?" No quotations from Becker except those relayed through these state's witnesses displayed anything like this degree of recklessness. Immediately after the Appeals Court decision a remark was made that fitted perfectly into the pattern the prosecution had established for the police lieutenant. It was made not by Becker but by his lawyer, Joseph Shay.

"I boldly predict that Becker will not be tried again," declared Shay in his moment of understandable pride and jubilation. Becker would not be tried, he said, because the only possible result of such a trial would be a triumphant acquittal. Publicly at least, Becker never associated himself with this prediction other than to say that he "sincerely believed" that he would one day be free. At the time Shay spoke, it appeared that the district attorney agreed with the defense counsel. "It became known," reported the *Times* in its story on the decision, "that Mr. Whitman did not believe a second conviction would be possible in view of the decision handed down by the court."

But the smug triumph of Becker's lawyer had infuriated all citizens who sincerely believed that justice had been cheated in the case ("Oh, he won't, won't he?"). Within a few days the remark was being described as "the boast of Becker and his counsel" and not long afterward had transmogrified into "Becker's taunt that Whitman would never dare try him again." The *World* was especially indignant. E. J. Kahn, Jr. insists that Swope's proprietary feeling about newsworthy events would cause him to

shout in a voice that carried the length of the city room, "Who's
writing up *my* snowstorm?" or "Who's covering *my* riot?" His
sense of identification would never be more intense than in the
Rosenthal matter—"*my* murder" beyond all murders—and Swope
undoubtedly felt personally insulted by the Court of Appeals
judgment.

Whitman's duty was clear, the *World* declared sternly. "Whitman must try Becker again. If this man Becker be turned loose
upon the community with the stain of Herman Rosenthal's blood
washed from his hands, the final responsibility. . . . must not
rest with the District Attorney of New York." The district attorney
of New York, his spirits rising, came to agree. Becker would be
tried again, after all, he announced a few days later, in spite of
the terrible handicaps under which the prosecution must now
labor.

Whitman's problems were imposing. Witness Rose, of course,
was available. Bald Jack was still plying the lecture circuit,
having worked his way down to Methodists and local YMCAs by
this time. As a professional reformed criminal he was naturally
only too glad to assist the district attorney once again. Harry
Vallon was more available than ever after reading Becker's
charge that he had done some of the shooting himself. Bridgey
Webber, however, gave the prosecution a hard time. He announced at the start that he had no intention of going on the
stand again. He and his brother-in-law now owned a thriving
paper box factory in Passaic, and he wanted to forget about the
Becker case. Three times an assistant district attorney traveled to
Passaic and vainly tried to talk him into changing his mind.
Finally Whitman had to make the trip himself. Possibly he
pointed out that murder is an extraditable offense. Late in April
he was able to report that Webber would come across the river
and testify after all.

Whitman's roster of corroborative witnesses was in an even
sorrier state. Although the Court of Appeals had described Sam
Schepps' testimony as "impeached," the district attorney announced in desperation that the former nonaccomplice would
again be a leading witness for the prosecution. At considerable
expense the East Sider was brought back from Vancouver, British
Columbia, put up at a hotel in the constant company of a member
of the prosecution staff, and paid a sizable cash bonus. He never

did appear in court, but this considerate treatment—and presumably some references to the immunity agreement—kept him out of the defense camp. Using the disbarred lawyer Hallen was out of the question in view of the language of the reversing opinion. Morris Luban, the other discredited corroborating witness, was an even more dismal prospect.

After Luban had testified in the first trial about the curious events in the Lafayette Baths steam room and been released from the New Jersey swindling charge "because of assistance accorded the District Attorney of New York County, N.Y.," he had gone on the payroll of Whitman's office as one performing "confidential services." The employment had lasted from November 1912 until the middle of the next January, during which period New York County had also bought him various items of clothing, had his teeth fixed, and paid a $625 board bill for him at the Broadway Central Hotel. Nevertheless, three months after he left the payroll, Luban had accompanied a friend of Becker's to a lawyer's office and in the presence of Lieutenant John Becker, who presumably made it worth his while, swore that there had not been a word of truth to the story he had told on the stand. Hearing of this development Whitman naturally mentioned the possibility of a perjury indictment, and a few days later the lawyer was told that Luban had changed his mind and wanted his affidavit back. It was returned but, as the prosecution no doubt suspected, the lawyer had taken the precaution of photographing it for his files. Luban clearly would not do.

In his distress over the way things were going, Whitman could hardly have been comforted by a statement quoted in the papers about this time from "a prominent Republican district leader" that Whitman's "availability" for higher public office would be dubious if he failed to convict Becker the second time. Whitman dealt with the witness situation as best he could. As usual his method of attack involved the press. He simply announced to reporters every few days in the weeks before the trial that one more, two more, four more witnesses ("one a woman") had been discovered who would fully corroborate the various stories of Rose and company. No less than six persons, "two of them former policemen," he declared just before the trial began, would support the story of the Harlem conference.

During April and early May 1914 at least four men (no women and no former policemen) were on the payroll of Whitman's office, apparently scheduled to be corroborating witnesses. Several were small-time crimnials. All of them, Becker and his lawyers believed, had been recruited by Morris Luban's older brother, Jacob. Jacob Luban's most recent conviction for forgery had resulted in a suspended sentence, and while he waited this one out he was on the district attorney's payroll for over two years, from November 1912 through December 1914, listed as a "confidential investigator." Unfortunately the sworn deposition of one of this stable of witnesses fell into the hands of the *American*, which published it early in April. Signed by one Jacob Goldman, a convicted forger, it established him as Morris Luban's intended replacement. Goldman, too, he was ready to swear, had happened to be in the Lafayette steam room to hear Becker order Bald Jack to "croak Rosenthal." When the *American* soon thereafter revealed that Goldman had been in jail in another state at the time of the alleged eavesdropping, Goldman's name was scratched from the prosecution's agenda. Probably Whitman took a closer look at the rest of Luban's recruits. In the end he never used any of them.

One nonwitness was worth a good deal to Whitman. This was Moe Levy, one of the two chauffeurs who had supposedly driven the gamblers to the Harlem conference and whose testimony was absolutely essential, the Appeals Court opinion had said, if a man was to be executed on the theory that the conference had occurred. Itch Schoenhaus, the other chauffeur, was either lying very low indeed or had left town. But in mid-April, 1914—ignoring Levy's previous affidavit that denied any knowledge of the Harlem meeting—Whitman began announcing in daily wrap-up stories about the case that Levy would testify for the prosecution that the Harlem conference had happened just as the gamblers had described it. He never did take the stand, probably on account of the previous affidavit. But because of the barrage of stories about his coming appearance it seems probable that many newspaper readers, possibly even some members of the jury, never quite realized this fact. Before and during the trial Levy slept each night in a hotel suite in the company of one of the district attorney's staff. When he agreed to testify for the prosecution

Whitman put him on the state payroll as an auto inspector. One way or another, Levy remained out of reach of the defense.

Besides coping with the witness problem, Whitman was busy during these weeks fending off efforts of the four gunmen to evade the death sentence. The Court of Appeals decision upholding their conviction (People vs. Seidenschner) had rejected their complaint that they were referred to throughout the trial by "opprobrious and insulting" nicknames. By their own testimony, the court pointed out, the four men had been known by at least twenty-three different names. The only possible error, said the opinion, was in allowing the addition of words to the nicknames "and such added words," said the court, presumably thinking of Gyp the Blood, "were not without evidence to justify their use." The gunmen's counsel, a former Tammany magistrate, made a last-ditch attempt to save them by appealing to Goff once again for a new trial on the ground of newly discovered evidence. Several witnesses appeared who were willing to place each of the gunmen elsewhere at the time of the crime. The plea failed.

A few days before the gunmen's scheduled execution Whitman pulled a trick that seemed repellent to nonlegal minds. Although he had stated repeatedly in recent weeks that the survival of the gunmen was irrelevant for Becker's coming trial, that there was no reason to delay their trip to the electric chair, he was advised that it would be prudent to have two of his witnesses reidentify them for the purposes of the case. With the cooperation of the warden, he brought to the Sing Sing death house Krause, the former waiter whom Whitman and Dr. Parkhurst's Society for Prevention of Crime had kept on their payrolls all this time, and Shapiro, the chauffeur, whose indictment for murder Whitman, with considerable foresight, had not yet got around to dismissing. Crouched in his cell, Gyp the Blood suddenly looked up to find the district attorney and his party peering in at him. Whitman turned to his witnesses expectantly. Krause and Shapiro were a study in confusion.

"Hello, Gyp," said the warden, helping out.

"That's Gyp all right," said Shapiro quickly.

By this time, with a howl of rage, Gyp and the other three gunmen in their adjoining cells had thrown themselves flat on their cots and pulled blankets over their heads. They refused to show themselves further until Whitman and his party had left.

Meanwhile, according to one possibly frivolous reporter, they kept shouting that Whitman would only identify them over their dead bodies. Whitman's baiting of men so close to death, whatever the legal point involved, brought him considerable criticism. By this time Italian and Jewish organizations on the East Side were beginning to make noises about ethnic discrimination. The district attorney's office, along with most right-minded New Yorkers, undoubtedly breathed a sigh of relief when the gunmen were finally executed early on the morning of April 13. Elaborate memorial services followed all over the East Side. A young social worker named Harry Hopkins, fresh from Iowa, was deeply shocked when he went to a settlement house boys' club meeting and found his charges standing in reverent silence honoring four thugs just electrocuted for murder.

Two hours before the execution Lefty Louie had asked to see Warden Clancy and begged him to do something to save Dago Frank who, he said, had left Forty-third Street before the shooting. Clancy found Frank just finishing his last confession to Father Cashin. He swore that he hadn't taken part in the murder. This testimony was not considered as interesting as his subsequent remark.

"So far as I know Becker had nothing to do with this case," he told his mother and sister, the warden, and Father Cashin. "I think it was just a regular gamblers' fight."

Cashin pointed out that Dago, now a good Catholic (there are few atheists in death row) would have known he would be in mortal sin if he told a lie between his last confession and the moment of his death. Lawyer Shay also had something to say. "That cinches it for Becker," he told reporters. "He will be acquitted without a doubt."

But the following day Shay announced his withdrawal from the case. He was too sensitive for criminal practice, he said. Also, he and John Becker, who was now active for the defense, weren't getting along too well. Again there was talk of calling in Jerome, but again he passed it up, and within a few days Martin Manton entered the scene as Becker's new counsel.

Manton, a Brooklyn Irishman, was then thirty-four years old and known as an energetic, though not particularly distinguished, Criminal Courts lawyer. His specialty (like Shay's) was negligence rather than murder cases. The year before he had become the law partner of W. Bourke Cockran, but this seems to have been mainly an office-sharing arrangement. Manton's own political connections at this time were meager. Cockran was usually referred to as "the famous Tammany orator," although his relations with Tammany had cooled by 1914. Like most members of the Wigwam, Cockran had little use for the most successful Democrats of his time, Grover Cleveland, Bryan, and Woodrow Wilson. Unlike most of his friends on Fourteenth Street, he had not always been satisfied just to sit out their national election campaigns. He had twice gone over to the other side. In 1896 he had actively supported McKinley and in 1912 had deserted Wilson for Teddy Roosevelt. For four years, beginning in 1905, he had been Grand Sachem of Tammany Hall, but he had then quarreled with Charles Murphy and been on the political sideline since early 1910. The ups and downs of his political career covered such a long period—he was elected to Congress in 1886, '88, '90, and '92; 1904, '06, and '08, and, after another hiatus, would be elected in 1920 and 1922—that one historian of the World War I period described him as being a leading Tammany orator "like his father before him."

But Cockran's relationship with Al Smith remained close, and he got on well with Smith's chief Tammany mentor, Tom Foley. Many people believed that someone from this old Tim Sullivan crowd had asked Cockran to take on the Becker defense and that, after declining the honor, he had suggested his young partner. Manton worked hard for his client during the next fifteen months but, unfortunately for Becker, he would underestimate the opposition.

X X

A month before the start on May 5 of Becker's second trial, the Brethren of the Amen Corner, a fraternity of local political reporters, held their annual dinner meeting. Among the six hundred guests was Whitman, who sat beside the incumbent New York governor, Martin Glynn. (William Sulzer, Tim Sullivan's man, had proved unco-operative about certain patronage matters, and Charles Murphy, in an impressive show of political muscle, had simply had him impeached.) As usual, the evening featured irreverent skits about prominent public figures. The most successful turn that night was one called "The Grand Jury Stunt." It depicted a meeting of the grand jury and had the foreman declaring, "We've got to indict ninety or a hundred men before the papers go to press or we won't get on the front page—at least the District Attorney won't." Finally he announced that an indictment had been agreed upon. Asked for the names of the criminals, he handed over a copy of the New York telephone book. All five million New Yorkers had been indicted at the insistence of the district attorney, the foreman announced. When a spokesman for the accused citizens stepped forward and asked to see the grand jury minutes on which their indictment was based, the foreman told him, "You're too late—the District Attorney has just given them to the reporters."

The district attorney of an American city has certain built-in advantages over the counsel for the defense, and now, as he had earlier in the weeks preceding the first trial, Whitman played them for all they were worth. At what seemed to some like shrewdly spaced intervals various of Whitman's off-and-on witnesses—Schepps, Rose, Vallon, and even the "worthless" Luban and self-impeached Margolies—announced, one after the other, that they had been approached by agents of Charles Becker and offered two thousand, five thousand, ten thousand dollars to testify for the defense. During the same period a rash of newspaper stories appeared, reporting, with the D.A.'s office as the source, that the Police Department was raising a Becker defense fund from criminals of all types. ("SYSTEM RAISES DEFENSE FUND TO SILENCE BECKER," "BIG BECKER DEFENSE FUND RAISED BY THREATS.") When these headlines grew repetitive—and when no evidence to support them appeared—stories hinted of startling testimony scheduled by the prosecution (to be given by those new witnesses who would never take the stand). And on a really dull day Whitman would mention that he had never told the full story of what had happened between him and Becker in the Forty-seventh Street station house just after the murder. If the defense pushed him too far . . .

There was still another ploy. Two days after the execution of the gunmen in mid-April one of the eleventh-hour witnesses for the gunmen swore out a statement, released by Whitman's office, saying that he had committed perjury in claiming that one or another of the gunmen had been elsewhere on the murder night. During the next two weeks two other such witnesses joined the procession of sworn perjurors. Each implied that someone had put him up to swearing falsely, someone who believed it was to Becker's advantage to have the gunmen remain alive. Almost daily the witnesses issued statements enlarging upon their accounts of subornment until, on the day before the trial began, one of them declared it had been Lieutenant John Becker who had talked them into it by threats of death and, alternatively, the promise that his brother Charley would pay them well. No evidence to support this charge by admitted perjurors was produced. (John Becker naturally denied it.) The routine preliminaries of the second Becker trial hadn't attracted anything like the press attention of its predecessor. But the successive stories indicating that bully boy Becker was up to his old tricks revived most New Yorkers' deepest suspicions, and international crises now took second place. The lead headline that members of the jury panel read on their way into the Criminal Courts Building the morning of the first day of the second trial was "PERJURY BOUGHT BY JOHN BECKER/ DEATH THREAT LAID TO BECKER CASE PERJURY."

The fact that counsel Manton had only been associated with the defendant in a capital case for two and a half weeks before the trial did not seem to concern anyone, and Manton did not ask for a postponement as the *personae* gathered once again in the same stuffy courtroom.

The trial's opening day brought a surprise for the prosecution, however. Not Manton but his more famous partner, Bourke Cockran, took the floor for Becker. Probably the main reason Cockran had not signed on for the case himself was because he had assumed that Becker was guilty as charged. But in the fortnight that his junior partner had been Becker's counsel Cockran had taken a closer look and decided there was dirty work afoot, a judgment he soon made retroactive to the beginning of the case. From this time on he was apparently convinced that Becker was innocent of the murder charge. His appearance on the first day of the trial was to make a series of motions, including one requesting that the judge hold Whitman in contempt of court.

"I have never seen his like or in some respects his equal," Winston Churchill once wrote of Cockran. On an afternoon in the early 1950s Adlai Stevenson was talking to Churchill. "I asked him something I'd always wanted to know," Stevenson told a friend afterward. "I asked on whom or what he had based his oratorical style." Churchill's answer had been: "It was an American statesman who inspired me when I was nineteen." Bourke Cockran was the name, he said. Stevenson was amused at Churchill's having called Cockran a "statesman"—"just an Irish politician with the gift of gab," the younger man thought privately—but the prime minister had reason to rate Cockran very high, at least for his discernment. "I firmly believe you would take a commanding position in public life at the first opportunity which arose. . . . I was so profoundly impressed with the vigor of your language and the breadth of your views . . . that I conceived a very high opinion of your future career," Cockran wrote to Churchill when the young Sandhurst graduate was twenty-one and considered unpromising by his fondest relatives. During the next decade Churchill wrote constantly to Cockran and visited him at intervals and, according to Randolph Churchill, "Cockran in some ways fulfilled a role that (his father) should have filled if he had survived." Churchill astonished Stevenson by quoting long excerpts from Cockran's speeches of sixty years before. "He was my model," he said.

Cockran's impact on his audience was not purely a matter of oratorical skill. Churchill mentioned "his enormous head, gleaming eyes and flexible countenance." "Who that ever saw it," asked the *Times* after Cockran's death in 1923, "can forget that tall, impressive figure, burly in later years, the deep-set eyes, with those curious, curved, almost Oriental eyelids, the powerful nose . . . the noble face with something Spanish . . . as well as Celtic, something a little strange about it anyway; with flashing from the eyes to the lips, above all the marvelous voice charged with mockery, with passion, always with music." A look of consternation crossed Whitman's face as the lion-headed Cockran moved toward the front of the courtroom where Charles Becker was for the second time on trial for his life.

There is a way of handling an imposing and venerable figure such as Cockran, however, and Whitman found it. "The gray-haired lawyer was in a rage," noted the *Times*. "The District Attorney's answer to the thrusts and gibes was a cynical smile. Even when the older lawyer's fist was clenched the District Attorney kept on smiling." The judge, Samuel Seabury, was of the same frame of mind: "He refused to take Cockran's arguments seriously."

The motions Cockran made asked for a change of venue on the ground that the judicial atmosphere had been perverted by the district attorney's recent actions and requested that "Charles S. Whitman be adjudged in contempt for deliberately giving out statements on the eve of this trial to injure the interests of this defendant." When Whitman said he had no control over the newspapers, Cockran pointed out that many of the sensational rumors had been spread by Whitman himself in a formal interview in the *World*. As for the story about John Becker's having commissioned perjury, that, Cockran said, had been "the culminating atrocity of the District Attorney." The alleged perjuror's affidavit describing John Becker as having "coached and trained" him had been "prepared in the office of the District Attorney and malevolently timed" for the afternoon before the start of the trial.

It had been given out to reporters in typewritten form by the
district attorney's office, Cockran added—quoting a *Morning
Telegraph* man in support—and the office had then slyly requested the reporters to say that the document had come not from
Whitman but directly from the prisoner in the Tombs.

"On my oath of office I deny that anything came from me," said
Whitman, rising to his feet.

"Your secretary gave it out," said Cockran.

Whitman, still smiling, said he knew nothing about that but
that "anyhow I believe the story about John Becker's part in
things." Cockran swerved toward the bench, clearly expecting a
reprimand for the prosecutor, but Judge Seabury said nothing. "I
didn't say it was true, I said I *believed* it to be true," said Whitman, with an amiable air of making amends. Nodding, Seabury
then denied each of Cockran's motions and ordered the selection
of the jury to begin. Cockran, his face purple, stomped up the
aisle and out of the courtroom. "I am through with the Becker
case, through with it," he told reporters who followed him into the
corridor. "This is not a trial, it is an assassination." He left town
that afternoon, and Martin Manton again took over full responsibility for Becker's defense.

In the prevailing opinion of the Court of Appeals Justice
Hiscock had commented at length on "the harmonious relations
which prevailed between the court and the prosecution." The
harmony continued in the second trial. Seabury and Whitman
had much in common. Both had practiced law on a marginal
basis for a few years, got into politics fighting Tammany Hall,
and first been elected to office on this platform. Each now had his
eye firmly fixed on a particular high office above the one he
presently held. In both cases their performance in the Becker trial
would have an important bearing on whether they got the office
they wanted. At this point it was not the same office, and although they were of the same generation—Seabury was five years
younger—they were not of the same party. They entered the
courtroom with a common purpose: to see that the record in the
second Becker trial was not subject to reversal by the Court of
Appeals, which would have been awkward for both of them. An
air of mutual deference and politeness prevailed between them
throughout the proceedings.

Seabury had run on the anti-Tammany ticket for the lowly City

Court in 1899 and been defeated. He had won in 1901, swept into office by Jerome's energetic campaign for the Fusionist reformers. In 1905 he had been elected to the State Supreme Court on a combined Hearst–Tammany ticket. His judicial career had been largely uneventful, and in 1912 when he had tried to move up from the State Supreme Court to the Court of Appeals he had been badly beaten. This was before he became associated in the public mind with that magic issue, the crusade against police grafters. In 1913, however, he attracted favorable attention for his conduct of the cases against several of the police inspectors netted in Whitman's (and Buckner's) celebrated crusade. As a result the Appellate Division of the State Supreme Court had chosen him to preside over the second Becker trial. He now had serious hopes of getting the Democratic nomination for the Court of Appeals in the fall election.

Seabury wore his prematurely white hair parted in the middle and looked older than his forty-one years. His usual expression was stern and dignified. His air of severe judicial probity gave the room a far different atmosphere from the days when the outrageous Goff had sat in the same high-backed chair. But it wasn't only the judge and the district attorney who contributed to the cool, deferential, bowing and smiling climate of the trial. Manton, unlike his formidable senior partner, was an unobtrusive Irishman. When he objected to a point, it was with an air of diffidence. When he lost, he simply sat down, ever disinclined, it seemed, to make trouble. His manner was probably a reflection of his belief that Becker would be a free man on Decoration Day. After the way in which the Appeals Court had dismissed the prosecution witnesses—who were now about to take the stand again—he apparently had no doubt of the verdict. Several times he said the defense might put on no witnesses at all.

The absence of acrimony and temper tantrums meant a far less exciting show. Nevertheless the crowds were even larger than they had been at the first trial. Passes were hawked for fat sums in the streets around the Criminal Courts Building. Visiting dignitaries again put the trial at the top of their list of sights to see in New York. And once more the crowds gathered each day below the Bridge of Sighs to watch Becker move back and forth from his Tombs cell to the courtroom. The newspapermen trotted out their old adjectives for him—stolid, steely-eyed, and apparently emotionless, except when he looked across the room at his wife, again seated out of sight of the jury.

Two weeks earlier, as in the first trial, Whitman had requested that a special blue ribbon panel be named from which the jurors in the case were to be selected. Manton had made no objection. Then as now, such panels consisted of better-educated citizens with some standing in the community. The three hundred names on the panel for the second trial had shown a high incidence of bankers, brokers, publishers, and presidents of manufacturing companies. Whitman now announced that his staff was conducting an investigation of every talesman on the panel to be sure that none had the faintest association with the Police Department or with persons who had ever been suspected of being supporters of the department.

A troubling question in the story of the Becker case is how two juries could have found him guilty (for of course that was also the outcome in the second trial), given the serious defects of the evidence against him as described in the Court of Appeals' reversal. For over two decades Americans and even many Europeans had been hearing the System deplored. But to a far more intense degree New Yorkers had been treated to details of its wickedness. The first trial and conviction of Becker, the personification of the System's grafting policemen, had seemed the culmination of a long moral struggle to many of them, particularly to public-spirited New Yorkers of a certain income, the well-brought-up, nonimmigrant local minority that would never under any circumstances have gone stomping through Madison Square shouting "Well, well, well! Reform has gone to hell!" To them the reversal of that verdict had represented not justice but justice undone. Such high-minded citizens were likely to be heavily in the majority on the blue-ribbon panels from which the arbiters of Becker's fate were chosen in both trials. (In 1965, after many attempts, downstate Democrats in the New York State Legislature would finally get a bill through both houses abolishing blue ribbon jury panels. In the words of its assemblyman sponsor, these rosters of better-off, "upright citizens" inevitably resulted in "convicting juries who could be expected to take an extremely self-righteous stand toward anyone accused of a crime.")

The selection of the jury took four and a half days this time. Nineteen months earlier, when the process had seemed painful enough, 187 were examined before the box was filled. This time 331 from two panels took the stand before twelve men were found who were willing to say they had not made up their minds as to Becker's guilt and who were acceptable to both prosecution and defense. The unobstreperous Manton used up only sixteen challenges to Whitman's twenty-six.

In his opening address the district attorney gave a highly unfavorable joint character sketch of the dead gunmen and promised to prove "beyond any doubt that the police lieutenant who is facing you today is the worst murderer of them all." The four gamblers, he said, were merely "middle men." The now familiar parade of witnesses then began. Patrolman Brady, Detective File, and waiter Krause told their stories. During Krause's time on the stand there was an unfortunate incident. A clerk in the office of the Court of Special Sessions had to be removed when he remarked in a loud voice that Krause certainly had been well drilled in his testimony, that the case was a frame-up from start to finish, but that Whitman would get to be governor with the help of such witnesses. As a sidelight, he added that Krause was wearing one of Whitman's suits. Manton would point out in his concluding speech that, whatever the prosecution's solicitousness for Krause had cost, it was rather a curious investment since all the waiter was testifying to was that a man had been murdered in front of the Metropole, a fact the defense was entirely willing to concede. Krause's real mission, said Manton, was to assert that Jacob Reich had been among the spectators that night. No one else had seen him there until later and no one knew exactly what it meant even if he *had* been there, but planting the question in the jury's minds was considered worth the investment.

When Bald Jack Rose took the stand on the eighth day of the trial he "acted like a man who is bored to death with repeating a story which rose from his mouth as easily as water from a spring," reported the *Times*. "He told in many different ways how Becker had threatened to kill Rosenthal and never varied the expressions used at the first trial." But if he always quoted Becker in the same language, his general account now had some variations that Manton pounced upon in cross examination. In his appeals argument he would list sixty discrepancies in Rose's testimony in the two trials. Rose also now recalled that during the Harlem conference Becker had given him five hundred dollars to bail out Zelig. He had not thought to mention this earlier. On cross-examination he agreed that Rosenthal had once sent Spanish Louis to shoot Sam Paul, but that Paul had bought the gangster off. Most important of all—so the defense would conclude—he acknowledged for the first time that it was Rosenthal who was maliciously spreading the word that Rose had framed gangster Zelig, which put Bald Jack in danger of being punished fatally by Zelig's henchmen and gave him a strong reason for wanting Rosenthal out of the way.

Manton was able to take advantage of some of Rose's literary confessions published between the trials. Rose agreed that he had written: "Well, I was in the gambling business. I knew hundreds of gangsters who, at a word from me, would have done my bidding with or without pay, save for a reasonable sum to make sure of their getaway and to pay expenses while they were trailing the victim." Rose declined to say what the victim he had written about was to be the victim of.

"When you were planning this murder did not your conscience prick you?" Manton asked him.

"My conscience was under the entire control of Becker," said Rose. This answer was considered a big score for the prosecution. A clatter of applause broke out in the courtroom and had to be silenced by Seabury.

The reluctant witness, Bridgey Webber, told his story as at the first trial except that he was now sure the Harlem conference had started at nine-thirty instead of eleven, the hour he had been so sure of earlier, having looked at his watch at the time. Manton had discovered that the only vacant lot at the corner of 124 Street and Seventh Avenue two years before had been an excavation thirty feet deep. Webber knew nothing of this but, after a hasty recess, insisted that there had been a small area along the edge where there had been room enough for the gamblers to stand. Vallon recalled that while they stood, Becker had sat on a plank balanced across two barrels. The fact that none of the gamblers remembered an adjacent excavation thirty feet deep apparently did not puzzle the jury. Vallon's other testimony was as before, except that he now recalled quite a bit more about "the little colored stool pigeon, Jimmy" who had approached Becker. The next witness, the chauffeur of the car Becker had borrowed on the murder night, proved rather unsatisfactory for the prosecution.

On cross-examination he testified that an assistant district attorney named Groehl had tried to make him promise to say he had driven Becker through Forty-third Street past the Metropole that night and that Becker had said if he saw Rosenthal he would shoot him down on the spot.

In almost every respect the prosecution's case seemed weaker than before until the last day of the trial. Schepps, the pseudo-corroborator, was absent. No one but the accomplices had heard Becker say or do anything that had any connection with the murder. No witness had heard him order Rosenthal croaked before the crowd at the Lafayette Baths (Rose did not even mention this episode in the second trial). No one had seen him at the murder epilogue on Forty-second Street or heard him plot the murder in Harlem except Rose, Vallon, and Webber, the same "degenerates and criminals" who, according to the Court of Appeals, "had made a bargain to save their own lives by helping to swear away that of the defendant."

But there were three other prosecution witnesses whose testimony would persuade the Court of Appeals in 1915 to uphold the verdict it had summarily rejected the year before, that would cause four of the seven members of the court to directly reverse themselves. The witnesses whose testimony distinguished the second prosecution case from the first, the court would hold, were Charles Plitt, former Police Deputy Commissioner Dougherty, and James Marshall.

Charles Plitt was the twenty-four-year-old hanger-on whom Becker had encouraged to keep the press informed of his strong arm squad exploits. Plitt's name had been brought into the first trial to explain why Becker would have wilfully raided Rosenthal's place, inflicting great damage on the furnishings a few weeks after he had given the gambler fifteen hundred dollars for a mortgage on those same furnishings, as the prosecution claimed. Late in March 1912, during a raid by Becker's squad at which the lieutenant was not present, a janitor had been shot to death. A witness had identified Plitt as the killer. According to Rose's testimony at the first trial, Becker had felt obliged to raise money for Plitt's defense and, furious when Rosenthal refused to meet a five-hundred-dollar assessment, had conducted the destructive raid. But Plitt's lawyers in the janitor-murder case (Plitt had been acquitted) had turned up as defense witnesses at

Becker's first trial and sworn that Becker would hardly have made such a pitch to Rosenthal since their full fee had been paid by the state.

In the months after the first trial Plitt had plied reporters with statements about the injustice of the verdict. In May 1913 he got more specific and, according to the *Times* that month, "tried to sell information to the newspapers which, if true, would have aided Becker in his fight for liberty." Within a few days he found himself arrested on a charge of having committed perjury during a civil damages suit once filed against him. In default of ten thousand dollars bail—unusually high for a man charged with perjury in a civil suit—he remained in the Tombs for six weeks. By this time it was mid-July again, and once more the heat was murderous. On July 18 Plitt went over to the other side. "Having vainly tried to sell his 'story' to the newspapers for five hundred dollars," said the *Times*, "he turned to Whitman in the hope the prosecutor would be kind to him." His hope was realized. That night the district attorney's office took various useful statements from Plitt and, like other helpful witnesses before him, he was quickly transferred from the Tombs to the West Side Prison, the old Whitman Ritz. Soon afterward his accommodations improved even more dramatically, and he spent the rest of the summer in an Atlantic City hotel at the county's expense. During this time, as he later testified, he also drew a weekly salary, not from the district attorney's budget but from "a private fund at the disposal of the District Attorney." Taking no chances with Plitt, however, the district attorney did not dismiss the perjury indictment against him until just before he testified for the prosecution in Becker's trial.

Plitt's most damaging charge against Becker was that on the afternoon before the murder the lieutenant had told him, "Above all stay away from Times Square tonight. . . . You will learn more tomorrow," showing Becker's "cognizance of a probability, at least, that something momentous was then likely to occur," as the Court of Appeals would put it. Plitt also testified that he had talked with Becker in the lavatory of the train on Becker's way to Sing Sing and that Becker had said, "If anything happens to me, I want you to kill that squealing bastard Rose," a little vignette put in presumably to reinforce the picture of the defendant as a vengeful and bloodthirsty man. Representatives of the sheriff's office denied on the stand that a discredited newspaper tipster would ever had been allowed to talk to the condemned man alone. This denial, the Court of Appeals said later, "enables defendant's counsel to invoke the maxim *falsus in uno falsus in omnibus* [if testimony is untrue in one respect it must be untrue in all] but the maxim is not mandatory, and it was for the jury to say how far they would believe him." One problem did seem to puzzle the second appeals court. "No satisfactory explanation is given," wrote the presiding justice solemnly, "of Plitt's change of attitude toward the defendant from one of devoted friendship to fatal hostility."

The second persuasive witness, according to the Court of Appeals opinion, was former Deputy Police Commissioner Dougherty, now back with the Pinkertons. In 1912 Dougherty had testified that on the morning Jack Rose had turned himself in Becker had told him he hadn't seen Rose for a month. In 1914 he quoted Becker as saying that he hadn't seen *or heard from* Rose for a month. (In either case Becker was lying, as he would later reveal. He had seen Rose the night before the murder.) It is hard to understand why the court would have made so much of this additional verb. There could have been a number of reasons why a not overly scrupulous police officer might deny having seen or heard from a criminal who had just turned himself in in a murder investigation, none of them necessarily proving that he had commissioned the murder himself. Apparently the court was not averse to applying the *falsus in uno falsus in omnibus* maxim where Becker's statements were concerned.

But the testimony in the second trial that above all else sent Becker to the chair involved the Harlem conference, that "pure fabrication," as Justice Miller had called it. Every day during the first half of the second trial, including the morning of the last day of the prosecution's case, word had continued to go out from Whitman's office that "Mr. Whitman expects to use Moe Levy . . . to clinch the Harlem conference testimony." Though the chauffeur never appeared, on that last afternoon Whitman came up with dramatic testimony that something had been discussed one June night at the corner of West 124 Street and Seventh Avenue. By now he had not only a specific date for the rendezvous —June 27—but a witness, James Marshall.

The prosecution had taken nearly two years to settle upon a date for the conference and to identify Marshall as their witness, although the June 27 raid was the only one made in Harlem by the Becker squad during the last weeks in June 1912, the period when the gambler witnesses had vaguely indicated that the crucial meeting might have taken place. Marshall's name had been mentioned in the police and court records and in newspaper accounts of the hearing given the crapshooters who had been raided that night. Nevertheless Whitman insisted at the second trial that his office had been unable to settle on a date or the identity of the witness until the spring of 1914. The reason for this fancy footwork involved certain technical regulations about introducing as new evidence at a second trial information that could have been available earlier.

James Marshall, the very important witness, was slight and black and had been twenty years old in June 1912. He had been found in Baltimore in 1914, working as a buck and wing dancer, and had been enticed to New York in April of that year by an assistant district attorney who had pretended to be a theatrical producer able to guarantee him a long engagement at the Palace. Becker had met Marshall during a raid on a Negro crap parlor in the spring of 1912 and had signed him on as his stool pigeon for the colored gambling houses in town. Marshall now testified that about ten o'clock on the night of June 27, 1912, he had seen Becker from across the street, standing at the northwest corner of 124 and Seventh. Becker had called him halfway across the pavement and said, "Jimmy, why don't you hurry?" Although it was nighttime, he had noticed that Becker was talking to a man wearing a brown straw hat whom he was able to identify nearly two years later as Bald Jack. (When he was wearing a hat and viewed at some distance, the defense would insist over and over, Bald Jack was no more memorable than any other casual bystander.)

"You must know," Becker would write in his last letter to Deacon Terry of the *American*, "that the testimony of the little crapshooting coon was pure and unalloyed perjury of the rankest kind as far as seeing Rose at 124th Street and Seventh Avenue was concerned. This little stool had the shortest lie to tell of any of the witnesses, yet his perjury was the most damaging. All he had to say was that he saw me talking to Rose on the other side of the street. It was very simple and had a basis of fact because he secured the evidence on which the warrants were issued and was present at the raid. . . . Marshall was not required to tell a lie very dangerous to him. I remember telling Rose of this little colored stool," Becker claimed in this letter to Terry. Rose, he said, had asked if he could be present at the raid—Negro places then had a somewhat exotic interest. But Becker had forgotten the arrangement and in any case, so he wrote, never saw Rose there.

The defense would point out frantically that all Marshall had testified to was having seen Rose talking to Becker. (And over half a century later a man who was then a member of the prosecution staff would say, shaking his head: "I cannot understand now how we could have sent a man to the electric chair because someone saw him talking to another man across the street!") Marshall had not claimed to hear any discussion of murder plans. If the other gamblers were on the scene, Marshall did not identify them.

But in the first trial Harry Vallon had mentioned seeing Becker greet a little colored boy during the Harlem conference. In trying to explain this, the defense naturally relied on those sociable sessions in the West Side Prison among the four gamblers (and men from the D.A.'s office) in which useful scraps of information were shuffled back and forth—"rehearsed" had been Judge Miller's word for it. Rose, they believed, had probably mentioned the little Negro, and the line about him had been given to Vallon to flesh out his testimony about the alleged conference. But the jury in the second trial and later the Court of Appeals would regard Vallon's statement as clinching evidence that everything the gamblers had testified to about the Harlem meeting was reliable (*verus in uno, verus in omnibus,* perhaps), and Becker's fate was sealed.

In February 1915, however, the prosecution staff would have some bad moments. Marshall was arrested in Philadelphia for beating his wife. In the station house she informed reporters for the local *Evening Ledger* and the *Telegraph* that he had often told her he had committed perjury in the Becker trial. Brought out of his cell, Marshall readily admitted to the reporters that he had lied on the stand. The *Ledger* editor wired Manton, who, within the hour, sent down a young assistant in the law firm, John B.

Johnston. Johnston announced on his arrival that, in order to avoid any charge of wrongful influence, he wanted never to be left alone with Marshall.

The dancer was then taken before a United States Commissioner and swore out a statement in the presence of several witnesses, including the *Ledger* editor. After he had been brought to New York in April 1914, Marshall said, he had been interviewed over and over by Assistant District Attorney Groehl and by Whitman. Groehl, he swore, "told me he wanted me to say I saw Becker at 124th Street and Seventh Avenue speaking to Jack Rose." Rose was then pointed out to him, he said, in the office of a theatrical agent in the New York *World* building. He was seeing him "so far as I knew for the first time." Groehl and another man from the district attorney's office "frequently . . . showed me a false affidavit which I had made and which was used at the time warrants were issued for one of the raids by Becker's squad. Groehl said he could send me to jail anytime for perjury. . . . I can positively state now that I could not possibly identify Rose as one of the men who was speaking to Becker, and I would never have identified the man as Rose were it not for what Groehl told me and what I read in the papers." In the six weeks before the trial, Marshall and his dancing partner had been kept in a hotel suite in the custody of representatives of the D.A.'s office working in three shifts, he said. He had also been paid various sums of money and had even been treated to automobile rides from time to time in Central Park.

Marshall signed every page of the retracting affadavit that afternoon in the *Ledger* office. The next day, after Johnson had brought him to New York, he was seized by detectives from the district attorney's office and by the end of the week had retracted his retraction. The Court of Appeals in its 1915 decision was content to believe his earlier testimony, mentioning only that the retraction in the newspaper office had been "somewhat inconsistent with his testimony upon the trial." "Accepting the testimony of Marshall as true," began a crucial paragraph of the opinion, "it shows that the defendant and Rose were together at a specific locality in Harlem . . . on the night of June 27, 1912. . . . The evidence . . . concerning the Harlem conference, as a whole, is much more convincing than it was on the first trial."

After young Marshall's appearance on the stand in the second trial counsel Manton did not panic, but there was no further talk of the defense not bothering to put in any evidence. As with the prosecution witnesses, the roster of defense witnesses was pretty much the mixture as before. The star defense witness once again was Jacob Reich. After his ten months in the Tombs and with a murder indictment still hanging over his head, he had had plenty of time to reflect on the consequences of testifying for Becker, but he was back again to describe the uncommon social life in the West Side Prison. Manton made much of the letter to him from Assistant District Attorney Frank Moss, threatening him with indictment if he did not support the stories of the other witnesses. ("Moss simply wrote letters as other men do," Whitman would later say.)

In his summing-up Manton would call Reich "the greatest character this city has seen in twenty years." He described the temptations that had been put in Reich's way, Whitman's threats ("I'm going to indict you tomorrow"), the long months in the dank cell in the Tombs. In *his* final speech Whitman would call Reich "a little monster. . . . whose own admissions showed him beyond doubt to be a murderer." But two days after the end of the trial when reporters asked the district attorney when Reich's murder trial would begin, Whitman said indifferently that he had no plans to prosecute Reich.

Several delegates from the East Side were now willing to testify for the defense that Rose and Webber had collected several thousand dollars from prominent Second Avenue gamblers to help remove Rosenthal from the scene, one way or another. But none of these witnesses was of impeccable moral character, as was brought out. On cross-examination Whitman accused one of them, Isadore Fishman, of having abandoned his rightful mate to go live with another woman. Fishman agreed obligingly that the abandonment had taken place seventeen years earlier and good riddance too. The prosecution counted on the members of the blue-ribbon jury not being able to imagine that a man who was living with a woman who was not his wife could still testify honestly about certain events. Just in case, however, all the time Fishman testified a woman with a terribly scarred face stood mutely just beyond the side door of the courtroom where the jury could see her if they craned their necks. Clinging

to her ragged dress was a small child. Their relationship to
Fishman was never established and the witness did not falter in
his testimony, but it was a maneuver for which those famous
legal stage managers, Howe and Hummel, would have expected
congratulations all around.

Among the district attorney's list of coming prosecution attrac-
tions had been several members of the strong arm squad who,
according to Whitman's pronouncements, had turned against
Becker and were ready to contradict him about the Harlem
conference. But the only squad members who took the stand were
defense witnesses who insisted they had been with Becker before,
during, and after the Harlem raid and had not laid eyes on Rose
or any of the other gamblers.

What was described as the biggest crowd in local courtroom
history stormed the Criminal Courts Building on this last day of
testimony. What had brought the crowds out was the prospect
that Becker would take the stand. After the first verdict, he had
expressed regret that his lawyers had persuaded him not to
testify, and following the Appeals Court reversal he had said that
of course he would take the stand the next time. But now, once
again, his lawyer announced that since the prosecution had
virtually no case, since it was relying on the words of "three
murderers and a little colored boy," there was no point in having
Becker testify.

The final day's testimony had one interesting sidelight. In the
course of the defense attempt to discredit Charles Plitt a certain
World reporter was briefly implicated as a principal figure in the
case. The source was the most dubious imaginable—though it
was one which the Court of Appeals would not hesitate to cite
respectfully. Swope's name had come up before. McIntyre had
asked Bald Jack at the first trial if it weren't true that he had first
learned of Rosenthal's having given his name to Whitman for
subpoena purposes from a newspaperman named Swope. If on
the afternoon before the murder Swope was spreading the word
among East Side gamblers that Rosenthal had put them on the
spot with the district attorney, his later recollection of his director's role in the case was understandable. But it now developed
that Charles Plitt had once charged this *World* employee with
playing an even more central role. (No one apparently doubted
that Plitt meant Swope. In his own mind and everyone else's he

was the only *World* man on the story.) In December 1912 Plitt had written a letter to the editor of the Summit, New Jersey, *Record.* It read:

> Now the New York *World* is the one that is responsible for Becker being where he is. For when one of there men who had close connections with certain gambling houses in the City was raided by Becker he went to the City Editor of his paper and said that Becker was collecting graft from gambling houses . . . this way back last May. When Becker was informed he said . . . I have nothing to fear at that time he asked to be removed from that office the Commissioner of the Department, Mr. Waldo said that you stay here and "I will stand by you," which he did when he tried to testify but was refused by the court who was in control by the Dist. Attorney and with whom he wined and dined at all times where had Becker any chance for it if it was any it was taken away before he went to trial. . . .

After this sample of Plitt's degree of literacy reporters on hand were grateful for the chance to include in their accounts Plitt's admission on the stand that, although he called himself a member of the press, he had never actually worked on the editorial staff of any paper.

XXI

"You heard Rose, Webber and Vallon and the colored boy on the one hand, and you heard the three policemen on the other. Which will you believe?" attorney Manton rashly asked the jury in discussing the central event of the prosecution's case, the Harlem conference. In his summing-up Manton also observed that his client had had "a fair and impartial trial." He spoke in his usual mild, conversational tone. Manton's performance throughout had been so unprovocative that in *his* closing address Whitman had to hark back to something John McIntyre had said in the first trial to suggest the outrages of the defense. Whitman's speech included the old chant: "The crack of the pistols on Forty-third Street was a defiance not only of our American institutions, but a challenge to our very civilization itself."

Justice Seabury's charge to the jury "was regarded as dealing heavy blows to the defense," noted the *Times*. "Most who heard it agreed that Becker had been damaged by it." The *World* hailed it as one of the great charges of history. Seabury, in fact, had put on a performance not very different from that of Judge Goff a year and a half before, but his tone was sober, unimpassioned, impressively judicial. In going over the facts he largely accepted the prosecution's case. When he posed questions that the jury should ask itself about the murder, his tone made it clear that the answers he had in mind were not helpful to Becker. For example, ignoring Justice Miller's statement that the question of whether

Rose had called Becker after the murder was of no significance since any acquaintance could guess he would be interested in the news, Seabury told the jury, "It obviously becomes a matter of great importance for you to determine whether Rose did call up the defendant. . . ." *Someone* (besides Hawley) had telephoned Becker. "What was the subject of that conversation?" he asked, moving his eyes portentously from one juror's face to another. Or later, in the same sort of voice, discussing Becker's statement to Dougherty that he had not seen or heard from Rose since the murder: "Did Becker lie to Dougherty? *If so, why?*"

Seabury's advice on the law involved was even more helpful to the prosecution. "If an accomplice was corroborated as to some material fact, the jury may infer that he says the truth. . . . A witness does not have to be corroborated in everything." (*Verus in uno, verus in omnibus* this time.) Irrelevant, apparently, was the law governing testimony by uncorroborated accomplices, which he did not discuss. To convict, the jury must be convinced of Becker's guilt "beyond a reasonable doubt," but "there is nothing human, probably, that can be said to be beyond all doubt. The law says . . . a reasonable doubt, not *all* doubt." As for harboring any sympathy for the defendant because of his long ordeal, a member of the jury "would be utterly unfit to occupy his position if he allowed his judgment in any respect to be influenced by any consideration of sympathy."

Because of the Court of Appeals' contempt for the major prosecution witnesses, Whitman's prospects for a second conviction had looked dim until the trial judge made his powerful charge, accepting their version of the murder. The defense lawyers weren't the only attorneys in the courtroom who had thought the prosecution's case a dubious one. At least one assistant district attorney, Billy De Ford, had been going about town saying it was a lucky thing for Whitman that he didn't have to submit the case to a jury of his own staff.

"SEABURY'S CHARGE HITS DEFENSE," the headlines proclaimed the next day. When Seabury finished speaking, young Manton had jumped to his feet. For the first time in the trial he spoke in a voice harsh with anger. "I object to the whole charge on the ground that it is an animated argument for the prosecution," he cried. His face was dark red. Seabury calmly noted his objection, and the jury filed out.

The question of whether the jury would believe policemen testifying for the defense was soon answered. A long wait for a verdict was expected, but the jury was back in four hours. In later years Edwin C. Hill's account in the *Sun* of what followed was often reprinted with admiration in journalism textbooks.

> Charles Becker to the bar! [it began] Once more the door that gives entrance toward the Tombs as well as to the jury-room was opened. A deputy sheriff appeared, then Becker, then a second deputy. One glance was all you needed to see that Becker had himself under magnificent control. His iron nerve was not bending. He swung with long strides around the walls and came to a stand at the railing. Those who watched him did not see a sign of agitation. He was breathing slowly—you could see that from the rise and fall of his powerful chest—and smiling slightly as he glanced toward his counsel.
>
> He looked for the first time toward the jurors. There was confidence and hope shining in his eyes. Coolly, without haste, he studied the face of every man in the box. Not one of them met his eye. . . .
>
> There was the most perfect silence in the court-room. The movements of trolley-cars in Centre Street made a noise like rolling thunder. . . . And yet such sounds and annoyances were forgotten, ceased to be of consequence, when Clerk Penny bent toward the foreman and slowly put the customary question:
>
> "Gentlemen of the jury, have you agreed upon your verdict?" . . . It was obvious that the foreman, having to express the will of his associates, was stirred by such feeling as seldom comes to any man.
>
> "Guilty as charged in the indictment," he breathed more than spoke.
>
> Becker's right hand was then gripped to the railing. He held his straw hat in his left hand, which, as his arm was bent backward and upward, rested against the small of his back. It is the plain truth that he took the blow without a quiver. After a second, it may be, he coughed just a little; a mere clearing of the throat. But his mouth was firm. His dark face lost no vestige of color. His black eyes

turned toward the jurymen, who still avoided his glance, who looked everywhere but at the man they had condemned. . . .

No crowd of Becker's friends and relatives had awaited the verdict this time. Alexander Williams was not there. Helen and Charles Becker had waited alone in the sheriff's office. When word arrived that the jury was ready and the deputy sheriffs came for Becker, she stayed behind. "I did not wish to face the crowd. I stood by the window, and after a time I saw people coming out from the courtroom slowly and dejectedly, and my heart sank, for I realized that we had lost again. I could see by the way they walked out that it was bad news. After good news, people walk briskly."

She was also absent when they brought Becker into court for sentencing, choosing not to hear intoned again the grim phraseology of the death sentence. Her husband was to be kept in solitary confinement "and sometime in the week of July sixth the . . . agent and warden of the State Prison is ordered to do execution upon you, Charles Becker, in the mode and manner prescribed by the laws of the State of New York."

Everyone understood that nothing would happen in the week of July sixth, that an appeal would be taken. The *Times* hailed the verdict as "the close of a terrible chapter in the history of the city . . . a story more revolting than the worst chapters in the history of the Renaissance. . . . Yet the danger is," the editors added, "that a miscarriage of justice is not yet impossible." In other words, the Court of Appeals had another chance to queer things.

This time Becker was driven to Sing Sing in the sheriff's own car. The sheriff explained he was afraid of the unsympathetic crowds that he understood were again planning to gather at Grand Central. Helen Becker was not allowed to ride with the prisoner. At Sing Sing he was put on the upper tier of the death house in a cell that hadn't been used in many years. "That's one of the hottest cells we got and it looks like a hot summer coming up," one of the keepers told the press matter-of-factly. In this cell Charles Becker would spend the rest of his life.

Soon afterward Helen Becker also changed her address. However many thousands of dollars Becker had stashed away in his strong arm squad days, his legal expenses had been very large, with or without an assist on McIntyre's fee. In the first trial three other lawyers had worked on the case. Shay had had two assistants in preparing the briefs asking for a new trial and for his later foray to the Court of Appeals. Several investigators were hired for weeks before each trial, including Val O'Farrell, a former policeman, who came high. Whatever the total cost, in the spring of 1914 Helen Becker signed over to Manton the deed to the Olinville Avenue house. She had no more money to pay his fee, she said. In the fall he put the house up for rent, and she moved into a small apartment in the Bronx building where a brother and sister lived.

After Becker's return to Sing Sing he took up the old routine. The only change was in the name of the chief warden who occasionally stopped by to see him. The new warden, Thomas Mott Osborne, was an unorthodox political sort. Independent, earnest, energetic, and rich, he had moved into politics as an upstate reform Democrat ever ready to make trouble for Tammany Hall. During a period when young Franklin D. Roosevelt was of the same mind, Osborne had backed his rebellion financially. His efforts had been rewarded by the anti-Tammany legislature with appointments to a series of public service sinecures—the Forest, Field and Game Commission, the Civil Service Commission, and finally the Commission on Prison Reform. Here he had found his life work and would spend his remaining years evolving policies, lecturing, writing, and serving in public roles that had to do with the treatment of criminals. His prison theories favored leniency, trust, and even a degree of self-government for the convicts. In 1914, presumably to annoy Tammany Hall, with whom he was on the outs, Governor Martin Glynn named him as the warden at Sing Sing. Osborne was a leader in the national society working to abolish capital punishment and made it clear that he had not changed his position. "You'll never see me in the death house when a man must go to the chair," he said.

Osborne at first didn't like Becker, seeing "something cruel in the handsome face," he said later. But the way "the doomed man would sit for hours at the door of his cell reading aloud to his fellow prisoners" touched him, and he changed his mind. Unlike most prisoners, he reported, Becker never pretended he had always been virtuous in his previous life or promised to be one of the Lord's saints if he should ever get out. Many elements of the Rosenthal murder were not in keeping with Becker's character, Osborne insisted. "If such a man had set his mind on murder, he would have made a better job of it."

In June 1914 Helen Becker had gone back to work, teaching summer school to make up for her long weeks away during the second trial. "As I look back over everything," she wrote that summer, "it seems as if my worst suffering has come, not at the tragic moments as when my husband was arrested or when he was sentenced or when I saw him first in the death house, but just at ordinary times when I have been alone in the home we no longer own, or perhaps with people about me. . . ."

Some of her worst times, she said, had come when she was riding to school on a White Plains street car.

> I often feel discouraged on street cars, I don't know why—perhaps it is because there is nothing to do but just sit there and think. [On one such ride] it seemed as if almost everything that could happen to me had happened. My husband was under sentence of death, I had lost my baby, our money was gone, my housekeeper had killed herself, my mother had died, my dog Bum had bitten a man and been shot, my pet canary bird had died. Then I thought: "Well, anyway, I am not blind. There's something to be thankful for, that I am not blind."
>
> The very next morning I woke up with a sore eye. That struck me as funny, and I wrote it to Charley in my next letter. I am glad I have a sense of humor. I think it has often saved me from suffering and it has made me see amusing things to put in my letters to my husband.

Becker's letters to her were usually short, she said. "He hasn't very much to tell me—it's the same monotonous life all the time." One that she allowed *McClure's* to reprint was dated three weeks after his return to Sing Sing. Possibly it was written to order, although its uxorious tone was no different from that of all his other published communications with his wife. It read:

> Queen of my heart: I've been thinking of you the best part of the night, in fact you are never out of my mind. . . . I think of you sitting on the porch, and in my mind's

eye you look lovely but sad. I try to fix in my mind how you'd look if you saw me coming in at the gate. You always were such a bunch of sunshine when I came home. I don't say this because it happens to be us, but I'm sure no two people ever lived who really understand and love each other as we do. I often think back to the dismal years before I met you, and I can't recall any pleasure in life except that which I've known since I met you. I love to sit in reverie and recall all the beautiful times and days we enjoyed together—the many talks, the drives, the places we visited, our homecoming, and the words you said, the question you'd never fail to ask, and when answered properly, the look of satisfaction I'd see on your face made me happy beyond words. I only got Friday's letters yesterday. I do hope you'll disabuse your mind about me, for I'm in fine fettle again. Sweetheart, let us not lose faith or heart. This must come right, and you and I live out our lives together. Charles.

If Charles Whitman wrote any letters to his wife that summer they did not deal with a monotonous life. He had easily captured the Republican nomination for governor, but the campaign that followed didn't always go smoothly. Some newspapers that had called him a hero for his conduct of the Becker case now attacked him for, as one of them put it, his "absolute brutality in the drive to build up a political career upon the stake of a human life." Whitman's response was to write an article for *Collier's* on the responsibilities of a prosecutor. "The man who is influenced in the conduct of the great office of district attorney . . . by motives political or selfish is violating the law of the land just as truly as does the criminal he prosecutes," he wrote sternly.

Teddy Roosevelt had been able to prevent his Progressive party from giving its nomination to Whitman. "The truth is not in him," he said of the district attorney and identified him as eligible for the Ananias Club, as Liars' Clubs were known in those more scripturally oriented times. Roosevelt also charged him with settling for Becker as the prime defendant in the murder and not going after the higher-ups in Tammany Hall for political reasons best known to himself.

Martin Glynn, the incumbent governor running against Whitman, was a Catholic. A Republican anti-Catholic, Know-Nothing splinter group sprang up during the campaign. Unlike many other Republican candidates, Whitman did not disavow their support and was accused of running a campaign that catered to bigotry. One of Whitman's problems was another kind of prejudice. He had discovered that the police vote, when one considered all friends and relatives, was no minor consideration at the polls. He had long since shifted his campaign from discussing only police graft to going after other issues that he had once labeled "unfortunate abstractions." Now he also began announcing from the hustings that some of his best friends were policemen.

Whether or not many members of the force voted for him, he did all right in other precincts, winning by 145,000 votes over Glynn. This was treated as a landslide although he had actually got less than half of the votes cast: Two other men in the race had received nearly 160,000 votes between them. In the last hurrah for the local Progressive party, their candidate had come in a very poor fourth. Asked to comment on Whitman's victory, Roosevelt, like Becker, had a Bible verse ready to hand, Timothy II, chapter 4, verse 4: "They shall turn away their ears from the truth and their ears will be turned unto fables."

In his victory, which excited interest throughout the country, Whitman had carried with him every Republican on the state ticket with one exception. The Court of Appeals candidate of the Democratic and Hearst parties, Samuel Seabury, had roundly beaten the Republican nominee, Emory Chase. Chase was one of the judges who had voted with the Court of Appeals majority to give Becker a new trial. Being on the right side in the Rosenthal murder case was clearly the way to win elections in 1914.

Whitman hadn't been governor-elect of New York for forty-eight hours before there was talk of him as the next Republican candidate for the presidency. This development may seem puzzling, especially in view of his minority of the total vote. But the idea of the New York governor having a lien on the presidency had not been a new one in 1906 when Jerome had had "both eyes on the governorship and at least one on the White House" or in the summer of 1912 when that distinguished political pundit Sam Schepps had remarked, "Whitman wants to be Governor—and then it's only one step to the White House." In thirteen out of the first twenty presidential campaigns after the Civil War one of the major party candidates was a present or former New York governor, and in 1944 *both* candidates—Roosevelt and Dewey—would have served time in the Albany State House.

Two days after the election wire agency stories out of Washington said, "President Wilson is convinced that Charles S. Whitman is likely to be his Republican opponent in 1916," and on the same day Republican Senator Gallinger of New Hampshire took up the chant: "It seems to me that District Attorney Whitman's great triumph in New York makes him not only the logical but the inevitable candidate for the Presidency in 1916." The enthusiasm engendered by this prospect in the western press was especially strong.

"The western newspapers accepting [Whitman] as the next presidential candidate will do him a favor if they refrain from putting such notions in his head. . . ." read a *Times* editorial a few days later. "It is Mr. Whitman's weakness that he makes a good impression until he begins to play politics, that when he does he plays it so as to chill his friends and that a very slight temptation is enough to induce him to embark on this dangerous game." The westerners did not understand, the *Times* went on, that Whitman's personal popularity hadn't won the election, that it had been won by religious prejudice and opposition to Charley Murphy. The trouble was that the Republicans had no other man in sight. "So it is possible, with the dearth of men who can really make an appeal, that the murder of a gambler in front of the Metropole may make a President of the United States."

XXII

THE law-and-order issue was not invented in the 1960s, of course, or for that matter in January 1915, when New York Republicans signified their intention of preempting it for Charles Whitman, their rising candidate for national office although he had just assumed his first statewide office. In his inaugural address the new governor dwelt at length on the dangers of the growing disregard for legal authority in the state and the nation. The city apparently offered no further problems in this area. At a dinner in his honor later that month Whitman's achievement in bringing this about was hailed by the venerable Joseph Choate. "We had reached a point where life was no longer safe in this city," he said. "We were at the mercy of a band of assassins. . . . Mr. Whitman changed all that."

As Whitman listened to the clamorous predictions of his brilliant political future or as soon afterward he sat as guest of honor at a dinner given by his Newport friends, Mr. and Mrs. Cornelius Vanderbilt, the hours he had spent trading favors with ex-cons in the Tombs must have seemed remote. Still, now and then there was a reminder. At a special hearing to consider the scandalously corrupt behavior of the U.S. minister to the Dominican Republic, James Mark Sullivan, Bald Jack Rose testified about how the lawyer had saved his skin two and a half years earlier. Worse than that, it turned out it was a letter of endorsement from Whitman that had cleared the appointment for the Tammany ambulance chaser. Sullivan's local political backing had been strong, but Tumulty, Woodrow Wilson's high-level patronage man, had been worried about his connection with the unsavory Rosenthal case. Whitman's letter, paying a debt, had reassured Tumulty, "I have found him honorable, upright and reliable." In the Rosenthal case Sullivan's "course was thoroughly professional and, I believe, in every way commendable." Within a week after he arrived at his diplomatic headquarters Sullivan was cabling his pals to come on down, "the pickings are fine." The New York *World* led the successful fight for his removal and frequently called attention to the New York governor's part in the national embarrassment. No doubt in his new eminence Whitman had proved less obliging about holding the phone until Swope got around to answering it.

Late in February 1915 Manton delivered a 540-page brief to the Court of Appeals. The new brief declared that Becker's conviction was "hopelessly against the weight of the evidence" and contrary to law since there was no testimony about his part in the murder except the word of accomplices. "The staging of this second trial in an atmosphere designed to be hostile to the defendant was highly prejudicial to his rights" and his conviction had been "brought about because of newspaper clamor, the zeal of the prosecutor, and the natural desire of the actual self-confessed murderers for their own preservation. . . ." Among the reversible errors cited were the admission into evidence of anonymous letters to the Police Department branding Becker a grafter, which were bound to be "highly prejudicial." The final two dozen pages attacked "the extreme partiality" of Seabury's "erroneous" charge. Manton's tone was no longer that of the well-behaved counselor who preferred not to make a scene. "Both the facts and the law were arranged and marshalled in a way highly inimical to the defendant's rights. . . . Whenever there was a discussion of a circumstance which might warrant the inference of guilt, the court presented the People's case with great force and minuteness of expression, but, on the other hand, when a circumstance warranting an inference of innocence was under discussion, it was passed over with the lightest possible reference."

As the Court of Appeals deliberated that spring Whitman often mentioned the political magic of the Becker case. "The judge who tried the case is now on the New York Court of Appeals and the

District Attorney who prosecuted him is now Governor of the state," he pointed out exuberantly to a reporter. "Nothing short of remarkable! Nothing to equal it has ever happened I believe!" Overexuberance and occasional inattentiveness were already being noted on occasion in the new governor. According to onetime *Evening World* editor Charles Chapin, Whitman had predicted shortly after his election that Congress would soon pass a national prohibition law. "I couldn't conceive of such a thing coming to pass in my lifetime and said so," reported Chapin. " 'There will be general prohibition in all of the states before my term of office as Governor has expired,' was his prophetic reply."

"At luncheon the following day, after drinking his wine," Chapin went on, "Whitman raised his empty glass and, looking me squarely in the face, exclaimed with considerable feeling: 'I assume that you . . . think that I drink more than I should. Then listen to what I am now saying. On the first day of January next I shall be Governor of the State of New York and from that day on I become a prohibitionist in fact as well as theory.' Governor Whitman," Chapin concluded, "prophesied accurately in regard to what Congress would do, but he missed fire in his prophecy about himself."

When in the same month that Manton's brief was delivered to the Court of Appeals, New York Law School gave a dinner honoring Seabury as its first alumnus to be named to the court, Whitman was naturally on hand. Even the toastmaster that evening was a man who had dealt with policeman Becker and come off well: Martin Littleton, Inspector Schmittberger's staunch defender of nearly a decade before. Among the laudatory speakers was Benjamin Cardozo who a few months earlier had been named to a temporary appointment on the Court of Appeals.

The Court of Appeals judgment was handed down on May 25, just a year after Becker's second conviction. This time all was different. In an opinion half as long as the February 1914 decision in his favor, the court's ruling was foursquare against the defendant. Expecting quite a different approach from the one the judges took, nearly two-thirds of both the defense and prosecution briefs had offered arguments about the facts in the case, that is the reliability of the evidence given against Becker, this subject being the one that had so troubled the court fifteen months earlier. In the new opinion, however, the judges virtually abdicated responsibility for this question. The contention that the three accomplices might have decided to hire the gunmen independently of Becker had been presented to the jury, said the court. The jury had rejected this argument, which settled the matter. The jury had also rejected the contention that Becker had had a motive not to commit the crime since "any attack upon Rosenthal at that time would almost certainly be attributed to his agency. It cannot be laid down as a matter of law that a jury is bound to hold that a specified event has not occurred because its occurrence involves unwise or foolish or blundering conduct on the part of the accused person. The propensity of criminals to blunder has long been recognized." As for the judges' own responsibility as they now saw it: "We are to see to it that the trial was fair and that there was sufficient evidence, within recognized rules of law, to support the verdict; this done, the responsibility for the result rests with the jurors."

The characters of the major witnesses against Becker had been known to the jury, said the opinion. "Of course they were very bad men; accomplices in murder always are." Moreover, "the case as presented upon the second trial differed materially from the case as presented upon the first." The court then cited the corroborating evidence of the dancer Marshall, of newspaperman Plitt, and of former Police Commissioner Dougherty, which it had found so persuasive. As for the defense claim that "immediately before the trial certain articles prejudicial to the defendant had been published in the newspapers and that affidavits in the record 'make it a matter of very strong inference that the highly objectional newspaper accounts emanated from the office of the district attorney'" (as the defense brief had put it), the court declared that "how any of the matters mentioned could have affected the defendant injuriously or how they constituted any 'staging' of the trial prejudicial to his interests it is . . . impossible to see. The case would be quite different," the court added, "if the record disclosed any substantial foundation for the suggestion that the district attorney or his agents were responsible in any way for any publication by which it was sought to influence the outcome of the trial. Such misconduct would not only merit the severest reprobation, but would be a good ground for summary removal from office." (It wouldn't be until 1966 that the U.S. Supreme Court would hand down its landmark decision on trial by newspaper, granting a new trial to convicted murderer Dr. Sam Sheppard on grounds that the prosecution had plied newspapers with damaging evidence against him that it knew was inadmissible in court, that it had made frequent reference to "bombshell" witnesses who were then never put on the stand, that, in sum, a massive campaign of "virulent publicity" before and during the trial had made a fair verdict impossible.)

In a similar way throughout the opinion, the court frequently stipulated as proven truth many of the prosecution assertions that the defense brief had worked hardest to throw doubt upon. There was nothing contrary to law in introducing accounts of numerous conversations between the conspirators and the gunmen implicating Becker when he was not present since Rose "was acting under general authority from the defendant to bring about the death of Rosenthal. The evidence . . . concerning the Harlem conference . . . is much more convincing," declared the court. "*Accepting the testimony of Marshall as true*, it shows . . ." The opinion this time did not discuss the ample opportunities for hashing over the evidence that the accomplices had had in their months in the same cell block, and ". . . the fact that Vallon knew the colored boy was there can hardly be accounted for unless Vallon was there himself." Plitt's change in attitude toward the defendant was puzzling "but if he is telling the truth now, it makes little difference what the reason is."

They rejected the claim that the trial judge's charge was "unfair, erroneous and highly prejudicial in many respects." On the contrary, "the most sedulous care to preserve the rights of the defendant was manifested not only in the charge but throughout the whole trial. The first judgment of death," concluded the court, "was reversed because (the defendant) did not have a fair trial. The judgment now under review is not assailable on that ground. . . . *Judgment of conviction affirmed*." Execution was set for July 16, the third anniversary of Rosenthal's murder.

By the time Deputy Warden Johnson gave Becker the news about dusk that day he seemed prepared for it, Johnson said, knowing that if the word had been favorable someone would have rushed to tell him earlier. Father Cashin, who arrived on Johnson's heels, reported that for several days thereafter Becker was "overcome by a frantic and futile anger." The *Times* commented that there appeared to be "undiminished public interest in the case." Reporters seeking comments from old members of the cast found Bridgey Webber in a sociable mood in his factory office in Passaic.

"Of course my sympathies are with Becker," he told reporters. "He made a mistake the same as I did and the same as the others, and I am mighty sorry for him." The man from the *Globe* mentioned that since Becker and he had made the same mistake Webber must feel fortunate to be sitting comfortably at his desk while Becker got ready to die in the electric chair. Bridgey shrugged his shoulders.

"Of course there's no chance for a pardon," he told his visitors. "Governor Whitman certainly can't pardon the man he prosecuted."

For of course this was the confounding situation, one that had never before occurred in the state or, apparently, in the nation. The only individual who could remove Becker from the shadow of the electric chair was the man who had put him there in the first place. Or, as Bourke Cockran would argue later before Justice Charles Evans Hughes, "whereas every person under sentence of death has a constitutional right to a final review by an impartial mind, in this case complaint or criticism of the manner in which (the defendant) was prosecuted . . . must be addressed to the very person of whom the complaint is made. Criticism of the characters of the witnesses on whose testimony the plaintiff . . . was convicted must now be made to the very man who bargained with them for the testimony they gave. . . ."

For some reason no one asked Whitman about this painful dilemma when the decision was handed down. In any case, though naturally gratified, the governor was distracted that day. Everybody at the mansion was busy packing. The next day Whitman, his wife, his four-year-old daughter, Olive, and about thirty political associates, their wives, and a few friends (including John W. Goff, Jr.) set off on a special train for San Francisco and the Pan-Pacific Exposition. Democrats grumbled that Whitman, who posed as a prime economizer in state budget matters, was now about to bill the state for thirty-five thousand dollars for a month-long junket undertaken mainly to further his national political career. The train made numerous stops going and coming so that Whitman could be interviewed by the local press and deliver a speech or two. His welcome was especially warm in the far west where the citizens had delighted in the long, continued story about the wicked eastern city and knew all about the hero who had put things right. He was often introduced as the next Republican candidate for president.

Back in New York there was hope that the complication of his having to rule on the right to clemency of a man he had prosecuted would be avoided. His client would never seek a pardon from Whitman, said Manton. What would be the use? On the other hand, Becker's former lawyer, Joseph Shay, predicted that Becker would never die in the chair "for that would be judicial murder." He also expressed astonishment that in two opinions on the same case the Court of Appeals had come to such different conclusions. In legal circles all over the state the reasons for this phenomenon were now being vigorously discussed.

The vote in the first People vs. Becker appeal—six-to-one to overturn the lower court denial of a new trial—had been exactly reversed in the second appeal and was six-to-one against the defendant. Only one of the seven judges, a Democrat from Syracuse named John M. Hogan, had voted as he had before. He voted against the prevailing court view in 1915 without writing a dissent. The 1915 court had not been exactly the same court that had taken part in the first judgment. Two judges in the first case had not participated in the second. One of these was William Werner, the single dissenter in 1914, the other, Nathan Miller, for whom even the hypercritical judgment of the earlier court had not seemed strong enough. The judges who replaced Miller and Werner in the 1915 deliberations, both from New York City, were the author of the second opinion, Chief Judge Willard Bartlett, and that comparatively new figure on the bench, Benjamin Cardozo. The four judges who heard both appeals and who directly reversed themselves in the second case were Emory Chase, Frederick Collin, William Cuddeback, and Frank Hiscock. Hiscock, of course, was the author of the first opinion that in such bald language had upheld Becker's right to a new trial.

To legal philosophers there is nothing startling about such reversals. In what most people outside the profession would consider an ideal world of law, the issue at each stage of the case should have been whether or not the defendant deserved to be electrocuted for the crime of first-degree murder. To many observers the evidence against Becker in the second trial seemed to be no more convincing than that offered in the first, in which the judges had said, "While no one doubts that in the great majority of cases the character and credibility of witnesses and the believability of testimony should be left to the final determination of a jury, yet the fact that the state imposes upon us the absolute duty of deciding whether a verdict in a murder case is against the weight of evidence would seem to make it equally plain that the law contemplates the possibility that a jury may be swayed or led into giving an unjust and unwarranted verdict and requires us to correct the error when it does occur."

But, traditionally, appeals courts consider their formal assignment to be that of deciding only whether or not the procedure of the lower court trial was so unfair that the defendant deserves another chance to prove his innocence. ("When will our appellate judges recognize that their duty is to do justice, not simply see that the judicial machine is run according to rule?" demanded the legal philosopher John D. Lawson, in his discussion of the Leo Frank case in *American State Trials*. "Not so long as in American courts Procedure is King; for while the claims of this tyrant are respected, it matters not what becomes of justice.") After devoting nearly half of its opinion to considering the evidence and the special interests of the prosecution witnesses against Becker, the 1914 court had formally relied on the ground on which the six judges supporting the court opinion were unanimous—the extraordinarily prejudicial conduct of the trial itself. In 1915, by conceding as the jury's province the reliability of the evidence against Becker, the court limited its attention to the question of the conduct of the trial. Since the procedure under Seabury was very different from that under John Goff, two separate sets of conditions had come before the court in succeeding years (taking the narrow view of things), and it was thus quite feasible for the four reversing judges to come to opposite conclusions about them.

Of course this shift of judicial approach from the active to the passive may have reflected only a sincere conversion of the judges to the view that no injustice had been done Becker after all. But there were outside forces influencing the second appeals court judgment against the former police lieutenant that had not been present in the decision a year earlier. Still ringing in the judges' ears, no doubt, was the public outcry over their first decision in the case. And this time the presiding judge at the lower court trial had not been an eccentric maverick like Goff but a respected partner of the deliberating judges. Although Seabury naturally didn't take part in the 1915 decision, he was sitting with his colleagues on the day word was handed down, and so far as they knew would be among them for the thirteen years that remained of his elected term. They would not be eager to reverse the case on the ground that their fellow judge had misconducted the trial or even—as the defense brief argued—that he had shown prejudice in his charge to the jury.

Another strong influence favoring the prosecution in the second appeal was the altered status of the prosecutor in the case. In 1914 Whitman had been still a New York City figure, and all seven judges on the appeals court had then been upstaters. By 1915 Whitman was the most powerful political figure in the state, and speculation that he might soon be the most powerful man in the nation was at its height. This circumstance and the possible political consequences of supporting the proposition that the governor of the state had played a dubious, even crooked, role in the conviction of a man for a crime punishable by death must have had an effect on the judges. And although the judiciary is supposed to be independent of the executive branch of government, it is often nothing of the sort. The chief figure in the Republican party in a state, for example, is bound to have a certain power over the selection of the Republican candidates for office. Frank Hiscock, the Republican judge who had offered such a scathing view of the credibility of Whitman's prosecution witnesses in the first judgment, apparently considered this an irrelevant point a year later. He voted quietly with the majority against Becker. Four months afterward, possibly in the ordinary course of things, he was named as the chief judge of the court and served as head of the Court of Appeals for the next decade.

To other judges on the Court of Appeals the good will of the man in the governor's chair was crucial for a different reason. Then as now a judgeship on the appeals court was an elective office, but any time the court was overworked or temporarily not up to strength because of illness or disqualification of members, the governor could appoint temporary replacements from the elected members of the lower State Supreme Court. Assignments to the Court of Appeals conferred not only prestige but additional income on those chosen (at this time the annual salary of a Court of Appeals judge was $13,600, which was $3,600 more than that of the governor). In the first Becker case appeal two of the judges sitting had been on temporary appointment by the governor. The two were Emory Chase and Nathan Miller. Chase, who in the 1914 election had lost to Seabury in a contest for a regular judgeship on the court, had served there as an interim appointee off and on since 1906 and presumably had some hopes for a more settled arrangement under Whitman, his fellow Republican, since the governor had the power to name lower court judges not only to temporary service on the Court of Appeals but as full-fledged members to fill out actual vacancies resulting from death or compulsory retirement. Although men so appointed had to run for the office in the next election, in practice they were often given bipartisan endorsement and were elected without opposition.

Chase's permanent appointment to the court never materialized, no doubt to his disappointment. Nathan Miller, the other temporary member of the 1914 court, could not be disappointed since he chose another option the second time around. After contemplating Whitman's new position of power and his own conspicuous part in the first Becker case decision that had given the new governor such a terrible scare, he apparently decided his chances for judicial advancement were not rosy. In the spring of 1915 he announced his retirement from the court and took no part in the second Becker appeal.

". . . Cardozo agreed with his associates . . . that the technicalities advanced by Manton carried no weight, that the chain of evidence led directly to Becker by way of his accomplices, who were in his power. The gentle Cardozo was not gentle when patent murder called for the sword of justice," George S. Hellman observes in his biography of Cardozo. Someone who is repelled at the idea that any man, however unworthy, should go to his death on the unsupported testimony of Bald Jack Rose and his friends may be unsettled to find the revered Cardozo among those voting with the majority in the second appeal. Cardozo had not had a judicial career of any kind until November 1913, when he had been elected to the State Supreme Court bench as a Fusion candidate. Such judgeships were not often won by the anti-Tammany crowd but, thanks to the Rosenthal murder, 1913 had been their year all the way. "The cold-blooded shooting of a gambler by thugs under orders of a police officer had . . . much to do with the popular indignation sweeping Cardozo into office," Hellman notes. Pointing out that it had done the same for Whitman and Mitchel, he adds, "Vagaries of chance indeed! Three fine public servants assisted in their careers by the bullets shot into a gambler by Whitey Lewis, Dago Frank, Lefty Louie and Gyp the Blood!" Before he went on the bench Cardozo had been an appeals lawyer and had written a book on practice before the Court of Appeals. To serve on that court was one of the dreams of his life. Within three months after he reached the State Supreme Court his dream was realized when Governor Glynn appointed him to a temporary Court of Appeals vacancy. The only Jew on the court, he had held this appointment for only a few months when the second Becker case was argued.

Cardozo's speech praising Seabury at the dinner in his honor had been more than a ceremonial gesture. They had been friends and mutual admirers for years. There was still another reason why Cardozo would have found it hard to overturn the lower court's decision. He preferred to stay as aloof as possible from any controversy involving Tammany corruption. "No record of his life would be complete without reference to what happened to his father," the *Times* would note at his death. Albert Cardozo had been a Grand Sachem of Tammany Hall in the days of Boss Tweed, who had put him on the State Supreme Court. During the Tweed Ring exposé a bipartisan committee of the legislature had recommended his impeachment for gross favoritism to Tweed and his associates. He had hastily resigned. The Cardozos were an old and proud clan, and Albert Cardozo's fall from grace was a deep stain on the family honor. A dissenting vote from Cardozo in the notorious Becker case might have invited comment that revived the old scandal. Cardozo voted with the Court of Appeals majority. Eighteen months later Whitman gave him a regular instead of a temporary appointment to the appeals court, and that fall, supported by both parties, he was elected to a full term on his own. In 1926 he succeeded Frank Hiscock as chief judge of the court. Six years later he replaced Oliver Wendell Holmes on the Supreme Court in Washington. If this diffident nonpolitical scholar had not won a judicial post in the freak election of 1913 and thus become eligible for appointment to the Court of Appeals, the last event might never have happened. Thus it is possible that, although it did not make a president of the United States, the murder of a gambler in front of the Metropole made a justice of the United States Supreme Court.

In mid-June 1915 Martin Manton, fighting back, asked the appeals court to hear a reargument of the Becker case. He now insisted that the charge of their colleague, Judge Seabury, had misled the judges of the Court of Appeals as well as the jury. Having announced that he would summarize the evidence, said Manton, Seabury had then misstated and distorted that evidence. He had never mentioned, for example, that Rose's testimony in the second trial showed he had blamed Rosenthal for spreading the word that Rose had caused gangster Zelig's arrest in May 1912, thus putting Rose in danger of being erased by Zelig's followers. On account of Rosenthal Bald Jack had been "in fear of losing his life," while Becker had been "only in fear of losing his position, possibly his liberty. The fact that the admitted assassin had a personal motive for accomplishing the crime vastly more powerful than the one attributed to the defendant is surely a feature of the case which should have been clearly submitted to the jury."

In his summary of what he called the facts, Manton went on, Seabury had referred to Becker as having "ordered" Webber and Rose to do various things, showing the jury, he said, Seabury's total acceptance of the prosecution's view of Becker as a man of enormous power over the gamblers. Also, Seabury had told the jury Rosenthal was *about to* expose corruption on the part of the defendant, and his colleagues on the Appeals Court had dutifully followed this tack, declaring in their opinion that at the time of the murder "Rosenthal had *just taken steps* to make public charges against the defendant by offering them to a prominent New York newspaper," which the court considered a powerful motive for Becker to arrange the murder. The court had apparently been misled, argued Manton, or had forgotten that Rosenthal's charges had already been published in the *World* two days earlier. "Obviously the defendant could not have planned the murder with a view to preventing the publication of charges that had already been published." Manton's plea concluded with a reminder to the judges that they were "in a very peculiar sense the last refuge open to the defendant" since "through the inexorable course of events the prosecutor of the defendant is now

Governor of the State." The Court of Appeals rejected the motion without comment.

Becker's own comment from Sing Sing was that he was used to bad news by now. He was exercising in his cell as strenuously as ever. One newspaper suggested that a man who really thought he was about to die would surely let himself go to flab. Father Cashin reported that the prisoner now was displaying "a marvelous calm." He had also requested quantities of writing paper, explaining that he planned to write an account of certain episodes in his life, not to be read by others until after his death.

Meanwhile Governor Whitman's train was making its triumphal way back from the coast. In city after city where it stopped editorials hailed him as the probable next president. The Salt Lake City *Herald-Republican* ticked off his qualifications for the high office: his outstanding record in the governorship, the fact that he was cordially hated by Tammany with all the virtues that signified, and the fact that by prosecuting the murderers of Rosenthal he had "so cleansed the New York Police Department that citizens of the metropolis for the first time in years feared the police less than the criminal."

A few days later the New York *Times* answered that one. To begin with, said the editorial, Whitman had been such a terrible governor that the ineptness of his Albany regime was being attacked not only by Democratic but by Republican and independent newspapers all over the state. And Tammany, far from hating him, had earlier made him their candidate for district attorney. The rest of the *Herald-Republican*'s editorial moved the *Times* to take a position that suggested the term "police grafter" might not in the future continue to have the emotional impact as the symbol of civic evil that it had had for so many years past. The Salt Lake City remarks were "an outrageous slander on the New York police force, which New Yorkers have always taken pride in as one of the best in the world." There might have been a few grafters among the bluecoats, but to say that New York "feared them more than it feared the criminals" was idiotic. As for Whitman's great achievement in cleansing the force, "there were ten thousand of them, and Mr. Whitman exposed and punished five."

XXIII

As the hot weather descended in 1915 the fight for life of another condemned murderer, Leo Frank, was also frequently in the national headlines. In the spring of 1913 Frank had been superintendent of a pencil factory in Atlanta. Respectable, married, a graduate of Cornell, Frank had come to the southern city from Brooklyn only five years earlier to manage the factory, owned by a relative. On a day the factory was closed a fourteen-year-old girl employee was found strangled, her clothes half ripped off, in the basement of the plant. A Negro sweeper who was in the basement at the time was the natural suspect. But when local authorities discovered that Frank had also been in the building, the chronic redneck mistrust of the Jewish outlander made another choice irresistible. Urged on by Atlanta newspapers, the police arrested Frank. The chief witness linking Frank to the murder was the Negro sweeper, who otherwise would have been in the defendant's chair himself. In the cause of anti-Semitism Southerners were for once eager to take the word of a black against a white man.

In a courtroom in Atlanta, as in his home territory, Charles Becker's name could now be used to scare little children and influence juries. A dramatic point in the prosecution's Jew-reviling final statement was the reminder that "when Lieutenant Becker wished to make away with his enemies, he sought men of [Frank's] race." Enormous crowds stood outside the courthouse chanting "Guilty! Guilty! Guilty!" as the jury deliberated and when this verdict came they danced a mass cakewalk in the square. But within a few months many local citizens, including newspaper editors and even the trial judge, had new thoughts. The Atlanta *Journal* campaigned for a new trial for Frank. This change of mind infuriated Tom Watson, political boss of the state and editor of a Know-Nothing hate sheet. Watson now began his own campaign to see that Frank did not escape the noose. ("Our Little Girl—ours by the Eternal God—has been pursued to a hideous death and bloody grave by this filthy perverted Jew of New York.")

Alarmed by his incitements to racism (which caused some Georgia Jews to leave the state, fearing for their lives), a group of prominent northern Jews took over the direction and expense of Frank's appeals. Albert Lasker, the pioneer advertising man, was organizer and largest contributor. Among the publishers he interested in the cause was Adolph Ochs of the New York *Times*. Attorney Louis Marshall finally argued the case before the U.S. Supreme Court, contending that Frank had not received a fair trial because of the climate of hatred in Atlanta. His citations included the first Court of Appeals decision in the Becker case with its mention of the hostile atmosphere of the trial. In April 1915 this decision went against Frank by a vote of seven-to-two, the dissenters being Oliver Wendell Holmes and Charles Evans Hughes, who had resigned as New York governor in 1910 to go on the court. The New York *Times* deplored the outcome as a travesty of justice. A few weeks later, after the second Becker decision by the Court of Appeals had come down, one southern newspaper went after the *Times* editors about this. The Knoxville *Sentinel* indicated its astonishment that the *Times* had "expressed complete satisfaction with the decision of the New York Court of Appeals in the case of Charles Becker while it has promoted and led the nationwide propaganda . . . to reverse the decision of the Georgia courts of appeal in the case of Leo M. Frank. What is the difference between the cases?" demanded the *Sentinel*.

In its answer the *Times* agreed that the two had some things in common. "Both men were convicted by the testimony of self-confessed accomplices, low in type, and the other evidence was largely circumstantial. But there the similarity ends. Becker had two trials, and the absolute fairness of both has never been impugned or questioned by anybody except Becker himself and his counsel" (a remarkable statement since the reason Becker had had two trials was because the first had been formally judged unfair). "There has never been even a whispered suspicion of any outside pressure to convict Becker brought to bear on judge or jury before which he was tried," the *Times* went on. "The testimony of Becker's accomplices was adequately corroborated at the second trial, as the law requires, and after neither of his convictions was there a trace of public dissatisfaction with the verdict."

The two cases inarguably had one thing in common in June 1915: The condemned man's fate in each instance was in the hands of the governor of his state. Frank's execution was more imminent, being set for June 22. Naturally his lawyers had made a plea for commutation, but nothing was expected to come of it. The governor of Georgia, John Slaton, had no reason to involve himself unduly. When he had been elected governor it was with Tom Watson's support. Many thought he would go even further in politics. Watson planned to support him for the U.S. Senate the next year. Editorials all over Georgia warned him that any move in Leo Frank's favor would bring out the mobs against him.

On June 21 Whitman's train arrived back in Albany at last. As he stepped off onto the platform, smiling broadly, he told a group of reporters he wanted to make it clear that in spite of all the newspaper stories he had never at any time during his trip discussed running for the presidency. The reporters had something else on their minds, however. The awkwardness of his position in case Becker should ask for clemency was beginning to disturb people. Had he given any thought to Martin Manton's latest proposal that he let the lieutenant governor preside over a clemency hearing?

"None at all," said Whitman, shortly.

That afternoon in Atlanta John Slaton commuted Leo Frank's sentence to life imprisonment. The commutation order was accompanied by a thirty-five-hundred-word statement reviewing the evidence in minute detail and dismissing it as contradictory and inadequate to warrant the taking of a man's life by the state. "I can endure misconstruction, abuse and condemnation," wrote Slaton, "but I cannot stand the constant companionship of an accusing conscience, which would remind me in every thought that I, as Governor of Georgia, failed to do what I thought to be right." Within an hour a mob was storming the governor's mansion, and the National Guard was called out to save his life. After his term of office ran out a few days later, Slaton left Atlanta and stayed away for several years. The next senator from Georgia was Tom Watson. Slaton never again held public office. His brave action did not even save Leo Frank, as it turned out. Two months later vigilantes kidnapped Frank from a prison farm and lynched him. Whitman had no comment on Slaton's act of clemency.

Martin Manton now visited Whitman in Albany to request that he designate some prominent citizen such as Elihu Root, Roosevelt's secretary of state, to rule on any plea Becker might make. Whitman rejected this suggestion. "I was elected governor and given this awesome responsibility," he said. "To turn it over to another man would be shirking my duty." Back in New York reporters asked Manton if he didn't think it would be wise for Becker now to tell all he knew about the city's grafting situation and at least win the support of reform groups.

"I believe 99 per cent of the public believe he is guilty, and I doubt that it would be possible under any circumstances to create favorable public sentiment," said Manton. The truth was that no matter what Becker's inclinations may have been in these last days, his chance to trade his inside knowledge for freedom had probably vanished long before. The testimony he might have given was out of date, and most of the people he could have implicated had prudently retired from the force, left town, or, as in the case of the big catch, Tim Sullivan, were in their graves.

Early in July, Bourke Cockran moved back into the case for the first time since the courtroom explosion when he had denounced the second trial as an "assassination." Immediately after taking over, Cockran announced that his first action would be to apply to the U.S. Supreme Court for a writ of error on the ground that the lower court had violated Becker's constitutional rights, in this case the due process and equal protection clauses of the Fourteenth Amendment. The high court was in recess for the summer months, so it was possible to apply for the writ to any one of the nine justices. The two likely candidates were Holmes and Hughes, the dissenters in the Frank case. Since Hughes had general jurisdiction over the New York area during the summer recess, Cockran apparently decided it would be politic not to bypass him in favor of Holmes although Hughes had been Whitman's political patron in earlier days. On July 9 Cockran argued the case at the Hughes' summer home in Rangley, Maine. Becker had been deprived of his constitutional rights, he said, because Whitman's dual role deprived the defendant of a final, impartial review, because Judge Seabury had evidence that Whitman had filled the newspapers with sensational stories against Becker as the trial began and had failed to hold the district attorney in contempt of court therefor, because a request for a change of venue had been disallowed without argument, because the immunity agreements with the gamblers had been given for the sole purpose of inducing them to swear falsely against Becker, and because "the proceedings on which Becker was convicted were not, in fact, an impartial trial . . . but were features of an elaborate plan, scheme or plot to obtain a verdict of guilty against him. Every witness," the brief went on, "was bribed to testify . . . either by promise of immunity from prosecution for crimes of which he was admittedly guilty—including the crime of murder—or by moneys paid by order of the district attorney." Late in the afternoon Cockran took the night train back to New York. Hughes had ruled there was no substantial federal question involved.

The day before Cockran's futile trip, Governor Whitman had paid a state visit to Sing Sing ostensibly to check on general conditions there but actually, the warden believed, to try to discover something to use against Osborne, whose prison theories Whitman considered coddling. This would be the last occasion when Osborne and Whitman exchanged civil words. Osborne's long history as a fighter of Tammany and prominent figure in prison reform made it hard for the governor to fire him out of hand. A few months after this tête-à-tête Osborne was indicted on six counts, including one of having committed sodomy with Sing Sing prisoners. ("I have just read 292 editorials on his death," wrote his Harvard classmate John Jay Chapman in 1926, "and only one stated what the precise charge was.") The prosecutor in the case was William J. Fallon, later Arnold Rothstein's lawyer. Osborne would spend seventy-five thousand dollars fighting the case, a large chunk of it going to Val O'Farrell, the private eye who had worked for Becker. This time Farrell dug up enough evidence to discredit the witnesses against his client, most of them prisoners who had been offered reduction of their sentences in return for their testimony. Osborne was reinstated as the Sing Sing warden. Rightly or wrongly, Osborne would blame Charles Whitman for having plotted this wretched episode.

Becker's date of execution had been postponed to allow time for the appeal to Hughes and was now scheduled for the week of July 26. The Police Department house organ suggested that Whitman reprieve Becker and leave the decision about the death sentence to a future governor, keeping the dilemma and Charles Becker himself in cold storage, as it were. They added that as district attorney Whitman had been responsible for enforcing the gambling laws, had failed to do so (unlike Jerome before him) and thus was "morally responsible to some degree for conditions that had led to the murder of Rosenthal." The current district attorney, Charles Perkins, whom Whitman had hand-picked for the job, pointed out a day later that, far from winking at lawbreakers, the D.A.'s office in recent years had been responsible for virtually wiping out the city's gangs. For instance, he said, Dopey Benny was awaiting sentence, Jew Murphy and Augie the Wop were already behind bars, and Joe the Greaser, Nigger Benny, and Little Doggie had left town. New York's gangster era was past history, said Perkins.

Meanwhile Cockran, Manton, John Johnston, and Helen Becker were conferring night after night at Cockran's office, sometimes joined by John McIntyre, Becker's much-abused first counsel whose peristaltic needs had once been a matter of procedural concern at the appeals court level. Their only slim hope was that one of the major witnesses against Becker would change his testimony at this eleventh hour. One very hot afternoon Helen Becker met Bald Jack Rose—now making films for Humanology Motion Pictures, of which he was president—by appointment at Sam Schepps' jewelry store on Broadway and vainly pleaded with him to tell the truth and save her husband. Schepps, grandiose as ever, announced afterward, "I hold the secret of the Becker case, and I will tell the Governor if he asks me. But," he added reasonably, "do you want that I should go so far as to bring Charley Becker back to Broadway and I take his place in the electric chair?" A few days later he decided he had talked too much. "If you want me to say anything, pay me for it," was his standard response. Morris Luban wasn't talking to anybody at any price.

He had just been sentenced to ten years in Sing Sing on a forgery charge. His brother Jacob would soon be there on a similar rap.

Of course there was always Changeable Charley Plitt, who had changed his story again. He now denied most of what he had testified to for the prosecution at the second trial, insisted that Becker must have another chance, and offered to sign any number of recanting affidavits. Becker *had* told him to stay away from Times Square the night of the murder, he said, but that was because Plitt liked to hang around Dowling's saloon, and Becker said he was afraid Plitt would lose the original of the Dora Gilbert affidavit that had seemed crucial at the time. Plitt issued his re-revised testimony from New Jersey because, he said, the New York district attorney's office was after him again, and he didn't dare come across the river for fear of being indicted for something. "The Negro James Marshall and myself are fully acquainted with the methods employed to secure testimony against Becker after the first conviction had been set aside." He had only testified against his good friend Becker, Plitt insisted, because he wanted to get out of jail and Whitman had promised he would pardon Becker once he was governor. But by this time no one was relying on the slippery young tipster for the truth about anything. Twelve men on a jury had done so, however, and six members of the highest court in the state, and that, unfortunately for Becker, would be all that signified.

A final Tombs eavesdropper was heard from. A Sing Sing prisoner named Joseph Murphy wrote to Osborne that he had been in the Tombs in July 1912 and had overheard Bridgey Webber tell the other gamblers the only way out was to frame Becker. He hadn't revealed this before, he said, being sure that Becker would get off. Whitman had Murphy brought to his Albany office where, according to Swope in the *World*, the governor had "shaken him like a terrier shakes a rat."

Nothing could save the prisoner now except some dramatic move that might force Whitman at least to stay the execution until something broke in the case. On July 20 the defense made such a pitch, a formal communication sixty pages long in Becker's handwriting. The first thirty-eight pages covered Becker's version of the events leading up to the murder. Accompanying this was a letter to the governor explaining how the events had been misunderstood. "Whatever effect it may produce (and I hope for very little) it will remain a public record," Becker wrote. The explanatory part of the document, Cockran said, had been "edited by Becker's counsel." The two-part letter was delivered by hand to Whitman and simultaneously released to the press.

In the newspaper world the foreign correspondents were now riding high. Richard Harding Davis was naturally with the British troops on the western front. Although recent Becker news had been well covered, news of the European war took the lead columns. On July 21, however, as would be true for the rest of the month, the Becker case was once again the biggest story in town. Just as in the old days, the *World* gave it the two right-hand columns on the front page, the whole of the second and third pages, and a good part of the fourth. The *Times* treatment was only a few columns less. The headline on one *World* story shunted into a secondary slot by the Becker case was "ONLY MIRACLE CAN SAVE WARSAW AS AUSTRO-GERMANS TIGHTEN THEIR GRIP."

Becker's version of the facts was in the labored style of the police report. "In the early part of Oct. 1911," he began, "I was directed by Com. Waldo to raid premises 155 2nd Ave." This was Bald Jack Rose's gambling house. Soon afterward he and Rose had made arrangements for Rose to get evidence for him so Becker could raid more places and build up a good record with Waldo. ("The stool pigeon's trade is treason. Surely Your Excellency . . . must realize the absolute impossibility that I could have trusted a stool pigeon like Rose with confidences involving my character and my life.") The handwritten story ended with the events of Becker's last day of freedom, July 29, 1912: "I went home to 165th Street at 9 a.m. I went in reserve at the 65th precinct, took the desk at 5 p.m., and was arrested at 8:30 p.m. . . ."

Old stuff like this would never have shoved the siege of Warsaw halfway across the *World's* front page. The furor his letter did cause proved that the excitement and controversy once set off by the name of Big Tim Sullivan weren't entirely of the past. For Becker's account included an admission of something that had been rumored from the very beginning of the case: the fact that Big Tim had been deeply involved in the negotiations that had preceded Rosenthal's murder. Because of these rumors, wrote Becker, "I am advised that to state the whole truth about those transactions is the most effective method of repelling darker insinuations calculated to blacken his memory."

Sometime in January 1912, he reported, Sullivan's half-brother Larry Mulligan had told him Big Tim would like to see him and thank him personally for the way he was enforcing the Sullivan Law. "That meeting was my first with the man so widely known as 'Big Tim,'" Becker wrote to Whitman. "Your Excellency may have some difficulty now in realizing the value which I then placed on this invitation to meet Mr. Sullivan, although your experience as District Attorney must have made you familiar with the extraordinary power he wielded. His influence in the Police Department, no matter who might be its head, was believed to be unbounded. A policeman who succeeded in enlisting his favor was considered sure of promotion."

Sullivan had something other than the Sullivan Law on his mind. He was under the impression—mistaken as it turned out—that he'd talked Waldo into letting his friend Herman Rosenthal alone if he opened up again in the Tenderloin and wanted Becker's promise not to queer things by staging a raid on his own. Becker told him he took his raid orders from Waldo, so everything should be all right. But what startled followers of the case was Becker's story of a further meeting with Sullivan the Sunday night before the murder. His account of this second meeting was endorsed and enlarged upon later that same week in an affidavit sworn to by Harry Apelbaum, Big Tim's assistant. Sullivan, wrote Apelbaum, had got into "a terribly unsettled mental condition by the summer of 1912" in which he "made mountains over molehills." He learned that Rosenthal was bragging that his pal Sullivan was back of his complaints to Whitman. "It worried Tim . . . he fearing that it would be made public that Tim loaned him money and that his position would be falsely construed." Aging and ill, Sullivan was no longer as cavalier about his reputation or his responsibility for others' misfortunes as he had been in the old Whyo days. Rosenthal's affidavit had then appeared in the *World*. Sullivan told Apelbaum to find Becker and bring him to see him that Sunday night so he could explain he had not put Herman up to it. Not knowing where Becker lived, Apelbaum had tracked down Bald Jack at Luchow's after the Sam Paul outing, and they had telephoned Becker soon after midnight. He had just arrived home from the long day at Brighton Beach but had bowed to the royal command. Apelbaum and Rose had driven to 165 Street in Tim's car and brought the lieutenant downtown. During the ride, according to Apelbaum, "Rose told me Herman had been talking about his wife. He was very bitter over it and made the remark that someone ought to croak Herman. 'No, they hadn't,' said Becker. 'If they do it will be blamed on me, and I can beat this thing all right.'"

"Herman must be crazy to carry on like this," Sullivan had told Becker, according to him and to Apelbaum. Sullivan would make sure Rosenthal couldn't get corroboration for his story. Apelbaum had been working on Herman for several days and would get him to lay off. "It is not only bad for you, but if it continues everything"—that is, all the city's gambling houses—"will be closed and many a poor feller will be thrown out of work," said Tim. Having demonstrated once again that he was just thinking of the other fellow, he had then asked Becker to promise never to speak of either of the meetings with him. "If you don't, I am all right."

"I made the promise not to do so, and I have kept that promise until now," Becker wrote with nutty pride in his letter to Whitman.

Sullivan had mentioned he would give any amount of money to stop Rosenthal but had apparently left the fund raising to others. "It was a matter of common reporting in every newspaper office," wrote Becker to Whitman, "that a sum of money had been raised . . . from the gamblers to get Rosenthal away, that Rosenthal refused the sum offered, but consented to go for a larger sum. It was for this . . . he is said to have been waiting at the Metropole when he was called out." Rosenthal had finally agreed to shut up and leave town for a while because that was the way Big Tim wanted it, said Apelbaum. Becker knew of this development because on the morning before the murder Sullivan had sent his assistant to tell the lieutenant about it. But at some point, they both believed, Bald Jack Rose had apparently decided it was a shame to waste all that cash on Herman when he could pay the gunmen their thousand-dollar rub-out price and keep the rest of the money for himself.

The second part of Becker's communication to Whitman began by quoting an editorial entitled "Whitman and Becker" that had providentially appeared three days earlier in the *Times*. In the contest between that paper's satisfaction that Lieutenant Becker had got what was coming to him and their dislike of Governor Whitman, the latter had temporarily got the upper hand.

"Should the innocence or even partial innocence of Charles A. Becker be demonstrated by a John Doe or any other legal proceeding," the editorial read, "the position of Governor Whitman will be most extraordinary. The Governor's entire political standing is based upon the convictions in the Rosenthal murder case. His uncompromising determination to send the culprits, and above all Becker, to the electric chair, is the very stuff of which his reputation as an unflinching public servant and antagonist of evil is made up. It was the second conviction of Becker that made him Governor. It would be most painful for him and his admirers to discover now that he had been the victim of blind zeal and misinformed prejudice." Whereupon, having done its worst, the *Times* concluded: "We refuse to give any credence to such a theory without overwhelming proof."

Becker's letter to Whitman did not request a commutation of his sentence. ("If I were given the choice between dying a felon's death in the electric chair and living a felon's life in a prison cell, I should certainly not be inclined to prefer the longer over the shorter agony.") However, said Becker, "I do revolt from being forced to bear, living or dead, the stigma of murder. . . ." In his appearance before Hughes, he noted, Cockran had accused the district attorney of New York of having conducted a trial which constituted "a conspiracy to bring about my conviction. Although it involves the unprecedented (perhaps some would say preposterous) proceeding of asking His Excellency Charles S. Whitman, Governor of the State, to review, reverse, and in some respects condemn the conduct of Hon. Charles S. Whitman, District Attorney of New York County," nevertheless, he requested the governor "to forbid execution of the capital sentence . . . on the ground that my guilt of the murder is not established so clearly as to justify the taking of a human life." He asked that execution be forbidden so that he might have time to find evidence of his innocence. If Whitman turned him down at least this account of events "will serve as a key to explain future developments certain to follow quarrels which will inevitably arise among the assassins whom you have allowed to save their own lives by swearing mine away." He assured Whitman he was "entirely free from anything

like personal resentment," and after that bare-faced lie moved
into the recessional:

> In these days when we read of men dying by tens of thou-
> sands every day in battle, the disposition that may be
> made of one poor human life seems scarcely worth the
> trouble which the perusal of these very voluminous papers
> must entail. But I do not feel I should withhold a single
> word that might by chance aid you in reaching a conclu-
> sion which will win approval of your own conscience and
> of the people who have intrusted you with the sovereign
> power to take my life or spare it.
>
> I have the honor to be, sir, Your Excellency's humble
> servant,
>
> CHARLES BECKER

Despite his lofty tone, Becker was still playing games in one
respect. In his long letter to Whitman he had continued to insist
with unbecoming righteousness that all tales of his having raked
in spoils during his strong arm squad days were slanders. It almost seemed that Becker believed there was still a chance he
would "beat this thing all right" and didn't want his victory
marred with an anticlimactic jail term for grafting. Or possibly
his attorneys advised this course, convinced that the public's response to the term "police grafter" remained so irrational that
he'd better stick to his story even if it meant losing the chance to
point out that grafting was not a capital offense.

Bald Jack the next day derided Becker's version of things and
naturally had no recollection of having himself proposed that
Rosenthal be croaked. Becker had ordered the murder all right
and afterward had "gone around town like a Judas looking for
someone to blame it on." (Rose was apparently not an authority
on the New Testament.) But he supported Becker's story of the
Elks' Club meeting and of the second interview with Big Tim. In
their last legal maneuvers Becker's lawyers would include Rose's
published statement as a defense document. If true, the account
of the second Sullivan meeting went a long way to prove the
contention of the defense that by the time of the shooting Becker
had known he had nothing more to fear from Rosenthal. The
World story had already appeared. Big Tim had now taken over.
The gambler would either pipe down or leave town, Sullivan's

crowd would see to that. If Becker had ever entertained murderous thoughts they had become irrelevant. Since this was the point the defense had worked so hard to establish, why had Becker kept his mouth shut about the interview until this moment?

All his attorneys insisted they had known nothing of the Big Tim story. Perhaps some of them were lying. It seems likely that Cockran had not known it for very long. At the opening of the second trial he had been in such a rage at Whitman that he would almost certainly have seized on it to devil the prosecution had he known it was available. He said his client had never mentioned it until June 1915. (On June 19 Becker had written him in his large round hand, "I should like to have a heart-to-heart talk with you." Cockran had motored up the next day.)

In the first trial Becker had had a problem about the Big Tim story. Who would introduce the subject if he didn't take the stand? If he took the chance of testifying, opening himself up to questions about grafting, then who would confirm the story? Not the loyal Apelbaum (Big Tim was still alive). Not the other witness, Bald Jack Rose, who had so much to lose if Becker's denials became more plausible. But by the time of the second trial Sullivan had been dead for nearly a year. Apelbaum now said he had urged Becker to take the stand in 1914. Perhaps Becker did not break his silence because he still thought his chances were so bright he didn't need to go into the Big Tim matter. When he got out of Sing Sing, it would be convenient to have the Big Feller's grateful friends to rely on.

Father Curry told reporters the former policeman had mentioned the Sullivan meetings to him nearly two years earlier, but since this was in the confessional he could do nothing about it. Becker's Police Department career, Curry pointed out, had almost exactly spanned the period of Big Tim's East Side reign, and he must have been foolishly overimpressed by his face-to-face encounter with the powerful Irishman. In addition, said Curry, Becker felt a special loyalty to Sullivan's memory since he believed Tim had died a martyr to his cause, that he had been cut down just as he was about to try to save Becker from the death house. No doubt the prisoner's silence also had something to do with his long determination not to be among the company of squealers. "However extravagant or ridiculous they may have been, these are . . . the reasons that actually governed me," said

Becker, clinging to his only explanation, that he had made Sullivan a promise and felt bound by it. Swope may have been right when he wrote contemptuously during the first trial: "Becker radiates strength, but it is a physical rather than a mental strength."

As expected, Whitman had not been moved by Becker's plea. The plans for the execution proceeded. However, a petition was circulating at the state constitutional convention in Syracuse asking the governor to leave the decision on Becker's fate to a state Board of Pardons, and Manton now proposed turning it over to a special commission made up of former chief judges on the Court of Appeals. Whitman rejected both suggestions. Before doing so, he announced, he had consulted with two of the most distinguished judges in the state. One of them was a former Appellate Court chief judge. The other was Samuel Seabury. Hearst's *American*, which until this time had been down the line against Becker, was distressed about the situation. "Practically all of New York has been convinced of his blood guiltiness," it said of Becker. But Whitman's "complete identification with the prosecution almost from the moment of the murder makes appeal to him as a last resort a ghastly jest." On the other hand, the *World* argued that Whitman should make the decision for that very reason: He had been with the case longest and knew more about it than anyone else.

Meanwhile Cockran was sifting through his unsolicited mail in the hope of a break in the case. The most promising communication described in detail Big Tim's frantic middle-of-the-night phone calls to the home of one of Whitman's assistant district attorneys in the summer of 1913, begging him to help Charley Becker, whose fate had become Sullivan's King Charles' head. Unfortunately the letter was unsigned. Cockran then made one last trip to the courts for Becker. He went before a State Supreme Court justice and asked that a new trial be granted on the ground of newly discovered evidence. Becker was now anxious to testify, said Cockran. Having been "the innocent victim of mistaken loyalty" to Big Tim, he had not been a witness before and thus had not had his day in court. "This pledge and its keeping constitute the most extraordinary chapter in the most extraordinary narrative in the history of our criminal jurisprudence." The evidence about the Sullivan meetings should have been put in before,

Cockran agreed, "but are you going to electrocute a man on a technicality?" Among the affidavits stapled to the claim of new evidence was one from a gambler, Benjamin Kaufman, who had been an occasional business partner of Rosenthal's. Three hours before the murder, he said, Rosenthal, standing at Forty-fourth and Broadway, had told him he had a date at the Metropole that night to pick up fifteen thousand dollars. "Who the hell is going to give you fifteen thousand dollars?" Kaufman had asked him. "What the hell is fifteen thousand to that gang?" Herman had responded. "It don't amount to a nickel apiece to them. . . . As soon as I get that money I'm going to beat it." In a homey touch Kaufman then quoted Rosenthal as saying he thought he wouldn't go back home just then: "She won't let me out again."

The execution was now scheduled for the early morning of July 30. State Supreme Court Justice John Ford took Cockran's plea under advisement on July 26. A ruling for Becker was not expected. Two days earlier linemen had begun stringing wires and setting up telegraph instruments in a shack opposite the Sing Sing death house. Formal invitations went out to public officials and to applicants selected from among the hundreds who had requested the privilege of watching Becker die. But the district attorney's office had had rude surprises before and, preparing for the worst, again set its well-oiled machinery in motion. Dozens of subpoenas bearing the old familiar names were held at the ready. Once again Jack Rose was seen moving with assurance in and out of the Criminal Courts Building. Sam Schepps declared himself available, as usual. Bridgey Webber said he wanted nothing more to do with the case, as usual. By the time reporters caught up with Harry Vallon out in Pittsburgh, he was in the custody of a man from the New York district attorney's office. "You going to make a statement before Becker's bumped off?" a reporter asked him.

"You bet I am," said Vallon, "and I'll make some people sit up and take notice." Did he mean Whitman? "That's just what I mean," said Vallon angrily. "They ain't treated me right." They had even scared his girl away by threatening him with the Mann Act, he complained.

Fortunately the prosecution didn't have to face the problem of putting Vallon on the stand again. Justice Ford handed down his decision late on July 28. To the surprise of many, nine out of ten of the telegrams sent to him while he deliberated had begged him to spare Becker's life. Properly ignoring the barrage, Ford had denied the motion for a new trial. None of the material submitted could be called new evidence, he pointed out. Becker himself had known of the Big Tim story all along. In any event the State Supreme Court had no inherent power to open up a capital case already decided by it and passed on by the Court of Appeals. In a case like Becker's, he concluded, "the safeguard against error is the pardoning power. That is the tribunal which properly can grant, if it sees fit, appeals of this sort."

Reached at the governor's mansion, Whitman, the man with the pardoning power, was glad to answer that question. "There never was a case more perfectly proved in the history of jurisprudence," he said.

In his cell Charles Becker spent most of his last days writing letters. Early in July, when he still had some hope, he had sent several to Jacob Reich, his *"fidus Achates,"* as he addressed him, showing off his Latin. "I wrote two letters to Deacon Terry," he told Reich, "and I wish you could get him to come out with the truth of what he knows; it might help some. . . ." In one letter to Terry, Becker ran down the list of perjuries against him. "You know how Goldman was suborned. Luban and Hallen also added their little mite to the whole perjured fabric, to say nothing of the others. . . . You must know that Plitt's absolute perjury against me was the price of his freedom on the other charge of perjury hanging over him. He was shown a way to get out . . . under the guiding hand of Groehl. . . . In view of what you positively know . . . I ask you to do all in your power to help me." Terry's only assistance was to see that a few hours before the execution the *American* printed the letter across the top of its front page with the footnote that Terry knew that all that Becker had written was true. Fred Hawley's job on the *Sun* hadn't lasted a day after he had openly supported Becker, and Terry didn't take that route.

On July 26, his forty-fifth birthday, Becker wrote farewell letters to old friends on the police force, to Jacob Reich, and to Father Curry. He told a former chief inspector that he had decided against a habeas corpus action in the federal courts because he didn't have the money to print the briefs. He thanked Reich for all he had done for him. "You know beyond all doubt that I am as much a victim of murder as was poor Rosenthal. Whitman is my murderer. . . . I am tired of the world and its injustice to me; my happy life is ruined," he wrote Curry. "My life has been made a sacrifice on the altar of Whitman." Two nights later news of Justice Ford's rejection of his motion for a new trial came to him, like so many revelations in the case, through the offices of the New York *World*. Fifteen minutes after the decision was handed down the *World* got through to Warden Osborne, who walked across the courtyard to the death house and told Becker.

" 'Denied! Denied!' " he murmured (according to next morning's *Sun*) and was silent for a long moment. Then he threw his shoulders back. " 'There's nothing more for me to say. . . . I'll die like a man.' " The nineteenth century was not a remote era to the feature writer of 1915. In times of stress his subjects still talked like characters out of a Ouida novel instead of, as today, like second-rate Hemingway heroes.

Helen Becker had left Sing Sing for the railway station ten minutes before the telephone call came. When she arrived at her Bronx apartment at midnight, a crowd of waiting reporters gave her the news. When they asked her whether she would make a personal appeal to the governor, she shook her head. Becker had said he would rather go straight to the chair than have his wife humble herself before Whitman. But by morning she had decided it must be done. Martin Manton put in a call to Albany for her. After some delay the governor's secretary reported that Whitman would see her at noon.

After the final legal escape was closed off for Becker the evening before, Charles Whitman had done a very curious thing. Perhaps the published telegrams to Justice Ford favoring a better deal for the prisoner had unnerved him by indicating there was a growing feeling around the country (of which he had plans to become chief executive) that the case against Becker was not quite the black-and-white morality play he had presented. The *World* had dismissed them all as "a bunch of cranks," and probably many of them were representing the anti-capital-punishment forces and had only a general interest in Becker. But in his three years behind bars Becker had steadfastly denied any part in the murder and, so far as was known, had kept his vow not to squeal on anyone to save himself. Now the imminence of death gave his pigheadedness a certain baroque dignity. Some newspapers were treating him almost as a sympathetic character.

Whitman did not care for this finale. Late on the evening of July 28, when the condemned man had less than thirty hours to live, the governor received Albany reporters in his State House chambers and loosed an attack on Becker that culminated in an additional charge of murder.

From the next day's stories it was clear that the writers had been told the interview was not for direct attribution. (Later Whitman unofficially dropped the masquerade.) It was evident from the story's prominence in the press that the source was no capitol clerk. The *World* account, occupying a box two columns wide at the top of the front page, declared that the paper had been able to learn from "those persons who are closest to the Governor" some of the reasons for his confidence that no mistake had been made in the Becker case. Each item thereafter was prefaced by "The Governor knows . . ." or "The District Attorney's office is aware . . ." although why the Manhattan district attorney's office took an Albany dateline was not gone into.

The governor knew, for example, that, far from protecting his fellow grafters to the death, Becker, through Manton, had given five names to Whitman and had promised to give evidence against these persons in return for clemency. Two of the men were dead, the news stories reported. Whitman had not said that one of them was Big Tim Sullivan and the other Mayor Gaynor, so it was not his fault if quite a few citizens jumped to this conclusion. Moreover Becker, far from having at all times maintained his innocence of Rosenthal's murder, had been "ready at any time to plead guilty to murder in the second degree." The reports also said that the governor had "known all along" of Becker's conference with Big Tim the Sunday night before the murder.

"Many women through the state"—the *World* story went on— "have been urging the Governor to commute Becker's sentence on the plea that Becker's family life was pure. This appeal, however, has not impressed Mr. Whitman." After all, it was known that Becker's second wife had been given a divorce on the ground of infidelity. And then came the eleventh-hour indictment. "The New York District Attorney's office has known that Becker's [first] wife died suddenly in a bathtub. . . . The District Attorney's office, the Governor knows, is confident that the Rosenthal murder was not the first with which Becker was concerned."

XXIV

WHEN the guards roused the prisoners in the death house the next morning, Becker was already awake, sitting upright on his cot. He asked whether the morning papers had arrived.

"Charley, don't bother about the newspapers today . . . You are facing eternity," Father Cashin pleaded when he stopped by a little later.

"I want to see them just once more," said Becker, the true addict.

Before the papers arrived, Becker wrote his wife a last love letter. "My heart's blood:" it began, "There is no way I can tell you all you are and have been to me. You are simply the flower of my life, the guiding star of my hopes, and my comfort in my anguish of soul. This I know, my spirit shall ever hover near you until we meet in the green pastures beside the still waters in the great beyond. Your lover, Charley."

About nine o'clock Father Cashin, looking apprehensive, brought him the New York papers. A moment after he read Whitman's remarks from Albany Becker let out a shout. Grabbing the bars of his cell, he demanded a stenographer so he could answer Whitman. He was promised a tablet and pencil. But first there were the grisly preliminaries of his execution. Part of his hair was shaved off, he was issued a black cotton suit of clothes with no metal buttons or snaps, and his shoes were exchanged for a pair of black felt slippers. Becker submitted to these ministrations with an almost absent air. Back in his cell, he began to write furiously.

A man can't read newspaper stories about himself for three years without acquiring some expertise about the logistics of the business, and it must have seemed to Becker that Whitman had cleverly arranged matters so that his charges would break before the papers had time to cover the scheduled execution and thus wouldn't be swamped by that dramatic event. He also must have suspected Whitman of counting on a man so close to death being in no shape to answer the charges. But Becker kept writing. About eleven o'clock the warden told him he would have to wait until the lawyers arrived in midafternoon before anything could be released to the press.

"I don't want to wait. I want my story in the afternoon papers," he cried passionately, according to the *World*. He wrote all morning between visits by Warden Osborne, the two priests, and the prison doctors who found that his hands were steady and his pulse seventy-eight, only a fraction above normal. At three when Manton and Cockran arrived he consulted with them in the warden's office. Reportedly they edited out of his letter many libelous references to the governor. Typed out on the warden's typewriter, it was then released to the press.

"It would be shocking to suspect that the governor of this state would stoop to assail with unfounded charges a helpless man in the very shadow of death," it began. "I prefer to believe that you have been misled." Becker fiercely denied that he had ever offered to plead guilty to a lesser charge. Two days later Whitman denied that he had made this statement. "If he'd ever offered to plead guilty, the D.A.'s office would have jumped at the chance," declared J. Robert Rubin, an assistant district attorney who had worked on the second case. Rubin also added the final accounting of Becker's graft haul. "There is another point that should be corrected," Rubin told the *American*. "Some papers have stated that Becker's 'graft bank accounts' totalled a hundred thousand dollars or more." The amount the district attorney's office had uncovered, he said, was $29,500.

In his letter to Whitman Becker also swore he had never authorized anyone to give the governor the names of grafters, and Manton denied he had done so. Manton had quite a different story. The names of some political figures had come up, he said, but it was because Whitman had listed for *him* the people he wanted to get some dirt on. Topmost on the list, Manton implied, was Mayor John Purroy Mitchel. But Becker, said Manton, had not obliged the governor.

Becker's letter denounced Whitman's suggestion that his first wife had died "under circumstances warranting the suspicion that I caused her death" as "cruelty almost inconceivable." Perhaps Whitman knew what he was talking about. But neither he nor the district attorney's office supplied any evidence for the charge (the next day Whitman refused even to comment on it). And there is at least one published recollection of Whitman that suggests he sometimes got a notion in his head that would bolster his side of a case, held firmly to it, and even passed it on as authoritative fact. In his autobiography Charles Chapin, the terrible-tempered city editor of the *Evening World*, reported that soon after Whitman was elected governor, the editor had mentioned to him that Rhinelander Waldo had never believed Becker was guilty. Whitman answered this, related Chapin, by telling

> with circumstantial detail, a story about the two men that made me gasp with astonishment. It was the story of an uptown raid, years before the Rosenthal affair, and, if true, explained in a way the hold Becker had on Waldo at the time all New York was clamoring for Becker's arrest.
>
> I took pains to carefully investigate the next day the story told me by Whitman and I learned that Becker was not concerned in the raid Whitman told about and that at the time of the occurrence Waldo was serving as an officer in the Philippines. A week later I told him the result of my investigation.
>
> "I told you the story exactly as it was related to me," was his only defense.
>
> "But you didn't tell it to me as a bit of hearsay gossip," I retorted. "You told it as a statement of fact, and coming from the lips of the District Attorney who prosecuted Becker and the gunmen and who is soon to be Governor of the State, I had every reason to believe it was true. I am glad I took the precaution to investigate what you told me, and I suppose you will be gratified to learn that it is

untrue in every particular, so that you will not again repeat as a fact what is really only a malicious, lying
scandal."

"Governor Whitman changed the subject," reported Chapin.
(Chapin's biography was written from a cell in Sing Sing where
he had been sent to serve a twenty-year term for having killed his
wife, to save her, he said, from learning of a terrible loss he had
taken in the stock market. The newspapermen under whom he
had worked for two decades on the *Evening World* always pretended astonishment at this outcome. They had known he would
be involved in a murder someday, they said, but had always
assumed he would be the victim.)
Concerning the wife murder charge that Whitman had brought
against Becker, Manton told the press that Whitman had mentioned in the spring of 1914 that he understood Becker had killed
his first wife. After investigating, Manton had been convinced this
was no more than a malicious rumor. Though Whitman had not
brought up the matter again, the defense had prepared a brief
dossier to refute the charge. They had also got in touch with the
priest who had given Becker's first wife the last rites of the church,
who was ready to testify that she had died in bed of tuberculosis.
Presumably Manton had brought the folder with him when he
came to Sing Sing this last day, which was why, in his reply
to Whitman, Becker had so ready to hand the details of the
almost classic little nineteenth-century pathetique.
"I was married to Mary Mahoney of No. 117 Washington
Street, Feb. 6, 1895, at St. Peter's Church on Hester Street," he
wrote. "Mrs. Becker caught cold on the night of our marriage. It
settled on her lungs and ten days later she was treated by Dr.
Turner of No. 30 State Street." He then gave the names and
addresses of three other doctors who had treated her in the next
months, including one at a Sullivan County sanitarium to which
she was moved for a while before being brought home to Washington Street to die. "Mrs. Becker died in her father's home
October 15, 1895, and was buried from St. Peter's Church where
she had been married eight months before." By the day of the
execution the newspapers had located several of Mary Mahoney's
relatives, who corroborated this account. "She was sick with hasty
consumption from the day she was married," said a niece. No one

from the district attorney's office had ever approached them to
check on any rumors of murder.

"When your power passes, then the truth of Rosenthal's murder will become known," Becker's last letter to Whitman concluded. But meanwhile "you have proved yourself able to destroy
my life."

With only a dim hope of changing this, Helen Becker and
Manton's young assistant, John B. Johnston, had taken the morning train to Albany, arriving just before noon at the State House
office where Whitman had agreed to see them. At the door they
were told that the governor had left the capital and gone to review
a detachment of the National Guard at Peekskill. Unfortunately
he had had to leave earlier than he'd expected, his military aide
explained nervously. He would not be back until evening. For four
hours Mrs. Becker sat in the lobby of a nearby hotel while
Johnston called the governor's office at intervals. At last word
came that Whitman would see her after all if she would come to
Poughkeepsie, five miles north of Fishkill. She and Johnston took
another train, arriving a little before six at a hotel called the
Nelson House where one of the second-floor parlors had been
reserved for the confrontation. Word of the meeting had preceded
them, and an immense crowd of people filled the street. Inside the
hotel, Johnston went in to see Whitman first to present the legal
arguments for a temporary stay of execution so that Becker's
attorneys could have time to review Justice Ford's decision. Whitman told him there was nothing he could do.

When Johnston finished his plea, Helen Becker was led in. The
natural summer evening light was almost gone, but no one had
turned on the lamps in the room. Whitman, flanked by two of his
assistants, stood when she entered, and she and the four men
remained standing throughout the brief interview.

"If there is anything you have to tell me, feel free . . ." Whitman began. Perhaps he was hoping for a last minute confession
of her husband's guilt. She said she had nothing to tell him and
asked for the temporary stay of execution. "My husband is not a
murderer," she said. Whitman repeated that there was nothing he
could do. It was clear to her that he had been drinking.

"Whitman was supported by two aides the entire time he spoke
to me," she told a reporter some time later. "He was in no condition to understand anything I said." One of the reporters Whit-

man spoke to after seeing Helen Becker described him as "leaning limply over the side of a chair" while the reporter talked with him. Photographers waiting outside to get a picture of her as she came down the hotel steps saw no sign that she had cried. Upstairs the dark windows of the room where she and the governor had met were suddenly ablaze with lights.

Discovering that a train from Poughkeepsie would not arrive at Sing Sing until after ten, Johnston hired a car to drive them to the prison. The car stalled in front of the hotel and, as the driver tried to get it started, brasher members of the crowd, now esti- mated at two thousand, clambered on the running board and peered in at their faces. Later the driver missed the Peekskill turnoff and went considerably out of his way. They took over three hours for the forty-two-mile trip. During this frantic jour- ney, fearful that she might arrive to find the prison gates closed and might never see her husband again, Helen Becker wrote out a statement to be given to the press after the execution and decided on the wording of the silver plaque she planned to attach to her husband's coffin.

Cockran and Manton had left for New York on the 5:30 train along with several of Becker's sisters who had come to say good- bye. Their places outside his cell were taken by his police lieu- tenant brother John and by John Lynch, his wife's brother. As the evening wore on the two men, understandably short of things to say to a relative about to die in the electric chair, merely sat and watched while he paced in his cell, his felt slippers making no sound. At about half past eight he asked the time and remarked that it was exactly three years since he had been arrested in the Bathgate police station. After Father Cashin joined the party about nine, someone began to sing "Rock of Ages." The two rela- tives gratefully took it up, as did the other prisoners in the block. Becker joined in the chorus. At ten he was moved to the head keeper's room. It was after eleven when his wife reached the prison. The gates were opened for the car, and Helen Becker and Johnston jumped out and ran to the warden's private entrance. Johnston said a brief good-bye and then, joined by John Becker, started back to the city.

In New York that evening John McIntyre had declared that in all his years at the bar he had never before doubted the verdict of a jury. "But in this case I say that if Becker is executed tomorrow

I will carry to my grave the conviction that at least one innocent man has suffered the death penalty." Now that it was almost over, none of Becker's lawyers showed a sign of defecting. "I believe that Becker is dying a martyr," said Joseph Shay, "and that his innocence will be established in time, perhaps by the deathbed confession of Vallon or Webber. Rose is too low to confess even on his deathbed." Reporters were covering all bases in this last gasp of the Becker case, and several were on hand at Grand Central as Cockran and Manton's train arrived there from Sing Sing.

"His hand is just as cool and his voice as steady as can be," Cockran told them. "Such a situation and he so calm! To think of executing a man like that for this crime! He is a most marvelous man . . . most marvelous. One would think that he was the Governor and someone else was about to die."

In the keeper's room at Sing Sing Helen and Charley Becker were left alone together for over an hour except for two guards at the door. No condemned man at the prison had ever had such sympathetic treatment, the *World* noted crossly the next day, or had "been given such comparative freedom" in his last meeting with his wife. Half an hour after midnight Warden Osborne told Helen Becker she must go. After a last embrace she left for the city with her brother. "Becker is beyond commiseration," read an editorial in the *Times* that was at this moment just beginning to hit the New York streets. His death "should be notice to the New York brotherhood of the knife and the 'gun' that the most brazen, cunning cutthroat may be beaten at last by limping justice." Except to "persons of too easy lachrymal ducts," the refusal of the state to prolong the proceedings any further "should give a sense of satisfaction to all of us who still believe in justice and honesty."

After his wife left, Becker returned to his cell. White curtains had been stretched across all the cubicles along the narrow corridor so the other inmates of death row would not see him as he started his long walk to the execution room. According to the keepers Becker did not sleep or even lie down in what was left of the night. He had rejected ahead of time the condemned man's traditional hearty meal. At two-thirty Warden Osborne, coming to say good-bye, found him sitting crouched on the end of his cot, his chin sunk in his hands. At four his visitors were the two priests.

"God, in permitting me to die must have some wise design," he told them, according to Father Curry, who then heard his last confession. Afterward Becker repeated his avowal of innocence in the murder and then added cryptically, "I am sacrificed for my friends."

Published the next day, this last statement naturally set off speculation over what friends Becker had meant. The whole East Side subdivision of Tammany Hall? Police inspectors such as Hughes and Hayes? Some thought he meant Winfield Sheehan, Waldo's shrewd and mysteriously affluent assistant. Waldo, perhaps? Probably he was just referring in a general way to all the politicians and higher ranking policemen known to be in on the gambling take whom he might have ruined—the same old "I'm no Schmittberger" routine from the debate of twenty years earlier in which he had cast his lot with Clubber Williams without realizing that the polemic in his case would turn into a death struggle. There were also those who suspected the partisan Father Curry of having made the statement up.

At five o'clock that last morning a death house guard named Patrick O'Toole appeared at the door of Becker's cell, carrying in one hand a long pair of shears and in the other a letter signed by all eighteen other inmates of the death house. "Your manly behavior during these trying days was a source of edification and inspiration to us all," it read. (An upstate schoolteacher who had murdered his wife was among the recent death row arrivals.) "Surely some day your case will be cited by historians of human progress as one of the best arguments against antiquated legal concepts, chambers of horrors, death houses, condemned cells, etc., remnants of ages gone by." The letter concluded with a paragraph that some newspapers omitted as blasphemous: "We are at a loss to offer you any consolation except the example of One who also was executed as a criminal and Whose last words were, 'Father, forgive them for they know not what they do.'" When Becker had read the letter the guard stood fingering his scissors until Becker sat down on the cot and held out his right leg so that O'Toole could slit his trouser leg to the knee.

Meanwhile a double line of guards was posted along the fence that separated the prison grounds from the road, and other guards poked long sticks at the crowd of several hundred people that stood outside the main gate, three hundred yards from the death house. For a man who abhorred the death penalty, Warden Osborne's quarters were not well situated. From the porch of his

house he had a clear view of the execution annex. Even at dawn
the day was already hot. Collars wilted on the thirty-five official
witnesses and newspapermen who had gathered on the porch as
the sun rose. The twenty newspapermen were busily bartering
background material: the fact that before 1891, for instance,
Becker would have been not electrocuted but hung by the neck in
the grimy yard next to the Tombs, that he would be the hundred
and sixteenth person to die in the Sing Sing chair.

When the four gunmen had been electrocuted fifteen months
earlier, Herbert Bayard Swope had sat in the front row, and other
reporters there insisted they were surprised he didn't at the last
moment step forward and pull the switch himself. But in April
1915 Swope had come down with rheumatic fever, and by the end
of July was still only back at the *World* city desk on a part-time
basis. He came down from his Riverside Drive apartment to
handle important stories and was certainly in charge of the
Becker execution story, but he was not in shape to travel to Sing
Sing. Another *World* reporter, carrying pages of handwritten
directions from Swope, was on hand this morning in his place, one
who had also known Becker when he was riding high. The hyper-
energetic and overbearing Swope was not always a popular figure
among competing newspapermen, but few could help feeling
sorry for him now, forced to be absent from the denouement of
the case in which he had been so important a figure.

Shortly after 5 A.M. Warden Osborne came out his front door,
wearing a blue blazer and white flannel trousers. True to his
promise that no one would catch him on the premises when a
man was about to go to the chair, he put on his straw bowler and
walked away from the scene to another part of the prison com-
plex. At five-thirty the company got word to move along. Motion
picture cameras ground away as the witnesses filed through the
exercise yard and into the execution chamber. The electric chair,
toward which all eyes turned, was brown and newly varnished.
Straps dangled loosely from its arms and legs, and above it a
twisted length of wire hung from a goosenecked iron fixture. Back
of the chair and a little to the left stood the executioner, a small,
sharp-featured man dressed in a gray sack suit with a pink striped
shirt, a winged collar, a purple scarf, and pointed patent leather
shoes. At five-forty-two the narrow red door at the back of the
death room swung open, and Becker entered. "The Lord have

mercy upon me," he was saying in a loud, clear voice. It was a response in the litany of the Holy Name being read by Father Curry and Father Cashin, who followed a few strides behind him. The prisoner carried a silver crucifix. The black cloth of his right trouser leg flapped wide as he walked "exposing Becker's powerful bare leg," noted a wire service reporter. Becker was "a tremendous animal physically," the story added. His short black coat was unbuttoned, and his white linen shirt and undershirt were open, revealing, according to the *World* account, "a great expanse of strong, outswelling chest."

Becker walked stiffly, his shoulders hunched forward. The old Becker, said the *World,* "a familiar figure in days gone by, indeed an acquaintance frequently met by the writer," had "carried his chin high, arrogantly—for he was arrogant." The press had been told that his hair had been cut short, but only a spot on each temple was shaved. "It was a surprise to see the old, rather intractable sweep of long, dark brown, almost black hair curving from left to right above his forehead." As Becker came near the chair, his eyes suddenly swerved toward the line of spectators until they reached the newspapermen, bunched together at one end. "He had turned away in an instant, but some of those who met his eyes felt that his gaze seemed to linger . . . for an appreciable, uncomfortable period."

Once Becker was in the chair, five prison guards began feverishly tossing heavy straps about and buckling them around his knees, ankles, wrists, elbows, and chest. "Because they were fond of Becker," according to the *Times* man, "and were in a hurry to get the whole thing over for him, they neglected to buckle one of the straps across his chest. As the blindfold was adjusted, Becker continued to give the responses to the litany."

The reports of Becker's demeanor at the moment of death varied somewhat. Most of the reporters there thought he had faced death almost as stolidly as when he had twice heard the verdict of "guilty" in court. "BECKER MET DEATH UNFLINCHINGLY" was the *American* headline. But the *World* insisted he had been "about to be overcome by sheer nerve panic." His brow had been furrowed, the *Times* pointed out. His voice had shaken on his last words, reported the *World,* and the hand holding the crucifix had trembled. Before "the merciful bandage went on," his eyes had "darted up, down, to the right, to the left." The delegate from the

New York sheriff's office insisted, however, that "Becker died game." To no one's surprise, the New York Police Department had the same impression. "He went to the chair as game as going to his dinner at home," declared a later history of the department.

All agreed that he continued to say the Catholic responses to the end and that his last words before a broad strap was pulled across his mouth were "Into Thy hands, O Lord, I commend my spirit." At that moment one of the prison physicians standing by gave a signal, the executioner took his hands out of his pockets, and there was a harsh, crunching sound as he threw the wooden lever that turned on 1,850 volts of current.

A nightmare followed. As the big body heaved upward the loose strap gave way, the body lunged forward, the head twisted about, and from the left temple an unexpected flame spurted and blazed steadily through the long full minute of the first jolt of current. When the lever was pulled back, the two prison doctors found that Becker's heart was not only still beating but pounding strongly. Becker was said to be the largest man who had been brought into the execution chamber, and the experts had misjudged the amount of current it would take to kill him. Now the loose strap was buckled, the priests and doctors stepped back on their protective rubber mats, and, over the droning of Father Cashin's prayers, the lever crunched again as another jolt was applied. When the doctors moved forward, they found the heart was still pounding. It was only after a third jolt that Becker, after further consultation, was finally pronounced dead.

The whole procedure, often described in later years as the clumsiest execution in the history of Sing Sing, had taken only nine minutes but, as the *World* reporter wrote, "to those who had sat in the gray-walled room and watched and listened to the rasping sound of the wooden switch lever being thrown backward and forward and had seen the greenish-blue blaze at the victim's head and feet and the grayish smoke curling away from the scorched flesh, it had seemed an hour." As a prison physician at last said, "I pronounce this man dead," most of the witnesses made a dash for the outdoors, the sunlight, and the fresh air.

"The giant died hard," the *World* agreed the next day. But the city editor who liked to talk of "*my* shipwreck" and *my* five alarm fire" refused to concede that *his* execution had been bungled in any way. "The rumor spread that a great botch had been made of the killing. There was a slight accident, it is true. But this was not important. As executions go," the *World* insisted, "this one was entirely a success." Today when state executions are virtually unknown in America, Swope's attitude and the details of the event itself seem to hark back to the Middle Ages instead of earlier in the present century.

Apparently no one found it unseemly for the doctor who had done the official autopsy to write a feature story on the experience in the next day's *American*. He began with some lines that suggested Whitman was right in detecting a dangerous rise of sympathy for Becker. The men in the death house weren't the only blasphemers that early morning. Having described the scene as the prisoner, still praying, climbed into the electric chair, the doctor added: "At the words 'God have mercy . . .' one couldn't help but think of the Nazarene who suffered a like punishment brooking the authority of the majority two thousand years ago." As for the autopsy, Becker, he wrote, "proved to be a perfect physical specimen of enormous development. . . ." The dead man's brain was also large, he added. "From a phrenological standpoint the measurements of Becker's head were slightly above the normal, especially in the area of constructiveness, acquisitiveness, combativeness and calculation."

The *World* had its own autopsy witness. Their reporter on the scene had not joined the stampede for the door when the execution was over. In a move that seems beyond the call of journalistic duty, but one that Swope presumably had specified in his directives, he went along as the body was removed from the chair and carried through a door to the autopsy room, "its arms dangling, its head hanging back, its lower legs swinging." And just as if it had been "Swope's execution," the *World* seemed impelled to prove that the quarry it had so relentlessly pursued had been indeed a prize. "It was a wonderful body from which the vital spark had been burnt away. . . . Such a pair of lungs, so deep, so broad, so unstained, the physicians had rarely seen, they said. Such a perfect heart, in as normal a condition as that of a healthy boy's, it had seldom been their experience to observe. And the brain, forty-five and a quarter ounces in weight, was likewise of perfect contour. . . . Neither vice nor disease had touched any part of this man, who . . . was 215 pounds of sinewy strength. He was physical perfection."

The *World* story on the execution began with a sentence that Swope had perhaps begun to formulate in his mind on another July morning in the Forty-seventh Street police station three years before: "The crooked trail upon which Charley Becker first set foot when a gambler's gold lured him from the straight way of his sworn duty led him today around the last corner and into an impasse from which there was no escape." After a description of the big body straining outward, the bared teeth, the frothing lips, it concluded: "That was the end of Charles Becker and of the Becker case which began one June night at 124th Street and Seventh Avenue, New York, when the man now dead, then in the flush of his police powers, said to those evil creatures of the underworld—Rose, Webber and Vallon—'Rosenthal must be croaked! Croak him!'"

Becker had meant to make a last statement in the execution room. He had written it out sometime during the night and memorized it. The wardens wouldn't permit this, however. Instead, copies of the statement were given to the press.

> I stand before you in my full senses knowing that no power on earth can save me from the grave that is to receive me, and in the presence of my God and your God I proclaim my absolute innocence of the foul crime for which I must die. You are now about to witness my destruction by the State, which is organized to protect the innocent. May Almighty God pardon everyone who has contributed in any degree to my untimely death. And now, on the brink of my grave, I declare to the world that I am proud to have been the husband of the purest, noblest woman that ever lived, Helen Becker. This acknowledgement is the only legacy I can leave her. I bid you all goodbye. Father, I am ready to go.
>
> **CHARLES BECKER**

"People ask how I have lived through these last two years— what has helped me," Helen Becker had said the summer before. "Is it religion? Or prayer? I tell them no. I have never been very religious. I go to church, but that hasn't helped me much. People have sent me all sorts of prayers to say . . . but that hasn't helped. How can it? Suppose they electrocuted my husband? Would religion do me any good? I would hate God, wouldn't I?"

After the execution Warden Osborne also gave the press a statement from the new widow, the statement she had written after her last interview with Whitman. It left God out of it.

> I shall never rest until I have exposed the methods used to convict my husband. Whether he was guilty or innocent, there never was any justification for the means employed to convict him. In all the ten years of our married life I never had occasion to regret that I was his wife. . . . He was not an angel, he never made a pretense of being one. He was just an ordinary human being, and that is why I loved him so.
>
> HELEN BECKER

The *World* opted for another soap-opera-type heroine on the day after the execution. Ignoring Helen Becker's statement it published instead an interview with Mrs. Lillian Rosenthal, in which she said that with Charley Becker dead she would now be able to sleep nights again. Governor Whitman's comment was "The Becker case is closed." He then departed to make a speech at a hopgrowers' outing in Oneida County. Only one relative of the four gunmen could be located, Samuel Seidenschner, father of Whitey Lewis. He had nothing to say about the execution. "The whole thing is over now," he said, "and I want to stop thinking about it."

Word of Becker's death was carried in an ordinary death notice the next day in the *Times*. It read: "BECKER. July 30, 1915, Charles Becker, dearly beloved husband of Helen Lynch. Funeral from his residence, 2290 University Avenue. Thence to the Church of St. Nicholas of Tolentine, Andrews Avenue and Fordham Road. Monday, August 2, at 10 A.M."

The hearse sent to bring Becker's body back to the city broke down four times on the way to Sing Sing and once on the way back because of an overheated engine. The story that had begun in terrible heat was ending in the same kind of weather. It was the hottest July 30 in forty-four years. Twenty thousand people spent the night on the Coney Island beaches. By the following morning Helen Becker's apartment was banked with wilting flowers. They had come from her fifth-grade class, from her fellow teachers, from all of Becker's lawyers, from Tim Sullivan's friend James March, from Warden Osborne and his deputy. A large wreath had arrived from former Inspector Williams, who also came to call each evening before the funeral. After the first conviction Becker's lawyers had felt that his public association with a notorious old grafter was a poor idea. Thereafter Williams had kept his distance. But now his wreath was prominently displayed at one end of the coffin. The ribbon across it read: "In Respect for Charley." Dominating the room were two much larger floral offerings, both crosses, both bearing no cards. On one of them the attached streamer read "To the Martyr." On the other the four-foot horizontal spelled out "Sacrificed for Politics."

An estimated five thousand people filed past the open coffin. Some of the visitors came out of friendship, some out of curiosity, and most of them to get a look at the silver plate, eleven and a half inches long, that was now attached to the end of the coffin. It read:

CHARLES BECKER
MURDERED JULY 30, 1915
BY GOVERNOR WHITMAN

A delegation of newspapermen and photographers came as soon as they heard. In their stories the next day they could cite only one similiar indictment, the case of a Syracuse man, executed for homicide, whose mother had had carved on his tombstone "Murdered by the State." The tombstone had not lasted long, nor did Helen Becker's silver marker. By the afternoon of July 31 the Bronx district attorney had been notified by telegram that "criminal libel against the Governor of the State is being committed in your jurisdiction," and a little later three policemen arrived, removed the plate, and took it back to Centre Street headquarters where it was locked up in the safe in case the governor should bring a libel action.

The *Times* was in a fury. "The offense is not palliated by the removal of the plate," it declared editorially. "The libel upon the Governor is an insult to the people of the state, and such a defiance of the majesty of the law as ought not to be ignored." Meanwhile the *World* printed the rumor that the Board of Education would remove Mrs. Becker from its teachers' rolls for her insult to the forces of justice. The superintendent of schools, however, announced that she would be welcome in her classroom as usual at the beginning of the fall term.

The church of St. Nicholas of Tolentine had seats for seven hundred people. Fourteen hundred crowded in in the steaming heat and, according to the busy head counters, another ten thousand milled about outside. Service on the Fordham Road trolley line ceased completely because of the sightseers on the tracks. No top echelon members of the Police Department were present though a former member of Becker's strong arm squad and five men on the force served as pallbearers. Again the implacable *Times* was indignant, calling their service in this capacity "a scandalous spectacle" since they had "deliberately proclaimed their sympathy for a former associate whose proved conduct brought disgrace upon their organization."

Two black horses drew the open victoria bearing the hearse to Woodlawn cemetery where Becker was buried beside his infant daughter as motion picture cameras whirred away, and in the broiling sun members of the crowd contended for vantage points on nearby tombstones. Six carriages bearing family and friends had followed the cortege. In the third carriage, directly back of those reserved for the Becker and Lynch families, rode old Alexander Williams. The management of the cemetery had refused to allow the cortege to enter the gates until the floral crosses reading "To the Martyr" and "Sacrificed for Politics" were removed. On top of the coffin as it was lowered into the ground lay Williams' wreath with its final salute, "In Respect for Charley."

XXV

"I don't believe . . . any evidence whatever—even though it were a revelation from heaven—could have sufficed to save poor Becker," Bourke Cockran wrote to Warden Osborne a few hours after the execution. "His death had become in the minds of certain politicians a stepping stone for their own advancement. . . ."

But in the editorial and letter columns of newspapers all over the country that week there were only expressions of relief that Charley Becker had paid his debt at last. Because of the long stretch of time since the murder, grumbled the local *Evening Post* in an editorial reprinted approvingly in the *Nation,* "the execution lost nine-tenths of its moral effect." "The effectiveness of punishment as a deterrent to crime is largely based upon the swiftness of justice rather than the severity of the penalty," *Outlook* magazine chimed in. "Such effect as may result from Becker's execution would have been trebled if his death had come soon after the crime." By which they apparently meant that if a man should one day think of ordering three men to order four other men to kill still another man, Becker's earlier death would have been three times as likely to persuade him against it.

The *Nation* called Becker's chaotic funeral "the final distressing detail in a disgraceful episode which the people of New York and of the country at large will be glad to forget." And so it worked out. With unseemly haste the Rosenthal murder case, so absorbing a topic for three long years, suddenly vanished from the news columns. When it came up again in conversation months later, it had already begun to sound *démodé*. The spectre of the itchy-palmed policeman as an evil that challenged civilization had faded. Apparently in the mind of the average citizen Becker's death at the hands of the state had taken care of the police grafting issue once and for all. But there were circles that did not entirely forget. The aftermath of the Leo Frank case was the formation by prominent American Jews of the Anti-Defamation League. The Becker case may have had another kind of consequence. "The inherent belief of all the police force from top to bottom that the press and public are prejudiced against them is working untold harm," Police Commissioner McAdoo had noted six years before the Rosenthal murder. The relentless pursuit and execution of Becker—the only American policeman ever put to death by the state—could not help but intensify this paranoid view and possibly had something to do with the familiar sight, generations later, of cops too young even to have heard Becker's name breaking heads open with the special rage of those who are convinced the dice are loaded against them.

Hopes for a new moral purity in the city and the nation had been touchingly high after Becker's conviction. The Philadelphia *North American* hailed its "salutary effect" and called the coming months "a time of regeneration." Of course the hopes were not fulfilled. The contrary result could not have surprised one *World* editorial writer who had predicted as much after Becker was sentenced to die. Although it reflected the personal attitude toward the gambling laws of the paper's star reporter Swope and other members of the staff, the slant of the editorial was unexpected since the *World* had been treating the arena of the police graft scandal as Armageddon. But with Charles Becker safely out of the way, the newspaper took a different view.

"The great function of a policeman is to protect life and property," said the editorial. "Morals are no concern of the Police Department." Before long, the editorial predicted, there would be "a new Becker, new gunmen, a new gang rule . . . a resurrection of all the evil which we think we are burying. . . ." This pattern would be repeated again and again, the writer declared, "so long as Anglo-Saxon hypocrisy persists in making felonious everything that it considers shocking, so long as it brands as

crimes those practices which other broader-minded and equally
civilized nations handle as public nuisances, so long as an Albany
legislature takes it upon itself to decree a rigid, standardized code
of manners and of morals for a city nearly half of whose inhabi-
tants come from foreign lands . . . so long as such a legislature
strives to create fiat chastity, fiat sobriety, and fiat frugality in
conformity with its own professed ideals and binds our local
authorities by oath to treat any divergence from these ideas as
crimes, just so long will human nature . . . evade such laws by
subterfuge and corruption. . . ."

Some things change, some remain the same. Over half a century later after grafting was once more uncovered in the local
gambling squad—as of course it has continued to be from time to
time in the decades since the Rosenthal crisis—the *Times* pointed
out that "if police take payoffs, someone gives the payoffs." They
do so because it is profitable, and it is profitable because "so many
people like to gamble. The hypocrisy that pervades some of the
nation's criminal laws, particularly those concerning such 'non-
victim crimes' as gambling, and the refusal of society to confront
this hypocrisy is actually a larger scandal than that of the police
payoffs. To effectively reform the police, it will be necessary to
reform the laws the police are asked to enforce." The *Times* editorial had been set off by the arrest of a group of present and
former members of the New York Police Department on charges
that they had taken about a quarter of a million dollars in graft.
In the 1960s, however, the police graft scandal stayed on the
front pages for exactly one day.

One of the men who presumably had read the 1912 *World*
editorial on spoilsport laws with satisfaction was old Alexander
Williams. He and his nemesis, Max Schmittberger, died in the
same year, 1917. Schmittberger's estate was six thousand dollars.
That of Clubber Williams amounted to $13.49. By coincidence
both men were buried in Woodlawn Cemetery, not far from
Charles Becker. Of the other members of the department whose
names had come into the Becker case, Inspector Hayes was dismissed after an altercation with Waldo, Hughes retired not long
afterward, and Captain Day was transferred from the bright light
district to a post in rural Brooklyn. Winfield Sheehan, on the
other hand, moved on to California where he became one of the
richest of the film producers in Hollywood's golden age.

Helen Becker never pursued her announced plan of exposing the methods that had sent her husband to the chair. For the rest of her life until her death at the age of eighty-eight, half a century after the murder, she lived quietly with her family, never remarrying. When she retired in the early 1940s she was assistant principal of an elementary school in northern Manhattan. For some years after the execution, friends insisted, she set aside a percentage of her salary to pay off legal debts. She always made it clear that none of this went to Bourke Cockran. A week after the funeral she had written to him: "I shall not attempt to . . . speak of the great debt which I owe you who fought my husband's cause without any compensation whatever. Indeed, I have found people who believed you were paid a great sum for your services. I shall only say that in all my life I have met no better, no greater man than W. Bourke Cockran." Possibly Cockran was rewarded in other ways by the old Big Tim crowd. But he would also prove himself capable of fighting for justice for an unpopular defendant whose appeal involved no local political advantage.

In the summer of 1916 a bomb had gone off during a Preparedness Day parade in San Francisco, killing ten people. A prominent labor leader named Tom Mooney was soon indicted. The committee arranging for Mooney's defense had heard of Cockran through the Becker case and persuaded him to take Mooney on. Once again Cockran, who was a rich man, worked without fee. From the defense point of view the Mooney and Becker cases had much in common. Of the Mooney trial the *New Republic* later wrote: "When a district attorney in an American city begins to hunt for evidence wherewith to convict a prisoner whom almost everybody dislikes and almost everybody thinks is guilty, he is almost certain to find it." "There isn't a scrap of [prosecution] testimony that wasn't perjured," the editor of the San Francisco *Bulletin* wrote at the time to Upton Sinclair. Mooney, like Becker, was convicted, and the district attorney in that case also immediately ran for governor. But Cockran helped persuade President Wilson to appoint a special federal mediation commission. Young Felix Frankfurter, its legal counsel, wrote the commission report and, possibly conditioned by his mistrust of the "politically-minded D.A." in the Becker case, declared the proceedings so unfair that a new trial was in order. In the end Mooney's death sentence was commuted to life imprisonment, and many years later he was pardoned. Cockran's obituaries in 1923 dwelt on his willingness to take on unpopular clients, "even Lieutenant Becker." His funeral was attended by four senators, thirteen congressmen and two governors, including his favorite politician of the last years, Al Smith, whom he had nominated for president at the 1920 Democratic Convention.

Indeed, despite the unpopularity of the cause, association with the Becker defense generally had no blighting effect on the professional lives of his lawyers. Lloyd Paul Stryker had a notable career as a trial attorney. John McIntyre went on the State Supreme Court bench in 1916, and John B. Johnston eventually was named to the Appellate Division of the same court. But the most distinguished judicial career of the onetime Becker defense team seemed for many years to be that of Martin Manton. Within a year after the execution he was named to the Federal District Court, possibly at the instigation of Cockran. Eighteen months later he was moved up to the U.S. Court of Appeals for the Second Circuit, often considered second to the U.S. Supreme Court in prestige and influence. In 1939, when he was the court's senior officer, Manton achieved a distinction of sorts by becoming the first federal judge ever criminally indicted for corrupting his office. Nothing like it had occurred, declared the presiding judge in the case, since the time of Sir Francis Bacon. Manton, referred to in knowledgeable circles as "Preying Manton," was accused of "running a mill for the sale of justice" and was convicted. He argued on appeal that it was against public policy to convict a high judicial officer since "it tends to destroy the confidence of the people in the courts." This brand of gall got him nowhere, and he served two years in the penetentiary.

Convicted with Manton of conspiring to obstruct justice was William Fallon, who in his youth had prosecuted Warden Osborne and who had later been Arnold Rothstein's lawyer. Often mentioned in the news accounts of the trial was State Supreme Court Justice Aaron Levy, whose financial arrangements with defendants before his court were being investigated. Involved in some of the bribery proceedings that brought Manton down was George Whiteside, one of Becker's first defense lawyers, who had represented a company paying a hundred-thousand-dollar bribe for a favorable verdict and Max Steuer, representing Albert Lasker, who put up the cash. It appeared that, a quarter of a century after the Becker case, stock in the company of prominent New York trial lawyers was still very closely held. Evidence at Manton's trial showed that in an eleven-month period in the early 1930s he had arranged to have his net worth condition shift from minus $710,000 to plus $750,000. His annual salary was ten thousand dollars. Presumably he looked back on his most famous client as a piker.

After the Mooney trial the prosecution witnesses who had placed Mooney at the scene of the crime recanted one by one, but Becker's prediction that quarrels among the four gambler witnesses would eventually unmask Whitman as a perverter of justice did not come true. Though Rose, Webber, Vallon, and Schepps fell out in four directions, they kept their mouths shut about the Becker case. After drifting from job to job on the East Side Vallon dropped out of sight entirely, but the other three achieved a modest prosperity outside the neighborhood of back-room stuss games. Schepps switched from jewelry to the antique furniture business. Webber went on making paper boxes in New Jersey. Jack Rose left off preaching and the cinema in favor of a successful catering career. In the course of this he gave his name to the Jack Rose cocktail, a combination of lemon juice, grenadine, and apple jack that has mercifully disappeared from most bar lists. He died in 1947 at Roosevelt Hospital a few blocks from Broadway where, like all the witnesses, he had often strolled in the years after the trials, despite the prosecution's promise that it could never happen, that the gunmen's friends would take care of them if they did.

The stirring days when Becker was on trial for the second time were not Judge Seabury's last official encounter with Whitman. "I want you on the Court of Appeals or as Senator or as Governor!" Theodore Roosevelt had written Seabury after the trial ended. A year and a half later Roosevelt was urging him to resign from the Court of Appeals and make the race for governor against Whitman in 1916. At a dinner meeting with the former president at Oyster Bay, Roosevelt, according to Seabury, promised that he and the Progressives would endorse the judge in that race, adding that in any event he could never support Whitman for reelection. "There is no truth in Whitman," he said once again. Seabury was nominated for governor by the Democrats and resigned his seat on the court. But soon afterward Roosevelt went back to the arms of the G.O.P., and he and what was left of the Progressives endorsed Whitman after all. ("There is no truth in Roosevelt," Seabury might have concluded.) Seabury was endorsed by Swope's *World*, now ferociously opposed to Whitman whom it had built up as a political hero. They reported with special glee the attacks on him by Thomas Mott Osborne, who had resigned as warden of Sing Sing in order to campaign against Whitman. In an open letter he blamed the governor for the fact that his name had been "linked in people's thoughts with the vilest of crimes." He had succeeded in putting the charge down, he said, "but I do desire to influence the future . . . to the end that no man so weak as yourself—so shifty, so selfish, so false, so cruel—may be entrusted with further power. . . ."

The rapport between Whitman and Seabury, so evident during the Becker trial, was missing in the bitter campaign. Seabury charged Whitman with incompetence, graft, nepotism, payroll padding, and general mediocrity. Whitman called Seabury a chameleon, a demagogue, and a tool of Tammany. Contrary to the last charge, the Sachems of Fourteenth Street, seeing no reason to go all out for a man who had often run for office as one of their severest critics, largely sat out the election, and Seabury was defeated. His revenge would come later. The factor in his defeat that Seabury indicated had depressed him most was Whitman's bloc vote from the Prohibitionists. The governor had unearthed the old news clippings telling of his impromptu enforcement of the saloon closing law in the Forty-seventh Street station house, and the drys had dutifully flocked to his support. It was nearly a decade and a half before Franklin D. Roosevelt, by then governor of New York, asked Seabury, long out of public life, to preside over a special investigation of Tammany Hall. The Seabury hearings were the most tumultuous since those looking into the evils of the Tweed Ring half a century earlier and culminated, of course, in the resignation of Tammany's Mayor Walker. Notably, the Seabury inquiry considered the problem of corruption in the whole Tammany-dominated city government and didn't try, Lexow-style, to expose bits and pieces of it as part of an investigation into malfeasance in the Police Department.

Charles Whitman's public career ended in 1918. The cause that had required the death of Becker had not been so glorious after all. Whitman's importance as a Republican candidate for the presidency had always assumed the unavailability of his popular and able fellow New Yorker, Charles Evans Hughes, who had taken the Supreme Court veil. In mid-1916 Hughes was persuaded to leave the high bench and return to active political life, and it was Hughes, of course, who got the Republican nomination for president in 1916. Whitman considered the setback a temporary one, however. "On the Republican side everything centers on the quiet campaign, already under way, to obtain a third term for Governor Whitman and place him in line for the Presidential nomination in 1920," reported the *Times* in February 1917. "Friends of the Governor believe the goal is already in sight."

The almost total eclipse of the Becker case in the public prints after the execution undoubtedly had suited Whitman, who must have tired of reading that his entire political career had been based on getting Charley Becker. Still, there were troublesome reminders from time to time. Jack Rose was said to have approached the governor in the interest of a friend of his, an East Side thug sentenced to Sing Sing for trying to kill gambler Dollar John. Whitman pardoned the man. In 1915 Jacob Luban, the long-employed nonwitness, was arrested on another charge of forgery. Although the district attorney's office put in a plea for leniency, Luban was sentenced to twenty years in Sing Sing. In the summer of 1917 he wrote friends that his sentence was about to be commuted from twenty years to thirteen months, the time he had already served. "This is the highest commutation ever handed down in this State or any other State," he boasted. Luban added that he expected to get an absolute pardon before long, and in January 1918 Whitman obliged. Inevitably a few people wondered why the governor of New York was anxious to be so accommodating to a recidivist felon, but the Becker case had faded in everyone's memory, and the matter was not pursued. Still, the awkwardness of Whitman's dual role at the time of the execution had left the public with some sense of uneasiness about the governor. And there was at least one talkative and influential New York lawyer, Emory Buckner, who firmly believed that Whitman was a man who would have no qualms about letting a prisoner go to the electric chair unjustly if it happened to suit him for private reasons.

Buckner, along with Max Steuer, was one of the two highest-priced trial lawyers in the country during the 1920s, but, undoubtedly to his regret, he never was elected to political office. His dislike of Whitman was lifelong. Jealousy had something to do with it, but there were other factors. In 1917 Buckner had as a client one of the two young men who had killed a woman in the course of a robbery. Both were convicted of first-degree murder. An appeal was taken to commute the death sentence to life imprisonment. According to Buckner's biographer, the lawyer was fearful of the effect his "bad personal relations" with Whitman would have on his client's fortunes and had another attorney present the case on appeal, Whitman nevertheless commuted the sentence of the other defendant but did not spare Buckner's client, though there was no significant difference in the two cases. Buckner always believed that Whitman had sent the boy to his death as a gesture of personal revenge.

"A strange land, this. Yet not strange enough, meseemth, for Whitman ever to be President of it," F.P.A. wrote about this time in *Harper's Weekly*. In the 1918 contest for the governorship, the hurdle Whitman had to get over to be in line for the presidency, the Democratic nominee, was Al Smith. Pleased by the dry vote in his race against Seabury, Whitman now made frequent appearances with the head of the Anti-Saloon League and uttered obliging-enough sounds in favor of Prohibition to impress the hardshell evangelist Billy Sunday, who endorsed him. "I hope every man and woman . . . will stand by your brave Governor," he said in a tabernacle sermon. "I hope Manhattan will go so dry you'll have to prime a man before he can spit," Sunday added wrathfully. Something went wrong that fall, however. Whitman was beaten by Al Smith who made no bones about enjoying a beer when he felt like it. Possibly word had reached some of the Anti-Saloon Leaguers that when Whitman said he favored a dry Manhattan he didn't necessarily mean what they meant. Many insiders blamed the outcome on what was now often called "Charley Becker's Revenge." The cop whose murder conviction had made Whitman governor had had the last word after all, the story went. For as more and more citizens became aware of the governor's problems with alcohol during his second term, it was said that he drank to escape the huge accusing ghost of the dead policeman, which, according to rumor, could be seen tramping its beat night after night along the stone battlements of the old Albany State House.

Whitman was hardly the first politician to drink too much, but Al Smith became a full-fledged wet, his friends said, out of contempt for the hypocrisy of Whitman who "had campaigned dry while personally bibulous." Smith used his onetime opponent as a horrible example in another respect. In the early twenties when someone asked him about running for president, he said that he wasn't going to make the mistake of Whitman "who went to Albany and instead of tending strictly to business sat up in the dome of the capital with his eyes glued to a pair of field glasses trained on the White House." Whatever the reasons, when it came time for the Republicans to name someone to run against Smith again in 1920 Whitman wasn't offered another chance at it. Probably to his special distress the candidate the Republicans settled on instead was a man who had also played a role in the Becker case, but one that was no comfort to the prosecution. The nominee was Nathan Miller, the former Court of Appeals judge whose concurring opinion had so savagely dissected Whitman's case against Becker in the first trial. Miller was elected governor in the Harding landslide. Two years later, however, Al Smith bounced back and defeated him. In the long run Miller, like Whitman, would hardly be mentioned in the history books except as an incidental and temporary obstacle in the rise of Al Smith, the fair-haired boy from Tim Sullivan territory.

After his defeat for the governorship in 1918 Whitman practiced law in New York, making some money and no history. He and his family spent much time in Newport, but he was no longer the guest of honor at parties at the Vanderbilts. In 1924, full of nostalgia and hope, the former leading candidate for the presidency doubled back on his career and ran for his old job as district attorney. He got less than one-third of the votes. In 1935 he was given a ceremonial appointment as one of several commissioners on the Port of New York Authority. In 1947 at the age of seventy-nine he died of arteriosclerosis in his room at the University Club where he had lived for many years. Even at the very end he was not allowed to escape his ties with the policeman executed a generation before. In its obituary the *Times* measure of his achievements in Albany was brief. "The outstanding event of his governorship," it said, "was his refusal to stay the sentence of death in the case of Lt. Becker."

After 1915 lawyers occasionally expressed private doubts about the case against Becker but only one man conducted a single-minded crusade to prove the policeman had been railroaded to the chair. Henry Klein, a former East Side reporter and press agent for Hearst, had covered the Rosenthal murder for the *American*, writing articles that were hardly less anti-Becker than Swope's. But in time information he picked up on lower Second Avenue made him change his mind. In 1917 when Hearst got him appointed the city's deputy commissioner of accounts he took advantage of the assignment to nose around in the D.A.'s office disbursement records and other documents left over from the Whitman era, adding the information to a dossier he was assembling to prove Becker's innocence. The *American* later published some of Klein's material, and in 1927 Klein put out a book entitled *Sacrificed,* made up of reports of the trial testimony pieced out with affidavits he had gathered. Included was a letter from Billy Sulzer, the Tim Sullivan protégé elected governor in 1912. Sulzer declared that "from certain facts that had come to my attention" he had known Becker to be innocent and had intended to commute the death sentence and then pardon the policeman if the Court of Appeals failed to reverse after the first trial. By the time the court had reversed, however, he was no longer governor. *Sacrificed* also contained such undocumented tidbits as the report that several years after the execution two of Whitman's former assistant district attorneys had got into an argument in General Sessions Judge Rosalsky's courtroom, that one of them had shouted to the other, a man closely involved in preparing the evidence against Becker, "I'll prove right now that Becker was framed," and that Rosalsky had quickly cut him short with, "Let sleeping dogs lie." In 1951 Klein and Swope jousted in the Letters column of the *Times* over Becker's guilt. Swope was given the last word, a situation he was not unused to.

Swope had moved up from city editor to executive editor of the *World* in 1920. The appointment only ratified a view of himself that once inspired a cartoonist for the old *Life* to show him strutting about the *World* building over the caption *"Le Monde, c'est moi."* Long before this promotion his energy and flamboyant style had made his name a national symbol for the enterprising modern newspaperman. By the late twenties, however, he was such a big wheel among the people who made the news (he was also a very rich man as the result of shrewd gambling in the stock market and elsewhere) that no daily journal was big enough to deserve his full attention. He resigned from the *World*. For the next quarter of a century his profession was technically that of highly paid consultant to a number of large American corporations, but he thought of himself as primarily a collaborator with presidents and major international statesmen in the great events of his time, an impression that wasn't entirely delusionary.

"He taught George Rex to put his crown on/ Queen Mary how to put her gown on . . . /And for the Pontiff, as a pal/ He's written his encyclical. . . ." the owner of the *World* wrote of Swope in 1931 in an admiring piece of doggerel. According to Stanley Walker in a 1938 article in the *Saturday Evening Post*, "Travelers returning from Europe have been known to report that the first question asked of them by high-placed foreign personages would not be 'How are conditions in the United States?' but 'How is Herbert Bayard Swope?' " Later E. J. Kahn, Jr. wrote a piece for *The New Yorker* with the title "What is Herbert Bayard Swope?" His sense of prerogative had long been so strong that he required all those present in his home—men, women, his own wife and grown children—to leap respectfully to their feet whenever he entered a room. The house rule stayed in force, but before he died in 1958 at the age of seventy-six, the fame, the power, and the money had sharply dwindled, and highly placed foreign personages had more interesting things to talk about.

To the end of his life Swope referred to the Rosenthal murder case as the most important story of his career, the one that had started him on his way, and liked to tell of his part in it over and over in letters and at the dinner table where what he had said to Rosenthal, how Becker had blanched when he spoke to him, and what he had told Whitman to do next might last all the way to dessert. In time he was remembering himself as having made virtually every significant decision and come upon every useful piece of evidence connected with it. He also altered the plot a bit. In an account of the Rosenthal affair that he gave one writer, Charles Becker had become co-czar with Big Tim Sullivan over all phases of New York criminal life and a man who had intended to succeed Sullivan as political lord of the East Side until Tom Foley beat him out. Zelig was Becker's gangster lieutenant, enforcing his iron rule over the underworld. Swope, of course, was still the hero who, with one hand tied behind him, had brought this fabled giant down. In these later years he thought of his feat in having made Whitman governor—as he described it—as a joke on all concerned. He was also inclined to play down his friendship with Rothstein, which had given him special insight into the murder story, although through the early 1920s he had continued to spend time with the gambler.

Back in 1915 on the early morning when Becker died, a sociable group including Rothstein, his lieutenant Nicky Arnstein, and Tad Dorgan, the well-known *Journal* cartoonist, had kept a vigil a block from the Metropole at Jack's cafe, still open around the clock as it had been on the night of the murder. On the white tablecloth beside Rothstein was a gold pocket watch with its case open. During the minutes while the hands reached and passed five-forty-five, the hour when Becker was scheduled to die, conversation at the table stopped.

Actually, whether the former policeman was executed or survived now made little difference to Rothstein. In the year or two while Big Tim had been losing his hold on sanity as well as on the New York graft situation and while the headlines over the Rosenthal murder had been showing up the often-erratic, every-man-for-himself character of the collection of tribute from the city's leading lawbreakers, Charles Murphy down at Tammany Hall had reportedly concluded that the use of members of the police force as major graft collectors was an antiquated concept. The whole vastly lucrative arrangement needed modern organization with perhaps one man acting as liaison among the politicians, the gamblers, and other dues-paying trade associations such as the brothel keepers. In the new system important cops would be taken care of, but they would no longer help run the show. When Tom Foley and Murphy worked out a political truce after Big Tim's death, Foley's smart friend Rothstein was recognized as the perfect man for the new executive post.

In the years between this designation and the night in 1928 when he was shot to death in a Broadway hotel—a murder that was never officially solved—crime in America turned into organized big business. With the connivance of his politician friends Rothstein became chairman of the board of the New York underworld, trafficking not only in all forms of gambling but also in illegal whiskey, stolen securities, drugs, labor union rackets, and the performance of the players in the 1919 World Series. Like Becker he became a literary footnote. In Scott Fitzgerald's *The Great Gatsby* he appears as Wolfsheim, the ruthless *padrone* of gangsters.

In the old days the gangsters had worked as hired thugs for the gamblers who in turn had worked for the police and the politicians. But from 1915 on—and especially after the coming of Prohibition, which turned the gangs into empires—it would be the men of the underworld who often called the turn on everybody. Gangster Frank Costello wouldn't be overheard expressing his undying gratitude to a politician in the early 1940s—it would be the other way around. Symbolically, the old nineteenth-century term "Tenderloin," left over from the age of all-powerful Irishmen and colorful, despotic cops, seemed to disappear from the language of the city about this time. Already, that early morning in July 1915, when Arnold Rothstein snapped the watch shut and, with a shrug of his shoulders, walked out toward Broadway, it was into a different world from the one familiar to Big Tim, to Herman Rosenthal, and to Charles Becker, who in any case were all now dead, every one.

INDEX